SAP® Interactive Forms by Adobe

 **PRESS**

Stefan Kauf, Viktoria Papadopoulou
Creating Forms in SAP ERP HCM
2009, 200 pp.
978-1-59229-282-0

Karl Kessler et al.
Java Programming with SAP NetWeaver
2008, 719 pp.
978-1-59229-181-6

Martin Raepple
Developer's Guide to SAP NetWeaver Security
2008, 552 pp.
978-1-59229-180-9

Rich Heilman, Thomas Jung
Next Generation ABAP Development
2009, 504 pp.
978-1-59229-139-7

Marcus Banner, Berthold Latka, Roland Scroth, Michael Spee
Developer's Guide to SAP NetWeaver Portal Applications
2009, 423pp.
978-1-59229-225-7

Jürgen Hauser, Andreas Deutesfeld, Stephan Rehmann,
Thomas Szücs, Philipp Thun

SAP® Interactive Forms by Adobe

Galileo Press

Bonn • Boston

ISBN 978-1-59229-254-7

© 2009 by Galileo Press Inc., Boston (MA)
1st Edition 2009

1st German Edition published 2009 by Galileo Press, Bonn, Germany.

Galileo Press is named after the Italian physicist, mathematician and philosopher Galileo Galilei (1564–1642). He is known as one of the founders of modern science and an advocate of our contemporary, heliocentric worldview. His words *Eppur si muove* (And yet it moves) have become legendary. The Galileo Press logo depicts Jupiter orbited by the four Galilean moons, which were discovered by Galileo in 1610.

Editor Stefan Proksch
English Edition Editor Stephen Solomon
Translation Lemoine International, Inc., Salt Lake City, UT
Copy Editor Mike Beady
Cover Design Jill Winitzer
Photo Credit Getty Images/Ray Massey
Layout Design Vera Brauner
Production Editor Kelly O'Callaghan
Typesetting Publishers' Design and Production Services, Inc.
Printed and bound in Canada

Contents at a Glance

Contents

8   Integration with Web Dynpro ABAP 335

9   Internal Service Request 459

10 ABAP PDF Object 553

11 Offline Scenarios via Web Services 573

This book describes the SAP® Interactive Forms by Adobe technology. It provides all of the required details for print and interactive scenarios and uses step-by-step examples to explain the usage of the relevant tools for working with SAP Interactive Forms by Adobe.

1 Introduction

In 2002, SAP and Adobe Systems entered a strategic partnership. The aim was to integrate interactive forms and Adobe's print and design expertise with the SAP NetWeaver technology platform and make them available to customers via SAP's business applications.

▶ At this time, Adobe already had the required technology: the Adobe LiveCycle® product group—whose core area is the conversion of form templates and their corresponding data into various output formats, such as different Printer Definition Languages (PDLs) or Portable Document Format (PDF) documents. In addition to the generation of output formats, Adobe focused on the design of forms. For this reason, Adobe provided the Adobe LiveCycle Designer®, a graphically interactive tool that enables users to create the layout of the form.

▶ For the integration of the tools with SAP NetWeaver, SAP contributed its knowledge gained from the development of SAPscript and SAP Smart Forms. SAP Smart Forms provided the outline for integrating Adobe technology with SAP applications. This facilitated the implementation of the new technologies for most developers.

Today, the development tasks are divided between Adobe and SAP to a large extent: While Adobe develops the core technology, SAP improves the integration and the frameworks that are based on the technology.

In 2005, SAP finally brought SAP Interactive Forms by Adobe to market. For the SAP NetWeaver 2004 release, SAP Interactive Forms by Adobe was available as an SAP NetWeaver solution extension for SAP customers for the first time. Today, it is used in numerous SAP customer projects and even SAP uses the new technology in its own applications. With each enhancement package for the SAP Business

Suite, SAP provides more and more converted print forms and changes to this new technology either from SAPscript or from SAP Smart Forms. With the release of Enhancement Package 4 for SAP ERP 6.0, SAP now provides more than 2,200 PDF-based print forms that use this technology. Therefore, now is the right time to become familiar with this technology. Reading this book is the best way to do so.

The benefits of the newest, PDF-based print forms technology are obvious: In addition to the mere print output, the generation of interactive PDF forms (that is, PDF files that provide interactive form fields when you open them with Adobe Reader®) allows for usage options that have not been available in the SAP world. Various SAP solutions use interactive forms. You can find numerous examples for SAP ERP 6.0 in the Financial and HCM areas. For example, as of version 5.0, SAP Customer Relationship Management (CRM) also provides an interactive form for Lead Management via a partner enterprise in the standard.

Structure of the Book

To give you a better overview of the book's topic, the following sections introduce the structure and content of the individual chapters:

- **Chapter 2**, "Use of SAP Interactive Forms by Adobe," lays the foundation for understanding the concepts and technologies underlying SAP Interactive Forms by Adobe. This chapter considers different usage scenarios for interactive forms and helps you select the appropriate scenario. One of the basic principles is understanding the integration of the Adobe technology with the SAP NetWeaver technology platform.

- **Chapter 3**, "Installation and Configuration," describes how you can download and install the software to work with SAP Interactive Forms by Adobe. It also details the configuration of the software components. This chapter guides you through the individual steps and indicates possible problems and their solution.

- **Chapter 4**, "Interface and Form Context," introduces the print form topic. It uses an example to explain the corresponding procedure, which you can reproduce in your system. You get to know the Transaction SFP, important concepts, and the relationship between interfaces, form context, and form design.

- In **Chapter 5**, "Creating Form Templates," you begin using Adobe LiveCycle Designer to design the layout of print forms. Based on the interface and the context of the previous chapter, this chapter provides step-by-step instructions on how to use Adobe LiveCycle Designer and helps you understand the underlying technology. In this context, it considers critical topics, such as the process of structuring forms by means of subforms and data binding of form fields.

▶ **Chapter 6**, "Form Output," introduces you to the development of print programs. Print programs generate the print output using the interfaces and context that were created in Chapter 4 and the form template that was developed in Chapter 5. This chapter requires some ABAP skills.

▶ Now that you are familiar with designing PDF forms, **Chapter 7**, "Advanced Form Template Creation," covers more complex topics, such as output formatting, pagination, and script programming. It also explains the usage of tables in forms and discusses the creation of interactive PDF forms in preparation for the following chapters.

▶ **Chapter 8**, "Integration with Web Dynpro ABAP," describes the integration of PDF forms with Web Dynpro ABAP. Web Dynpro is the first of two environments that this book considers. It enables you to implement online scenarios. An example explains how you can integrate an interactive form with a Web Dynpro view and implement a value help. Further examples show how you can upload forms. This allows for implementing a combination of online and offline scenarios. This chapter requires some basic Web Dynpro ABAP skills.

▶ **Chapter 9**, "Internal Service Requests (ISR)," introduces the ISR framework whose technology is based on Web Dynpro. It describes the usage of this framework within the SAP infrastructure and creates a plain example. In the next step, the customizing and programming of complex scenarios are explained. This chapter concludes with links to additional technical documentation.

▶ In **Chapter 10**, "ABAP PDF Object," we leave the framework world and introduce you to a deeper level of ABAP programming. This chapter also uses programming examples to show how you can use the functions for PDF forms through the PDF object in ABAP. Among other things, it focuses on the implementation of offline scenarios.

▶ **Chapter 11**, "Offline Scenarios via Web Services," demonstrates an alternative method for integrating PDF forms with an SAP system via Web services, which can be used to implement offline scenarios. It discusses the two possible approaches to using Web services: The first approach is directly supported by Adobe LiveCycle Designer, the second approach uses the Simple Object Access Protocol (SOAP) object in JavaScript.

Depending on your special fields of interest, you can jump to different chapters in this book. The following list provides an overview of which chapters are relevant regarding particular concerns and interests.

▶ **Installed system available**
If you already have a completely installed and configured SAP system and are not interested in the installation, configuration, and administration, you can skip Chapter 3.

▶ **Creating PDF forms**
The procedures for creating print forms and interactive forms are largely identical. Chapter 5 introduces the creation of PDF forms. If you're already familiar with this, you can skip this chapter and only read Chapter 7, which addresses the advanced form designer.

▶ **Implementation of print outputs**
If you want to focus on the creation of print outputs, read Chapter 4 and Chapter 6. The process of designing forms is described in Chapters 5 and 7.

▶ **Implementation of interactive online scenarios**
If you are interested in the implementation of online scenarios, you can proceed with Chapter 8 and Chapter 9. To design forms, refer to Chapters 5 and 7.

▶ **Implementation of interactive offline scenarios**
If you are interested in offline scenarios, read Chapter 10 and Chapter 11. You can refer to Chapters 5 and 7 to read more about designing forms.

System Requirements and Sample Files

If nothing is specified, the descriptions in this book are based on SAP NetWeaver 7.0 SP 15, including version 8.0 of Adobe LiveCycle Designer and version 8.1.2 of Adobe Reader. If you have a newer support package for SAP NetWeaver, you can use this one. If your system is older, you can set up a test system as described in Chapter 3 to become familiar with the new developments introduced in this book.

You can find the form templates and listings that were created for this book at *www.sap-press.com*. Furthermore, you can also download a transport for the Web Dynpro ABAP examples here, so that you can directly reproduce the exercises in your system.

Acknowledgements

The writing of this book was quite a complex project, and the description of the composite integration with the SAP environment was no easy task and could only be mastered with a team of authors. That's why I am particularly glad that I could enlist the appropriate expert for each topic. At this point, I would like to thank my coauthors, Andreas Deutesfeld (Chapter 4, Chapter 6, and Chapter 10), Dr. Stephan Rehmann (Chapter 9), Philipp Thun (Chapter 3), and Thomas Szücs (Chapter 8) for their excellent cooperation.

A team of authors also depends on experts' counterchecks. We were provided with valuable feedback that contributed to the book's quality. For this, we would like to thank Christina Vogt, Martin Plummer, Ralf Ruth, and Dr. Simon Hoeg.

Additionally, we would also like to say thanks to Les Woolsey, Matthias Zeller, Blair Powell, Dave Welch, and Inder Narang at Adobe. At SAP, we would like to thank Dr. Wolfgang Weiss, Yasuo Nagao, Markus Meisl, and Dirk Michael Schulze. They contributed considerably to the success of SAP Interactive Forms by Adobe.

A special thank-you also goes to Stefan Proksch and Stephen Solomon, our editors at Galileo Press, for their excellent collaboration.

Dr. Jürgen Hauser
Adobe Product Manager for SAP Interactive Forms by Adobe

This chapter introduces SAP Interactive Forms by Adobe and discusses various application scenarios. It also specifies the software components used and the architecture for integration with SAP NetWeaver.

2   Use of SAP Interactive Forms by Adobe

This chapter introduces you to the basic terminology associated with the use of SAP Interactive Forms by Adobe, such as Portable Document Format (PDF)–based print forms and interactive forms. A classification of online and offline application scenarios is outlined for interactive forms; additionally, you are provided with support for deciding in which cases you should use interactive forms. Furthermore, this chapter compares Adobe Acrobat® and Adobe Reader and explains why it is sufficient to deploy Adobe Reader for the use of SAP Interactive Forms by Adobe. Finally, this chapter introduces the software components of Adobe, Adobe Live-Cycle Designer, and Adobe Document Services and their integration with the SAP NetWeaver stack.

2.1   PDF, PDF-Based Print Forms, and Interactive PDF Forms

The following sections detail PDFs and the two main concepts of this book — PDF-based print forms and interactive PDF forms.

2.1.1   PDF File Format

In the early 1990s, Adobe Systems launched the first version of PDFs. At that time, Adobe was well-known for its PostScript printer language, Adobe Illustrator (a vector-based drawing tool), and Adobe Photoshop (image editing). The idea behind PDF was to develop a platform-independent file format that enabled high-quality exchange and printout of documents. Here, the primary focus was on the exchange of documents and not on an editable document format.

The specification of PDF is published and therefore everyone can get an overview of this file format. Currently, PDF has been filed for standardization at the International Organization for Standardization (ISO). The PDF/A format for archiving documents is already an ISO standard; however, it has not become a part of SAP Interactive Forms by Adobe yet.

PDFs enable you to flexibly describe the structure of individual pages of a document; it is a flat file format and only knows the concept of a page as the structuring element. Compared to PostScript, it is a pure descriptive language and therefore contains no programming language constructs.

The most commonly known use of PDF is the high-quality print output: A document is converted into a PDF file and can then be displayed or printed on different platforms and operating systems via Adobe Reader. The presentation of a document as PDF ensures that the document always has the same layout regardless of the user's operating system or platform. The user only requires a PDF display tool, for example, Adobe Reader.

In addition to the pure display and printout, you can also use PDF documents for data entry. To do this, forms that are based on PDF contain interactive form fields that enable the user to interact with the PDF document. This way, you can enter data and execute calculations that are based on this data directly during entry. For this reason, Adobe Reader supports JavaScript as one of the scripting languages.

2.1.2 PDF-Based Print Forms

Forms are a well-known structuring method for data output (for example, a telephone bill) or data entry (for example, official application forms). One of the essential aspects of forms is a uniform layout that enables and supports the recognition of forms. The structure of each telephone bill is identical and the customer knows where to find certain information on the bill—just like annual tax forms.

This requires the form designer to use a clear and comprehensible layout for the form. The layout describes what information is located at which position on the form. It must also specify how to handle large amounts of data records, which is usually done by distributing them to multiple pages.

The task of a form designer is to create form templates. Based on the form template, a specific form is generated and—in most cases—filled with data during the generation process. Consequently, the form template plays a central role in all form-based processes. Therefore, the form designer must be optimally supported in his task with a user-friendly and intuitive tool.

Forms can be output both on paper and electronically, however, the electronic output has significant gains (for example, electronic transmission or archiving). For this reason, SAP Interactive Forms by Adobe enables you to output forms in different printer languages or as PDF files.

Supported Printer Languages

The printer languages supported include Adobe PostScript® (PS), Printer Command Language® (PCL) developed by Hewlett-Packard®, and Zebra Programming Language® (ZPL) for printing barcodes on Zebra label printers. Printers must be able to process one of the aforementioned printer languages to ensure that they are supported by SAP Interactive Forms by Adobe.

Supported Printer Languages

SAP Interactive Forms by Adobe supports the following printer languages:

▶ Adobe PostScript Levels II and III, where Level III is the default setting. To create Level II, the corresponding XML Device Configuration (XDC) file must be copied and customized (see Section 3.6.5, XDCs).

▶ PCL 5 in monochrome and color.

▶ ZPL-II is supported in different resolutions, for example, 200, 300, and 600 Dots per Inch (DPI).

The print output and the PDF file are created based on Adobe XML Forms Architecture (XFA) technology, which is a specification published by Adobe. This specification describes the XML-based structure of a form template and the behavior of display and conversion programs at runtime. The XFA specification is a very good source of information and can be downloaded from the Adobe website (*http://partners.adobe.com/public/developer/xml/index_arch.html*).

Support of Barcodes

Another important area supported by SAP Interactive Forms by Adobe includes barcodes. A barcode encodes information that can be read by a scanner and then processed. You can find barcodes on virtually every product package read at a checkout counter. Here, you can determine the scanned product and its price based on the information encoded in the barcode.

SAP Interactive Forms by Adobe supports most of the common barcodes. Currently, there are 34 different barcodes, including EAN8, EAN13, and Code 128, for example. There are also barcodes that can only be supported by the printer itself. If in this case the output is done as a PDF file and a gray rectangle is displayed instead of the barcode. It is also possible to exclusively create a barcode and print it on a barcode printer. Currently, this is supported for Zebra label printers.

There is no way to define barcodes yourself. For barcodes that are not supported you have to rely on their support in one of the more recent releases.

Simplex and Duplex Printing

The double-sided print output and paper tray selection are supported as of SAP NetWeaver 7.0 SP 13. Simplex and duplex printing, that is, single-sided and double-sided printing, are controlled by means of the page sets and master pages. The form designer assigns the individual form pages to master pages to specify whether a page appears on the front side or the back side. Very complex scenarios are possible here (for example, combining simplex and duplex prints in one form) that require skillful use of master pages and conditional page breaks.

Paper Tray Control

The selection for the paper tray control requires multiple configuration steps because the corresponding control codes need to be determined for the printer and assigned to the available paper types. The control codes are contained in the XDC files and their assignment is carried out by editing the XDC files located on the server.

PDF-Based Print Forms, SAP Smart Forms, and SAPscript

The print output, which is based on PDF-based print forms, provides an alternative to the SAPscript and SAP Smart Forms technologies provided by SAP. There is no full equivalence with regard to functions and properties between the technologies due to the technological differences. The option to navigate to a callback of an ABAP function during the layout creation is not possible for PDF-based print forms due to technological reasons.

> **SAP Smart Forms versus SAP Interactive Forms by Adobe**
>
> SAP Note 1009567 describes the functional differences between SAP Smart Forms and SAP Interactive Forms by Adobe.

SAP Interactive Forms by Adobe provides advanced and complex innovations, such as enhanced layout options (for example, rectangles with rounded corners) or support of a scripting language (for instance, implementing calculations and validations in interactive PDF forms). These enhanced options can impact the performance and file sizes; for example, shadings affect the output in PCL format.

Another innovation compared to the already-existing technologies is the option to create interactive PDF forms. These are described in greater detail in the following section.

2.1.3 Interactive PDF Forms

PDF documents provide much more than just the known display and print functionality: They can contain interactive form fields. These fields are called "interactive" because the user can make changes by means of the mouse or the keyboard.

Possibilities

Interactive form fields include input fields for text and numbers that are entered via the keyboard. Moreover, you are provided with radio buttons or checkboxes, which are primarily operated using the mouse. In addition, more complex fields, such as the date selection field (a calendar appears for simplified selection), list boxes, and dropdown lists are available. List fields or dropdown lists are particu-

27

larly helpful if the user of the form is supposed to select an input value from a predefined list. The list can display all list entries so that the user doesn't have to remember all possible input options.

Interactive PDF forms are used for structured data entry by the user. If multiple users enter data, this is called *mass data entry*. In this case, electronic support is especially beneficial because the processing and saving of data can be automated.

Interactive form fields enable the user to interact directly with the document. Data that is stored in the interactive PDF form is changed during the interaction. For integration with electronic processes, you can extract or insert data on the server side. In specific cases, this is also possible at the user's work station, for example, if only the data contained in the PDF form are to be sent by email.

For SAP Interactive Forms by Adobe the XFA-based technology is used. Here, the form template is stored in XML format and the data contained in the PDF form is stored as an XML data record.

Static and Dynamic PDF Forms

For interactive PDF forms, you can differentiate between static and dynamic PDF forms depending on whether the form layout changes during the interaction or not. An example is dynamic tables in which users can insert new rows or delete old rows. Another example is to hide parts of the form depending on the previous entries. This is only possible for dynamic PDF forms.

For dynamic PDF forms, the form layout is created directly in Adobe Reader. This is done based on the form template and the data contained therein. As of Adobe Reader version 8.1, the display of dynamic forms is considerably faster than in older versions. It is recommended to use Adobe Reader version 8.1 or higher if you utilize dynamic functions intensively.

2.1.4 Accessibility of PDF Forms

Because you can use interactive PDF forms as a part of user interfaces, the accessibility of PDF forms is of significance. Interactive forms enable you to create accessible PDF forms. Accessible means, for example, that visually handicapped users can also utilize the PDF form. Although Adobe Reader provides a function for reading PDF documents out loud (VIEW · READ OUT LOUD), third-party software, such as JAWS® from Freedom Scientific®, is usually used. Accessibility also means that mobility-impaired users can work with an application or a document (for example, by means of the voice control).

The accessibility impacts the size of the PDF file because additional information needs to be added. This information must be generated on the server during the creation of the PDF document, which also requires extra time. Because of this, you should consider whether a PDF form should always be accessible or not. A user-specific control is one option to avoid additional work. For example, you can use the user settings for the print preview in SAP GUI.

The form layout does not always result in an accessible form. The design tool to form templates supports you in the creation of accessible forms—for example, for the positioning of form fields, which influences the sequence. However, if the layout of the form is so complex that it is difficult to use, it is predictable that accessibility problems occur. In such cases, it is extremely helpful to reconsider and revise the form layout.

2.1.5 Using Interactive PDF Forms

You have been introduced to several significant properties of PDF forms. A PDF form may or may not be interactive. If not, it is a PDF-based print form. In addition, a PDF form can be static or dynamic. These properties are either determined by the individual frameworks that integrate the PDF forms, for example, in Web Dynpro ABAP it is a preset that creates dynamic PDF forms, or these properties are available as parameters in the programming interfaces.

The benefit of interactive PDF forms in electronic business processes in the SAP environment is that you just need Adobe Reader and a web browser or email program to use them. The wide distribution of Adobe Reader and the common email programs and web browsers facilitate their use considerably.

2.2 Adobe Reader and Adobe Acrobat Family

Adobe offers two products for displaying PDF files: the free Adobe Reader and the Adobe Acrobat family that is subject to charge. The Adobe Acrobat 8 family comprises three separate products: Adobe Acrobat Professional, Adobe Acrobat Standard, and Adobe Acrobat 3D.

Note

Adobe Reader is sufficient for the use of SAP Interactive Forms by Adobe! Most notably, it is not necessary to purchase Adobe Acrobat licenses. Adobe Reader is distributed by Adobe Systems and not by SAP, that is, it can only be downloaded from the Adobe website (*http://www.adobe.com/reader*).

Adobe Reader 8.1.2 is used throughout this book. If you use an older version of Adobe Reader, you should update Adobe Reader to this or a higher version after you've read this chapter.

The fee-based products of the Adobe Acrobat family provide more functionality than the freely available Adobe Reader. Section 2.2.1, "Comparing Adobe Reader and Acrobat Professional," details why it is still sufficient to use Adobe Reader.

Interactive Forms on Mobile Devices

SAP Note 1002905 describes the supported mobile devices and the existing restrictions from the point of view of SAP Interactive Forms by Adobe. Currently, interactive forms are supported by Adobe Reader for Pocket PC. Refer to the Adobe website to obtain a general description on this topic (*http://www.adobe.com/products/acrobat/readerfor-ppc.html*).

2.2.1   Comparing Adobe Reader and Acrobat Professional

The Adobe Acrobat products provide more functionality than the freely available Adobe Reader. This functionality includes, for example, the creation of PDF documents and their manipulation. Adobe Acrobat 3D enables the conversion of different 3D formats into a PDF document.

Parts of this functionality are also included in Adobe Reader; however, they are hidden and must first be activated. For their activation, a PDF document must be provided with a corresponding ID, called usage rights, during their creation.

Figure 2.1 shows a simple interactive PDF form in Adobe Reader 8.1, which contains interactive form fields. After a change has been made in the first form field, the dialog shown in the figure appears. It notifies the user that the data entered cannot be saved using Adobe Reader. In Adobe Acrobat, this functionality is always activated.

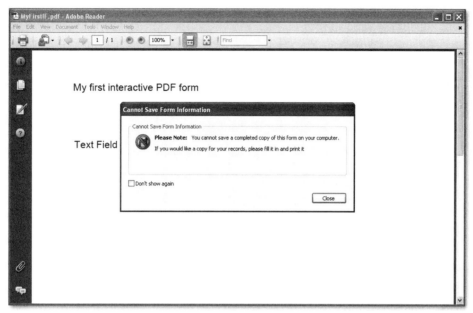

Figure 2.1 Interactive Forms in Adobe Reader (Without Embedded Usage Rights)

Usage Rights for Adobe Reader

By embedding usage rights into the PDF itself you can activate the following additional functions in Adobe Reader:

▶ **Saving of interactive PDF forms**
This eliminates the behavior of Adobe Reader described earlier, in which data entered in an interactive PDF form cannot be saved.

▶ **Digital signature**
If the PDF form includes a signature field, the user can digitally sign the PDF, provided that this functionality has been activated.

The qualified digital signature required in Germany, for example, is not supported in the standard version of Adobe Reader. This functionality can be added by using a plug-in.

▶ **Add comments and markups**
This functionality enables you to comment on the opened PDF document. To do this, you are provided with sticky notes that allow you to enter free text (see Figure 2.2). In addition, you can use custom stamps.

Commenting on dynamic PDF forms is not possible presently.

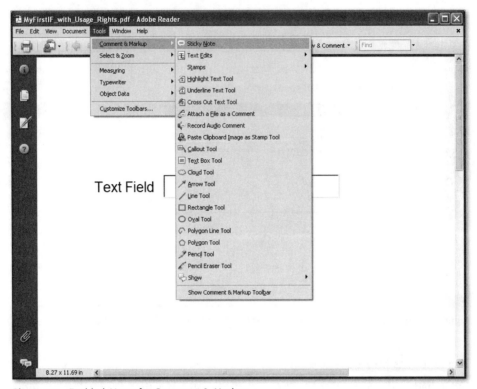

Figure 2.2 Enabled Menu for Comment & Markup

▶ **Add PDF file attachments**

You can add file attachments to PDF documents. Two types of file attachments are distinguished here: There are document-wide file attachments and file attachments on specific pages and in specific positions (also referred to as *file attachment comments*). A setting exists for these file attachments that prevents the file attachment from opening at the click of a mouse. This setting can be found under EDIT · PREFERENCES · TRUST MANAGER.

For dynamic PDF forms, you are only provided with document-wide file attachments.

▶ **Call Web services**

Calling Web services is also a functionality that can only be used with usage rights.

Figure 2.3 shows the same PDF form as was displayed in Figure 2.1. The difference is that usage rights are now embedded. You are provided with additional information about the currently opened document if you click on the blue I symbol in the top-left corner. The information for the example shown in this figure indicates that the document contains interactive form fields and lists the embedded usage rights in descriptive form.

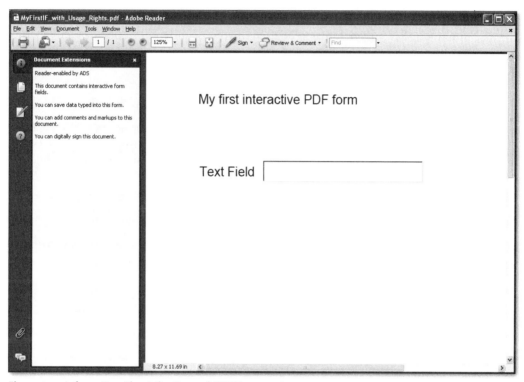

Figure 2.3 Information About the Opened PDF Document

The intention for SAP Interactive Forms by Adobe is to add usage rights to the interactive PDF forms. Therefore, Adobe Reader is sufficient for viewing.

For adding usage rights you must install a *credential* in SAP NetWeaver together with SAP Interactive Forms by Adobe. This credential is not required for PDF-based print forms. Chapter 3, "Installation and Configuration," describes how you can obtain this credential and how it is installed in the SAP NetWeaver stack.

2.2.2 Selecting the Appropriate Adobe Reader Version

New releases of SAP Interactive Forms by Adobe usually include new functions. Because of this, there is a recommended minimum version number for every release of SAP Interactive Forms by Adobe to utilize the entire functionality.

For a project that uses SAP Interactive Forms by Adobe you must always determine the Adobe Reader version(s) to be used. If you use different Adobe Reader versions it is recommended to test them (for example, a new version of Adobe Reader may correct errors of older versions).

Selecting the Adobe Reader Version

If you use functionality that was introduced together with a specific SAP NetWeaver support package, you must consider the lowest version number. New Adobe Reader versions are downward compatible, that is, you can always use a newer version of Adobe Reader.

If you use Adobe LiveCycle Designer 7.1 and SAP NetWeaver 7.0 with a support package that is lower than Support Package 15, it is recommended to use Adobe Reader 7.1.0. As of Support Package 15, and if you use Adobe LiveCycle Designer 8.0, you should use Adobe Reader 8.1.2 or higher. You must also observe whether an integration environment (such as Web Dynpro) specifies the Adobe Reader version to be used.

It is also useful to visit the Adobe Systems website (*http://www.adobe.com/reader*) to obtain information about the latest Adobe Reader version. There you can find new versions if, for example, a security problem occurred that was remedied by a new version.

2.2.3 Useful Settings of Adobe Reader

In Adobe Reader, there are some preferences that enable you to customize the behavior of Adobe Reader for the use of interactive forms. These preferences can be found under the menu path EDIT · PREFERENCES....

▶ Under the Forms category you can find multiple options with regard to the display and behavior for filling out an interactive PDF form. The ALWAYS HIDE FORMS DOCUMENT MESSAGE BAR option is particularly interesting. You can select this option if document messages (for example, that the document contains interactive form fields) are sensitive or if you want to provide more space for the form itself.

▶ In the INTERNET category you can find the DISPLAY PDF IN BROWSER option. This option specifies whether Adobe Reader is started embedded in the browser. Users frequently search for this option when they find out that Adobe Reader always opens externally and want to change this setting.

2.3 Examples of PDF-Based Print Forms and Interactive PDF Forms

If you have an SAP system at hand that is already installed and configured for the use of SAP Interactive Forms by Adobe, you can continue to the following two examples. If you don't have such a system, you can set up a test system as described in Chapter 3, and then follow the examples. The first example demonstrates the print output; the second example creates an interactive PDF form that is prefilled with data.

2.3.1 Example for Print Output

This example is intended to demonstrate the integration of the print output with the SAP NetWeaver stack via PDF-based print forms. To do this, you call a print program, enter the parameters, and then create a print output. You can display the print output as a print preview instead of sending it to a printer.

The example assumes that the flight database is filled with data. If required, the flight database can be filled by executing the SAPBC_DATA_GENERATOR program in Transaction SE38.

The print output is viewed at runtime when the print program and the form design have already been created. The print program performs the data retrieval and its preparation and then initiates the creation of the print output. The print output can either be a printer language (PS, PCL, or ZPL) or a PDF.

1. Log on to the SAP system via the SAP GUI.
2. Start Transaction SE38 to open the ABAP Editor.
3. Enter FP_TEST_03 as the name of the program. Figure 2.4 shows what the screen must look like.

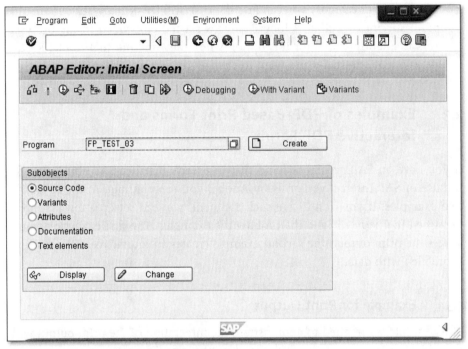

Figure 2.4 Selecting and Starting a Print Program

4. Then, start the program by clicking on the corresponding icon in the toolbar (the clock with the green checkmark) or by pressing the `F8` key.

5. The print program is now executed and the screen shown in Figure 2.5 is displayed. You can accept the displayed parameters. After you've run the example, you can change the parameters.

6. You could also select another form by changing the FORM parameter in this screen. However, you can't select just any form, only forms with the same interface. Chapter 4, "Interface and Form Context," provides detailed information on this topic.

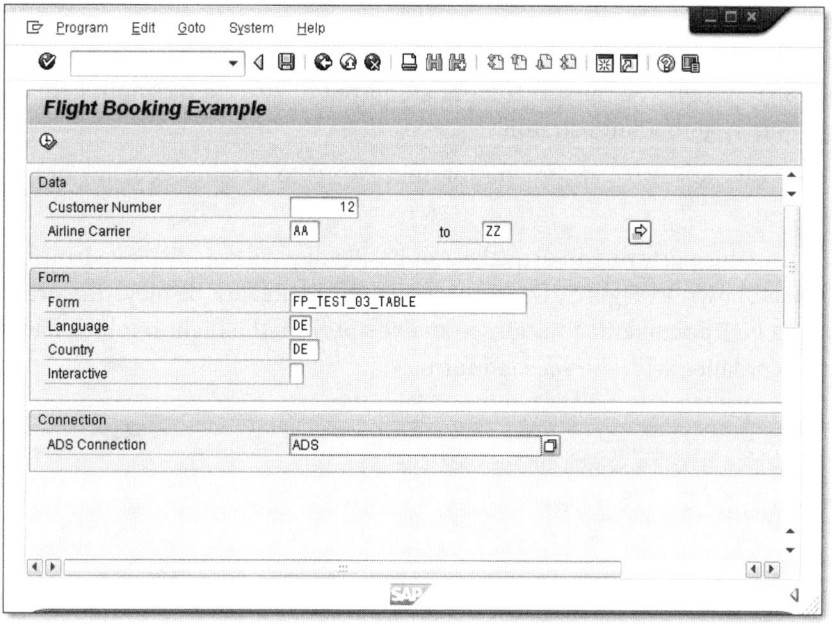

Figure 2.5 Entering Parameters for the Print Program Example

For example, select FP_TEST_03 or FP_TEST_03_TABLE. Again, click the clock icon or press the F8 key to run the program. This opens the PRINT dialog for selecting the output device (see Figure 2.6).

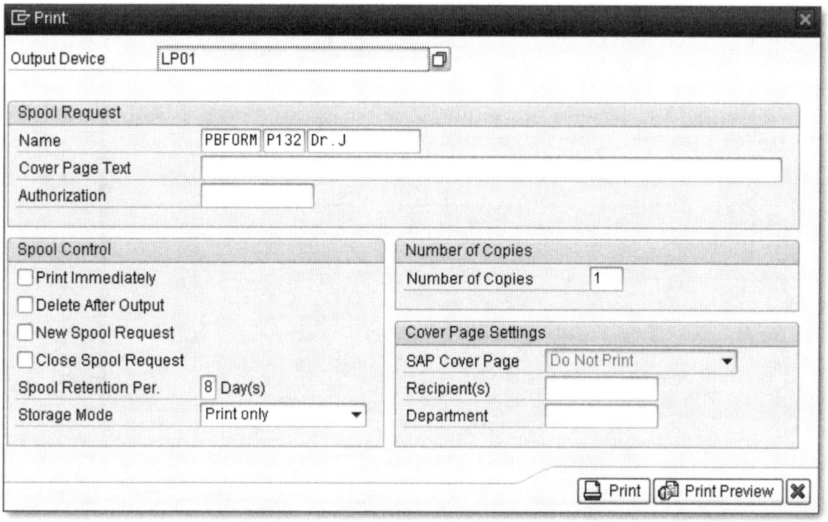

Figure 2.6 Dialog for the Print Output

7. In this dialog, you must select an output device. You can enter LP01 as text; LP01 is a sample printer present in many SAP systems. If this printer is not available on your SAP system you must search for an output device via the input help or contact your system administrator.

8. Next, click on the PRINT PREVIEW button (not PRINT) to obtain a preview of the print output.

9. If all steps were performed correctly, Adobe Reader will be displayed in the SAP GUI as shown in Figure 2.7. In this case, Adobe Reader displays the print output as a PDF document. You can see an excerpt from the flight-booking database in accordance with the selected form.

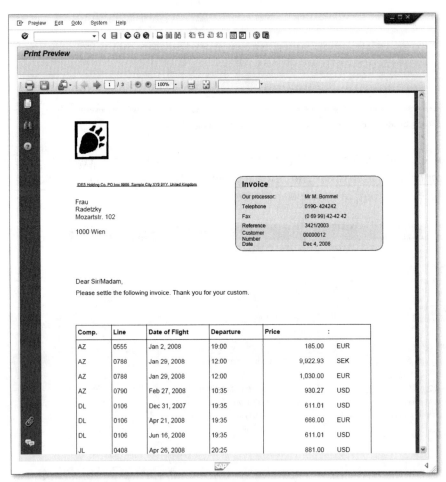

Figure 2.7 Print Preview of the Print Output via Adobe Reader

This example indicates which parts of the print output are identical for all forms. On one hand, this includes the form layout that describes the appearance of the formatted output and, on the other hand, the structure of data. The data quantity per form output is the only variable that is changeable and thus changes at runtime during the various calls. This is based on parameters and therefore different data is selected from the database and processed.

2.3.2 Creating an Interactive PDF Form

The second example considers the creation of an interactive PDF form. SAP provides a test program for this as well. You can test it as described here:

1. Go back to the initial screen of the ABAP Editor (see Figure 2.4).

2. In contrast to the print example, start the FP_TEST_IA_01 program. You can change the parameters for the test in the following screen.

3. Don't make any changes in the FORM area for the initial test.

4. In the DATA area you can set individual parts of the form to EDITABLE or LOCKED (READ-ONLY).

5. You can change the values that are used for filling the individual form fields during creation. You can accept these defaults or change them as shown in Figure 2.8.

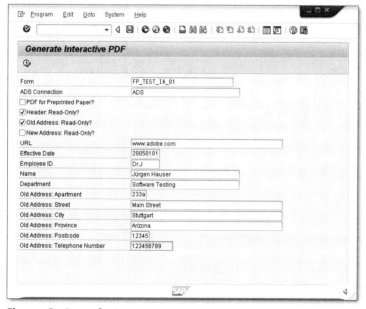

Figure 2.8 Screen for Entering Parameters

6. Start the program.

7. In the subsequent PRINT dialog, select a configured printer—just as in the print example—and click PRINT PREVIEW to confirm.

An interactive PDF form as shown in Figure 2.9 is displayed in the preview of the print output. This form is used for a change of address of an employee. Accordingly, the form includes an area that provides general information such as name and department and an area with the old, currently saved address. The NEW ADDRESS area contains interactive form fields for entering a new address.

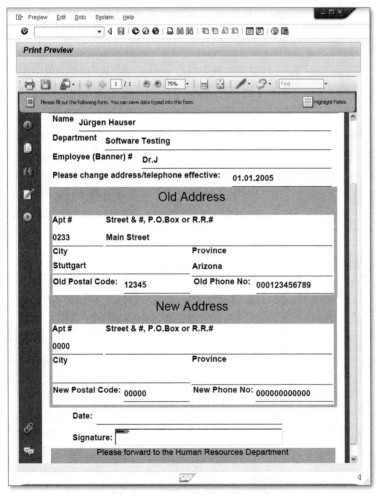

Figure 2.9 Preview of the Interactive PDF Form Example

Below the NEW ADDRESS area, there are two more form fields that you can test. The first field is a date field that provides a convenient date selection screen. The second field is the field for a digital signature. At this point, you may test the procedure for applying a digital signature. To do this, a certificate must be installed on your PC; Adobe Reader indicates the certificates available. You can also check which usage rights have been added to the form (see Section 2.2.1 for more details).

2.4 Using Interactive Forms in Business Processes

The creation of interactive forms is the second important application area in addition to the print output. Interactive forms can be used to optimize individual steps of a business process. In this case, optimizing processes means:

- ▸ **Increasing the data integrity**
  Errors can occur whenever data is transmitted or processed manually. If, for example, the handwriting on a paper form is illegible or can't be read entirely after transmission by fax, this may result in problems during further processing.

  So what are you supposed to do if you want to enter the data into the system? In most cases, you would simply guess. This may result in higher costs, if, for example, electronic bank transfers fail or a second manual revision is necessary. A consistent electronic entry of data can remedy this problem.

- ▸ **Eliminating manual steps**
  Manual entry of data must be carried out by a person. However, before this person can start entering data, the data must be sent to the person in paper form. The transfer of data to the entering person can be done by fax or by mail. Frequently, the documents are scanned in and the data is then provided in electronic form.

  Another example is the entry of data during a telephone call (for instance, telephone orders). Usually, you can't control the data entered on either side.

  All of these manual steps result in processing delays. This ultimately prolongs the overall duration of the business process, which means that products are delivered with a delay and suppliers receive their payment later, for example. Consistent electronic processing can considerably accelerate business processes by eliminating manual steps.

For the use of interactive forms in business processes, there are two different types of scenarios: online scenarios and offline scenarios. In this case, the concepts online and offline don't indicate whether the users have network access, but whether the users are logged on to an SAP system or not.

2.4.1 Online Scenarios

Online scenarios mainly feature the following two characteristics:

▶ **Direct access to an SAP system is required and possible**
During the use of a PDF form it is possible to call an SAP system, for example, to perform validations, implement a value help, or carry out complex calculations. This requires that the user is known in the system and that he is logged on to an SAP system.

▶ **Integration with other user-interface technology**
PDF forms are never displayed alone. They are displayed in a web browser and are surrounded by other web technology that calls Adobe Reader embedded in an (HTML) page.

A typical online scenario may look like the following: The user is logged on to SAP NetWeaver Portal. In the portal, he can view the pages of a Web Dynpro application in an iView. Web Dynpro enables you to integrate a PDF form with a view as a user-interface element and supports the implementation of value helps, validations, etc., for PDF forms.

2.4.2 Offline Scenarios

Offline scenarios may be characterized as follows:

▶ **No access to an SAP system possible or required**
When the user processes a form, he cannot (and doesn't have to) call an SAP system. Therefore, value helps, validations, and simple calculations must be contained in the PDF form by means of a scripting language. When the processing of the PDF form is completed, it is transferred to an SAP system. This is done either indirectly (for example, via an email that contains the PDF form as an attachment) or directly by logging on to the SAP system and uploading the PDF form to an application.

For example, if the user is not logged on to the company intranet, it is usually not possible to access an SAP system. If the user is logged on to the intranet, he can send the PDF form, or the data contained therein, to an SAP system via a Web service or HTTP call.

▶ **Independence of other user-interface technologies**
PDF forms are opened and processed with Adobe Reader exclusively. Therefore, integration with another technology for creating user interfaces is not necessary.

These two characteristics only require that the PDF form contain all of the necessary information (such as value helps and data). This may result in larger PDF files, which can impact the transfer time. This is important if the network connection is slow, for example.

The fact that all necessary information is already contained in the PDF form and that no access to an SAP system is required entails very interesting application options. Let's consider the following implementation example of an offline scenario:

A user receives an email including a request for increasing the budget of a cost center. The details of this request (currently approved budget, requested budget, and already-spent budget) are contained in an interactive PDF form that has already been sent to the user as an email attachment. Therefore, this interactive PDF form provides all of the necessary information for making a decision. Additional access to an SAP system is not required to fulfill the task. After the decision has been made (approval, rejection, or approval of a different budget), the form, including all changes, can be transferred as follows:

▶ It is returned to the SAP system via email for further processing.

▶ Or the PDF form can be sent to the user as an attachment to a proposal for an appointment. At the customer's site, you can then enter all of the relevant data in the form. Subsequently, it is returned to the SAP system for updating.

▶ A portal can also provide the option to download an interactive PDF form, fill it out, and start a process when it is returned to the SAP system.

An example of this is when a customer places an order with a mail-order business. If the user logs on to the system, the form should already be filled with important customer information. This information can be, for example, name, address, customer ID, and the last order as an initial value. Filling in business data in advance ensures that the user can conveniently use the interactive forms.

2.4.3 Combining Online and Offline Scenarios

Another approach is to provide the user with an option to go offline midway through the process. This constitutes a mixture of offline and online scenarios. Examples of this include the entry of travel expenses or working time.

When planning a business trip in the enterprise portal, you can prepare the entry of travel expenses. One step of the business process could be the display of a PDF form in which the user can enter the expenses. Depending on the process implementation, the user could download the form or receive it via email. During the business trip, he can fill out the PDF form on his laptop. The user interface for travel expenses enables the business traveler to upload the PDF form via a portal upon his return. It is then displayed for checking, the entries are validated, and possible confirmations are displayed. Corrections to the form can be done online.

2.4.4 When Do You Use Online and Offline Scenarios?

In addition to the question about the functioning and programming of the technology, you must also consider when you want to use interactive forms. To do this, the following lists provide some support. Interactive forms are suitable as a method for implementation if at least one of the following criteria applies:

▶ **Imitating the layout of well-known forms**
A well-known form implies that the user already knows how to handle it. This enables a fast transfer of the former paper-based process into an electronic process. The (re)use of a well-known form can reduce training costs.

▶ **Simple user interface for occasional SAP users**
Interactive forms allow for the creation of simple interfaces for occasional users of SAP systems. Instead of logging on to an SAP system, the user receives all of the necessary information for the operation in a compact PDF form. This enables a fast and convenient participation in the business process.

▶ **Creating a document for archiving**
In contrast to other technologies (for example, all HTML-based web technologies), completed PDF forms are available for further use. This way, they can be archived to fulfill regulatory requirements of traceability.

▶ **Local print output of the form**
PDF forms enable you to quickly create high-quality prints on site. For many

user-interface technologies (for example, HTML) this is only possible with some difficulty and extra effort.

▶ **Support of digital signatures**
PDF forms can contain fields for digital signatures. However, country-specific requirements must be taken into account. You can insert multiple digital signatures into a form within workflows (the respective fields must be contained in the form).

▶ **Several persons are required for data entry**
PDF forms support data entry that cannot be implemented by one single person. Frequently, forms cannot be completed by one person only, because the required information must be provided by several people (for example, information on products and finances).

You should consider the implementation of an offline scenario if one of the following criteria is met:

▶ **Integration of external users**
A person that is not an employee of the enterprise is supposed to participate in a business process, but must not have access to the enterprise's SAP systems.

▶ **Offline use of a form**
The user group of the form is in the service field or on a business trip and therefore has no access to the intranet and hence no access to the SAP system.

An alternative approach is the analysis of existing business processes. If you can identify manual steps or detect intermediate statuses in processing that are similar to the following two examples, you should consider the use of interactive forms for process optimization:

▶ **Conversion of existing paper-based processes**
It is possible that today's paper-based forms can be replaced with electronic versions. With the introduction of electronic forms, you can digitize parts of or complete processes.

▶ **Approval processes**
In approval processes, you either change or create new system data, for example, master data. However, this modification is supposed to become effective in the system only after it has been approved. In this case, interactive PDF forms are highly suited as data containers. The data saved in the PDF form are transferred to the SAP system only after approval.

If you compare the various options available in online and offline scenarios, you will notice that the full efficiency of interactive PDF forms is utilized in offline scenarios. The necessity to integrate external users with business processes indicates that an implementation using interactive forms makes sense. This ultimately results in a faster execution of the business process and higher data quality and therefore optimized process costs.

2.4.5   Notes on the Use of Interactive Forms

The why and the how play a decisive role in the use of interactive forms in the implementation of business processes.

Note for Offline Scenarios

In offline scenarios, the usability of interactive forms primarily depends on the forms' size. The larger the forms are, the more difficult it is for the user to navigate within the form. For this reason, it is useful to use the concepts of dynamic forms.

Depending on the data (for example, marital status, nationality, or answers to yes/no questions) some parts of the forms can either be hidden or displayed. This way, you can reduce the size and the complexity of the form. In extreme cases, you can implement a navigation with tabs that is similar to user interfaces.

A welcome side effect is that the behavior with regard to performance sometimes considerably improves if, for example, large dynamic forms (more than ten pages) don't have to be constantly re-created in Adobe Reader.

Notes for Online Scenarios

Online scenarios entail that you ensure a balance between the user interface parts of the embedded technology (for example, Web Dynpro) and the interactive form. Let's consider some extreme examples to illustrate this:

▶ If an interactive form with multiple pages is embedded in Web Dynpro and if the Web Dynpro screen doesn't include any interface elements, the user faces a complex navigation in the interactive form.

▶ Another extreme example is multiple dynamic tables—tables in which you can insert or delete rows—which are distributed to multiple pages.

A possible solution for these cases is to reduce the complexity—just as for offline scenarios. In both cases you should check why interactive forms are used (see Section 2.4.4, "When Do You Use Online and Offline Scenarios?") to ensure that interactive forms are not used just because they are easy to implement.

Interactive Forms are not a Replacement for Complex User Interfaces

SAP Interactive Forms by Adobe is a form technology that is oriented toward the creation of forms. There are fewer functions provided, particularly in comparison to user-interface technologies; for example, it is not possible to program a form entirely in JavaScript without creating a form template in Adobe LiveCycle Designer.

Therefore, you should use SAP Interactive Forms by Adobe for form-based scenarios and not as a replacement for a user-interface technology. You will encounter difficulties if you still use forms as a replacement for user interfaces.

Notes for Combined Online/Offline Scenarios

If you combine online and offline scenarios, for example, to map the completing and processing of a form, you should carefully consider whether you use one and the same form in both scenarios. Consider the notes provided in Section 2.4.4 to check whether an interactive form is required for the online scenario. Keep in mind that the effort saved for the design and the implementation of the application interface usually entails a higher development and maintenance effort.

2.5 Software Components and Architecture

Now that you've learned what PDF-based print forms and interactive forms are and when they can be used, let's look at the required software components and their integration with SAP NetWeaver. SAP Interactive Forms by Adobe mainly consists of three software components, which can only be used after they've been integrated with different SAP environments. They are:

▶ **Adobe LiveCycle Designer**
Adobe LiveCycle Designer is used at design and implementation time.

▶ **Adobe Reader**
Adobe Reader is required on the user's PC at runtime.

▶ **Adobe Document Services (ADS)**
ADS must be installed and configured in the SAP NetWeaver stack at runtime.

Adobe Reader must be downloaded from the Adobe website. ADS and Adobe LiveCycle Designer are available directly from SAP. They are provided via the SAP Service Marketplace (*http://service.sap.com*).

2.5.1 Adobe LiveCycle Designer

Adobe LiveCycle Designer is a tool that the form designer uses to create the layout of forms. The layouts of PDF-based print forms and interactive forms are created in the same way. The same tool, Adobe LiveCycle Designer, is used for both types of forms. Figure 2.10 shows how you can use Adobe LiveCycle Designer as a desktop application.

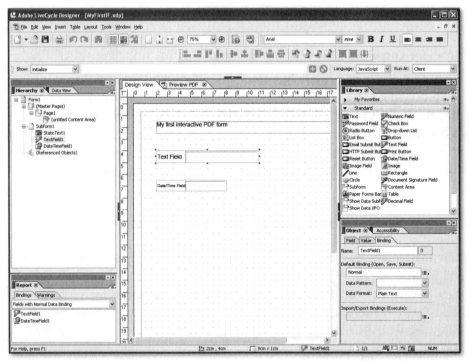

Figure 2.10 Adobe LiveCycle Designer

Adobe LiveCycle Designer is a graphical interactive tool; many of the required steps can be implemented using the mouse. The layout of the form is displayed graphically at design time (the window shown in the middle of Figure 2.10). Changes, such as the positioning of form fields, are carried out using drag and drop.

In addition to the layout, Adobe LiveCycle Designer graphically displays the form hierarchy and the data context:

▶ The form hierarchy indicates the structure of the pages that consist of the form fields used and the subforms. Subforms are structuring elements that enable you to create and maintain more complex forms. Nested subforms therefore constitute a form hierarchy.

▶ The data context describes the data structure of the form. Technically, a form is based on an XML data structure with a corresponding XML schema. In the SAP environment, Adobe LiveCycle Designer is used almost exclusively in the context of a framework. These frameworks create the XML schema at design time. During runtime, the XML data required for form output is generated automatically.

Adobe LiveCycle Designer provides all of the available form fields in a library. From this library, you can insert new form fields into the form layout using drag and drop. After a new form field has been added to the form, you can define additional properties using the palettes. Some examples are the appearance of buttons or edit and display patterns. The appearance determines whether a button has a border or a 3D effect. The edit and display pattern can be used to format figures, times, or a date.

Very complex behavior of forms can also be implemented using script programming. Forms are based on an event model and you can create a script program for many predefined events (for example, `initialize` for the time of initialization of a field).

You can choose between two different scripting languages:

▶ The first option is JavaScript, a scripting language from web programming. It allows for easy access to script programming for form creation.

▶ The second option is Adobe's proprietary scripting language, FormCalc. FormCalc has a higher performance rate than JavaScript. In particular, calculations that are based on tabular data structures can be implemented easier with FormCalc than JavaScript.

Most PDF-based print forms can be used without any script programming. Interactive forms with dynamic behavior, however, often require scripts to implement this dynamic behavior (for example, inserting or deleting table rows).

SAP Version of Adobe LiveCycle Designer

You must use the SAP version of Adobe LiveCycle Designer for the development of PDF-based print forms and interactive forms, and not the version available from Adobe (for example, as part of Adobe Acrobat Professional or other Adobe LiveCycle products). Therefore, you must download Adobe LiveCycle Designer from the SAP Service Marketplace.

Embedding Adobe LiveCycle Designer in SAP Development Environments

Adobe LiveCycle Designer is already embedded in the development environments for the use in the SAP environment. This results in the following benefits:

- Adobe LiveCycle Designer is integrated with the development process and can be called at the right point and at the right time.
- Adobe LiveCycle Designer is always called in the context of the current development work. Therefore, the form to be processed is already opened and the data view already displays the underlying data structure.

As a result, the form design must be saved in the surrounding development environments. Therefore, the embedded Adobe LiveCycle Designer does not provide any FILE menu. You can't find the menu item for file properties under FILE · FORM PROPERTIES... as is the case in the independent Adobe LiveCycle Designer; instead, it is available under EDIT · FORM PROPERTIES...

Figure 2.11 shows the embedding of Adobe LiveCycle Designer in the SAP GUI. Here, Adobe LiveCycle Designer is integrated with Form Builder. Form Builder is the environment in the ABAP Workbench that bundles all of the development tools required for the use of SAP Interactive Forms by Adobe.

Figure 2.11 Adobe LiveCycle Designer Embedded in the SAP GUI

To check to see if your installation is correct, you must call Form Builder and navigate to the form template shown in Figure 2.11.

1. To do this, start the SAP GUI and call Transaction SFP. The screen shown in Figure 2.12 should appear.

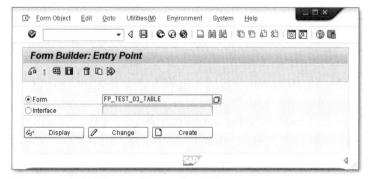

Figure 2.12 Initial Screen of Transaction SFP

2. Enter the name of the form in the FORM input field—in this case FP_TEST_03_ TABLE.

3. Then click on the DISPLAY button.

4. In the following screen, select the LAYOUT tab to go to the screen shown in Figure 2.11.

For the sake of completeness, Figure 2.13 shows how Adobe LiveCycle Designer is embedded in the SAP NetWeaver Developer Studio. The SAP NetWeaver Developer Studio is an Eclipse-based development tool that is usually used for development in Java.

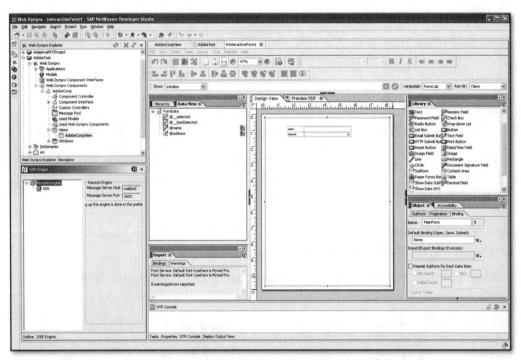

Figure 2.13 Adobe Designer Embedded in the SAP NetWeaver Developer Studio

In SAP's Java world, there is only one integration of SAP Interactive Forms by Adobe, that is, the integration with Web Dynpro Java. This book focuses on development using ABAP because multiple integrations exist here. For this reason, the main focus is on integration with Web Dynpro ABAP and not with Web Dynpro Java.

2.5.2 ADS

ADS is the server component that is installed on the SAP NetWeaver stack; strictly speaking, it is installed on the Java stack and comprised of Java and C++ coding. It must be configured after the installation and prior to the first usage. A configuration is also necessary on the ABAP side. In a nutshell, the ABAP stack must be notified which ADS installation is to be used and how it can be reached. Only after these two configurations have been completed, can ADS be used by ABAP.

ADS and Adobe Document Server

ADS is a software component of SAP Interactive Forms by Adobe. Do not confuse this component with Adobe Document Server.

Adobe Document Server is an Adobe product that is only maintained within the framework of warranty services and will be taken off the market soon. Adobe LiveCycle provides a similar scope of functions.

Let's first consider how you can use ADS within the ABAP and Java world (see Figure 2.14). On both sides, there is a PDF object that represents the lowest usable interface. The PDF object calls ADS.

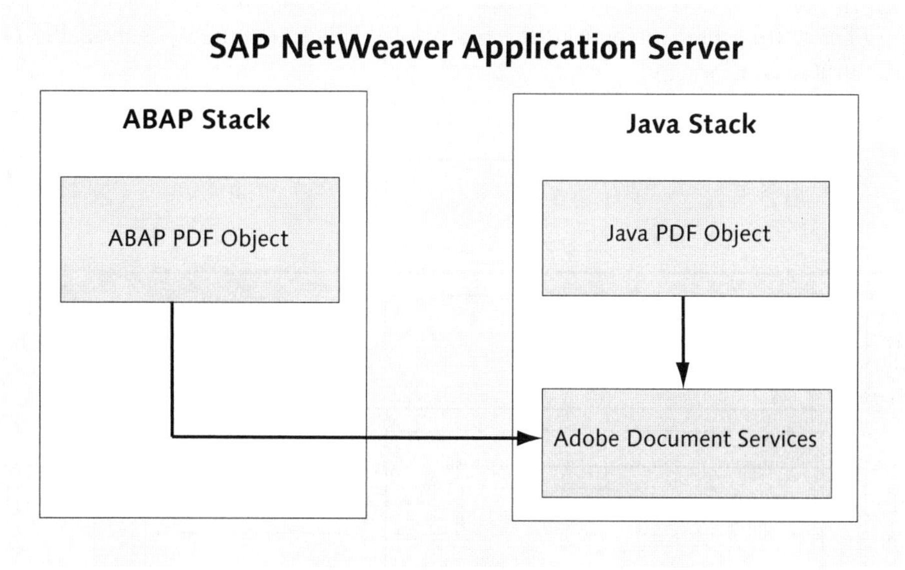

Figure 2.14 Main Components from the Developer's View

The PDF object is used exclusively whereby you can only use the functionality existing in the respective PDF object. Currently, the PDF object in ABAP provides considerably more functionality. The Java PDF object is mainly used in Web Dynpro runtime; the ABAP PDF object, however, calls ADS from the Java stack. The Java stack is still required for ADS for applications that are completely implemented in ABAP.

ADS Requires the Java Stack

ADS constitutes an SAP NetWeaver solution extension that can only be installed and operated on the Java stack of SAP NetWeaver Application Server. So, you need a Java instance in your system landscape, even if the PDF forms are only used in the ABAP world.

Using ADS

Figure 2.15 illustrates which frameworks are based on the two PDF objects or on other frameworks.

The PDF object is the lowest layer. Web Dynpro is based on the PDF object in both worlds (ABAP and Java). In the ABAP world, you are also provided with Form Builder and the Forms Processing runtime. You can also develop custom applications that use the PDF object directly. In this case, Form Builder is used to create the PDF forms and save them in the repository. This functionality is available in SAP NetWeaver directly.

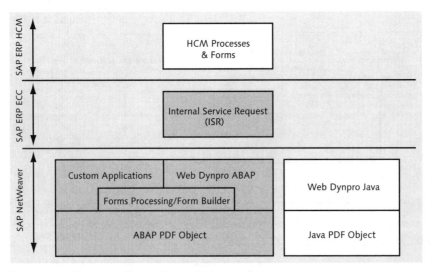

Figure 2.15 Hierarchy of Integration and Frameworks

SAP Enterprise Core Component (ECC) contains the Internal Service Request (ISR) framework, which is based on Web Dynpro. In more recent releases of SAP NetWeaver it is based on Web Dynpro ABAP; in the past, it utilized Web Dynpro Java. ISR supports the implementation of online scenarios using a workflow integration.

This book considers all integrations that are displayed in gray in Figure 2.15. It imparts the necessary basics that also apply to the frameworks and application options not considered within the scope of this book. These are briefly explained in the following text for the sake of completeness.

▶ HCM Processes & Forms is a framework that has been developed specifically for personnel administration. It is part of SAP HCM and allows for the implementation of processes in personnel administration using interactive PDF forms. It is a specialization and further development of the ISR framework. For this reason, this book only considers the ISR framework because it provides all necessary basics.

▶ Guided Procedures is the second framework that is not considered. Guided Procedures is a complex tool for creating business processes without any programming. This framework includes an integration of interactive PDF forms for implementing individual offline steps of a process. A process is either started by processing and sending an interactive PDF form (to the SAP system) or an offline step is required midway through the process flow. In this case, an interactive PDF form is sent to the user who then participates in the process. The process is stopped until the user has processed the PDF and returned it to the system.

▶ There is also indirect integration. Indirect integration includes all options in which interactive PDF forms are not integrated with a technology or framework directly; however, they can be integrated with an existing framework using another technology. An example would be the integration of a Web Dynpro application with SAP Business Workflow or with Guided Procedures. This way, the two frameworks can be used to support online scenarios. For the implementation, you need a working knowledge about the frameworks with which you want to integrate and about the integration of interactive PDF forms with Web Dynpro. This book provides details about the latter. However, it would go beyond the scope of this book to describe SAP Business Workflow or Guided Procedures.

Communication between PDF Objects and ADS

PDF objects are implemented either in Java or in ABAP. The communication structure with ADS is illustrated in Figure 2.16; it is identical for both languages.

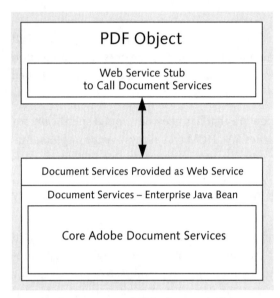

Figure 2.16 Interaction of PDF Object and ADS

The communication between the PDF object and ADS is carried out by calling a Web service. The PDF object implements a Web service stub, which is utilized to call ADS.

The PDF object itself does not contain a lot of logic. Its main task is to correctly call ADS via the Web service stub based on the parameters and the required functionality. Both the PDF objects and ADS are located on the SAP NetWeaver Application Server (AS). ADS is always installed on the Java stack.

Structure of ADS

ADS is comprised of two components, Document Services and Core Adobe Document Services (see the lower part of Figure 2.16):

▶ Core Adobe Document Services provide the main functionality for the server side. This includes, for example, the creation of a PDF or various printer languages, extraction of data from the PDF, insertion of a server-side signature, or adding of usage rights for a PDF. Functions, such as the administration of fonts or certificates stored on the server, are part of Core Adobe Document Services.

▸ Document Services are on the next abstraction level. These utilize the functions made available by Core Adobe Document Services; however, they provide an application programming interface that is comprised of more than just simple basic functions. This enables you to perform multiple tasks in one Document Services call. Document Services ensure that basic functions are used in the correct sequence and that you only require one Web service call. You can save a lot of administration and communication effort with just one single call. This would be particularly significant if you call multiple fast functions individually.

Interface to ADS

Document Services are combined and managed in an Enterprise JavaBean. The interface of these JavaBeans is provided as a Web service and the interface of the Web service via a Web Service Definition Language (WSDL file) . The Web service stub for the PDF objects can be created from the WSDL file. This is illustrated in Figure 2.16.

The Web service of ADS is a public Web service that cannot be used directly. You can find it in developer and administration tools within SAP NetWeaver without any problems—the documentation of the Web service and its parameters, however, is not published. Ultimately, it is the interface agreed upon by SAP and Adobe.

The PDF object abstracts from this Web service interface and is the lowest interface to ADS that is released for application development. This abstraction provides SAP and Adobe a wider scope for future developments.

2.5.3   Interaction of Components

Up to now, this chapter described individual software components and the interaction of PDF objects and ADS. The following sections detail the overall architecture of the integration both at development time and at runtime. You need this information for the following chapters to, for example, understand and solve problems or comprehend why certain decisions were made in frameworks.

Considering Development Time

First, let's consider the development time. Figure 2.17 illustrates how you can use the development environment to create a form template (which is based on a specific context) and make it available for further use.

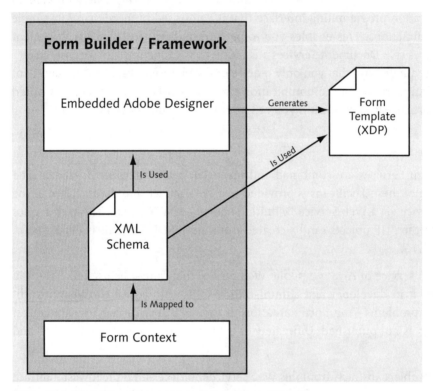

Figure 2.17 Interaction of Components at Development Time

- At development time, Adobe LiveCycle Designer, which is integrated with the SAP environments, is used to create form templates, which are then converted into PDF documents or print outputs at runtime. This form template corresponds to the description of a data structure.

- All development environments have a form context (often also referred to as context). In most cases, this context must be set up manually prior to the actual form template creation. The context is the intermediary element between the SAP framework and the Adobe components.

▶ The development environment creates an XML schema that is based on the context. This XML schema includes the description of the data structure, which is based on the form template. This description is transferred to Adobe Live-Cycle Designer and is displayed in the data view of the form designer's screen. This is done automatically.

▶ Now, the form designer creates the form template. To do this, Adobe LiveCycle Designer, which is embedded in the development environment, is started. The form template includes the form layout; for interactive PDF forms, you must specify the behavior and integrate the form with the data structure. By integrating the form template with the data structure, you always create a form template for a specific data structure.

If you change the data structure, you may also have to change the form template; this is the case for structural changes of the data hierarchy. Adding new data nodes does not require a modification of the form template; however, if you want to use the data node you must extend the form template accordingly.

▶ When you save the form template, it is returned to the SAP development environment that embeds Adobe LiveCycle Designer. The development environment then ensures that the form template is stored at the correct position with the correct name (for example, in ABAP Repository). There are several reasons for this automation, such as facilitating the form designer's work or ensuring that form templates can be referenced and retrieved.

Considering the Runtime

Every framework has a specific runtime environment in addition to a development environment—for PDF-based print forms it is the Forms Processing runtime and for Web Dynpro the Web Dynpro runtime.

▶ At runtime, form data must be created that corresponds to the data description and therefore to the context and the XML schema.

▶ The data can be read from the database or is already available in the framework, for example. Before the data is transferred to the PDF object, it must be prepared and converted into XML format, which must correspond to the XML schema.

▶ In the next step, the runtime must locate the form template required for the current task and transfer it to the PDF object.

▶ For the actual call of the PDF object, the runtime environment decides on the required output format or whether usage rights should be added in case of an interactive PDF form. It then calls ADS via the PDF object.

Figure 2.18 summarizes the steps at runtime up to the call of the PDF object.

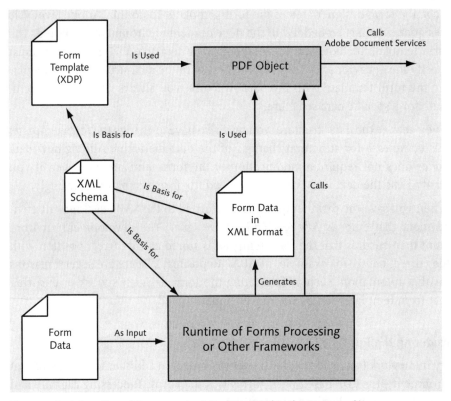

Figure 2.18 Interaction of Components at Runtime (Within the Framework)

Figure 2.19 summarizes how input data (form data and form templates) is transferred to ADS using the PDF object at runtime.

▶ The PDF object uses the form data and form template that were provided by the runtime environment.

▶ In this process, the PDF object calls ADS. The data, the form template, and the parameters are transferred to ADS in accordance with the interface definition.

▶ ADS processes the data and form templates according to the parameters and thus creates the required output format.

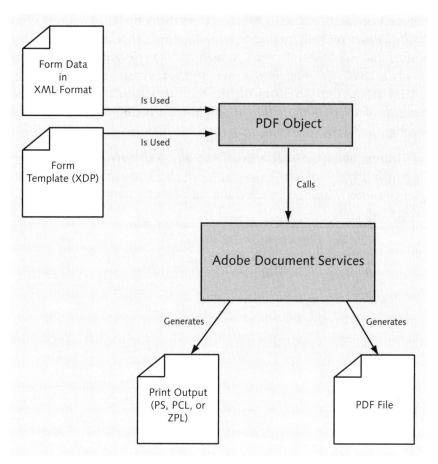

Figure 2.19 Interaction at Runtime (Call of ADS)

2.6   Summary

This chapter briefly introduced you to the terminology used for PDFs. In this context, two central concepts, PDF-based print forms and interactive forms, were detailed.

The knowledge about the classification of application scenarios in offline and online scenarios enables you to select the correct framework for your implementation. Furthermore, you were provided with decision support for assigning business processes to scenarios. This chapter also provided support to answer the question whether you should use interactive forms at all.

Users who participate in business processes comprising interactive forms must install Adobe Reader on their computer. In this context, this chapter compared Adobe Reader and Adobe Acrobat and pointed out the relevance of the various versions. Adobe LiveCycle Designer was presented as tool that you can use to create form templates during development. The form templates and data from the SAP systems are converted into different output formats (printer languages and PDF) at runtime using ADS.

Finally, you learned about the integration of ADS with SAP NetWeaver. This information is particularly useful for Chapter 3. It can also be beneficial for troubleshooting. If you already have an installed and configured system at your disposal, you can skip Chapter 3.

This chapter details how to install and configure the required software for using SAP Interactive Forms by Adobe. It also gives an overview of the scenario-dependent configuration of the runtime components and of optional setting options.

3 Installation and Configuration

This chapter details how to set up a development environment for SAP Interactive Forms by Adobe. In this context, you use trial versions of the required SAP software components. Their installation enables you to create and test forms in a local environment. In addition, this chapter provides useful information on the use of Adobe Document Services (ADS) and analyzes typical (configuration) error situations and their elimination.

3.1 Preparations

To work with SAP Interactive Forms by Adobe, you need ADS and Adobe Live-Cycle Designer. ADS is integrated with the SAP NetWeaver Java application server; however, you also need an ABAP application server to reproduce certain scenarios that are described in this book. Chapter 9, "Internal Service Requests," details the requirements for the creation of ISR scenarios.

Downloads

You can download the SAP NetWeaver 7.0 trial versions (Java and ABAP) that were used for this book via the SAP Interactive Forms by Adobe page in the SAP Developer Network (SDN).

1. To do this, go to *https://www.sdn.sap.com/irj/sdn/adobe*.

2. Log on or register to the SDN.

3. Download the Java and ABAP trial versions for SAP NetWeaver 7.0 via their respective links.

The following sections explain the installation and configuration based on these trial versions. The descriptions also apply to other versions of SAP NetWeaver 7.0; however, depending on the support package, they may differ slightly. Therefore, you should read the provided installation and configuration documentation when using another version.

SAP NetWeaver 7.0 (2004s)—Java Trial Version

In addition to the Java application server, the SAP NetWeaver 7.0 (2004s)—Java Trial Version contains the SAP MaxDB database. ADS is also part of this installation. You also need Sun® Microsystems Java™ 2 Standard Edition Software Development Kit (J2SE SDK). To avoid later installation problems, you should download and install one of the versions that were tested and specified in the documentation provided.

SAP NetWeaver 7.0 (2004s)—ABAP Trial Version

The SAP NetWeaver 7.0 (2004s)—ABAP Trial Version contains the ABAP application server and the SAP MaxDB database.

Credentials and Password for SAP Interactive Forms by Adobe

You can download a ReaderRights credential, which is valid for a limited period and required for the generation of interactive forms, via the SDN.

1. To do this, go to *http://sdn.sap.com* and log on or register.

2. In the main navigation, select DOWNLOADS and then SOFTWARE DOWNLOADS • SAP NETWEAVER MAIN RELEASES. You can also access this page directly via *http://www.sdn.sap.com/irj/sdn/nw-downloads*.

3. From the software packages available, you need CREDENTIALS AND PASSWORD FOR SAP INTERACTIVE FORMS BY ADOBE. The download includes an archive file (*.zip*) that contains a password-protected private key (credential). The file format corresponds to the Public Key Cryptography Standards (PKCS) #12 specification; the file has the extension *.p12* or *.pfx*. In addition to the key, the ZIP archive also contains a text file (*.txt*), which stores the corresponding password.

Adobe LiveCycle Designer 8.0

You can download version 8.0 of Adobe LiveCycle Designer from the SAP Service Marketplace.

1. To do this, go to *http://service.sap.com/installations* and log on with your S user.
2. Then, select the Entry by Application Group menu entry.
3. Navigate to SAP NETWEAVER • SAP NETWEAVER • SAP NETWEAVER 7.0 • INSTALLATION AND UPGRADE • <OPERATING SYSTEM> • <DATABASE>. Here, you can specify any combination of operating system and database, because it is a local PC application.
4. Use the Adobe LiveCycle Designer 8.0 entry in the Downloads tab to download the software.

3.2 Installation of the Java Application Server and ADS

To install the Java application server, including ADS, you must unpack the downloaded archive to a directory of your choice. Open the *start.htm* file, and read the displayed documentation. It contains important notes on the system requirements and the software license. The INSTALLATION menu entry takes you to a short description of the installation steps. You can also use it to navigate to the installation program directory. Call the *sapinst.exe* application here.

3.2.1 SAPinst

1. After having started the SAP installation program (see Figure 3.1), select the DEVELOPER WORKPLACE WITH MAXDB option, and click NEXT.
2. You must then accept the license terms to proceed with the installation. Now, the installation program automatically searches for the J2SE SDK versions that are installed on the system. If it finds a supported version, this version is used for the installation. It then asks you for the Java Cryptography Extension (JCE), which you can download from the Sun Microsystems website. The installation of the package allows for cryptography, authentication, authorization, the usage of a public key infrastructure, and other functions with unlimited strength.

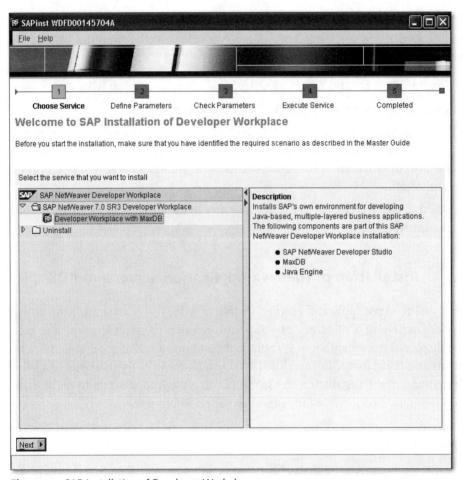

Figure 3.1 SAP Installation of Developer Workplace

3. Then, the installation program asks for further specifications, such as the SAP System ID (SAPSID) and the Database ID (DBSID). Here, you should use J2E respectively, because it enables you to extend the license of 90 days at a later stage. You also need a master password, which is assigned to all technical users that are created during the installation process.

4. If the media browser prompts you to specify the location of particular software packages, you must select the corresponding subdirectory from the installation directory that you use. The package name indicates the respective directory. For example, the directory that contains the SAP MaxDB Relational Database Management System (RDBMS) begins with MAXDB.

5. You don't need the System Landscape Directory (SLD) to use SAP Interactive Forms by Adobe. Therefore, you should select the No SLD Destination option.

6. Before the program initiates the actual installation, it displays an overview of all installation parameters. This overview includes the specifications made by you and the default values for additional parameters. When you scroll down to the end of the list, you can view the password of the ADSUSER user as an additional parameter (see Figure 3.2). This is a technical user who is authorized to call the ADS Web service. Section 3.4.1, "ADSUSER," provides more information on this user and its relevance to SAP Interactive Forms by Adobe.

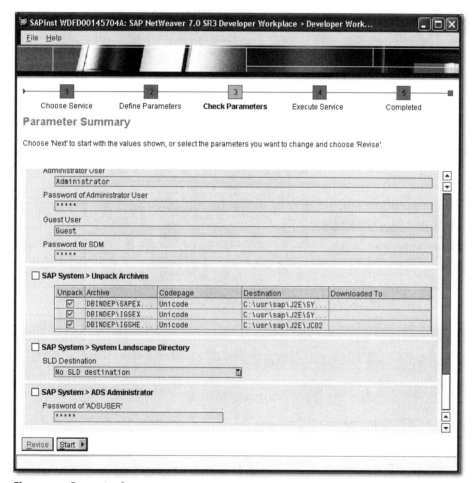

Figure 3.2 Parameter Summary

7. You can now start the installation. The installation program displays the individual phases of the installation and the current progress. One of the installation phases is called CONFIGURE ADOBE DOCUMENT SERVICES. During this phase, the system automatically implements the basic configuration of ADS. You can also view a detailed log. To do this, follow the FILE • VIEW LOG menu path (see Figure 3.3). Note that the installation takes some time. The START JAVA ENGINE phase in particular takes several minutes, even on powerful machines.

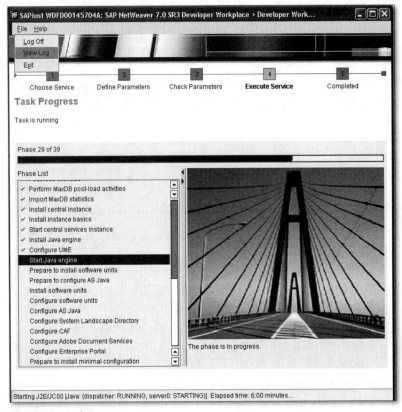

Figure 3.3 Task Progress

3.2.2 SAP Management Console

When the installation is complete, you can call the SAP Management Console from the Windows™ start menu (see Figure 3.4). It is a plug-in for the Microsoft® Management Console (MMC). This program enables you to start and stop the database and the application servers.

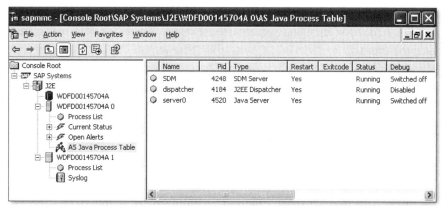

Figure 3.4 AS Java Process Table

1. When you select the first subnode of the SAP system that is displayed in the console, an administrator interface for the database (WEB DBM) opens. When the system prompts you to enter a password, enter the master password that you defined during the installation process. The ONLINE and OFFLINE buttons (see Figure 3.5) enable you to start or stop the database. You won't need to know any more regarding the database systems for this book.

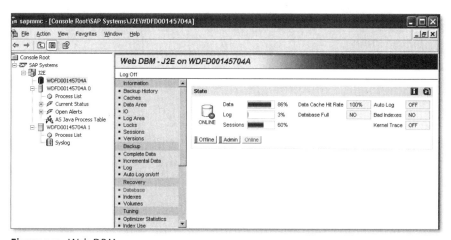

Figure 3.5 Web DBM

2. The second subnode that is displayed in the console represents the actual Java application server. The AS JAVA PROCESS TABLE displays the following processes:

▶ **Software Deployment Manager (SDM)**
This is a tool for managing software packages. You can call a user interface for this service (SDM GUI) with the *C:\usr\sap\J2E\JC00\SDM\program\ RemoteGui.bat* file. Then, click on the CONNECT TO SDM SERVER button to connect to the server process after you have entered the master password. The hostname and port are already predefined in the logon screen. The SDM REPOSITORY tab displays all of the components that are deployed on the Java application server (see Figure 3.6).

▶ **dispatcher**
The dispatcher process is responsible for the central communication tasks of the system, such as the distribution of incoming HTTP requests.

▶ **server**
Applications are executed in server processes that are similar to ABAP work processes. To scale a system according to the load requirements, you can configure various server processes and distribute them across different computers, if required. You don't have to use this scaling method for ADS. Instead, you can configure how many process instances the individual services can use simultaneously (see Section 3.6.3, "Service Properties").

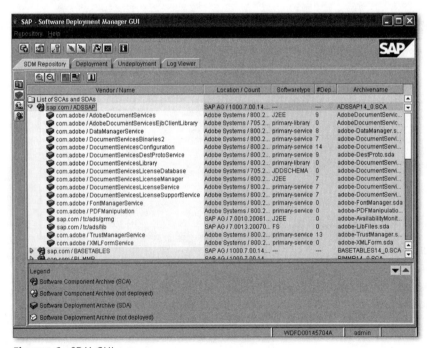

Figure 3.6 SDM GUI

3. The third subnode that is displayed in the SAP Management Console enables you to access the central SAP processes, message server and enqueue server.

3.2.3 Smoke Test

To ensure that the installation was successful, you can call the start page of the Java application server (see Figure 3.7) in a web browser via *http://localhost:50000*.

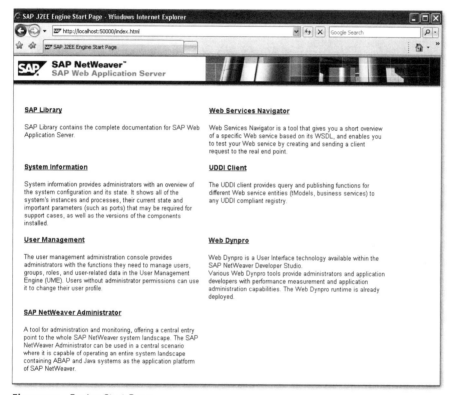

Figure 3.7 Engine Start Page

If there are already other SAP systems installed on your computer, the next free instance number is assigned to the previously installed Java application server. You can recognize it by the directory name *C:\usr\sap\<SAP system ID>\JC<instance number>*. Here, you must enter the SAP system ID and instance number respectively. By default, the Java instance of the trial version is located in the *C:\usr\sap\J2E\ JC00* directory. In addition, the instance number is displayed in the SAP Management Console after the corresponding node.

3.3   Installation of the ABAP Application Server

Before you can install the ABAP application server, you must unpack the downloaded archive to a directory of your choice.

1. Call the *start.htm* file and read the displayed information on the system requirements and license. You can call the installation program directly using the Installation menu entry (see Figure 3.8). Alternatively, you can start *setup.exe* in the *image* subdirectory.

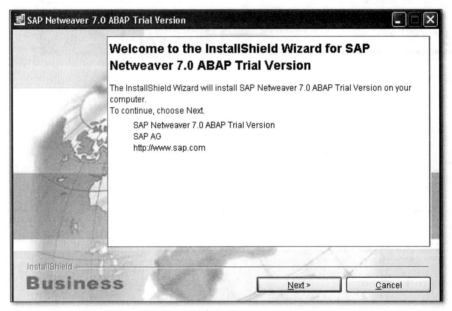

Figure 3.8   SAP NetWeaver 7.0 ABAP Trial Version

2. In the installation program, you must first specify a directory for the installation and then define a master password.

3. If you call the installation program of the ABAP application server while the previously installed Java application server is running, the system provides a list of all processes that you must stop before you can start the installation (see Figure 3.9). To stop the running processes, you must first stop the Java application server via the SAP Management Console. Then, call the console that manages the Windows services through the services.msc Windows command (START • RUN...) and stop the SAPDBWWW service there (see Figure 3.10).

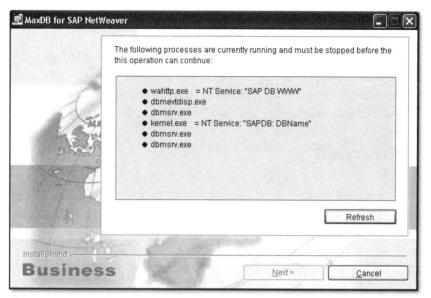

Figure 3.9 MaxDB for SAP NetWeaver

Figure 3.10 SAP DB WWW Properties

4. Now if you click the Refresh button in the SAP installation program, the previously displayed processes should disappear, and you should be able to proceed

with the installation process. Click on Install as soon as the system displays a summary of the specifications you made.

5. After the installation process has been completed, you are provided with the option to install the SAP Management Console. Because it has already been installed together with the Java application server, you should deselect this option (Install SAP Management Console). Then, restart the computer.

SAP Management Console

When you start the SAP Management Console (see Section 3.2.2, "SAP Management Console"), it now displays the NSP system (see Figure 3.11), a database, and an instance node. Below the instance node, there is a table that includes information on the configured work processes (AS ABAP WP TABLE).

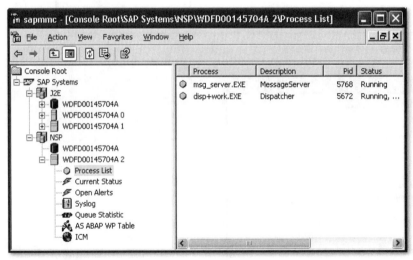

Figure 3.11 Process List

SAP GUI

To log on to the ABAP application server, the SAP GUI must be installed on your computer. The *SAPGUI* subdirectory contains the corresponding installation program (*SapGuiSetup.exe*). Alternatively, you can also use an already-installed SAP GUI installation.

1. To connect to the system, create a new system entry in the SAP Logon Pad (see Figure 3.12). Enter "localhost" as the APPLICATION SERVER and "NSP" as the

SYSTEM ID. The SYSTEM NUMBER depends on the SAP systems that are already installed on your computer. For example, if you have installed the Java application server with instance number 00, the system automatically assigns the system number 02 to the ABAP application server. You can find the corresponding number in the SAP Management Console.

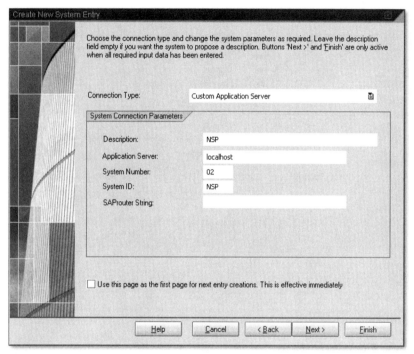

Figure 3.12 SAP Logon Pad

2. Then, call the newly created system entry and log on to the ABAP application server (see Figure 3.13). Several users are available:

   ▶ **BCUSER**
   You can use this user to create new development objects.

   ▶ **DDIC**
   This user is provided with administration authorizations and is therefore used for the configuration, which is described in the following sections.

   ▶ **SAP***
   You require the superuser to import an extended trial license.

   The password for all of these users is "minisap."

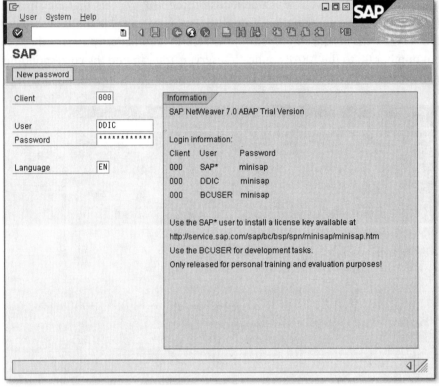

Figure 3.13 Logon Screen

3.4 Basic Configuration

This section describes the individual steps that are required to set up ADS. In this context, it is distinguished between the basic, scenario-dependent, and optional configuration. This section also introduces the tools used and check options for each configuration aspect.

You can call ADS via a Web service interface. The provided function is wrapped in the Portable Document Format (PDF) object that is available in both the ABAP and the Java environment. Therefore, to use ADS, access to the Web service must be configured. This general configuration was already implemented during the installation process of SAPinst (see Section 3.2.1, "SAPinst"). The following sections, however, provide further details on the individual configuration aspects to give you an understanding of possible errors and how to eliminate them.

3.4.1 ADSUSER

1. Start the Visual Administrator by calling the *go.bat* file in the *C:\usr\sap\J2E\ JC00\j2ee\admin* directory. A Java Swing application opens, which you can use to manage both local and remote systems.

2. Follow the menu path CONNECT • LOGIN and click on the Connect button to establish a connection to the local server (Default). Enter the master password that you defined during the installation, and click on CONNECT again.

3. After the connection to the server has been established, the left area in the Cluster tab displays two nodes for the dispatcher and the server process.

4. To find the configured ADSUSER user, navigate to SERVER... • SERVICES • SECURITY PROVIDER. Then, select the USER MANAGEMENT tab, and switch to the tree display (TREE). There, you can find the ADSCALLERS user group that also contains the ADSUSER user (see Figure 3.14).

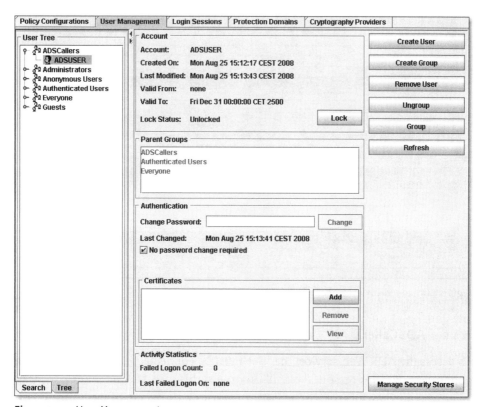

Figure 3.14 User Management

5. The AUTHENTICATION area indicates that the NO PASSWORD CHANGE REQUIRED option is selected for this technical user. If this option is deselected, the password would change after a certain amount of time; the password can be changed in the edit mode.

6. You can also call the user administration via *http://localhost:50000/useradmin*. A Web Dynpro application opens that also displays information on ADSUSER (see Figure 3.15).

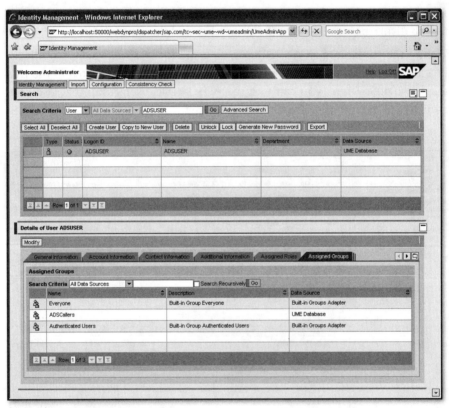

Figure 3.15 Identity Management

3.4.2 ADSCaller

To access the ADS Web service, the user must be connected to the corresponding application. For this reason, the application—in this case ADS—defines a security role. You can view this role in the POLICY CONFIGURATIONS tab of the Security Provider service in the Visual Administrator. Select the COM.ADOBE/ADOBEDOCUM

ENTSERVICES*ADOBEDOCUMENTSERVICES ASSEMBLY.JAR component here and then the SECURITY ROLES tab on the right. It shows that the ADSCALLER security role is linked to ADSUSER (see Figure 3.16).

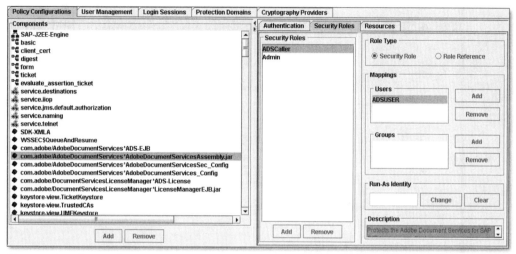

Figure 3.16 Policy Configurations

3.4.3 Web Service Test

The previously described configuration steps that have already been automatically performed allow for a password-protected call of ADS. You can test this via the Web services navigator.

1. To do this, go to *http://localhost:50000/wsnavigator*, and log on as the administrator using the previously defined master password.

2. From the displayed list of the available Web services, select AdobeDocumentServices. This navigates you to a page that describes the Web service.

3. Click on Test, select the rpData operation, and then click on the Send button without specifying any parameters. The page that opens prompts you to enter a user name and password. Enter ADSUSER and the master password.

4. By clicking on Submit, you receive the response of the Web service call (see Figure 3.17). Because no data was transferred for this test, the Results parameter contains an error message (*com.adobe.ProcessingException: Required stream: "PDF-Document" not found in request OR its length is zero*). However, this does indicate that the Web service call has been successful.

Figure 3.17 Web Services Navigator

3.5   Scenario-Dependent Configuration

Section 3.4, "Basic Configuration," described the basic configuration of ADS that all scenarios require. The following sections detail the configuration steps that are necessary for the different usage options. Figure 3.18 illustrates the components that are relevant for form processing. They are discussed along with the communication channels that these components use.

The Web service of ADS was already described in the context of the basic configuration. Two different client categories access this interface: the Remote Function Call (*RFC*) *destination* (ABAP application server) and the *Web service proxy* (Java application server).

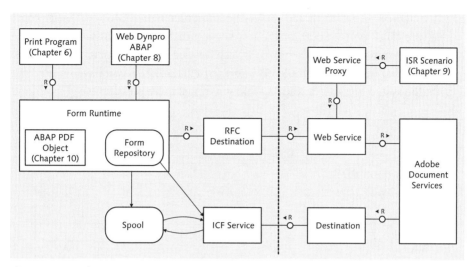

Figure 3.18 Architecture

Both ABAP print programs and applications in Web Dynpro ABAP use the *ABAP PDF object* at runtime. This object requires a *configured RFC* connection (*RFC destination*) to communicate with ADS. Form scenarios that are executed on the Java application server, such as applications in Web Dynpro Java, and ISR scenarios access the ADS Web service via a proxy (*Web service proxy*).

There is an additional callback channel for the ABAP form runtime—the Internet Communication Framework (ICF) service. To access this interface, a *destination* must be configured for ADS. The system uses this feedback channel to reload form templates, because ADS buffers these templates and reads them only if necessary. This communication channel is also used to transfer application data and documents that were generated by ADS. That is, the Web service call itself only contains control data in these scenarios.

3.5.1 RFC Destination

To call ADS from an ABAP application server, an RFC connection must be configured, which is done in Transaction SM59 (Configuration of RFC Connections).

1. Click on the CREATE button and enter a name for the connection. The default connection must be called "ADS." You can also configure additional connections. The application program controls the ADS call by transferring a connection name. Select G (HTTP CONNECTION TO EXTERNAL SERVER) as the connection type.

2. In the TECHNICAL SETTINGS tab, enter the computer name into the TARGET HOST field, the HTTP port (50000 for the test version that you have installed) into SERVICE NO., and the path of the ADS Web service (/ADOBEDOCUMENTSERVICES/CONFIG?STYLE=RPC, see Figure 3.19) into PATH PREFIX. After you have entered the path, the system displays a warning that you can skip by pressing the Enter key.

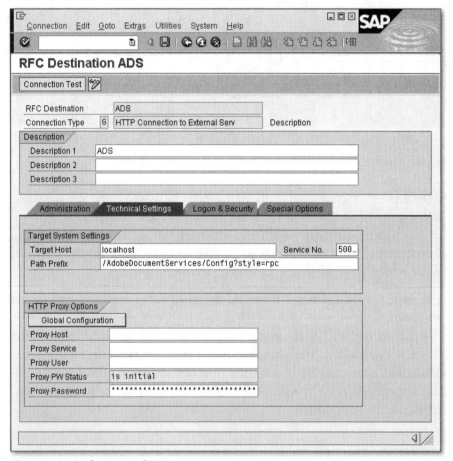

Figure 3.19 Configuration of RFC Connections

3. Navigate to the LOGON & SECURITY tab, and select the Basic Authentication option. Enter ADSUSER for the user and the master password in the Logon area. Click Save to complete the configuration.

4. You can then test the RFC connection using the FP_PDF_TEST_00 program. The connection test that Transaction SM59 provides does not work here, because it

doesn't support Simple Object Access Protocol (SOAP). Therefore, call Transaction SA38, and run the FP_PDF_TEST_00 program by specifying the RFC connection that you have configured. If a connection has been set up successfully, the system returns the internal version number of ADS.

3.5.2 Destination and ICF Service

While ADS is called through a SOAP protocol via the RFC connection that is configured in Transaction SM59, the actual user data, such as form templates and business data, is transported via a separate HTTP connection. This enables the ADS to cache form templates, because the call contains only a reference to the used template. The system thus uses a time stamp to decide whether the local cache needs to be updated or whether the already-cached template can be used. Moreover, the separate connection enables you to bypass SOAP restrictions, because this protocol is not designed for the exchange of large data volumes.

ADS_AGENT

First, you must create a service user that is used for the communication between ADS and the ABAP application server. The following two roles are assigned to this user:

▶ SAP_BC_FP_ICF

▶ SAP_BC_FPADS_ICF

1. To start, you must generate the roles for this profile. Call Transaction PFCG (Role Maintenance) to display the roles.

2. Then, navigate to the AUTHORIZATIONS tab, and click on the DISPLAY AUTHORIZATION DATA button on the MAINTAIN AUTHORIZATION DATA AND GENERATE PROFILES area (see Figure 3.20). The system now displays all authorizations for this role. You can use the Generate button to generate a current profile.

3. After the system has generated both profiles, call Transaction SU01 (User Maintenance) to create the user. Enter "ADS_AGENT" as the name and click on Create.

4. In the ADDRESS tab, you must fill the Last Name field; you should repeat the user name here. Go to the LOGON DATA tab, and select the Service user category. Configure a password.

5. Navigate to the ROLES tab, and assign the two previously mentioned roles to the user (see Figure 3.21). Finally, click on the SAVE button.

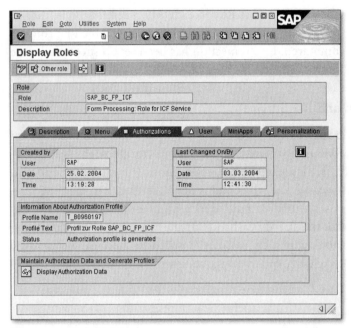

Figure 3.20 Role Maintenance

Figure 3.21 User Maintenance

SICF

Then you must activate the two ICF services:

1. To do this, call Transaction SICF (Maintain Services), and click on the Execute button.

2. Navigate to the DEFAULT_HOST • SAP • BC • FP node, and select the ACTIVATE SERVICE option from the context menu.

3. Repeat this step for the DEFAULT_HOST • SAP • BC • FPADS node (see Figure 3.22).

Figure 3.22 Service Maintenance

Testing the ADS_AGENT User and the ICF Services

You can use a web browser to test the ICF service, which is used to access the ABAP form repository. To do this, you must first determine the computer name and the HTTP port of the ABAP application server.

1. Call Transaction SICF, click on Execute, and then select the PORT INFORMATION entry from the Goto menu. The system displays a table in a dialog box. In the Protocol column, search for the HTTP entry, and write down or copy the corresponding entries in the Host Name and Service columns.

2. Start the web browser, and enter the following URL: *http:// <computer name>:<HTTP port>/sap/bc/fp/form/layout/FP_TEST_03_TABLE.XDP*. The name of the computer is identical to the previously determined host name and HTTP port. The URL of the test version—that has been locally installed with the instance number 02—of the ABAP application server begins with *http:// localhost:8002*.

3. When you call this URL, the system prompts you to enter a user name and password. Enter "ADS_AGENT" and the password that you previously defined. If the authentication has been successful, you can view an XML file. This file is the FP_TEST_03_TABLE template that is stored in the ABAP form repository in its original language (see Figure 3.23).

Figure 3.23 FP_TEST_03_TABLE

Destination

After you have configured the ABAP application server for access by ADS, you must create a destination on the Java application server that refers to the released services.

1. To do this, start the Visual Administrator (see Section 3.4.1), and log on to the system. Select the server process in the Cluster tab, and navigate to SERVER... • SERVICES • DESTINATIONS. In the tree structure of Destinations, navigate to DES-TINATIONS • HTTP and click New.

2. The system displays a dialog box (Enter destination name) where you must enter the name. This name follows a naming convention and is composed as follows: FP_ICF_DATA_<SAP system ID>. You must replace the SAP system ID accordingly. For the test version, the name is therefore FP_ICF_DATA_NSP. Establish the connection by clicking on the OK button.

3. Now you can maintain the connection details (see Figure 3.24).

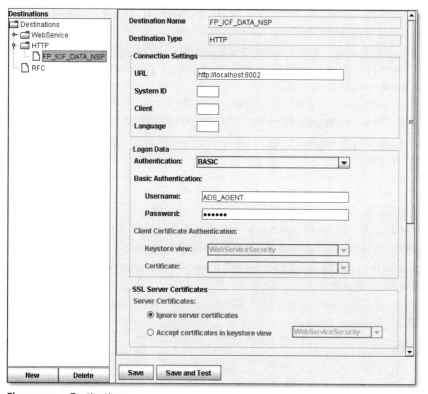

Figure 3.24 Destinations

You must specify the URL (in the CONNECTION SETTINGS area), set the AUTHENTICATION to BASIC and fill the USERNAME and PASSWORD fields (in the LOGON DATA area). The URL is composed of the *http://* protocol prefix, the name of the computer, and the HTTP port of the ABAP application server. We have already described how you can determine these details. Enter the previously created ADS_AGENT user and the defined password in the ABAP application server. Use SAVE to save the settings.

Testing the Destination

The connection test from the Visual Administrator does not work here, because the URL only stores the name of the computer and the HTTP port. The path specifications for the respective service are not added until runtime. To perform a test anyway, you can temporarily extend the stored URL.

1. Add the */sap/bc/fp/form/layout/FP_TEST_03_TABLE.XDP* path to the URL, and click on Save and Test. If the test has been successfully executed, the system displays an Info screen with the following message: HTTP GET response code 200, Content type text/xml.

2. Then, remove the path and save the connection once again. This test simulated that the FP_TEST_03_TABLE form template from the ABAP form repository was read.

You can also test the configuration from the ABAP application server.

1. To do this, call the FP_CHECK_DESTINATION_SERVICE test program (Transaction SA38).

2. Enter the name of the configured RFC connection and select the With Destination Service option.

3. When you click on Execute, the system calls ADS, which then generates a PDF form. For this process, the callback channel that you have previously configured is used, and the system displays a brief Info message (...bytes transferred) in the case of a successful result.

3.5.3   Web Service Proxy

The Java PDF object accesses ADS via a Web service proxy. To use applications in Web Dynpro Java and ISR scenarios, the proxy must be configured on the respective client system. This may either be a local call of the same system or a remote

Java application server. The local call was already automatically configured during the installation of the test version so that the following list can be used to check the configuration and any possible changes.

1. Start the Visual Administrator, and set up a connection to the locally installed server (see Section 3.4.1).

2. Select the server process in the Cluster tab, and navigate to SERVER... • SERVICES • WEB SERVICES SECURITY. From the tree structure, select the SECURITY CONFIGU-RATION • WEB SERVICE CLIENTS • TC~WD~PDFOBJECT • COM.SAP.TC.WEB DYNPRO.ADSPROXY.ADSPROXY*CONFIGPORT_DOCUMENT node (see Figure 3.25).

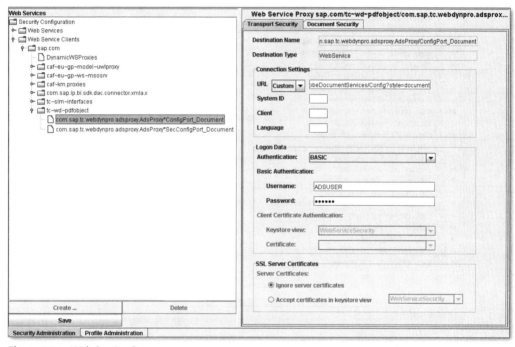

Figure 3.25 Web Service Proxy

3. In the TRANSPORT SECURITY tab that opens, enter a URL in the CONNECTION SET-TINGS area after having first selected the CUSTOM entry. Change the name of the computer and the HTTP port according to the target system that is supposed to be used. The resulting URL is as follows: *http://<computer name>:<HTTP port>/ AdobeDocumentServices/Config?style=document*.

4. In the LOGON DATA area, select BASIC for AUTHENTICATION, enter ADSUSER as the USERNAME, and enter the master password that you have previously defined into the PASSWORD field. Save the specified data by clicking on the SAVE button.

5. You must then restart the Java PDF object so that the changed settings for the configuration can take effect. To do this, select the DEPLOY service in the Cluster tab. Select the APPLICATION option, and then select the SAP.COM/TC~WD~PDFOBJECT component (see Figure 3.26). Click on the STOP APPLICATION and START APPLICATION buttons, and confirm these actions in the dialog boxes.

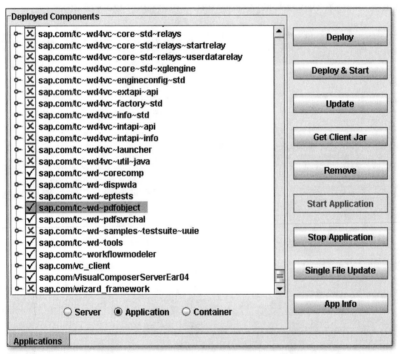

Figure 3.26 Applications

3.5.4 ReaderRights Credential

To generate interactive forms with usage rights, a private key is required—the ReaderRights credential. Based on the usage rights, additional functions are released in Adobe Reader. You can download the corresponding key with a trial period for evaluation and test purposes from the SDN (see Section 3.1, "Preparations"). To obtain a ReaderRights credential to use the product, follow the instructions in SAP Note 736902.

To configure the key, you must perform the following two steps:

1. Store the file in the *credentials* directory on the server
2. Register the corresponding password via the configuration service

ADS manages credentials, certificates, and Certificate Revocation Lists (CRLs) in the subdirectories of the global system directory. The directory path for the locally installed test version is: *C:\usr\sap\J2E\SYS\global\AdobeDocumentServices\TrustManagerService\ trust*. The TRUST directory contains three additional directories for the following file categories (see Figure 3.27):

▶ *credentials*

▶ *certificates*

▶ *CRLs*

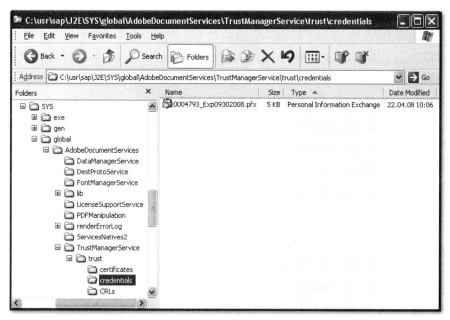

Figure 3.27 Trust Directory

1. First, copy the ReaderRights credential into the *credentials* directory to complete the first configuration step.
2. Next, start the Visual Administrator, and set up a connection to the locally installed server (see Section 3.4.1). Select the server process in the Cluster tab, and navigate to SERVER... • SERVICES • DOCUMENT SERVICES CONFIGURATION.

3. Select the Credentials tab. In addition to a list of already-configured files, the system displays a form for the registration of additional keys (see Figure 3.28).

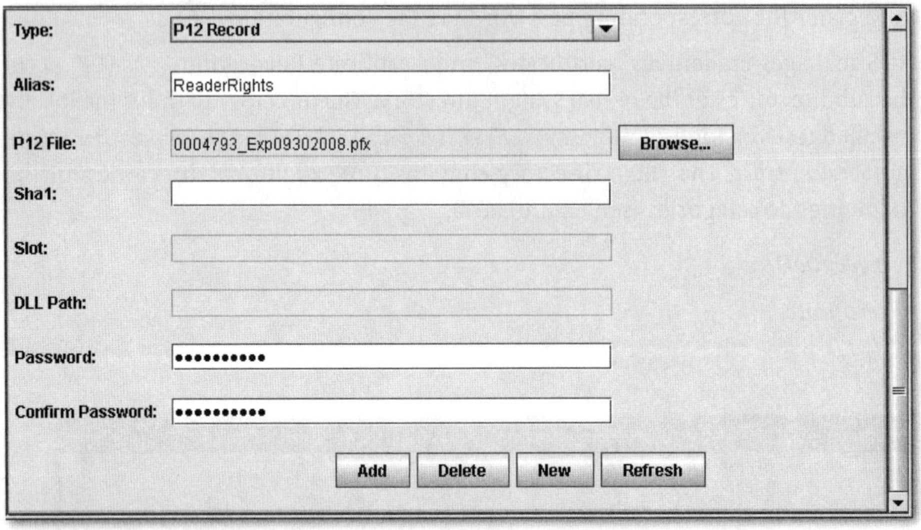

Figure 3.28   ReaderRights

4. Because the file that is supposed to be registered is a PKCS#12 key, select P12 RECORD for TYPE. Enter READERRIGHTS in the ALIAS field. Pay particular attention that you use the correct spelling, because this name is a predefined name that cannot be changed.

5. Click on BROWSE... next to the P12 FILE field to open a dialog box that displays all of the files that are stored in the *credentials directory*. Select the respective entry, and click the SELECT button.

6. Then, enter the corresponding password in the PASSWORD and CONFIRM PASSWORD fields. For keys that have been downloaded from the SDN, the password is included in the provided text file. Click ADD to complete the registration.

7. The ReaderRights credential is now displayed in the list of the registered keys (see Figure 3.29). The EXPIRY column indicates the end date of the validity period.

8. To use an added key, you must restart the following two services, which are also a part of ADS:

   ▶ DOCUMENT SERVICES TRUST MANAGER

   ▶ PDF MANIPULATION MODULE – LOW ENCRYPTION

To do this, select the respective nodes in the Cluster tab, and click on the Stop service and Start service buttons.

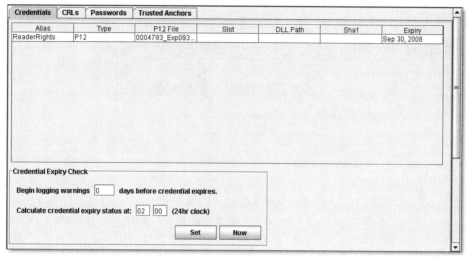

Figure 3.29 Credentials

Testing the ReaderRights Credential

You can test whether the ReaderRights credential has been installed correctly with the FP_TEST_03 program. Call this test program in Transaction SA38, and select the X (Interactive Form with Additional Usage Rights) option for the FORM • INTERACTIVE parameter. If you then display the print preview of the form, Adobe Reader indicates that it is an interactive form.

3.5.5   FPCONNECT

You can make additional settings for the previously configured RFC connection (see Section 3.5.1, "RFC Destination") in the FPCONNECT table.

1. Call Transaction SM30 (Maintain Table Views). Enter "FPCONNECT" in the Table/View field, and click on the Maintain button. You can skip the warning displayed (Caution: The table is cross-client).

2. To add settings for an RFC connection, click on NEW ENTRIES. Then, enter the respective name (for example, "ADS," see Figure 3.30) in the RFC DESTINATION column.

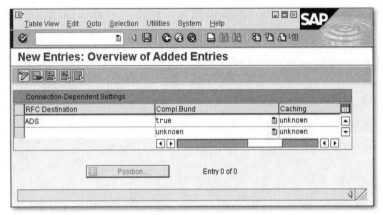

Figure 3.30 Table View Maintenance

3. In the DIR_GLOBAL column, you can specify whether the installation is a dual-stack system, in which case the ABAP and Java application server share a global directory. However, this does not apply to the test version described here. Nevertheless, if it is a dual-stack installation, you must set the value to True. Therefore, the data is directly exchanged via the global directory.

4. The Compl.Bund column allows for the cross-system control of form bundling. To activate this function, select the True value. This significantly reduces the runtime of print jobs with a lot of small or medium-sized forms as long as the print program outputs these forms in one print job (see Section 6.6.1, "Bundling Forms"). This is a cross-system setting; alternatively, ABAP print programs can control the form bundling via a parameter.

5. To save the changes of a table entry, click the Save button. For all other table columns, you should use default values.

3.6 Optional Configuration

This section discusses additional settings of ADS.

3.6.1 Licensing

To generate customer-specific, interactive forms, you require an additional license. ADS provides a component that monitors the usage, subject to licensing, and allows changing of the license status.

1. To view the corresponding usage data and make changes to the status, start the Visual Administrator, and set up a connection to the locally installed server (see Section 3.4.1).

2. Then, select the server process in the Cluster tab, and navigate to SERVER... • SERVICES • DOCUMENT SERVICES LICENSE SERVICE (see Figure 3.31). On the right, you can view the number of the forms that were processed on this system. These forms are divided into the following three categories:

   ▶ **Number of SAP Forms**
   This number indicates how many forms have been processed that were delivered by SAP and were not or only slightly changed. These forms don't require an additional license.

   ▶ **Number of Customer Forms**
   Customer forms are custom developed, interactive forms or SAP forms that have been changed to a large extent. Fundamental changes include a customization of the data binding, which is required for adding new data fields, for example.

   ▶ **Number of Draft Forms**
   Forms that are generated from nonproduction systems or clients are not considered in the determination of the license status.

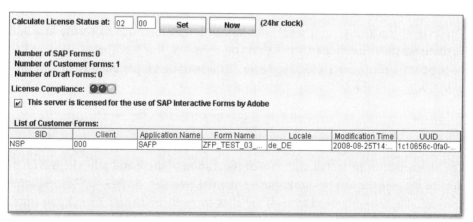

Figure 3.31 License Service

3. Once customer forms that require a license have been processed, the status (LICENSE COMPLIANCE) changes from green to red. When you purchase a license, you can configure this in the system by selecting the corresponding field (THIS

SERVER IS LICENSED FOR THE USE OF SAP INTERACTIVE FORMS BY ADOBE). Then the status changes from red to green again. In addition to displaying the license status in the administration interface, ADS writes a log entry when a license is required but the status has not been configured.

4. The LIST OF CUSTOMER FORMS table in the bottom area of the user interface displays all customer forms that require a license and any additional information, such as the SAP system ID and client from which ADS was called, and the name of the form and calling application.

3.6.2 Credentials, Trusted Anchors, Certificate Revocation Lists

You can use ADS to generate and check digital signatures. In this context, you must distinguish between certification and signature. When a PDF document is certified, it is assigned an invisible signature that ensures the integrity of the form; that is, once the PDF document has been manipulated, the certification is regarded as invalid—both in Adobe Reader and by ADS. You can add any number of signatures to the document, which can be inserted in business processes for approval steps, for example. To use digital signatures, you need credentials, trusted anchors, and certificate revocation lists.

Credentials

The PDF object (ABAP and Java) provides different methods to certify and add signatures. These methods also enable you to specify the key that is supposed to be used via a configured alias. However, if these optional parameters are not provided, ADS uses the following default values:

▶ `DocumentCertification` as the alias for the certification

▶ `ServerSignature` as the alias for the digital signature

The approach for the installation and configuration of these and other keys is identical to the one for the ReaderRights credential (see Section 3.5.4, "ReaderRights Credential"). You only need to spell the alias correctly and enter a valid password. As already mentioned in the description of the ReaderRights credential, you must restart the Document Services Trust Manager and PDF Manipulation Module— Low Encryption for additional keys.

The CREDENTIALS tab displays a table of all registered keys. ADS checks the expiration dates and write log entries daily when the current date approaches or exceeds the expiration date. Therefore the system administrators do not have to regularly check the expiration data of the keys via this user interface. Instead, they only have to monitor the log files.

In the Credential Expiry Check area, you can configure the settings for the log entries. For example, you can customize the time of the daily executed check process. You can also define the period for which warnings are supposed to be written to the log file before a key expires (see Figure 3.29).

Trusted Anchors

ADS enables you to check signatures in PDF forms. To do this, you need to configure trusted certificates that are either the public key of a private key that is used for a signature or the public key of the issuing authority—a so-called root certificate. These public keys are managed via the TRUSTED ANCHORS tab.

1. To register a key, it must be stored in the *certificates* directory (see Section 3.5.4). You can use the BROWSE... button to open a dialog box next to the CERTIFICATE FILE field, and then select the file that is supposed to be registered.

2. After having confirmed the selection with Select, you define what the certificate is supposed to be used for via the checkboxes (TRUSTED FOR):

   ▶ **Signatures and as trusted root**
   You use this option to define whether the certificate is supposed to be used to validate signatures.

   ▶ **Certified Documents**
   If you want to use the public key to check certified PDF forms, you must select this field.

   ▶ **Embedded high privilege JavaScript**
   Interactive forms may contain JavaScript statements. You can use this option to define whether such PDF forms can also be considered trustworthy if they are certified. This field becomes active when you select CERTIFIED DOCUMENTS.

3. Complete the registration of the public key by clicking on ADD. This key is then listed in the TRUSTED ANCHORS table (see Figure 3.32).

4. Restart the two services, Document Services Trust Manager and PDF Manipulation Module—Low Encryption.

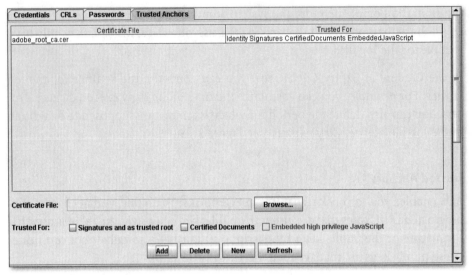

Figure 3.32   Trusted Anchors

Certificate Revocation Lists

Certificate revocation lists enable you to retroactively select keys as invalid that you have initially categorized as trustworthy. You maintain these lists in the CRLs tab.

1. To use such a list, you must copy it to the *CRLs* directory (see Section 3.5.4), and then select it via the BROWSE... button and the displayed dialog box.

2. After you have confirmed the selection by clicking on the Select button, you must fill in the URL field. This is a unique identifier, which is contained in the keys (`crldp` field) that can be revoked via this list. Usually, the certificate revocation list can also be called via this URL.

3. Click on the ADD button to complete the registration. The CRLs table now displays the list (see Figure 3.33).

4. After having configured the certificate revocation lists, you must restart the two services, Document Services Trust Manager and PDF Manipulation Module – Low Encryption.

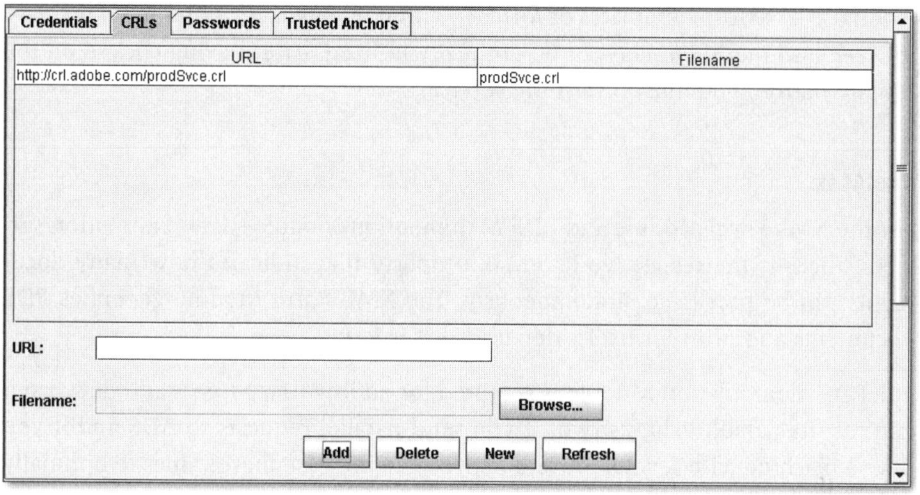

Figure 3.33 Certificate Revocation Lists

Secure Sockets Layer (SSL)

To use certifications and signatures, the ADS Web service must be called via a secure SSL connection. This book does not cover the aspects of an SSL configuration; you can find a detailed description of how to perform the necessary configuration steps in the SAP Help Portal (*http://help.sap.com*). There, navigate via SAP SOLUTIONS • SAP NETWEAVER • SAP NETWEAVER 7.0 to the Adobe Document Services Configuration Guide. The "*Configuration of the Web Service SSL Connection*" chapter describes the SSL configuration.

3.6.3   Service Properties

You can change some of the ADS' properties with the Visual Administrator.

Destination Cache

As mentioned in Section 3.5.2, "Destination and ICF Service," ADS has a local cache, which is used to store form templates. To modify the size of the cache, call Document Services DestProto Service, and change the value for the Cache property in the Properties tab. Its unit is kilobyte, the default value is 4,096.

If you use large form templates or forms in different languages, you should increase this value so that the cache can be optimally utilized. After having clicked on the Update button, you must restart the service.

PoolMax

For the XML Form Module and PDF Manipulation Module—Low Encryption services, there is the respective PoolMax property that indicates how many documents can be processed simultaneously. The XML Form Module generates PDF documents and print forms. Its default value is four.

The PDF Manipulation Module is required for adding usage rights and digital signatures. Its default value is two. If you send parallel requests to ADS and if you have a machine with several processors, you can increase these values to optimally utilize the resources.

3.6.4 Fonts

The installation of ADS comprises numerous fonts, which are stored in the following directory: *C:\usr\sap\J2E\JC00\j2ee\os_libs\adssap\FontManagerService\fonts\ adobe*. To use additional fonts for the form output, you must make the respective fonts available to the Document Services Font Manager.

1. To do this, create a *fonts* subdirectory in the *C:\usr\sap\J2E\SYS\global\AdobeDocumentServices\FontManagerService* directory. Then, create another subdirectory, customer, in the *fonts* subdirectory.

2. Copy the font files to this directory. The following types are supported:

   ▶ OpenType® (*.otf*)

   ▶ TrueType® (*.ttf*)

   ▶ PostScript® Type 1 (*.pfb*, *.pfm*)

3. Before you can use the newly installed fonts, you must restart two ADS components. Call the Visual Administrator, and set up a connection to the locally installed server (see Section 3.4.1).

4. Select the server process in the Cluster tab, and navigate to SERVER... • SERVICES • DOCUMENT SERVICES FONT MANAGER. Click on the Stop service and Start service buttons.

5. Select the Deploy service and then the Application option. Select the com. adobe/AdobeDocumentServices component, and click on the Stop Application and Start Application buttons.

3.6.5   XDCs

To generate form outputs, you need the ADS XFA Device Configuration (XDC) files. They are XML files that describe the printer or output to the printer. The XDC files are located in the *C:\usr\sap\J2E\SYS\global\AdobeDocumentServices\lib* directory.

You can add modified or additional XDCs by copying the files to this directory. However, the provided XDCs should remain unchanged. Section 6.3, "Device Types for the Output," provides more information on XDC files and the necessary assignment to device types on the ABAP application server.

XDC Editor

You can use the XDC Editor to edit XDC files (see Figure 3.34). You can download this editor through the SDN.

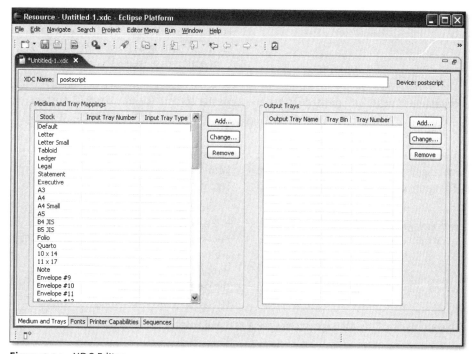

Figure 3.34   XDC Editor

1. To do this, go to the *http://sdn.sap.com*, and log on or register.

2. In the main navigation, select Downloads and then Application Server Tools. From the available downloads, select XDC Editor for SAP Interactive Forms by Adobe.

3. After you have downloaded the ZIP archive, unpack it to a directory of your choice, and follow the installation instructions in the *XDCEditor_Readme.htm* file.

SAP Note 1122142 describes in detail how you can edit XDCs using this tool. The application help (HELP • HELP CONTENTS) contains further information.

3.7   Error Analysis

This section discusses typical error messages and possible causes for these problems. The overview in Table 3.1 enables you to easily find common (configuration) errors and eliminate them.

Errors when Calling ADS from the ABAP Application Server	
The Enter Logon Data dialog box opens.	Possible causes: Either the ADSUSER user is locked (see Section 3.4.1) or you have entered a wrong password for the RFC connection data (see Section 3.5.1).
The *HTTP receive failed with exception communication_failure* message is displayed (possibly, as a part of a more detailed error message).	Possible causes: You have entered a wrong computer name or HTTP port for the RFC connection data (see Section 3.5.1).
The *HTTP send returned with status code* message is displayed (possibly, as a part of a more detailed error message).	Possible cause: You have entered a wrong path for the RFC connection data (see Section 3.5.1).
The error message contains *com.adobe. ProcessingException: Problem accessing data from destination...*	Possible causes: The ADS_AGENT user is either locked or does not have the necessary authorizations. The ICF services are not activated. You have entered a wrong computer name or HTTP port for the destination or the password is not correct (see Section 3.5.2).

Table 3.1   Typical Error Messages when Calling ADS and Possible Causes

Errors when Calling ADS from the Java Application Server	
The *com.sap.tc.Web Dynpro.pdfobject. core.PDFObjectRuntimeException: Service call exception* message is displayed (possibly, as a part of a more detailed error message).	Possible causes: Either the ADSUSER user is locked (see Section 3.4.1) or you have entered the wrong details in the Web service proxy (password, computer name, HTTP port, or path). The Java PDF object was not restarted after changes had been made to the configuration (see Section 3.5.3, "Web Service Proxy"). Usually, the stack trace, which includes the previously mentioned exception, contains further information that indicates the cause of the error.
General Errors when Calling ADS	
The *User ADSUSER does not have access to method rpData* message is displayed (possibly, as a part of a more detailed error message).	Possible cause: The ADSUSER user is not linked to the ADSCaller role (see Section 3.4.2, "ADSCaller").
General Errors when Calling ADS	
The *com.adobe.ProcessingException: Could not retrieve a password for credential: ReaderRights* message is displayed (possibly, as a part of a more detailed error message).	Possible causes: The ReaderRights credential has not been configured or has been configured with a wrong alias (see Section 3.5.4).
The *com.adobe.ProcessingException: Not allowed by credential error while applying usage rights to PDF* message is displayed (possibly, as a part of a more detailed error message).	Possible cause: The ReaderRights credential has expired (see Section 3.1).
The error message contains *com.adobe. ProcessingException: Credential login error while applying usage rights to PDF.*	Possible cause: The two services, Document Services Trust Manager and PDF Manipulation Module—Low Encryption, were not restarted after changes had been made to the configuration (see Section 3.5.4).

Table 3.1 Typical Error Messages when Calling ADS and Possible Causes (Cont.)

3.8   Using ADS

This section covers critical aspects of the usage of ADS. This includes monitoring the individual components and settings, and logging or tracing errors.

Monitoring

1. Start the Visual Administrator, and set up a connection to the locally installed server (see Section 3.4.1). Then, select the server process in the Cluster tab and navigate to SERVER... • SERVICES • MONITORING.

2. Select the ROOT • SERVICES • DOCUMENT SERVICES EJB MONITOR node in the MonitorTree tab. This monitor group provides the following data:

   ▶ Config Versions
   The system displays a list of the installed XDC files and the version number contained therein (see Section 3.6.5, "XDCs").

   ▶ Credential Alias Entries
   The system outputs a table with information on the installed private keys (see Section 3.5.4, and Section 3.6.2, "Credentials, Trusted Anchors, Certificate Revocation Lists").

   ▶ Credential Status
   A status monitor indicates the current status of all installed private keys; that is, this monitor is automatically informed about the expiration of these keys.

   ▶ Exceeded EJB Instances
   This monitor compares the number of EJBs simultaneously instanced by the ADS with the PoolMax value (see Section 3.6.3). The value indicates how many documents can be processed in parallel. These comparison figures enable you to determine whether the sizing process needs to be optimized.

   ▶ Request Count and Request Duration
   These monitors are for statistics only. They indicate how many requests were processed by ADS in which period of time.

3. If a monitor doesn't display any values but outputs the *No value has been reported yet* message, right-click on it, and select the UPDATE option from the context menu.

Log Configurator

You can use the Log Configurator service, which is available in the Visual Administrator, to configure which components are supposed to write how many logs or traces. To obtain detailed processing information from ADS, proceed as follows:

1. Select the LOCATIONS tab, and navigate to the ROOT LOCATION • COM • ADOBE node (see Figure 3.35).

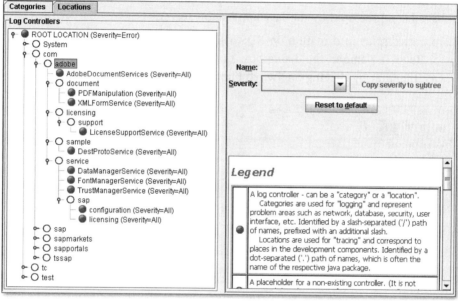

Figure 3.35　Locations

2. Select the All value for SEVERITY, and click on the COPY SEVERITY TO SUBTREE and APPLY buttons. This means that all subcomponents of ADS write the maximum number of traces, which can be helpful for troubleshooting.

3. To return to the default setting, click on the Installation defaults button.

Log Viewer

You can use the Log Viewer service to view log and trace files in the Visual Administrator. You can also use a separate tool, which is located in the *C:\usr\sap\J2E\ JC00\j2ee\admin\logviewer-standalone* directory. Call the *logviewer.bat* file here. The *Logviewer_Userguide.pdf* file in the same directory contains a detailed documentation on this program.

Performance Tracing

To obtain information on the runtime of the requests that have been processed by ADS, use the Performance Tracing service that can also be called via the Visual Administrator.

1. Go to the JARM tab in this service, and select REQUEST OVERVIEW (see Figure 3.36).

2. Clicking on the Actualize all information button opens a list of all requests that have been processed by the Java application server.

3. To only display information on ADS, click on Filter settings and enter "ADS:*" for Request Name in the dialog box. Confirm this by clicking on Ok, and activate the filter by clicking on Switch filter on.

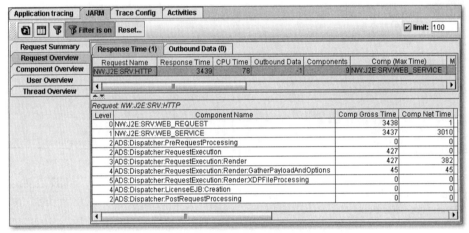

Figure 3.36 JARM

4. To obtain detailed information on a request, select the respective request. This opens a list that includes all components involved and their percentage of the total time.

3.9   Installation of Adobe LiveCycle Designer

To install Adobe LiveCycle Designer, you must first unpack the downloaded archive (see Section 3.1, "Preparations") to a temporary directory. Then, open the setup program contained therein, and select the ADOBE LIVECYCLE DESIGNER 8.0 option (see Figure 3.37).

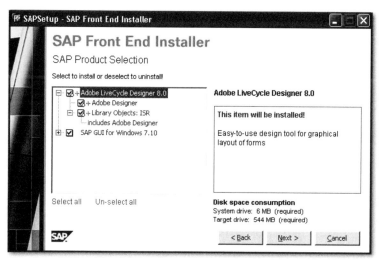

Figure 3.37 SAPSetup

Once you have confirmed the installation directory, the program components are installed. You can now use Adobe LiveCycle Designer together with the SAP GUI.

3.10 Summary

This chapter explained how you can set up a development and test environment for SAP Interactive Forms by Adobe. This environment is required to reproduce and test the examples that are described in the following chapters. The chapter also gave an overview of the individual components of the solution and their interactions. Moreover, it provided information on critical aspects of using ADS and enabled you to trace and eliminate typical (configuration) errors yourself.

To create forms or extend existing forms, you need to understand the struc-
ture of a form and its components. This chapter provides you with basic
information on interface and context.

4 Interface and Form Context

The following sections detail and describe the structure of a form and the maintenance of individual components. The main focus of this chapter is data definition
and form logic.

4.1 Structure of a Form

A form describes the appearance of a document, that is, the structure of the pages
and the positioning of objects, such as texts, graphics, fields, or even tables. Most
forms use fields that the application must fill with data at runtime. The number of
rows in a table depends on the data available for a specific document. Therefore,
a form constitutes a dynamic object that can only create the finished document in
conjunction with the application.

The form designer defines an interface so that you can assign the application data
between an ABAP program and a form. This interface is an independent form
object; the form itself consists of a context and a layout. Within the context you
can access data of the interface where you determine the hierarchy of the data.
Through the context you define a schema, which is available later on for layout creation. This means that there are two form objects: the interface and the form. Form
objects are maintained using either the Object Navigator of the ABAP Workbench
(Transaction SE80) or directly via Form Builder (Transaction SFP). As Workbench
objects they can be transported, have a package assignment, and can be translated.
Interface and form are independent objects that are maintained separately.

The interface defines what data is maintained by a print program and can be used
in multiple forms. An interface is referenced from a form whereby the form uses
this interface for the print program. The form itself comprises the context and the
layout—they form a unit.

Figure 4.1 shows the interaction of interface and form where multiple forms can exist for one interface. The form contains the context and the layout.

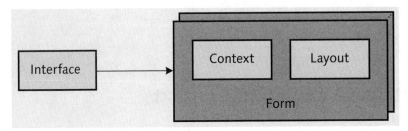

Figure 4.1 Interface and Form Context/Layout

It doesn't make any difference whether you process a form in the ABAP Workbench or directly in Form Builder. Form Builder provides direct access and the screen offers more space for processing.

In the ABAP Workbench, you can navigate within the packages and have an overview of multiple form objects from which you can select one by double-clicking on it. Additionally, the ABAP Workbench provides you with a where-used list that is very important if you want to know which forms use a specific interface. This way, you can determine which forms should be adapted if you want to extend an interface.

If you know the name of a form, you can work in Form Builder directly. The ABAP Workbench provides a good overview of the contained form objects in case you assign packages to your forms. This book uses direct access to Form Builder.

4.2 Interface of a Form

The interface of a form has a unique name and is defined in Form Builder. All application data that is supposed to be transferred to a form is listed here and typed accordingly.

There are three different types of interfaces:

▶ **ABAP Dictionary-based interface**
The ABAP Dictionary-based interface is the most commonly used interface and is therefore described in great detail within this chapter.

▶ **XML schema-based interface**
The XML schema-based interface is relevant for applications that work with an XML schema without any ABAP Dictionary reference.

▶ **Smart Forms–compatible interface**
The Smart Forms–compatible interface is generated during the migration of a Smart Form into a Portable Document Format (PDF)–based form.

For a better understanding, let's create an interface.

1. Start Transaction SFP, click on the INTERFACE radio button, and enter the name, Z_IFBA_BOOK_DDIC_01 (see Figure 4.2). Then, click on CREATE.

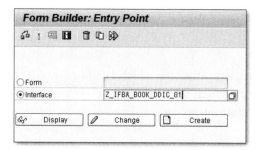

Figure 4.2 Creating an Interface

2. In the following dialog box, enter a description and keep all other values unchanged (see Figure 4.3). Choose SAVE.

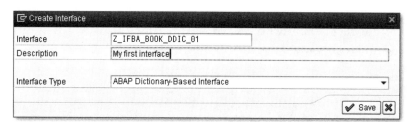

Figure 4.3 Specifying Interface Properties

3. An interface is a transportable object with a package assignment, so you are asked for a package. If you enter a package, you must assign a transport request. For these examples, however, it is sufficient to use local objects because they can't be transported and are only used locally on the system on which they were created.

4. Click on LOCAL OBJECT, or enter "$TMP" as the package. Save your entries (see Figure 4.4).

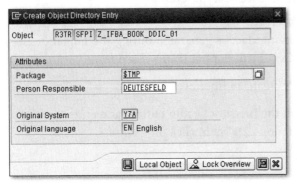

Figure 4.4 Package Assignment

Form Builder now shows the newly created interface, which is still empty (see Figure 4.5) and saved locally. It will be extended later on. On the left-hand side, you can see the different elements of an interface:

▸ Form interface

▸ Global definitions

▸ Initialization

▸ Currency/quantity fields

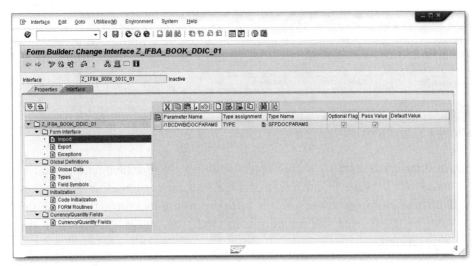

Figure 4.5 Interface

The following sections describe the purpose of the individual categories and the properties that can be specified.

4.2.1 ABAP Dictionary-Based Interface

The name of the ABAP Dictionary-based interface derives from the fact that all parameters have an ABAP Dictionary reference and are based on tables, structures, or data elements that are defined in the ABAP Dictionary. When you created an interface in Section 4.2, "Interface of a Form," and accepted the default values in the dialog box shown in Figure 4.3, the ABAP Dictionary-based interface had already been selected as the interface category by default. This interface category is the most important one for most applications. For this reason, it is described in great detail within the scope of this book.

You can make comprehensive definitions within an interface, where the definition of the import parameters is the most significant one. Here, you specify the application data to be maintained. This data is relevant both for the design of the form and at runtime when a print program wants to transfer data to the form.

The present interface must be extended by other parameters, which is detailed based on an example. In addition, you are provided with various processing options. The interface will use structures and tables from the flight-booking model (SCUSTOM, SBOOK, and SPFLI), which are employed in numerous SAP examples. In Section 4.3, "Context of a Form," you will use this data model to establish the context of a form to enable a tabular output. The layout of the form is developed in Chapter 5, "Creating Form Templates," while Chapter 6, "Form Output," discusses the output of the form.

Form Interface

Import and export parameters and exceptions are identified within the form interface. More notably, you can define new import parameters here. The export parameters and exceptions are predefined and can neither be changed nor extended.

Import Parameter

When you double-click on the IMPORT entry in Form Builder (see Figure 4.5), the system displays a parameter on the right that is predefined in every interface: /1BCDWB/DOCPARAMS TYPE SFPDOCPARAMS. By double-clicking the SFPDOCPARAMS type name you can navigate to the definition of this Dictionary structure; the system now displays the components of the structure (see Figure 4.6).

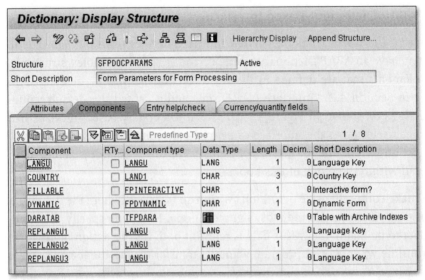

Figure 4.6 Defining the Default Parameter of an Interface

Table 4.1 describes the meaning of the individual fields in the default parameter.

Component	Meaning
LANGU	Output language of the form
COUNTRY	The country and the language is relevant for the formatting of dates and figures
FILLABLE	Indicator for whether the form is to be created as an interactive form
DYNAMIC	Property of interactive forms
DARATAB	Archive information if optical archiving is requested for the output
REPLANGU1	Replacement language if the form is not available in the requested language
REPLANGU2	Another replacement language
REPLANGU3	Another replacement language

Table 4.1 Components of the Default Parameter

You will come across these fields again if you want to write a print program and output a form. For now, you don't have to consider these fields.

Now that you know how to navigate to the definition of a parameter using a double-click; next we'll define some parameters for setting up a form context in the following examples.

1. In Form Builder, you are provided with various buttons which you can use to process an interface (see Figure 4.5). They enable you to append, insert, delete, or duplicate rows.

2. To add a new parameter, click on Append Row. The system creates an empty row below the default parameter.

3. Enter CUSTOMER as the parameter name, TYPE as the type assignment, and SCUS-TOM as the type name. The result is shown in Figure 4.7.

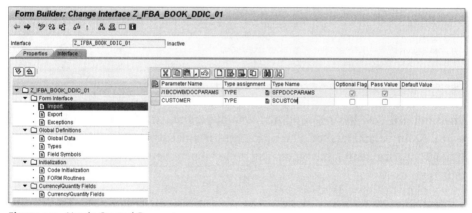

Figure 4.7 Newly Created Parameter

The structure of the import parameter is similar to a function module interface; and you can reference different Dictionary categories, for example, data elements, structures, or table types. In fact, you will generate a function module interface from the form interface later on.

You can use the two checkboxes, OPTIONAL FLAG and PASS VALUE, to specify whether a parameter is required at runtime and whether it is transferred as a value or as a reference. If you set the parameter to OPTIONAL FLAG, it doesn't have to be transferred by the application when a form is called. You will require most parameters; however, you can provide an additional optional parameter that can be transferred by the print program at runtime. A pass by value is usually not considered for structures and tables because, in most cases, it is more efficient to just refer to the data.

TYPE is the only type assignment permitted for ABAP Dictionary-based interfaces.

4. Now create two more parameters: BOOKINGS with the data type, TY_BOOKINGS, and CONNECTIONS with the data type, TY_CONNECTIONS.

5. You are supposed to transfer an elementary field of the Date type as another optional parameter. To do this, create a DATE parameter with the SYDATUM data type, and select the OPTIONAL FLAG checkbox for this parameter (see Figure 4.8).

Parameter Name	Type assignment	Type Name	Optional Flag	Pass Value	Default Value
/1BCDWB/DOCPARAMS	TYPE	SFPDOCPARAMS	☑	☑	
CUSTOMER	TYPE	SCUSTOM	☐	☐	
BOOKINGS	TYPE	TY_BOOKINGS	☐	☐	
CONNECTIONS	TYPE	TY_CONNECTIONS	☐	☐	
DATE	TYPE	SYDATUM	☑	☐	

Figure 4.8 Completed Interface

The interface now has one optional default parameter, /1BCDWB/DOCPARAMS, and four custom parameters, of which CUSTOMER is a flat structure, and BOOKINGS and CONNECTIONS are both table types. The optional parameter, DATE, is an elementary data type.

> **Navigating to ABAP Dictionary**
>
> The definition of the data types can be displayed at any time by double-clicking the type name. The system displays a message if you haven't saved the interface yet. You can now go to the ABAP Dictionary to navigate to the next step or back to Form Builder.

Export Parameter

The system displays the export parameters if you double-click Export on the left-hand side. For the ABAP Dictionary-based interface, only one parameter (/1BCDWB/DOCPARAMS) exists that you can't change—custom export parameters. The predefined parameter is used in some application programs, for example, to process a generated PDF.

Exceptions

You can view the exceptions by double-clicking Exceptions. There are three predefined exceptions for each interface:

▶ **USAGE_ERROR**

The USAGE_ERROR exception is triggered at runtime if the transferred call parameters don't enable form creation, for example, an unknown form or an invalid output device.

▶ **SYSTEM_ERROR**

The SYSTEM_ERROR exception indicates a runtime error, for example, if errors occur for the connection definition for Adobe Document Services (ADS).

▶ **INTERNAL_ERROR**

The INTERNAL_ERROR exception is reserved for unforeseen errors.

Meaning of the Interface at Runtime

As mentioned previously, the interface definition forms the basis for a function module interface in which you can find the import parameters, export parameters, and exceptions. For this reason, a form interface must always be in line with the application program (except for the optional parameters). A program terminates if parameters that are expected by the interface are not transferred.

Activating the Interface

You should activate the interface prior to discussing the other components, because only then can you use it in a form.

1. To do so, select the ACTIVATE button as shown in Figure 4.9.

Figure 4.9 Activating the Interface

2. If you made an error in the definition of the interface, for example, if you used an unknown data type, the system notifies you accordingly during activation.

3. You can check the interface at any time. To do so, select the Check button, which is positioned on the left side of the activation icon. The system checks whether all data types used exist and displays error messages, if necessary.

Global Definitions

The global definitions include global data, types, and field symbols. Here, you can define custom fields that you can use in the entire form to, for example, implement calculations that are not provided by the application program.

Global Data

Global data usually provides data that is required for the creation of sums.

1. In the present example, you define a SUM_BOOKINGS table and specify it as the TY_BOOKINGS data type.

2. To do so, double-click GLOBAL DATA on the left-hand side, and insert a row on the right, similar to the procedure used for the import parameters.

3. Now enter SUM_BOOKINGS as the variable name and TY_BOOKINGS as the type name (see Figure 4.10).

Variable Name	Type assignment	Type Name	Default Value	Constant
SUM_BOOKINGS	TYPE	TY_BOOKINGS		☐

Figure 4.10 Global Data of an Interface

Types

For the Types, you can define custom data types if no corresponding ABAP Dictionary type exists and you want to address multiple fields at the same time. The data types are recorded in the source code, just like in the ABAP program.

Field Symbols

Field Symbols are an efficient option to use pointers in nested tables or for large data quantities. By using field symbols you don't copy any data that improves the memory requirement and the runtime. This is illustrated in Listing 4.1.

Initialization

The initialization enables you to process data from the interface and initialize global data. An interesting option is that you can select data from a database depending on the interface parameters. You can therefore output more data on a form than is intended by the SAP application without having to modify the application program. `SELECT` statements can read data from the SAP database in initialization coding whose result is stored in global data. You can then use and output this data in a form even though the actual application program would not. The interface between the application and the form remains unchanged. You only fill global data and can then use it in the context and the layout of the form.

> **Extending Data Retrieval**
>
> If you need more data than provided in the standard, it is more efficient to extend the data retrieval in the application program, for example, by adding or enhancing an existing `SELECT` statement in ABAP. Because if you read data during initialization, this basically constitutes another database access; you must decide which procedure is best suited for the concrete case.

Code Initialization

Under Code Initialization of the interface, you can enter the initialization code in an ABAP Editor. Here, you specify the input parameters that you want to access in read-only mode and determine which output parameters to fill. The output parameters are global data that you created for the global definitions.

In this example, you fill the internal table, `SUM_BOOKINGS`, with sums from the import parameter `BOOKINGS`. To do this, you perform a currency-dependent summation to sum different currencies individually.

1. Click on Append Row and define the input parameter, `BOOKINGS`.

2. Again, select Append Row for the output parameters and enter the name, `SUM_BOOKINGS`.

3. A type assignment of the parameters is not required because the system automatically determines the assignment to the interface parameters or the global data.

4. For the summation, use the `LOOP` statement in ABAP and the `COLLECT` command (see Listing 4.1).

```
FIELD-SYMBOLS <lfs_bookings> TYPE sbook.
DATA lv_sums LIKE LINE OF sum_bookings.
LOOP AT bookings ASSIGNING <lfs_bookings>.
  lv_sums-forcuram = <lfs_bookings>-forcuram.
  lv_sums-forcurkey = <lfs_bookings>-forcurkey.
  COLLECT lv_sums INTO sum_bookings.
ENDLOOP.
```

Listing 4.1 Initialization Code

5. As a result, a row is created for each FORCURKEY currency (EUR, USD, etc.) in the SUM_BOOKINGS table and the FORCURAM values are summed separately for each of these currencies.

6. In the Editor, you can use the Pretty, whose button is positioned on the left-hand side of the Editor. There, you can also find the button for PATTERNS, which you can use to insert various statement patterns into your coding.

7. The results should appear as illustrated in Figure 4.11. Save the interface.

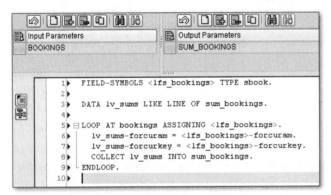

Figure 4.11 Initialization Code

Form Routines

If your initialization codes contain recurring program sections, you can outsource and call them in FORM routines, as it is common in ABAP. The Editor is the same as the one you already know from the initialization code. For this example, there is no need for form routines because it is rather simple.

Currency/Quantity Fields

The CURRENCY/QUANTITY FIELDS are a special case with regard to data: They are particularly important in business documents and require additional information for the output, which you as the form developer must pay special attention to.

Currency fields have the Dictionary data type, CURR, and the quantity fields the data type, QUAN. These fields each contain the amount; for the correct output, however, you also require the unit. For this reason, the currency is stored in a field of the CUKY data type and the quantity unit in a field of the UNIT data type.

1. Let's take a look at the SBOOK database table in the ABAP Dictionary. To do so, start Transaction SE11 and enter SBOOK in the database table field. Select DISPLAY to view all fields of the table.

2. The FORCURAM field comprises the S_F_CUR_PR data element and CURR as the data type (length 15, decimal places 2). Now, you can process any currency in this field.

   The definition specifies two decimal places; however, this is only the internal display and this value is not relevant for the output. For example, the Euro (EUR) has two decimal places, whereas Japanese currency (JPY) does not require any. The definition of decimal places for each currency is specified in the TCURX table.

3. If you now output the FORCURAM field, the currency is taken from the assigned reference field, which is defined in the SBOOK table.

4. By clicking on CURRENCY/QUANTITY FIELDS (see Figure 4.12), you can see that the FORCURKEY reference field is also contained in the SBOOK table. This field provides the currency (EUR, JPY, USD, etc.) and the runtime environment can implement the formatting correctly.

   The same applies to quantity fields. The LUGGWEIGHT field has the WUNIT reference field in the same SBOOK table.

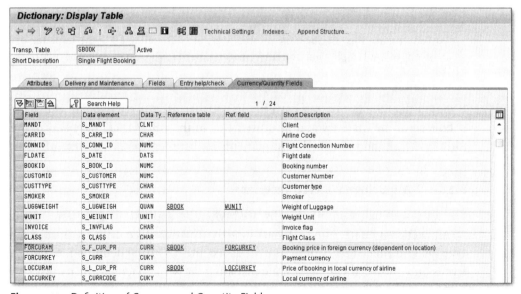

Figure 4.12 Definition of Currency and Quantity Fields

The special feature of both cases is that the amount and unit are stored in the same table. Therefore, the system automatically implements correct formatting.

However, if the unit (CUKY or UNIT) is stored in a separate table, the system cannot establish the reference automatically. In this case, you must reassign the reference fields for the interface definition.

1. To do this, select CURRENCY/QUANTITY FIELDS in the interface.

2. Enter a field name, such as TAB1-FELD, and specify an assigned reference field, TAB2-REFFELD.

3. Select CURR or QUAN as the data type, depending on whether a currency or quantity is involved (see Figure 4.13).

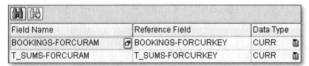

Field Name	Reference Field	Data Type
BOOKINGS-FORCURAM	BOOKINGS-FORCURKEY	CURR
T_SUMS-FORCURAM	T_SUMS-FORCURKEY	CURR

Figure 4.13 Defining Reference Fields

4. Remember to activate the interface!

Amount and Unit from Different Tables

If you don't make this specification and the fields are not contained in the same table, the system will not implement correct formatting. In this case, no error message is output.

If these values are not output correctly in your forms, it is advisable to check the definition of the currency and quantity fields in the ABAP Dictionary and in the form interface and to make the assignments in the interface, if required.

4.2.2 XML Schema-Based Interface

The XML schema-based interface is used when an application does not process ABAP Dictionary data, but XML data directly. This interface category is used for Web Dynpro ABAP that defines its own data context. During definition, the interface is only provided with a local file including the XML schema, which must correspond to the W3C standard.

1. Now, create a new interface, Z_IFBA_BOOK_XML_01, and select XML SCHEMA-BASED INTERFACE as the interface category (see Figure 4.14).

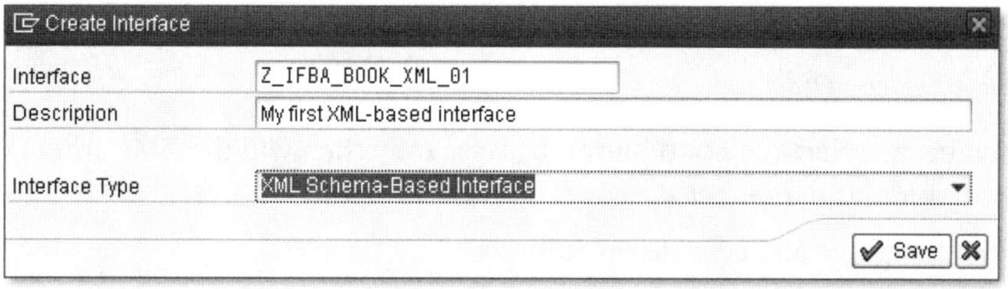

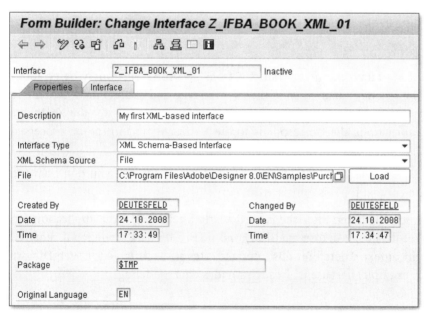

Figure 4.14 XML Schema-based Interface

2. Save the interface as a local object.

3. Now go to the properties of the interface, which look completely different compared to the ABAP Dictionary-based interface (see Figures 4.5 and 4.15).

Figure 4.15 Properties of an XML Schema-based Interface

4. There are two different settings for the source: File and Generated. You can't make any manual selections here because the Generated setting is intended for applications that generate an interface via Application Programming Interface (API), such as Web Dynpro ABAP.

5. Enter the complete path to the XML schema file in the FILE input field using the input help. Select an XML schema file via a dialog.

   Relative to the installation directory of Adobe LiveCycle Designer, you can find a sample file you can use under *EN\Samples\Purchase Order\Schema\ Schema\Purchase Order.xsd*.

6. Remember to select the LOAD button because only then will the XML schema be loaded into the interface.

7. You can then save and activate the interface.

8. The system displays the XML schema if you select the INTERFACE tab. However, you cannot make any changes here.

9. As usual, you can display the import and export parameters and the exceptions on the left-hand side. However, adding further parameters or exceptions to an XML schema-based interface is not possible.

10. The XML schema-based interface has two import parameters:

    ▶ `/1BCDWB/DOCPARAMS`

    ▶ `/1BCDWB/DOCXML`

You already know the first parameter from the ABAP Dictionary-based interface. The second parameter is of the `XSTRING` type and exports the XML data in binary format at runtime. The calling application must transfer the XML data with a formatting that corresponds to the XML schema and can be processed by ADS.

The XML schema is the final format of the form design and you don't have to define a context for this interface category.

The XML schema-based interface is particularly interesting if the application can provide the data in XML format already and no further data modeling is required via a form context. Therefore, this interface category is suitable for Web Dynpro ABAP, for example, because it already provides data modeling.

4.2.3 Smart Forms–Compatible Interface

Finally, you are provided with information on the last interface category, Smart Forms–compatible interface. Its name suggests that forms with this interface can be called by applications that have used Smart Forms previously.

Normally, such interfaces are created by migrating a Smart Form into a PDF-based print form; however, you can also create an interface of this category yourself. The Smart Forms–compatible interface contains the same parameters and exceptions as the interface of a Smart Form.

1. Therefore, create a Z_IFBA_BOOK_SF_01 interface as usual and select the category as illustrated in Figure 4.16. You can't change the predefined import parameters.

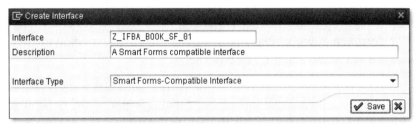

Figure 4.16 Smart Forms–Compatible Interface

2. The parameters are different to those of the ABAP Dictionary-based interface. Another difference is that you are now provided with tables (see Figure 4.17), which are transferred to a function module as table parameters at runtime. In ABAP Dictionary-based forms, this is done by directly transferring the table types using the import parameters.

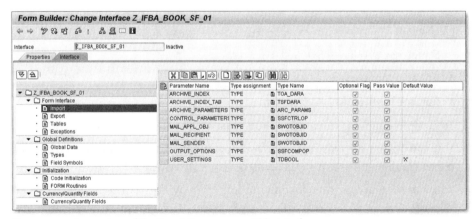

Figure 4.17 Parameters of the Smart Forms–compatible Interface

3. You can define custom export parameters for the Smart Forms–compatible interface. You already know the global definitions, initialization, and currency/quantity fields from the ABAP Dictionary-based interface.

The benefit of this interface category is that you can address it from existing Smart Forms print programs (for example, by migrating a Smart Form); however, this interface doesn't provide all of the options available in the SAP Interactive Forms by Adobe solution. Therefore, this interface category is only used in rare cases.

4.2.4 Documentation of a Form Interface

You can document your own form interface to store information about their significance. The documentation is integrated with the normal documentation environment that you can access using Transaction SE61.

If an interface is transported, its documentation is transported as well. It is also taken into account for other activities, such as copying, deleting, or renaming. You can consult the documentation of predefined interfaces to see if it provides valuable notes for the form development (provided that the interfaces are documented).

1. To record the documentation, enter the Z_IFBA_BOOK_DDIC_01 interface in the initial screen of Form Builder and follow the menu path GOTO • DOCUMENTATION • CHANGE.

2. You can now document the interface. To do this, you are provided with the following categories (see Figure 4.18):
   - Use (&USE&)
   - Structure (&STRUCTURE&)
   - Enhancements (&ENHANCEMENTS&)
   - Further hints (&FURTHER_HINTS&)

3. To complete the documentation, you must set the status to active.

4. You can access an existing interface documentation from the Form Builder menu via the path GOTO • DOCUMENTATION • DISPLAY.

5. You can also access the documentation from within Form Builder. Simply select the menu path GOTO • DOCUMENTATION. The system displays the documentation or you can edit it, depending on whether you are in display or edit mode.

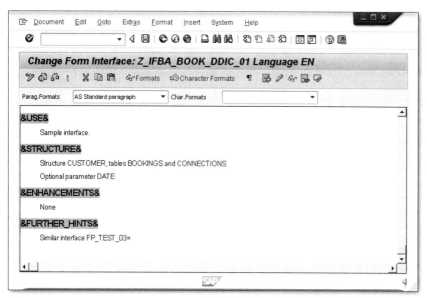

Figure 4.18 Documentation of a Form Interface

4.3 Context of a Form

The context of a form constitutes the form object only in conjunction with the layout and is thus not an independent object (like the form interface). The following sections focus on the context while Chapter 5 describes the creation of the layout.

Forms are maintained in Form Builder or in the ABAP Workbench—just like the interfaces. They can also be transported, have a package assignment, and can be translated. To create a new form, you need an existing and active interface. The different interface categories, along with their properties, have already been discussed in Section 4.2; from now on, only ABAP Dictionary-based interfaces are used. Forms with an XML schema-based interface don't require any context, the schema is sufficient to enable form layout creation. Forms with a Smart Forms–compatible interface are not discussed in further detail within the scope of this book because the descriptions focus on the SAP Interactive Forms by Adobe solution and its new options.

The context defines what data from the layout is available for the layout; the main task of the context is the data modeling. The ABAP Dictionary data of the interface is mapped in a hierarchy and constitutes the logical data model of the form. You can consider the context as a modeling tool that transforms a lot of input data (structures, tables, and elementary fields from the interface) into a data schema. In this process, you create an XML schema that is available for Adobe LiveCycle Designer.

However, you don't just use the context to include data into a hierarchy, but also to add additional objects, such as texts (SAPscript include texts and Smart Forms text modules), graphics, or addresses. The selection of these objects may depend on the interface data. An address is typically generated from an address number that is transferred to the form by the application print program via the interface. You can also add texts dynamically depending on the transfer values. Additionally, you can reference graphics or transfer their content in binary form. These objects are specified in detail later on. For now, it is only important that the form context constitutes the link between application data and the form layout.

4.3.1 Creating a Form

You can now create a form to establish the context. To do so, you use Form Builder again.

1. Start Transaction SFP and click on FORM. Enter Z_IFBA_BOOK_FORM_01 as the name.

2. Then click on CREATE (see Figure 4.19).

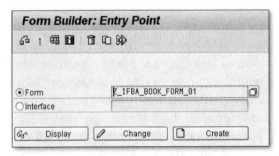

Figure 4.19 Creating a Form

3. Enter a description in the dialog box that opens (see Figure 4.20). Additionally, you must select the form interface for the form. You can use the Z_IFBA_BOOK_ DDIC_01 interface that you created in Section 4.2. If you know the name of an interface, you can always enter it directly.

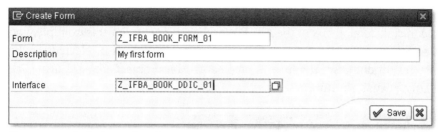

Figure 4.20 Assigning an Interface

Alternatively, you can also utilize the input help. To do so, simply press the ⌷F4⌷ key when the cursor is in the input field of the interface or the icon is on the right of the input field. A dialog box opens in which you can search for interfaces of a specific author or enter the creation or change date, for example.

4. If you only know a specific part of the interface name, you can enter it in the dialog box (see Figure 4.20). For example, the existing interfaces start with the letter Z and contain the term BOOK. So, enter "Z*BOOK*" as the name of the interface and press the ⌷F4⌷ key (see Figure 4.21).

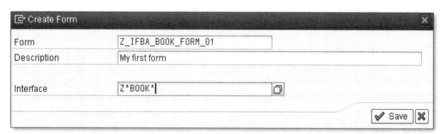

Figure 4.21 Searching for an Interface

5. Double-click Z_IFBA_BOOK_DDIC_01 to select the interface (see Figure 4.22) and click on SAVE.

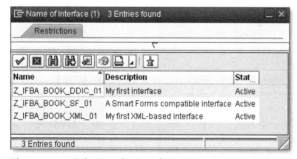

Figure 4.22 Selecting the Interface Using the Input Help

6. Because a form is a transportable object, you must make a package assignment. To do this, the dialog box of the ABAP Workbench opens. For this example, you can select the package, $TMP (see Figure 4.23), which you also selected for the interfaces. In doing so, the form is created as a local object. You can also click the LOCAL OBJECT button.

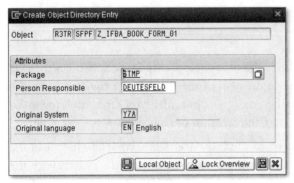

Figure 4.23 Package Assignment

7. Form Builder now displays the empty context of the created form (see Figure 4.24); the form itself was stored locally. The following sections detail how to define the context of the form.

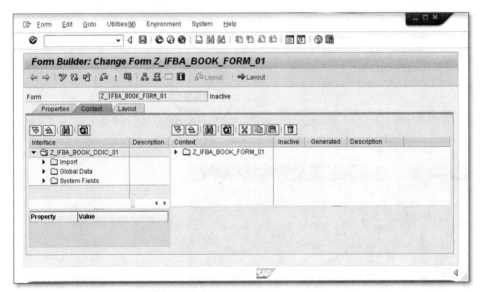

Figure 4.24 Empty Context of the New Form

4.3.2   Structure of a Form

You can see three tabs for the elements of a form:

▸ **Properties**
In the PROPERTIES tab, you can view general information, such as the assigned interface, the creator, the last processor and the corresponding time stamps. In addition, you can find information on the package assignment and the original language of the form. The original language is always the language you logged on to the SAP system with during creation. The form should only be changed in this language later on.

▸ **Layout**
The LAYOUT tab is not considered at this point. Feel free to click on this tab— Adobe LiveCycle Designer is started within the Form Designer.

▸ **Context**
The CONTEXT tab is selected by default. On the left side, you can see the form interface (in this case Z_IFBA_BOOK_DDIC_01), the context itself is displayed on the right. It is still empty, which is why you can only see the root node, Z_IFBA_BOOK_FORM_01.

The following steps describe how you can obtain information about the interface and the field definitions within the form.

1. On the left side, you can expand the parameters of the interface by clicking on the small arrows or selecting the EXPAND SUBTREE button (see Figure 4.25). To do this, you must position the cursor on a subtree; in doing so, you can expand the import parameters only or the entire interface, for example.

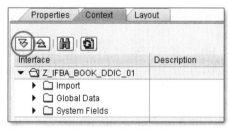

Figure 4.25 Expanding the Interface

For this interface, this still makes sense to some extent; for complex and comprehensive interfaces you should only expand the part that is relevant for your work to keep a better overview. You can compress individual subtrees again at any time. Figure 4.26 show the fully expanded interface.

Interface	Description
▼ 📁 Z_IFBA_BOOK_DDIC_01	
▼ 📁 Import	
▼ 🔲 CUSTOMER	Flight customers
· 🔲 MANDT	Client
· 🔲 ID	Customer Number
· 🔲 NAME	Customer name
· 🔲 FORM	Form of address
· 🔲 STREET	Street
· 🔲 POSTBOX	PO Box
· 🔲 POSTCODE	Postal Code
· 🔲 CITY	City
· 🔲 COUNTRY	Country code
· 🔲 REGION	Region
· 🔲 TELEPHONE	Telephone number of flight customer
· 🔲 CUSTTYPE	Customer type
· 🔲 DISCOUNT	Discount rate
· 🔲 LANGU	Language Key
· 🔲 EMAIL	Customer e-mail address
· 🔲 WEBUSER	Web user name for customer
· ▦ BOOKINGS	Table for Flight Bookings
· ▦ CONNECTIONS	Table of Flight Connections
· 🔲 DATE	Current Date of Application Server
▼ 📁 Global Data	
· ▦ SUM_BOOKINGS	Table for Flight Bookings
▼ 📁 System Fields	
▼ 🔲 SFPSY	System Fields
· 🔲 DATE	Current Date of Application Server
· 🔲 TIME	Current Time of Application Server
· 🔲 USERNAME	User Name
· 🔲 SUBRC	Return Value of ABAP Statements

Figure 4.26 Expanded Interface of the Form

2. You can see the import parameters and the global data as you have defined them in the interface, Z_IFBA_BOOK_DDIC_01. A CUSTOMER structure exists whose fields are all shown; additionally, there are two tables, BOOKINGS and CONNECTIONS, and an elementary field, DATE. The different object types, such as structures, tables, or fields, are marked by a corresponding icon. The global data shows a SUM_BOOKINGS table that you created as well.

3. Double-click a field to view the properties in the field list in the lower left. Figure 4.27 shows the full name of the CUSTOMER-CITY field, its description, and its type information.

Property	Value	
General		
Name	CUSTOMER-CITY	
Description	City	
Type Information		
Type Category	Dictionary Type	📄
Type Name	CITY	

Figure 4.27 Properties of an Interface Field

The type information includes the type category and type name. The following type categories exist:

- Built-in type (for example, STRING)
- Dictionary type (reference to a data element)
- Flat structure (a structure without a hierarchy)
- Deep structure (a structure with subelements, for example, tables)
- Internal table

The CITY type name is underlined for the CUSTOMER-CITY field. Double-click the underlined name to navigate to the definition of this data element in the ABAP Dictionary.

By double-clicking CUSTOMER, you can view in the field list that it has a flat structure; by double-clicking the SCUSTOM type name you can navigate to the definition. A double-click on BOOKINGS displays its properties; they indicate that it is an internal table of the TY_BOOKINGS type. This way, you can view the definition of tables, structures, and fields at any time without displaying the interface separately or searching for the data types in the ABAP Dictionary.

Below the interface, there are some system fields that you have not defined yourself; they involve the SFPSY structure, which provides some useful fields (see Table 4.2).

Field Name	Meaning
DATE	Current date
TIME	Current time
USERNAME	Name of the logged-on user
SUBRC	Result of a single record node

Table 4.2 System Fields

The SFPSY-SUBRC field can only be evaluated according to a single record node. This node type is discussed in detail in Section 4.3.10, "Single Record Nodes."

The following sections describe the individual node types on which the form context is based. All nodes are created below the root node, which is a folder that may contain any number of nodes. Node types are listed in Table 4.3.

Node Type	Meaning
Structure	Data structure
Data	Field
Text	Smart Forms text module, SAPscript includes text or dynamic text
Graphic	Graphic (reference or content)
Address	Address from the central address management
Alternative	Alternative subtrees, depending on the condition
Loop	Table with recurring elements
Single record	Direct access to an individual table row
Folder	Grouping option for multiple nodes

Table 4.3 Different Node Types

In addition, there are conditions that can be defined for almost every node type (except for the alternative node type). If a condition is defined for a node, that node is only processed when the condition is met.

The different processing options of the context are indicated based on the structure node type.

4.3.3 Structures

The simplest way to add a node to the context from the interface is to drag and drop.

1. For example, drag the CUSTOMER structure from the import parameter list to the root node of the context; as a result, the CUSTOMER structure is added to the context and displayed as expanded (see Figure 4.28).

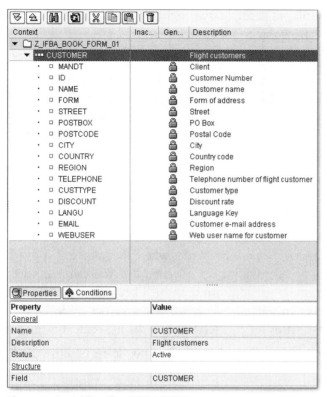

Context	Inac...	Gen...	Description
▼ ☐ Z_IFBA_BOOK_FORM_01			
▼ ▪▪▪ CUSTOMER			Flight customers
· ☐ MANDT		🔒	Client
· ☐ ID		🔒	Customer Number
· ☐ NAME		🔒	Customer name
· ☐ FORM		🔒	Form of address
· ☐ STREET		🔒	Street
· ☐ POSTBOX		🔒	PO Box
· ☐ POSTCODE		🔒	Postal Code
· ☐ CITY		🔒	City
· ☐ COUNTRY		🔒	Country code
· ☐ REGION		🔒	Region
· ☐ TELEPHONE		🔒	Telephone number of flight customer
· ☐ CUSTTYPE		🔒	Customer type
· ☐ DISCOUNT		🔒	Discount rate
· ☐ LANGU		🔒	Language Key
· ☐ EMAIL		🔒	Customer e-mail address
· ☐ WEBUSER		🔒	Web user name for customer

🔍 Properties	🔷 Conditions	
Property		**Value**
General		
Name		CUSTOMER
Description		Flight customers
Status		Active
Structure		
Field		CUSTOMER

Figure 4.28 Adding the CUSTOMER Structure

2. Alternatively, you can right-click the root node and select CREATE • STRUCTURE from the context menu.

3. A dialog box opens in which you can use the input help to display all available structures. In this case, CUSTOMER and SFPSY are provided.

4. Double-click CUSTOMER to select it and choose NEXT. The result is identical: The CUSTOMER structure has been added to the context as is illustrated in Figure 4.28.

In the context, you are provided with a number of different processing options. You can delete, cut, copy, or paste nodes or subtrees. This is done either using the context menu or via the toolbar above the context. You can search for nodes and expand or collapse subtrees for more convenient processing.

The node properties are displayed at the bottom right if you double-click a node in the context. Each node has two important properties:

▶ **Generated**

A generated node can't be deleted because it is an elementary part of a superordinate node. After you've added the CUSTOMER structure, a lock icon is displayed for every field of the structure. Because these fields are part of the structure they can't be removed from the context. You can only delete the entire structure; therefore no lock icon is displayed for the CUSTOMER structure.

▶ **Active/Inactive**

Initially, all nodes you insert are ACTIVE. An active node can be used for creating a layout and is provided with data at runtime.

You can set a node or subtree to Inactive by right-clicking it and selecting Deactivate. This can also be done via the node properties where the status is displayed. You can set it to ACTIVE or INACTIVE via the selection list. You can also select multiple nodes simultaneously—hold down the ⌗Ctrl⌗ key to select additional nodes. Use the ⌗SHIFT⌗ key to select whole areas. When you've made all your selections, you can set the status for all selected nodes via the context menu.

Note that you can set generated nodes to INACTIVE, but not delete or move them.

Why Is It Important to Deactivate One or More Nodes?

Structures often contain numerous fields of which only a few are necessary for the form output. You should always set the status of unnecessary fields to INACTIVE so that the data schema becomes clearer for Adobe LiveCycle Designer, that is, so the fields are not displayed at all later on and the creation of the layout becomes more comprehensible.

The status of the fields is also relevant at runtime. Only the fields with an ACTIVE status are provided with values and transferred to ADS. So, if you deactivate fields that are not required, then this results in less data being created and transferred. Therefore, you can reduce the memory requirement and improve the performance. This is particularly important for complex structures or tables.

---

1. In this example, you only need the following fields: ID, NAME, FORM, STREET, POSTBOX, POSTCODE, CITY, COUNTRY, and EMAIL.

2. For all other fields, set their status to INACTIVE.

   You don't have to set all fields to Inactive if they are not used. But you should do so if large data quantities or entire substructures can thus be hidden. If you are not sure whether you'll require a field in the future, you can keep its status set to ACTIVE.

3. The context should now look as illustrated in Figure 4.29.

Context	Inactive	Generated	Description
▼ ☐ Z_IFBA_BOOK_FORM_01			
▼ ••• CUSTOMER			Flight customers
• ☐ MANDT	✖	🔒	Client
• ☐ ID		🔒	Customer Number
• ☐ NAME		🔒	Customer name
• ☐ FORM		🔒	Form of address
• ☐ STREET		🔒	Street
• ☐ POSTBOX		🔒	PO Box
• ☐ POSTCODE		🔒	Postal Code
• ☐ CITY		🔒	City
• ☐ COUNTRY		🔒	Country code
• ☐ REGION	✖	🔒	Region
• ☐ TELEPHONE	✖	🔒	Telephone number of flight customer
• ☐ CUSTTYPE	✖	🔒	Customer type
• ☐ DISCOUNT	✖	🔒	Discount rate
• ☐ LANGU	✖	🔒	Language Key
• ☐ EMAIL		🔒	Customer e-mail address
• ☐ WEBUSER	✖	🔒	Web user name for customer

Figure 4.29 Setting Nodes that Are not Required to Inactive

4.3.4 Data Nodes

You can also include individual fields into the context. These can already be contained as such in the interface or originate from the structures. The difference is, however, that the field is dragged separately into the context. This is particularly useful if you only need one field from a structure. To include the entire structure and deactivate all of the fields not required would be too cumbersome and would decrease the clarity of the context. Therefore, you can add individual fields to the context.

1. You can add the DATE field from the SFPSY structure of the system fields. (You can also include the complete SFPSY structure and set the status of the fields not required to Inactive; however, this example is intended to show you how to work with individual fields in the context.)

2. To do this, expand the system fields and the SFPSY structure. Drag and drop the DATE field to the root node of the context, Z_IFBA_BOOK_FORM_01. The system displays an individual field, DATE, below the CUSTOMER structure.

3. If you collapse the CUSTOMER structure you obtain a better overview of the context. Below the root node, it contains two objects: the CUSTOMER structure and the DATE field.

Double-clicking the DATE field displays its properties below the context. Under DATA, the system shows that the field is provided with data from the SFPSY structure. However, its name is DATE and it is addressed with this name in the context and in the layout.

4. Because there is a DATE interface parameter that you want to use in the context, rename the parameter you just added by overwriting the DATE name with SYSTEM_DATE in the properties and by pressing the ENTER key. The name is updated in the context (see Figure 4.30).

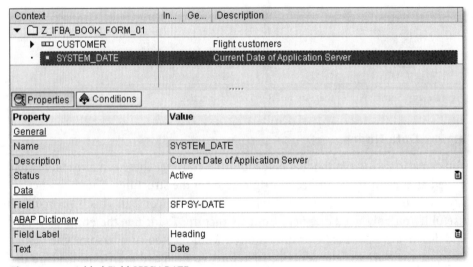

Figure 4.30 Added Field SFPSY-DATE

Uniqueness of Field Names

If you insert a field multiple times, it is automatically renamed by the system (for example, DATE1) to ensure uniqueness. The data binding, which you can check in the properties, remains the same.

You can also create a field via the context menu.

1. To do so, right-click the Z_IFBA_BOOK_FORM_01 root node of the context.

2. Select CREATE • DATA. A dialog opens where you use the input help. All fields you can directly add to the context are displayed. In this example, these are all fields of the two structures, CUSTOMER and SFPSY.

3. Double-clicking SFPSY-DATE displays the same result as previously.

Fields that you add to the context are not generated. No lock icon is displayed in contrast to the structure fields; therefore, you can delete these fields directly.

4.3.5 Text Nodes

A form doesn't just output data—rather, texts including additional information are important for the form. On one hand, these texts can be defined in the layout directly, which is discussed later on. On the other hand, they can also be provided via the context. To do this, three different text sources are supported:

▶ Smart Forms text modules

▶ SAPscript include texts

▶ Dynamic texts

SAP Smart Forms and SAPscript are existing form solutions from SAP and include texts that can be integrated with both solutions. SAP Smart Forms also enable the maintenance of text modules. Both text types can be used within SAP Interactive Forms by Adobe.

The Smart Forms text modules and SAPscript include texts that are stored in the database and can be used in forms.

Smart Forms Text Modules

Smart Forms text modules (in the following only referred to as text modules) are maintained using Transaction SMARTFORMS. They have a unique name, can exist in multiple languages, have a transport connection, and are client independent.

A text module contains frequently recurring texts, such as the footers of a form, for example, to output the business connection. For the present form, you use the SF_ADRS_FOOTER text module. You can also display this text directly.

1. Start Transaction SMARTFORMS and click on TEXT MODULE.

2. Enter SF_ADRS_FOOTER in the input field and click on Display. An address and bank details are now displayed. This text is supposed to be included in the form, which is why you add it to the context.

3. Right-click the root node of the Z_IFBA_BOOK_FORM_01 context and select CREATE • TEXT. In doing so, you append the text to the end of the form.

4. You should select a meaningful name and a description for the properties of the text so that you can identify the text in the context. To do this, overwrite the value "TEXT" with "FOOTER" and enter a proper description, for example, "business connection."

5. The status is displayed as another property, so you can set text modules to Inactive as well.

You now must specify the text module to be used so that the text can be added to the output at runtime.

1. Open the input help for the TEXT NAME field to display all text modules available on the system.

2. If you double-click the SF_ADRS_FOOTER entry, the system adds the name to the properties. You can also enter the name directly. Note, however, that you enclose the name in single quotes (see Figure 4.31).

Text	
Text Type	Text Module
Text Module	
Text Name	'SF_ADRS_FOOTER'

Figure 4.31 Text Name Enclosed in Single Quotes

If you enter SF_ADRS_FOOTER directly without the single quotes, the system notifies you that the SF_ADRS_FOOTER field does not exist. The system also checks whether a text module that you specified exists and displays an error message if the text can't be found.

Specifying the Text via a Field

A name without single quotes indicates a field; the name of the text module would be determined only at runtime. This way, it is possible to drag texts depending on fields that are transferred via the interface by the application.

3. In this example, you don't have to determine the language because the text is requested in the language of the form.

4. If you want to specify a text using a field, you can simply drag and drop the field to the text name from the interface. It is then entered in the properties. However, the system can't check whether the text already exists because the value of the field isn't known until runtime.

   Therefore, you can specify for the properties of a text module whether a runtime error should be triggered if a text module can't be found during output. In this case, select the No error if text not available checkbox.

5. The system also provides the Copy Style From Text Module Checkbox and an input field for the style as further properties. Each text module is assigned with a style that defines the paragraph and character formats that can be used in a text. The style enables you, for example, to specify the fonts and different paragraph properties, such as the alignment.

   In this case, select the Copy Style From Text Module checkbox and leave the STYLE field empty. As a result, the system uses the style that was statically assigned to the text; for the SF_ADRS_FOOTER text it is the SAPADRS style.

Limitations to the Use of Text Modules

Within SAP Interactive Forms by Adobe, not all components are supported in text modules and style properties; this applies to the following properties and elements:

- Page protection
- Outline paragraphs
- Superscript and subscript
- Barcodes
- Special characters
- Hyperlinks
- Smart Forms system fields

There are limitations for the tabulators and the SAP characters.

Details about the limitations can be found in the SAP online documentation for Transaction SFP under PDF-BASED PRINT FORMS • DESIGNING FORMS WITH FORM BUILDER • CONTEXT IN FORM BUILDER • INSERTING A TEXT• ENTERING TEXT MODULE PROPERTIES.

---

6. If you want to assign another style later on, you can simple use the input help for the STYLE field and select a style by double-clicking on it.

7. The context now appears as shown in Figure 4.32.

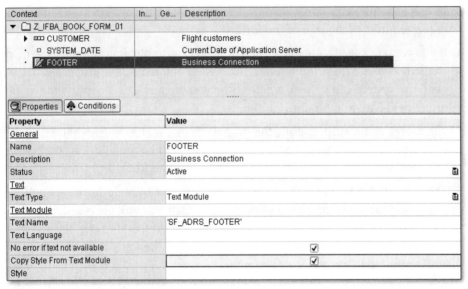

Figure 4.32 Inserted Text Module

SAPscript Include Texts

SAPscript include texts can be used in SAPscript forms and in Smart Forms. These are texts that are maintained in application transactions or in Customizing, for example, request texts, document texts, or vendor texts. They are classified in various text objects. In addition, you are provided with standard texts comprising the TEXT text object, which are maintained using Transaction SO10.

SAPscript include texts are client-dependent and can exist in multiple languages; they are not transported automatically. The key of SAPscript texts comprises four fields:

- Text name
- Text object
- Text ID
- Text language

The text object classifies the application, whereas the text ID enables the subgrouping within a text object. Each text has a name and can exist in multiple languages. The client is another key field that you may not define in the form. The text is always read in the client in which the application program is executed.

The key for an SAPscript include text contains the aforementioned fields, TEXT NAME, TEXT OBJECT, TEXT ID, and TEXT LANGUAGE. In contrast to the text modules, which only include a name and a language as the key fields, these texts also include the TEXT OBJECT and the TEXT ID.

1. To use an SAPscript include text, create a text in the context as has been described in Section 4.3.5, "Smart Forms Text Modules."

2. Select INCLUDE TEXT as the text type. The result is displayed in Figure 4.33.

Property	Value	
General		
Name	TEXT	
Description	Text Node TEXT	
Status	Active	🖹
Text		
Text Type	Include Text	🖹
Include Text		
Text Name		
Text Object		
Text ID		
Text Language		
No error if text not available	☐	
Standard Paragraph		
First Paragraph		
Style		

Figure 4.33 Properties of an SAPscript Include Text

3. You can display the definition of the text objects using Transaction SE75. You can view the corresponding text ID by double-clicking a text object.

   If you want to create your own SAPscript include text for testing, simply use an SAPscript standard text, which you can create by means of Transaction SO10. TEXT is predefined as the text object; you can use the ST standard value as the text ID. This includes a general standard text.

4. For this example, you don't require any SAPscript include text. You can also insert a text via the input help.

5. The No Error If Text Not Available checkbox (see Figure 4.34) has the same meaning as for the text modules. If you select this checkbox, no runtime error occurs if the desired text is not available. You can specify the text key statically (with single quotes) or dynamically using fields. In this process, a specific part of the key (for example, the text object and the text ID) can be static and only the name specified in a field.

Property	Value	
General		
Name	TEXT	
Description	Text Node TEXT	
Status	Active	🗐
Text		
Text Type	Include Text	🗐
Include Text		
Text Name	'ADRS_FOOTER'	
Text Object	'TEXT'	
Text ID	'ST'	
Text Language	'EN'	
No error if text not available	☑	
Standard Paragraph		
First Paragraph		
Style		

Figure 4.34 Inserting an SAPscript Include Text

6. Again, you can define a style that describes the formatting properties of the text. Note that you can only use a Smart Forms style, not a SAPscript style. This style must provide the required paragraph and character formats.

7. You can select a paragraph format in the STANDARD PARAGRAPH field and therefore override the standard paragraphs in the SAPscript include text.

   The FIRST PARAGRAPH field enables you to format the first paragraph of an include text using this paragraph format. If you haven't specified a standard paragraph, all standard paragraphs of the text are also formatted with this format.

Limitations for the Use of SAPscript Include Texts

Not all elements can be supported for the use of SAPscript include texts. The properties not supported include the following:

▶ SAPscript styles (A Smart Forms style must be used.)

▶ Control commands

▶ Page protection

▶ Outline paragraphs

▶ Superscript and subscript

▶ Barcodes

▶ Special characters

▶ Hyperlinks

▶ SAPscript system icons and standard icons

There are limitations for the tabulators and the SAP characters.

Note that no control commands are evaluated, they are simply ignored. As a result, both branches are output in the case of an IF/ELSE statement, for example. INCLUDE statements are not executed.

Dynamic Texts

It is sometimes possible that an application has already read the text from the database and transferred it to the parameters. In some cases, the text can also originate from a source that the text-reading functions of SAPscript and Smart Forms texts can't access. If your applications make use of such texts and you want to transfer the text content into the interface, you need a dynamic text.

1. To use dynamic text, create a text in the context as it has been described previously.

2. Select DYNAMIC TEXT as the TEXT TYPE. The result is displayed in Figure 4.35.

Property	Value
General	
Name	TEXT
Description	Text Node TEXT
Status	Active
Text	
Text Type	Dynamic Text
Dynamic Text	
Field	
Text Language	
Style	

Figure 4.35 Dynamic Text

3. In the STYLE field, define the style to describe the paragraph and character formats.

4. You should specify the text language because it may be relevant for the text display.

5. Enter the text under FIELD; an internal table of the TSFTEXT type is expected here. The structure of this table type is TLINE, which includes the fields TDFORMAT and TDLINE (see Figure 4.36).

The components, TDFORMAT and TDLINE, describe the text in Interchange Text Format (ITF) format. For more information on the structure of this format, refer to the SAP online documentation about the SAPscript topic via the help of Transaction SO10.

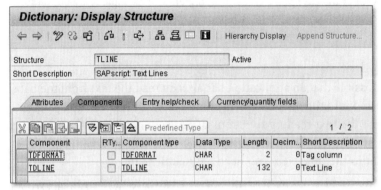

Figure 4.36 Structure of a Dynamic Text

4.3.6 Graphic Nodes

Graphics are frequently used in forms, for example, to output a company logo. You can use scanned drawings, scanned signatures at the end of a document, or small images in item lists showing a material.

You are provided with various options to insert graphics into a document. For example, you can provide a graphic via the data or specify it in the layout of the form. In the former case, the context provides the option both to transfer the content of a graphic, that is, its binary format, and to reference the graphic via a URL.

Because this chapter is limited to the context of the form, it describes the two alternatives of how a graphic can be specified within the context. The graphic node is available for this reason.

> **Note**
>
> Because the sample form doesn't use any graphics in the context, you can skip the following descriptions. The graphic nodes created here will be deleted again.
>
> If required, you can come back to this section if you want to transfer graphics into your custom forms using a program, for example, because you read them from a repository. In this case, the graphic node in the context is the only option.
>
> However, a general example can't be provided because it depends on your system environment. You can still provide such a graphic in your form context and insert it in the layout.

1. Right-click the root node of the Z_IFBA_BOOK_FORM_01 context and select CRE-
ATE • GRAPHIC to insert a graphic node at the end (see Figure 4.37).

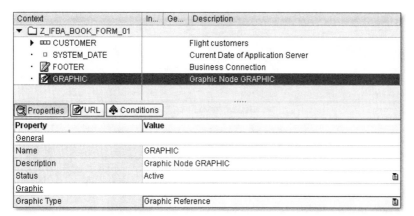

Figure 4.37 Graphic Node

2. You already know the properties of a graphic node from the other node types. Like all of the other node types, it has a name, a textual description, and a status (ACTIVE or INACTIVE).

3. You can specify the graphic type as another property. It is set to GRAPHIC REF-ERENCE by default. You can switch between GRAPHIC REFERENCE and GRAPHIC CONTENT using the input help.

4. Press the ENTER key after you've made your selection in the input help. An additional dialog box opens in which you must confirm your selection because the additional attributes detailed next will get lost.

Graphic Reference

In Figure 4.37, you can see the URL button on the right-hand side of the PROPER-TIES button.

1. Let's assume your company logo is available at *http://www.addressofyourcom-pany.com/images/companylogo.jpg.*

2. Select the URL button, insert a new row using the APPEND ROW button, and enter the URL in single quotes as illustrated in Figure 4.38. Remove the DELIMITER.

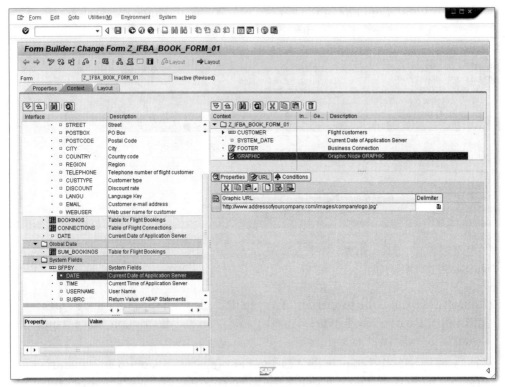

Figure 4.38 Static URL with Reference to the Graphic

3. If you want to specify the graphic reference dynamically, you can also use fields that refer to the graphic at runtime. A part of the URL can even be static, whereas only the name of the graphic is dynamic.

Therefore, it could be possible that all graphics are available at *http://www.addressofyourcompany.com/images/* and that you transfer the value (*company_logo.jpg*) at runtime in a GRAPHIC field, which must exist in your interface. Then, you would only have to enter the static part 'HTTP://WWW.ADDRESSOFYOURCOMPANY.COM/IMAGES' in the first row (see Figure 4.39), select the slash / as the delimiter, and insert a second row, which only contains the GRAPHIC field.

Figure 4.39 Compound URL for a Graphic

Graphic Content

If you changed the properties to graphic content (see Figure 4.40), the URL button is no longer displayed. Instead, you are provided with additional fields for the properties of the graphic content. These involve the two fields, FIELD and MIME TYPE.

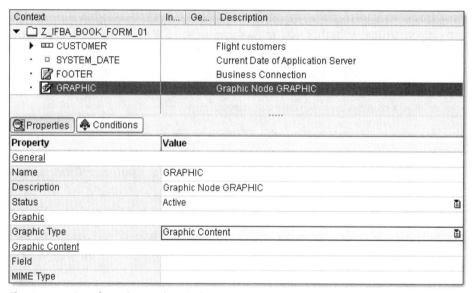

Figure 4.40 Specifying the Graphic via the Content

▶ Under FIELD, you can specify a parameter from your interface or the global data, which includes the content of the graphic in binary form. The data type of the field must be of the XSTRING type. The STRING data type is also supported; in this case, however, the data must be Base64-coded. If your interface provides such a field, you can drag and drop it to this position. It is the task of the application program to read the graphic from the corresponding source, for example, from the database or the MIME Repository, and to make it available via the form interface.

▶ The MIME type indicates the graphic format and has the "image/gif" form here. The list of supported formats is available in the Adobe LiveCycle documentation. You can also define the MIME TYPE dynamically via a field, which should be provided by the interface.

4.3.7 Address Nodes

Addresses are used in various forms, for example, invoices or delivery notes. Usually, not all fields, such as name, ZIP code, and city, are transferred; instead, the system uses addresses that are managed and formatted via Business Address Services (BAS).

An address in a form not only depends on the correct values, but also on the correct formatting. Whether you must position the ZIP code on the left or right side of the city, whether you must add a country key in front of the ZIP code, or whether you must print a country name in a specific language below the address depends on the regulations of the respective country and whether a document is sent within a country or from one country to another.

This complex logic can't be reproduced in every form—instead you are provided with BAS whose task it is to retrieve the relevant information and to visually format the address. The application only obtains an address number and can specify some additional information.

To obtain more detailed information about these services, call the help of Transaction SFP, select PDF-BASED PRINT FORMS • DESIGNING FORMS WITH FORM BUILDER • CONTEXT IN FORM BUILDER • INSERTING AN ADDRESS, and then click on the Business Address Services link in the help text.

> **Note**
>
> This section describes the information required for address formatting and the existing configuration options. For the sample form, you only position some address fields directly in the layout. Therefore, you can skip the rest of the section initially.
>
> The following sections, however, describe how you can search for an address number in your system via an input help. If you have found an address you can extend your form context by one address and position the address in the layout.
>
> You can find address nodes in many forms provided by SAP, which is why the following is particularly important and should be kept in mind.

There are three different types of addresses (see Table 4.4):

Address Type	Internal	Description
Company addresses	1	A typical business address that is specified by an address number.
Personal addresses	2	A personal address that is specified by a person number. Because a person can have multiple addresses, you must also define an address number additionally.
Workplace addresses	3	The address of a contact partner within an enterprise. Again, you must specify a person number and an address number.

Table 4.4 Address Types

To insert an address in a form, right-click the root node of the Z_IFBA_BOOK_FORM_01 context and select CREATE • ADDRESS. An address node is added at the end and can be moved to another position in the context using the mouse. Figure 4.41 illustrates the properties of an address node.

Property	Value
General	
Name	ADDRESS
Description	Address Node ADDRESS
Status	Active
Address	
Address Type	Organization, Company
Dynamic Address Type	
Address Number	
Person Number	
Handle for Address Number	
Handle for Person Number	
Additional Specifications	
Number of Lines to be Used	'10'
Sending Country	
If PO box and street exist	PO box has priority over street
Dynamic Priority	
Fixed Language for Country Indicator	
Different Recipient Language	
Country Indicator in Recipient Language	☐
Uppercase/Lowercase Spelling	☐
Priority of Lines	
Person Above Organization	☐
SAP Business Partner Details	
Time-Dependent Business Partner Name	No
Dynamic Time Dependency	
Time Stamp	
Business Partner Number for Organization, Company	
Business Partner Number for Person	

Figure 4.41 Properties of an Address Node

► Under ADDRESS TYPE, the company address is specified by default, which you can change using the input help. You can also select this property dynamically; however, you must provide a field that contains the address type at runtime. To do this, select DEFINE DYNAMICALLY as the address type in the address node—the DYNAMIC ADDRESS TYPE field is now ready for input. The values must correspond to the values provided in Table 4.4.

► The PERSON NUMBER is only ready for input if the address type is PRIVATE ADDRESS or CONTACT PARTNER ADDRESS.

> ### Addresses Must be Available at Runtime
>
> The address number and, if applicable, the person number are mandatory values. An address can't be formatted without these values because the corresponding data can't be read. Because addresses are usually specified dynamically this can't be checked in Form Builder. If the values are not available at runtime during the creation of the form, runtime errors occur and the print job is canceled.

► The fields HANDLE FOR ADDRESS NUMBER and HANDLE FOR PERSON NUMBER, are intended for temporary addresses. Refer to SAP Note 1059819 if these fields are not displayed on your system.

► You can use the address number's input help to search for addresses on your system. To do so, extend the form interface by a field for the address number (AD_ADDRNUM data type) and use this field in the address node of the context.

► During your initial tests you can leave the ADDITIONAL SPECIFICATIONS of the address node unchanged. However, you must enter a SENDING COUNTRY in any case. If this value is missing you can't activate the form and an error message is displayed.

► The NUMBER OF LINES TO BE USED is set to ten by default. You can enter a smaller value. During formatting via BAS, the program attempts to suppress lines.

► Under ADDITIONAL SPECIFICATIONS, you can detail how the address is to be formatted if both a PO Box and a street are available. Here, you can also determine language settings for the country names. The UPPERCASE/LOWERCASE SPELLING checkbox is also interesting. If it is not set, then the city and country are output in uppercase letters.

► In the last section, you can define properties of a business partner. For detailed information, refer to the BAS documentation.

4.3.8 Alternatives

Forms include a lot of dynamic content, for example, some objects are supposed to be output only under certain conditions. For this reason, alternatives are available. An alternative is a node that comprises a condition and two subnodes. Under Condition, you can check and logically link different fields. The names of the two subnodes are TRUE and FALSE and are carried out if the condition is met (TRUE) or not (FALSE). The TRUE/FALSE branches can contain any number of subnodes, which are processed accordingly.

There is an optional parameter, DATE, in the interface as has already been described in Section 4.2.1, "ABAP Dictionary-Based Interface." This value can be transferred by the application program at runtime; however, the form may not rely on it because it is optional.

A simply structured example illustrates the use of the alternative node. If the optional parameter, DATE, doesn't contain any value, use the system date that you already added to the context as the SYSTEM_DATE field (see Figure 4.30).

1. To add an alternative to your form, right-click the root node of the Z_IFBA_BOOK_FORM_01 context and select CREATE • ALTERNATIVE. An alternative node is added at the end and can be moved to another position in the context using the mouse.

2. Move the alternative further upward by dragging it to the SYSTEM_DATE field.

3. Rename the node ALT_DATE and enter an appropriate description. The result is displayed in Figure 4.42. Before expanding the two branches of the alternative, you should first set the condition for the alternative.

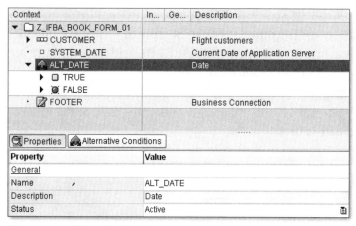

Figure 4.42 Alternative Node

4. Select the ALTERNATIVE CONDITIONS button and then APPEND ROW in the new screen.

5. You want to check whether the optional parameter, DATE, has a value or not. To do this, drag the DATE field from the interface and drop it in the first field, OPERAND; the equals sign (=) is already proposed as the relational operator.

6. In the second OPERAND field, you can check against another field or a concrete value. Because you want to test whether the value is initial, you can enter INITIAL directly into the field. You probably already know this concept from ABAP programming. The result should look like the one illustrated in Figure 4.43.

Figure 4.43 Alternative Condition

7. Different relational operators are available and you can interlink various conditions. For example, insert multiple rows and specify the operator, AND or OR, for each row. In the first row, the operator field remains empty.

This completes the condition for the alternative and you can now expand the two subnodes, TRUE and FALSE. If the condition is met at runtime, this means that the optional parameter, DATE, contains no value. For this reason, you use the system date that you already inserted in the context as the SYSTEM_DATE field.

1. Simply drag the SYSTEM_DATE field to the TRUE node where it is inserted as a subnode by using the mouse.

2. The FALSE branch now contains the DATE field, because in this case it provides the value you want to use. For this reason, drag the DATE field from the interface to the FALSE branch. The result is shown in Figure 4.44.

3. You can insert the fields below the TRUE or FALSE node via the context menu as usual. Through the alternative, either the value of the DATE field or the value of the current system date is used.

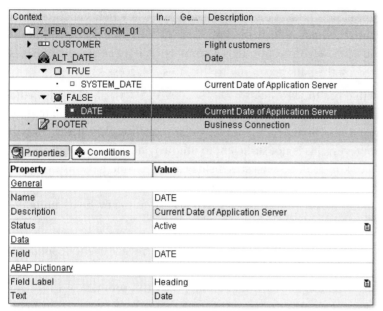

Context	In...	Ge...	Description
▼ ☐ Z_IFBA_BOOK_FORM_01			
▶ ▭ CUSTOMER			Flight customers
▼ ▲ ALT_DATE			Date
▼ ☐ TRUE			
· ☐ SYSTEM_DATE			Current Date of Application Server
▼ ☼ FALSE			
· ■ DATE			Current Date of Application Server
· ▱ FOOTER			Business Connection

🔍 Properties	♣ Conditions	

Property	Value	
General		
Name	DATE	
Description	Current Date of Application Server	
Status	Active	📄
Data		
Field	DATE	
ABAP Dictionary		
Field Label	Heading	📄
Text	Date	

Figure 4.44 Expanded Alternative Node

4.3.9 Tables or Loops

You come across tabular output of data in many forms, for example, in invoices, order confirmations, and delivery notes. In this regard, tables in forms means internal ABAP tables that are provided in the import parameters or global data of the interface. The number of table rows has not yet been specified at design time because the corresponding rows are not provided until form output depending on the application data. The column structure determines which fields can be output within a row.

Tables can also be nested, whereas multiple subitems can exist for an item row. However, it is also possible that the interface contains two (internal) tables. Here, a foreign key dependency exists between the data: In the second table, a data record exists for each item of the first table. Both data records form a common table row in the output table of the form.

This is exactly the case in the sample interface, where there are two internal tables, BOOKINGS and CONNECTIONS:

▸ The CONNECTIONS table contains the CARRID and CONNID key fields and defines a quantity of flight schedules, which are described by the two fields, CARRID (airline carrier) and CONNID (connection ID). A connection between two airports is uniquely defined by the pair; according to this, it is an access key.

▸ The BOOKINGS table has the key fields, CARRID, CONNID, FLDATE, and BOOKID, and is the table of the actual flight bookings. To describe a booked flight, you require the flight connection. Therefore, the table contains the two key fields, CARRID and CONNID. However, this is not sufficient to uniquely describe the flight booking. An actual booking is done on a specific day and multiple persons can book the same flight. Therefore, the booking table also provides the two key fields, FLDATE (flight date) and BOOKID (booking ID). These four key fields uniquely identify a booking.

Because both tables include the client in the key, the entries are client dependent. In this example, this is not significant because you only obtain different values at runtime depending on the client used for running the print program.

If you want to output the booking table, you may need information from the connection table. So, this section details how you can read information from a table during the output of another table, for example, the flight time.

1. To add the booking table to your form, drag and drop the BOOKINGS table from the interface to the context. The table is inserted at the end of the context.

2. You can move the table upward, for example, by dragging the FOOTER text node to the BOOKINGS table. Text node and table swap the sequence and the BOOKINGS table is fully expanded automatically.

   The icon on the left side of the node name indicates that it is a table. A DATA node is automatically generated below the table node, which you can identify as a structure based on the icon. The table node encapsulates a lot of similar data records, which are described by a structure.

3. Disable the fields you don't need for the output. Particularly for tables, you should disable all fields that are not relevant later on. Set all fields to Inactive except for CARRID, CONNID, FLDATE, FORCURAM, and FORCURKEY. The result of your work is displayed in Figure 4.45.

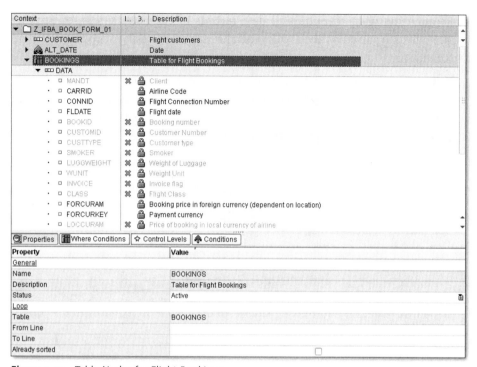

Figure 4.45 Table Nodes for Flight Bookings

You can also create a table via the context menu.

1. Right-click the root node of the Z_IFBA_BOOK_FORM_01 context and select CRE-ATE • LOOP.

2. A dialog opens in which you enter the table name directly or use the input help to select from the available tables.

3. For the properties of the table node in the lower part of Figure 4.45, you can see two fields, FROM LINE and TO LINE. Here, you can limit the value range to be output. The ALREADY SORTED checkbox is discussed later on, together with the control level.

4. The WHERE CONDITIONS button enables you to specify limitations for the output. This basically corresponds to the WHERE conditions, which you already know from the LOOP statement in ABAP. You can define conditions to limit the data quantity.

Because you want to output all data records of the BOOKINGS flight booking table that are passed by the application at runtime, you don't specify any Where conditions.

5. However, you can add such a condition to your form. If, for example, you want to suppress all data records that are in the past you can set the FLDATE fields of the BOOKINGS table in relation to the DATE field of the SFPSY system structure. The comparison could appear as illustrated in Figure 4.46.

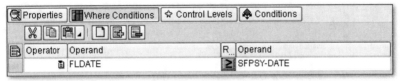

Figure 4.46 Limitation via a Where Condition

Avoiding Input Errors

The best way to avoid errors during input is to drag and drop the fields to the corresponding positions.

You now create a control level for groups according to one or more data fields. For example, a grouping according to airline carrier would make sense.

1. Select the CONTROL LEVELS button and insert a row. Drag the CARRID field to the field and check the SORT IN ASCENDING ORDER checkbox (see Figure 4.47).

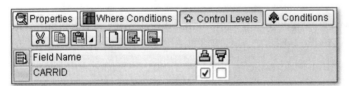

Figure 4.47 Control Level with Ascending Sorting

2. This changes the structure of the context. The CARRID field is positioned at the very top, whereas all other fields grouped via the control level are below the GROUP node.

Figure 4.48 shows the context after the control level has been created.

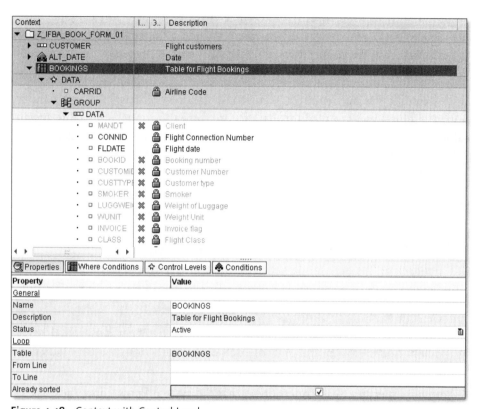

Figure 4.48 Context with Control Level

3. Now select the ALREADY SORTED checkbox (in the properties area of Figure 4.48). You leave it up to the application program to transfer the data already sorted by the airline carrier. As a result, the runtime environment won't carry out a new sorting again.

4. In the interface, you are provided with an additional table, SUM_BOOKINGS, for the global data whose values have been calculated in the initialization code (see Listing 4.1). Add this table to the context and position it directly after the BOOK-INGS table. Drag and drop the SUM_BOOKINGS table to the context and move it within the hierarchy, if required.

4.3.10 Single Record Nodes

Section 4.3.9, "Tables or Loops," stated that the CONNECTIONS table contains information about a flight connection. The table including the flight bookings requires information from the connections table, so you can nest the CONNECTIONS table in the BOOKINGS table.

In this case, this is not required because one data record exists for each connection. Therefore, you can read this data record from the connections table specifically and add the data via the single record node that is provided for this purpose. In ABAP, a single record node corresponds to a READ TABLE <tab> WITH KEY <key> statement.

You now read the flight time for each booking from this table. To do so, you add a single record node to the table output.

1. Expand the BOOKINGS table in the context, if you haven't done that yet.

2. Right-click on the DATA node and select CREATE • SINGLE RECORD.

3. In the subsequent dialog box, enter the CONNECTIONS table directly or use the input help to select the table from the value list.

4. Figure 4.49 illustrates that the single record node has been positioned below the DATA node. This means that for each data record from the BOOKINGS table one data record is read from the CONNECTIONS table.

5. You must specify a read condition so that the system knows how the CONNECTIONS table is to be accessed. If you double-click on the single record node, you can select the WITH KEY CONDITIONS button in the lower part of the screen.

6. The two fields, CARRID and CONNID, link the two tables. Initially, drag the CARRID field from the context of the CONNECTIONS table and drop it in the left OPERAND field.

7. Create a second row and add the CONNID field.

8. On the right side, specify the comparison fields, BOOKINGS-CARRID and BOOK-INGS-CONNID, which you can drag and drop from the BOOKINGS table of the context. You can also enter the field names directly.

9. Set the status of the fields not required to Inactive. Because you only want to read the flight time, set all fields to inactive except for FLTIME.

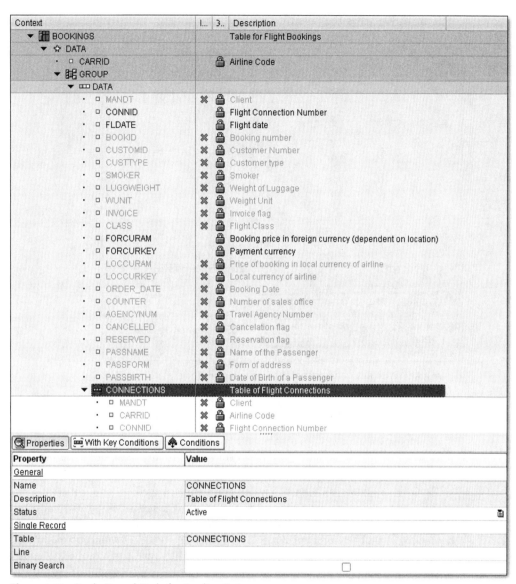

Context	I...	3..	Description
▼ ⊞ BOOKINGS			Table for Flight Bookings
▼ ☆ DATA			
· ▫ CARRID		🔒	Airline Code
▼ 🔠 GROUP			
▼ ▭ DATA			
· ▫ MANDT	✖	🔒	Client
· ▫ CONNID		🔒	Flight Connection Number
· ▫ FLDATE		🔒	Flight date
· ▫ BOOKID	✖	🔒	Booking number
· ▫ CUSTOMID	✖	🔒	Customer Number
· ▫ CUSTTYPE	✖	🔒	Customer type
· ▫ SMOKER	✖	🔒	Smoker
· ▫ LUGGWEIGHT	✖	🔒	Weight of Luggage
· ▫ WUNIT	✖	🔒	Weight Unit
· ▫ INVOICE	✖	🔒	Invoice flag
· ▫ CLASS	✖	🔒	Flight Class
· ▫ FORCURAM		🔒	Booking price in foreign currency (dependent on location)
· ▫ FORCURKEY		🔒	Payment currency
· ▫ LOCCURAM	✖	🔒	Price of booking in local currency of airline
· ▫ LOCCURKEY	✖	🔒	Local currency of airline
· ▫ ORDER_DATE	✖	🔒	Booking Date
· ▫ COUNTER	✖	🔒	Number of sales office
· ▫ AGENCYNUM	✖	🔒	Travel Agency Number
· ▫ CANCELLED	✖	🔒	Cancelation flag
· ▫ RESERVED	✖	🔒	Reservation flag
· ▫ PASSNAME	✖	🔒	Name of the Passenger
· ▫ PASSFORM	✖	🔒	Form of address
· ▫ PASSBIRTH	✖	🔒	Date of Birth of a Passenger
▼ ▭ CONNECTIONS			Table of Flight Connections
· ▫ MANDT	✖	🔒	Client
· ▫ CARRID	✖	🔒	Airline Code
· ▫ CONNID	✖	🔒	Flight Connection Number

🔍 Properties	▭ With Key Conditions	🔥 Conditions	
Property	**Value**		
General			
Name	CONNECTIONS		
Description	Table of Flight Connections		
Status	Active		📄
Single Record			
Table	CONNECTIONS		
Line			
Binary Search	☐		

Figure 4.49 Single Record Node for Reading Data

Figure 4.50 shows the result.

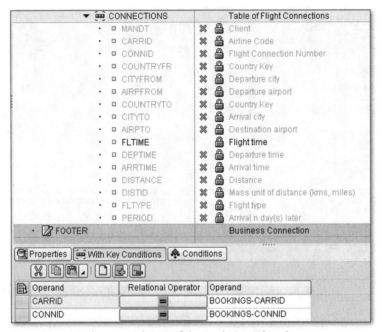

Figure 4.50 With Key Conditions of the Single Record Node

Act with Caution for Fields with Conversion Routines

If you implement a form check (CHECK button), a warning is displayed that informs you that the CONNECTIONS-FLTIME field has a conversion routine. See SAP Note 796755 for more information.

A conversion routine can perform a formatting at runtime and create a value that doesn't correspond to the schema definition. The FLTIME field is defined as 4-byte integer in the ABAP Dictionary; however, the SDURA conversion routine is defined in the assigned domain, S_DURA. Therefore, the CONVERSION_EXIT_SDURA_OUTPUT function module is called at runtime to implement the data formatting. The result is transferred to Adobe Document Services in the data stream.

If you call this function module in the single test and, for example, enter the value 250 (the value is expected in minutes), the result is 4:10, that is, four hours and ten minutes. The display of 4:10, however, is not a valid number value because it contains a colon. Therefore, you must pay special attention to fields with conversion routines with regard to the definition of the layout and set the data type to a character type in Adobe Live-Cycle Designer.

4.3.11 Conditions

You have already come across different forms of conditions in the previous node types, for example, the conditions for a table, the single record node, and alternatives. By means of a condition, you influence the behavior of the form at runtime depending on specific values.

For each node type (except for alternatives) you can also define a condition in the properties. You can do this via the CONDITIONS button as shown in Figure 4.50, for example.

If you define a condition for a node, a decision is made at runtime whether this node is processed or not. Therefore, a text node can only be output under certain prerequisites. The output of a graphic can depend on different conditions or you can suppress a complete table.

Processing Conditions

Note that if a condition is not met both the node itself and its subnodes are not processed and are thus not displayed in the layout.

In the creation of the layout, you learn more about the options to efficiently and effectively hide and display parts of the form by means of the form design and the conditions.

You can now add a condition to the form. To do this, take a look at the definition of the BOOKINGS table (SBOOK structure): You can see the CANCELLED field, which identifies all flights cancelled. Now, you are supposed to suppress all data records for which this indicator is set.

1. Because you are supposed to suppress the complete table row, you define the condition for the DATA node below the control level in the BOOKINGS table.

2. Double-click on the DATA node and select the CONDITIONS button in the node properties.

3. Select the APPEND ROW button. Drag and drop the CANCELLED field to the first operand field and enter an X enclosed in single quotes ('X') in the second operand field.

4. Set the relational operator to NOT EQUAL TO ('). The result is displayed in Figure 4.51.

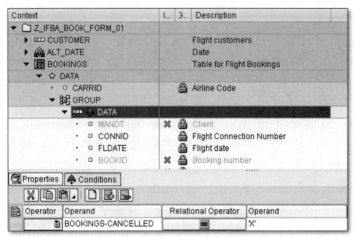

Figure 4.51 Condition for a Node

5. Different relational operators are available and you can interlink any number of conditions using AND or OR.

6. A corresponding icon in the context tree, which is displayed between the actual node icon and the node name, indicates whether a condition is defined for a node. If data is missing in the output of your forms you should check the corresponding conditions in the context.

4.3.12 Folders

The folder is described as the last node type (see Figure 4.52). Folders are required to structure the context and you can combine various node types in one folder. You can also group multiple folders into one folder.

You already know the property to group different elements: For an alternative, you can group multiple elements into the TRUE and FALSE branches. The root node of the context also constitutes a folder. Here, the folder is used not only for the structuring and clarity, but also to support you in the development of the form.

Like all other node types, the folder has the status ACTIVE or INACTIVE. If you set the status to INACTIVE, no subnodes are output so that you can temporarily set some parts to inactive during the test phase. If you create a folder retroactively, you can drag and drop already-existing node types to the folder.

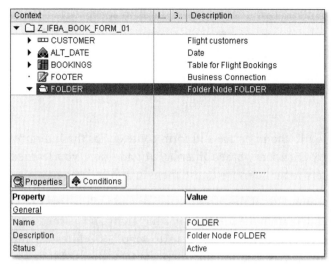

Figure 4.52 Folder

4.4 Documentation of a Form

You can document your own forms to store information about their significance. The documentation is identical to the procedure described in Section 4.2.4, "Documentation of a Form Interface." For existing forms, you can refer to the documentation to find notes about possible extensions if you use a form provided by SAP as a template.

1. The documentation is available via the initial screen of Form Builder. Select the Form radio button and enter Z_IFBA_BOOK_FORM_01 as the name. Use the following menu path: GOTO • DOCUMENTATION • CHANGE.

2. You can now document the form. To do this, you are provided with the following categories:

   ▶ Use (&USE&)

   ▶ Constraints (&CONSTRAINTS&)

   ▶ Call (&CALLUP&)

   ▶ Context (&CONTEXT&)

   ▶ Layout (&LAYOUT&)

   ▶ Further hints (&FURTHER_HINTS&)

3. To complete the documentation, you must set the status to active.

4. You can also access the documentation from within Form Builder. Follow the menu path GOTO • DOCUMENTATION.

4.5 Summary

This chapter introduced you to the interface and form context. For the interface, the focus was on the ABAP Dictionary-based interface. In addition, you learned how you can add parameters to an interface to use them in a form later on.

This was followed by a presentation of the form context as a modeling tool of the interface data. You mapped data from the interface in a hierarchy and learned how to enrich the context with various objects, such as texts, graphics, addresses, and conditions. Particular attention was paid to tables because they are used in many forms and provide interesting functions, for example, control levels.

Chapter 5 describes how you create the layout based on a form context using Adobe LiveCycle Designer.

This chapter introduces you to the design of form templates. The techniques that are explained here can be used for print forms and interactive forms. This chapter describes step-by-step how you can use Adobe LiveCycle Designer to create form templates.

5   Creating Form Templates

In Chapter 4, "Interface and Form Context," you created an ABAP Dictionary-based interface and used it as the basis for the form context. This chapter describes step-by-step how you can create a form template that is based on this context.

During the course of this chapter you will learn how to use Adobe LiveCycle Designer and design a form template to you become familiar with the basic principles of creating one. However, let's begin with an introduction to Adobe LiveCycle Designer and its integration with the SAP GUI.

5.1   Adobe LiveCycle Designer

To use it in SAP environments, Adobe LiveCycle Designer is integrated with the SAP GUI and SAP NetWeaver Developer Studio. This section describes how Adobe LiveCycle Designer is integrated and used with the SAP GUI to help you create a form template for print output. The first feature of Adobe LiveCycle Designer is that it doesn't have a FILE menu; you save the form template using the SAP GUI or SAP NetWeaver Developer Studio.

Figure 5.1 illustrates how Adobe LiveCycle Designer is embedded in Form Builder (which can be accessed with Transaction SFP) and thus in the SAP GUI. Adobe LiveCycle Designer provides its own menu bar and toolbar.

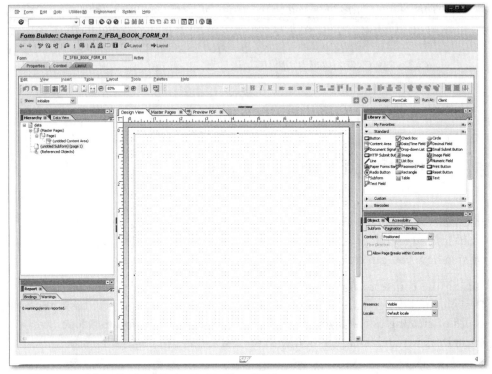

Figure 5.1 Adobe Designer Embedded in Form Builder

Adobe LiveCycle Designer and the SAP Version of Adobe LiveCycle Designer

Adobe LiveCycle Designer, which is embedded in the SAP GUI and SAP NetWeaver Developer Studio, has a slightly different menu structure compared to the standalone version. The WINDOW menu is called PALETTES, there is no FILE menu, and required menu items were moved to the EDIT menu. Therefore, the toolbar has fewer icons.

In addition to the obvious visual changes, the SAP version of Adobe LiveCycle Designer provides additional libraries for Web Dynpro and the Internal Service Request (ISR) framework. This version is also synchronized with the Adobe Document Services (ADS) version, that is, you need a particular version of ADS to use all of the functions for generating (print) outputs. This also applies to Adobe Reader; however, if you don't use any new features, Adobe Designer is backward compatible.

For example, you can use Adobe Designer 8.0 to create PDF forms for Adobe Reader 7.0, but you cannot customize the appearance of checkboxes, because this is not supported by Adobe Reader 7.0.

If you develop forms in the SAP environment, you must use the SAP version of Adobe Designer.

The following sections provide an overview of the relevant areas of the Adobe LiveCycle Designer user interface.

5.1.1 Menu Bar and Toolbar

Adobe LiveCycle Designer provides its own menu bar and toolbar (see Figure 5.2). Thus, as shown in Figure 5.1, there are two menu bars and several toolbars available.

Figure 5.2 Menu Bar and Toolbar

As already mentioned, Adobe LiveCycle Designer does not have a File menu. The NEW DATA CONNECTION…, FORM OBJECT COLLECTIONS…, and FORM PROPERTIES… menu items were moved from the FILE menu to the EDIT menu. The environment that embeds Adobe Designer loads the form templates.

For the SAP GUI this means that form templates are saved via the menu bar or toolbar of the SAP GUI itself. In Figure 5.1, for example, you can see the disk icon for saving in the top toolbar.

There is a toolbar directly below the menu bar. This toolbar enables you to quickly and easily call frequently required functions. Like most programs, Adobe Designer also allows hiding and displaying individual toolbars. Section 5.8.1, "Customizing the Toolbars," provides you with tips for the configuration of the toolbar.

5.1.2 Script Editor

As you can see in Figure 5.3, Adobe LiveCycle Designer offers a script editor in which you can enter scripts for the two supported script languages, JavaScript and FormCalc. The LANGUAGE screen element provides a dropdown list for selecting the corresponding language.

Figure 5.3 Script Editor

Various events occur while forms are generated and edited. You can create specific script programs for the respective events at the level of the individual form elements. The SHOW screen element enables you to select the scripts you want to display. In addition, you can create and edit so-called script objects, which you can use to combine and reuse individual script programs.

Script programming is further discussed in Chapter 7, "Advanced Form Template Creation."

5.1.3 Hierarchy and Data View

The HIERARCHY and DATA VIEW represent two different aspects of the form template in a tree structure. You will often switch between these two views during the creation of the form.

The form hierarchy shown in Figure 5.4 illustrates the structure of a form template. Because the information on the structure of a form template is required in various areas (for example, for binding form fields to data or for script programming), it is very helpful to display the information accordingly. As in most tree structures, you can expand or collapse individual branches.

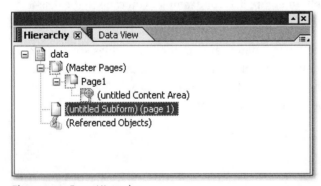

Figure 5.4 Form Hierarchy

The DATA VIEW (see Figure 5.5) is a critical source of information for the creation of the form template, because it displays the structure of the data that is supposed to be output via the form template. The information on the data structure is also required for data binding and script programming.

In addition to the structure of the data, DATA VIEW can also display the structure of request and response parameters for Web services.

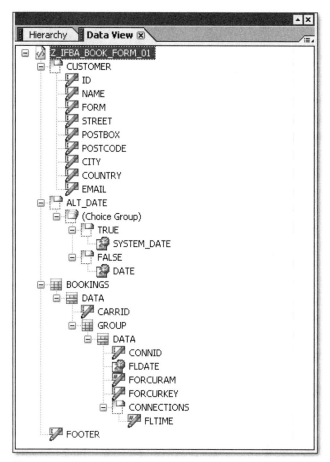

Figure 5.5 Data View

Data Structure for Forms/Data Connections

Every form is based on exactly one XML-based data structure. This is generally defined by an XML schema-based data connection. You can also set up data connections based on sample data. However, in these cases—compared with XML schemas—structure information is missing.

The two remaining types of data connections (OLEDB-based and Web Service Definition Language (WSDL–based) are not designed to describe the data structure on which a form is based. OLEDB-based data connections are not discussed in this book, but Chapter 11, "Offline Scenarios via Web Services," provides more information on WSDL-based data connections.

In addition to the structure, the system displays further information, such as the identified field type, in the form of icons to the left of the name of the data node. For XML schema-based data connections, for example, Adobe LiveCycle Designer can determine this information automatically.

Section 5.3.1, "Defining the Data Binding," describes how the data view uses an icon to indicate which data nodes are bound to form fields. Thus, in the data view, you can easily determine to what extent you actually use the data that is transferred via the interface.

5.1.4 Library and Object Palette

The right side of the Adobe LiveCycle Designer interface contains two other important palettes, for example, the LIBRARY palette (see Figure 5.6). The STANDARD library displays all available form field types:

▶ So-called static form fields (image, text, line, or rectangle)

▶ Form fields for the input and output of data (text field, decimal field, or checkbox)

▶ Interactive form fields (buttons or dropdown lists)

Figure 5.6 Form Field Library

This chapter and Chapter 7 explain the usage of nearly all form fields by means of examples. At this point you should take your time and have a look at the form fields illustrated in Figure 5.6. This figure gives a first overview of the functions that you can implement in forms.

The BARCODES library contains all supported barcodes. A look at this library shows which barcodes are supported by SAP Interactive Forms by Adobe; however, you cannot define your own barcode types.

One of the most important palettes is the OBJECT palette. This palette, illustrated in Figure 5.7, provides different tabs depending on the form object selected. In these tabs you can define the properties of the form fields.

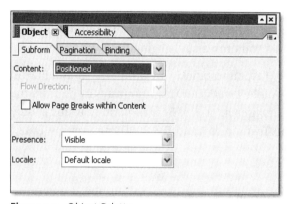

Figure 5.7   Object Palette

To speed up the work with Adobe LiveCycle Designer, you should know on which tabs you can find the corresponding properties. At the beginning of this chapter, you are guided to each tab; however, later on, it is no longer described in detail how you can navigate to the respective tab.

5.1.5   Form Design Area

The form design area (see Figure 5.8) is the most important area. For this reason, it should also occupy the largest part of the screen. The DESIGN VIEW and MASTER PAGES tabs provide an exact view of the form template's layout.

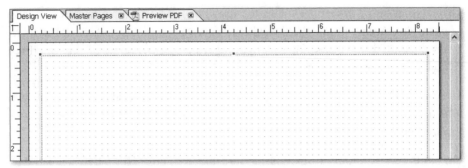

Figure 5.8 Form Design Area

Figure 5.8 shows the DESIGN VIEW in which you define the layout of the individual pages. In the MASTER PAGES tab, you can create the background of the pages that can be used for multiple form pages. Both views enable you to add form fields in a graphical interactive way via drag and drop and changing the layout.

The PREVIEW PDF tab is extremely helpful to quickly view the output as a PDF in Adobe Designer. For this reason, Adobe LiveCycle Designer creates a PDF from the form template and displays it in its user interface. Bear in mind that this is only a preview. Sections 5.2.2, "Using Text Fields," and 5.3.2, "Using Preview Data," discuss this aspect in more detail.

5.2   The Basic Principles of the Form Template Design

You already created the interface and context for the first form template in Chapter 4. In the next step, you prepare a form template that corresponds to the context. You are also already familiar with Form Builder from Chapter 4. This section now describes the options that the LAYOUT tab provides in more detail.

If you are not in Form Builder yet, execute Transaction SFP to start Form Builder. To begin creating the form template, perform the following steps:

1. Select FORM, and enter "Z_IFBA_BOOK_FORM_01" to select the form object that you created in Section 4.3, "Context of a Form."

2. Start to edit it by clicking on the CHANGE button.

3. Then, select the LAYOUT tab. The screen should now appear as illustrated in Figure 5.1.

4. Ensure that DESIGN VIEW is selected for the form design area. If it is not selected, click on the DESIGN VIEW tab. This design view displays an empty form template. Within the blue frame, you can add form fields.

The alternative, MASTER PAGES, is discussed in Section 5.5, "Using Master Pages and Rich Text Fields."

5. Now, close all libraries but the STANDARD library. The library should now appear as illustrated in Figure 5.6.

6. Select the hierarchy, and take a closer look at it. The form template has a master page—Page1—and an unnamed form page (UNTITLED SUBFORM) (PAGE 1).

In Section 5.2.1, "Getting Started," you begin creating your first form template. Figure 5.9 illustrates what the form template is supposed to look like at the end of this chapter.

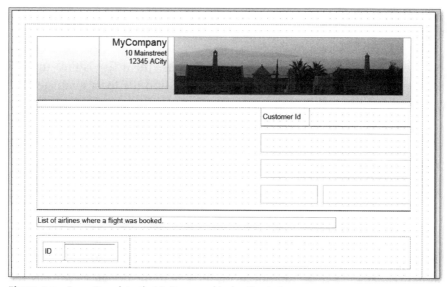

Figure 5.9 Form Template that is Supposed to be Created

5.2.1 Getting Started

Begin creating the form template as follows:

1. First, drag and drop an IMAGE form field from the Library palette to the first page of the form. You can position the image wherever you like. The correct positioning is discussed in Section 5.2.2.

2. Then, select the OBJECT PALETTE. It contains the DRAW tab (see Figure 5.10) that displays the input field for the URL of the image data. Next to the input field, there is a button to select the corresponding file. Select any image from your hard drive. For the example in Figure 5.9, we chose an image of a landscape.

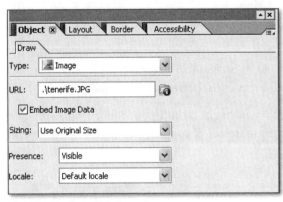

Figure 5.10 Draw Tab for an Image

3. Then, select the EMBED IMAGE DATA option. Because the image is the same for each form output, embed the data for the image into the form template. The reason for doing so is that the system is not supposed to access the image data to import or transfer it via the form context for each generation process.

4. Define that the size is supposed to be copied from the image file. To do this, select the USE ORIGINAL SIZE option for the size.

The letterhead is supposed to contain the name and address of the company. For this, a static text object is used as follows:

1. As the next object, you drag and drop a TEXT form field from the Standard library to the form template.

2. You can change the size of the form fields directly in the design view using the mouse. To do this, select the previously added text if it is not selected yet. As you can see in Figure 5.11, the system now displays an object frame for the form field. You can use this frame to adjust the size of the form field.

Figure 5.11 Object Frame for a Text Field

3. Enlarge the TEXT form field until it has about the same height as the image. Confirm the next dialog with OK. It is not relevant in this context.

4. You can change the position of a form field in a page in a similar way via drag and drop. To do this, click on the form field, and keep the left mouse button pressed. Now, move the mouse and change the position of the form field in the page.

5. In the next step, add a line to visually separate the areas of the form.

6. In the DRAW tab of the OBJECT palette, set the width of the line to "0.015in" (see Figure 5.12).

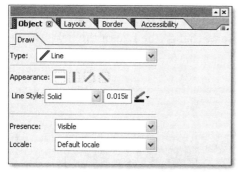

Figure 5.12   Draw Tab for a Line

7. Move the line to the left border of the blue rectangle, and extend the line over the entire page.

8. Now, add a rectangle to the page.

9. In the DRAW tab of the OBJECT palette, select the LINEAR—TO BOTTOM fill. Then, select any shade of white as the first color and any shade of grey as the second color. Set the LINE STYLE to NONE (see Figure 5.13).

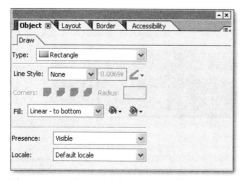

Figure 5.13   Draw Tab for a Rectangle

Gradients and PostScript Level 2

When a form is output in the PostScript Level 2 printer language, gradients are emulated, because they are not directly supported by PostScript Level 2. Therefore, you should avoid using gradients for performance reasons.

10. Select and right-click on the rectangle.

11. Select the Send to Back menu item in the context menu that opens. This way, you define that the rectangle is positioned behind all other form fields.

To check the first steps, compare your form template with the example shown in Figure 5.14. Note that you have not yet arranged the form fields; arrange them now as illustrated in Figure 5.15. If necessary, change the size of the fields. Now, the layout of the letterhead is defined.

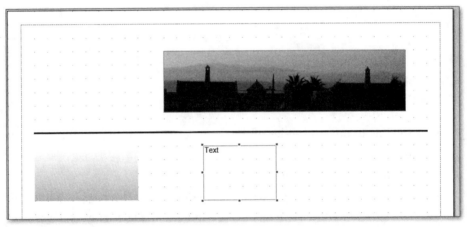

Figure 5.14   First Preliminary Result

Figure 5.15   Form Template After Having Arranged the Fields

5.2.2 Using Text Fields

Text fields are the easiest option to output data in a form. To output information on the customer, such as customer ID and address, you must enhance the form template in the example as follows:

1. Add a text field to the form template. To do this, drag and drop a text field from the STANDARD library to the page of the form template, and arrange the text field below the line.

2. Next, change the caption of the text field. To do this, double-click on the TEXT FIELD caption of the previously added text field, and enter "Customer Id" as the new caption.

3. Take a closer look at the text field. You can see a vertical yellow line between the caption and the input field (see Figure 5.16). It can be used to split the available space between the caption and the input field.

Figure 5.16 Text Field

Use the mouse to move this line to the right to increase the distance between the caption and the input field.

4. Navigate to the Field tab of the OBJECT palette for the text field, and make sure that the text field is selected. Here, select the NONE option for appearance to remove the frame for the input field of the customer ID.

The frame is quite helpful for interactive forms, because it is easier for the user to recognize the fields that require input. For the mere print output, this doesn't look very nice in most cases.

To further edit the form template, you require additional palettes.

1. Display the two palettes, LAYOUT and BORDER, by selecting the two corresponding menu items in the PALETTES menu.

2. Select the previously added text field.

3. Navigate to the BORDER palette, and select the EDIT INDIVIDUALLY option for Edges. Then, select SOLID for the bottom border.

4. Add another four text fields to the form design.

5. After having configured the properties for these four fields, you must align them as required. To do this, perform the following steps for each of the four fields.

   ▶ Select the corresponding text field, and navigate to the Object palette. In the Field tab, set the appearance to NONE.

   ▶ Then, navigate to the LAYOUT palette, and also set the POSITION in CAPTION to NONE (see Figure 5.17).

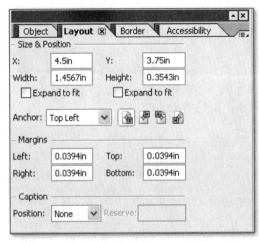

Figure 5.17 Layout Palette for a Text Field

Aligning Form Fields

This section shows you how to arrange the text fields for the customer information in the form in an appealing way. To make it easier to align the form fields, you can decrease the mesh size of the grid according to where the form fields are aligned.

1. To do this, open the drawing aids by calling the DRAWING AIDS menu item via the PALETTES menu. This menu enables you to activate and deactivate the grid and define the distance of its grid lines (see Figure 5.18).

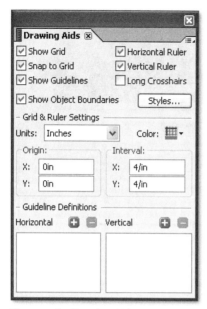

Figure 5.18 Drawing Aids

2. In INTERVAL, set the distance for X and Y to "8/in" respectively.

3. Close the DRAWING AIDS palette.

The grid is also required for the tabbing order and for accessible forms, because the order of the form fields is also defined by their position in these two cases. In this context, the position is evaluated from the top left to the bottom right. Therefore, you must position the form fields exactly.

Drawing Aids

In addition to the grid options, the drawing aid also provides the option to specify the used units of measurement. Available units of measurement are inches, centimeters, millimeters, and points.

In the next step, we'll align the text fields. Proceed as follows:

1. Arrange and size the fields in accordance with the example shown in Figure 5.19.

2. Insert the line that you can see in the figure below the fields.

3. Set the width of the line to "0.015in."

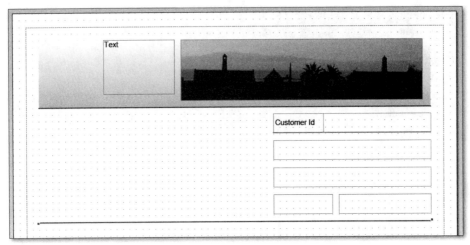

Figure 5.19 Alignment of the Text Fields

Naming Form Fields

Finally, you assign names to all form fields; however, don't confuse names and captions of form fields. The captions are visible in the form, while the names of the form fields are part of the structure of the form template.

1. To do this, select all of the added form fields consecutively in the hierarchy and either press F2 or open the context menu with the right mouse button and select the RENAME OBJECT menu item.

2. Rename the form fields sequentially: "CustomerID," "Name," "Street," "ZIP," and "City." During this process, check which text field you have selected in the design view to generate a correct address at a later stage, that is, ensure that the street is displayed in the correct position.

3. Compare your hierarchy with the one shown in Figure 5.20. This enables you to determine whether you have added and named all form fields correctly.

Naming form fields is particularly critical for advanced form development. Theoretically, you can also create form templates without naming the form fields.

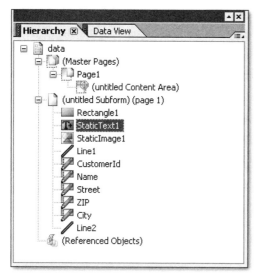

Figure 5.20   Hierarchy After Having Renamed the Fields

Naming Form Fields

Assigning names to form fields has the following benefits: A form template becomes much clearer when you use meaningful names for form fields (for example, Street instead of TextField3). Meaningful names also enable third parties to easily understand the structure of the form. In addition, writing scripts is much easier, because you can use the logically meaningful names of the form fields in the script programs.

Therefore, clear names considerably facilitate the maintenance of your form.

Using the Preview PDF Option

In the next step, the form template is displayed as a PDF document.

1. To do this, select the PREVIEW PDF tab in the form design area.

2. Above the PDF, there is a note highlighted in purple that indicates that you cannot save data that is embedded in the form. In the top right of the screen, a button for selecting fields is displayed. Click on this button and wait. The fields for the address are highlighted.

   The system has generated a preview of an interactive PDF. Adobe LiveCycle Designer cannot assign usage rights to this PDF form, which means that you cannot store the embedded data.

3. Because this chapter doesn't discuss interactive PDF forms, you will change the PDF preview to a print form in the next step. Call the FORM PROPERTIES... menu item in EDIT.

4. Navigate to the DEFAULTS tab. In the Preview area, set the PREVIEW TYPE to Print Form (One-Sided).

5. Call PREVIEW PDF again. As you can see, the note and the button are no longer displayed (see Figure 5.21).

PDF Preview in Adobe LiveCycle Designer

The Preview PDF option in Adobe LiveCycle Designer is used to test form templates. As you have already seen, no usage rights are assigned to PDF forms.

However, the forms need to be generated via ADS to be used in applications. This is done by the frameworks that are also responsible for assigning usage rights.

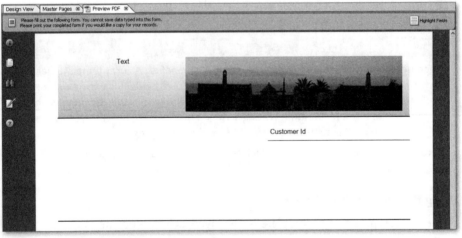

Figure 5.21 Form Template as a PDF Document

5.2.3 Formatting Texts

You must now again edit the Text form field that you inserted at the beginning. To do this, you must display two additional palettes if they're not visible yet: the FONT palette and the PARAGRAPH palette. You can display them by selecting the corresponding menu items in the Palette menu.

To edit the text, proceed as follows:

1. Enlarge the field using the object frame, and position it in such a way that it attaches to the image with only a small distance on the left.

2. Select the field by double-clicking on it. This way, you select the entire existing text so that you can easily delete it by pressing the `Del` key.

3. Enter each of the following three texts into a new line (you can go to the next line by pressing the `ENTER` key): "MyCompany," "10 Mainstreet," and "12345 ACity" (see Figure 5.22).

4. Select the first line by double-clicking on it, and navigate to the FONT palette.

5. Here, set the font size to 14 and the style to BOLD. Then, select the third line in the text, and set the font size to 14 here, too.

6. Finally, edit the paragraph, because the text is supposed to be right-aligned. To do this, select the text (the form field) and navigate to the PARAGRAPH palette.

7. Here, select the icon for the right-aligned text and the icon for ALIGN VERTICAL CENTER.

The text should now look as illustrated in Figure 5.22.

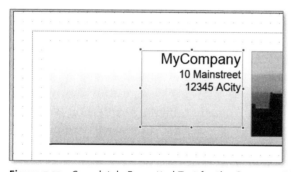

Figure 5.22 Completely Formatted Text for the Company Address

5.3 Data Binding for Form Fields

To define exactly where the form data is supposed to be output from the SAP system, you can link form fields to the data structure by means of data binding. In the next step, we'll bind the address fields of the customer to the data structure.

5.3.1 Defining the Data Binding

To define the data binding, proceed as follows:

1. First, select the text field for the customer ID.

2. Navigate to the OBJECT palette and select the BINDING tab.

3. The BINDING tab contains an input field for the default binding. On the right of this field there is a button. Click on this button, and follow the menu path Z_IFBA_BOOK_FORM_01 • CUSTOMER • ID. Figure 5.23 shows this selection.

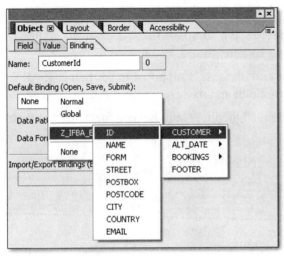

Figure 5.23 Selecting the Default Binding

4. The field of the default binding now contains a binding expression ($record. CUSTOMER.ID) that indicates where the data for the customer ID can be found in the data structure.

   Z_IFBA_BOOK_FORM_01 is the name of the data binding that is also displayed in the data view. For the binding expressions, it is replaced by record. This is followed by the path in the data hierarchy separated by a period (.). You could have also entered this binding expression directly with the keyboard.

5. If the message box for the binding properties is displayed, select the DON'T UPDATE ANY RELATED PROPERTIES and DON'T SHOW AGAIN options, because you're supposed to perform all of the steps of in this example manually.

6. The DATA VIEW displays an icon for bound data nodes after the ID data node. Navigate to the data view, and compare it with Figure 5.24.

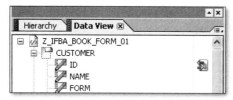

Figure 5.24 Icon for Bound Data Nodes

You can also define the default binding directly from the data view via drag and drop. To do this, you must first select the data view and expand it until the fields below the CUSTOMER node are visible. For the remaining four fields, you should use this alternative and proceed as follows:

1. You can find the data nodes that are supposed to be bound under the CUSTOMER node. This includes child nodes, such as NAME, STREET, POSTCODE, and CITY.

2. Now, select a first node (for example, NAME), and keep the left mouse button pressed. Move the mouse pointer to the text field below the customer ID in the design view, and release the left mouse button.

3. You have now defined the data binding for the second text field. You can check this by selecting the BINDING tab in the OBJECT palette and viewing the binding expression. Here, you should find an expression that starts with $record.

4. Proceed in the same way for the remaining three text fields.

As you can see, the second method for defining the data binding is quicker and easier than the method that was described first. However, there are various steps involved in the creation of form templates for which you must use the first method, for example, the usage of floating fields or the manual creation of tables or sub-form structures, if required.

Section 5.5 introduces a method that further simplifies this process: generating a form field with the correct binding directly from the data view.

5.3.2 Using Preview Data

To create the PDF preview, Adobe LiveCycle Designer generates a PDF from the form template. During this process, it may also process data; however, this must be explicitly defined for the preview. To do this, Adobe Designer allows you to refer to a data file.

1. Define the name and the path to the file in the FORM PROPERTIES dialog, which you call via the menu path EDIT • FORM PROPERTIES....

2. Then, navigate to the DEFAULT tab. Here, the PREVIEW area includes an input field for the name and for the path of the data file (see Figure 5.25).

Figure 5.25 Default Tab of the Form Properties

3. Next to the input field, there is a button to open a file search dialog. You can select a data file from the file system directly; this should be an XML file that corresponds to the XML schema used in the form template. If this is not the case, the system displays an error message when you switch to the PDF preview. You can also use a local file; however, if others want to open your form and view it in the preview, this file may be missing.

Note

Section 6.5.1, "Trace and PDF with Additional Information," shows you how you can retrieve sample data that was used to generate the output via a print program. You can then store this data locally and use it for your preview.

4. As of Adobe LiveCycle Designer 8.0, you are provided with the option to have the system generate a data file. To do this, the DEFAULTS tab of the form properties contains the GENERATE PREVIEW DATA...; click on this button (see Figure 5.25). The dialog that opens again displays the structure of the data. Click on the Generate button to generate a data file.

5. After already having bound the address fields to the data and being provided with the data for the preview, call the PREVIEW PDF option again. As you can see, all fields are now filled with data, and the form is no longer an interactive PDF form (see Figure 5.26).

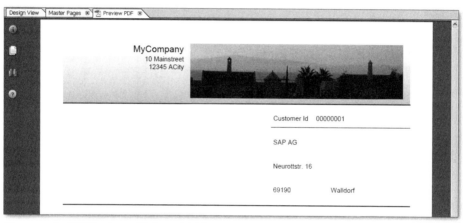

Figure 5.26 PDF Preview with Bound Address Data

5.4 Structuring Form Templates with Subforms

Take a closer look at the form hierarchy in Figure 5.20: All form fields are now below the node for page 1 of the form template; it is a flat hierarchy.

Subforms are an option to combine several form fields and structure the form hierarchy. It makes sense to combine logically associated form fields in a subform, because this helps the form designer keep the overview of the form template.

Because the individual data nodes are usually also logically grouped in the data structure, it is often helpful to assign a similar structure to the form hierarchy.

5.4.1 Adding a Hierarchy

In the next step, we'll add all of the address fields to a subform.

1. Use the mouse to select the text fields by clicking in the upper-left part of the text field for the customer ID, keeping the left mouse button pressed, and selecting all fields via the "rubber band." Move the mouse until you are to the right, below the text field for the city. Release the left mouse button. Now, all of the fields should be selected.

2. To add all of the fields to a subform, press the right mouse button, and select the WRAP IN SUBFORM menu item from the displayed context menu (see Figure 5.27).

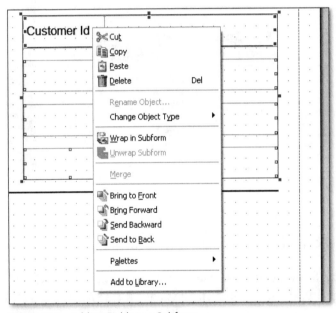

Figure 5.27 Adding Fields to a Subform

3. To include the form fields of the letterhead in a subform, you must perform the same steps for the respective form fields.

4. Drag and drop the hierarchy to add Line 2 to the UNTITLED SUBFORM. To do this, select Line 2 and keep the left mouse button pressed. Then, move the mouse upward. Move the mouse upward until the UNTITLED SUBFORM is highlighted

(see Figure 5.28). Now, release the left mouse button. You can see that the sub-form has been increased in the form design area.

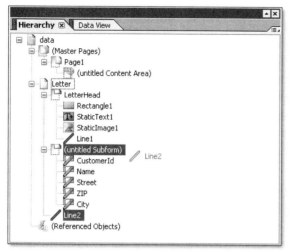

Figure 5.28 Adding the Line to the Subform

5. Now, assign a name to the two subforms. Depending on their content, name them "Letterhead" and "Address."

6. You should then take a closer look at the form hierarchy. The plus (+) and minus (–) signs to the left of the subforms enable you to display or hide the content of subforms. Hide the content of the Letterhead and Address subforms.

7. Now, select the two new subforms consecutively in the hierarchy by pressing the Ctrl key.

8. If you then right-click on them, the context menu opens (see Figure 5.29). Select the WRAP IN SUBFORM menu item to add the two subforms to a new subform.

It is also possible to create subforms in the hierarchy. The most complex way would have been to add the subforms to the form template from the Standard library, and then add the fields to the subforms.

1. Next, assign the name "Introduction" to the new template.

2. Now, assign the name "Letter" to page 1.

3. Accordingly, change the default binding of page 1 in the BINDING tab of the OBJECT palette from NORMAL to NONE.

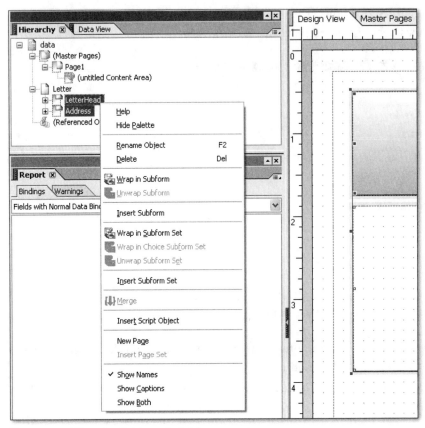

Figure 5.29 Wrapping Subforms in Subforms

If you have performed these steps correctly, your hierarchy looks like the one illustrated in Figure 5.30.

You have only changed the structure of the form template but not the layout. At this point, you can call the PDF preview and check this. The result is identical to the output in Figure 5.26.

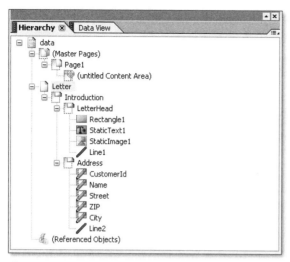

Figure 5.30 Hierarchy After Having Implemented the Subforms

5.4.2 Extending the Form Template

Subforms can be used for much more than structuring the form hierarchy. The following sections discuss the usage of subforms in more detail.

1. Add another Text form field to the form template.

2. Position the form field with a small distance below Line 2 and on the right-hand side of the left border of the design area of the form template. Increase the width of the form field, and enter the following text: "List of airlines where a flight was booked." Then, drag and drop a subform from the Standard library to the form template. Position the subform directly below the previously added form field. Increase the width of the subform until it covers the entire page. Finally, name it "AirlinesList."

3. In the next step, drag and drop a second subform from the Standard library into the first subform.

4. Name the second subform "Airline."

Creating Form Fields with Correct Data Binding from the Data View

Next, we'll add a text field to the second subform for specifying the flight line ID. Proceed as follows:

1. Navigate to DATA VIEW.

2. Search for the `CARRID` data node, which you can find under `Z_IFBA_BOOK_FORM_01` • `BOOKINGS` • `DATA`. Figure 5.5 already shows the entire data hierarchy.

3. Select `CARRID`, and drag and drop it to the second subform (see Figure 5.31).

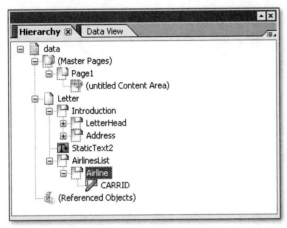

Figure 5.31 Hierarchy with Unnamed Subforms

4. The newly created area of the form template should now look as illustrated in Figure 5.32.

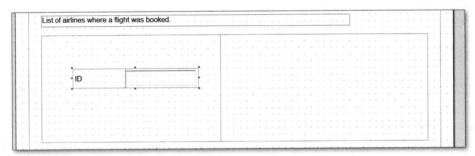

Figure 5.32 Extending the Form by Subforms

In addition to defining data connections from the data view via drag and drop, you can also use the drag-and-drop method to directly generate fields. To do this, the information from the XML schema is evaluated to determine which form field type is supposed to be used. The data view directly displays the result of the evaluation in the form of an icon to the left of the node name.

In this context, take a closer look at the data view. You can see icons for text fields, date fields, subforms, tables, and table rows. In addition to the type of the form field, its data binding is also known and set. In the case of CARRID, the system automatically creates a text field with the correct data binding.

In addition to the two procedures mentioned in Section 5.3, "Data Bindings for Form Fields," this is the third procedure for defining data bindings of form fields. It is also the easiest method, because you can create the form field and the data binding in one step.

For form templates that are based on ABAP Dictionary-based interfaces, this procedure provides even more benefits. The generated XML schema contains the caption that is already defined in the ABAP Dictionary. You can easily test this by adding the Z_IFBA_BOOK_FORM_01 • CUSTOMER • FORM data node to the form. The system automatically assigns the FORM OF caption to the text field.

After having tested this, delete the field from the form template again.

Completing the Layout of the Airline List

Next, we'll edit the AIRLINE subform and the CARRID text field.

1. Reduce the size of the CARRID text field and the caption area.
2. Then, move the text field to the upper-left corner of the subform for the airline.
3. Finally, reduce the size of the subform for the airline. However, the subform is still supposed to be larger than the text field.
4. If you have used Adobe LiveCycle Designer to generate preview data, you should now refresh the data. To do this, call the FORM PROPERTIES dialog via the menu path EDIT • FORM PROPERTIES..., and navigate to the DEFAULT tab. Generate the data as described at the beginning.
5. Now, call PREVIEW PDF. The result should be similar to the one shown in Figure 5.33, which displays the airline ID of the first airline.

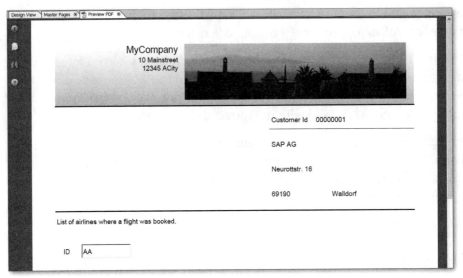

Figure 5.33 First Output Airline ID

Defining the Data Binding of the New Subforms

In this step, we'll output the complete list of the airline IDs. To do this, edit the default binding for the AIRLINE subform as follows:

1. Select the subform, and navigate to the BINDING tab of the OBJECT palette.

2. Click on the icon to the right of the input field for the default binding.

3. Follow the menu path Z_IFBA_BOOK_FORM_01 • BOOKINGS • DATA. Ensure that you select the first option for which no submenu is displayed (see Figure 5.34).

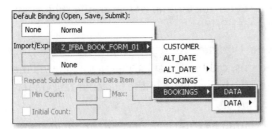

Figure 5.34 Data Binding for the Airline Subform

4. Have a look at the binding expression of the subform, which is $record.BOOK-INGS.DATA[*]. The expression contains an asterisk with square brackets ([*]), because Adobe LiveCycle Designer has determined from the data structure that

the DATA data node under BOOKINGS is a node that can be repeated any number of times. This was defined in Chapter 4.

The Airline subform was bound to the DATA node under BOOKINGS. The DATA node itself does not represent any data values, it is only used to structure the data.

5. Select the AirlinesList subform, and navigate to the SUBFORM tab of the OBJECT palette (see Figure 5.35).

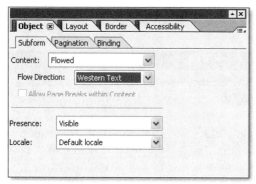

Figure 5.35 Subform Tab of the Object Palette

Regarding the content, the tab provides two options (POSITIONED and FLOWED) to define how the form fields that the subform contains are arranged in the form area. The first option, POSITIONED, defines that the form fields have an absolute position based on the X and Y coordinate. The positioning takes place at the design time of the form template.

6. Select the second option, FLOWED, for the form template. The FLOWED option defines that the form fields that are contained in the subform during the creation of the form output are positioned. However, you must still specify how the form fields are supposed to be positioned. To do this, the FLOW DIRECTION input field has been activated (see Figure 5.35). This field provides two options to define the order (TOP TO BOTTOM and WESTERN TEXT). For this form template, select WESTERN TEXT.

7. Then, have another look at the data binding of the Airline subform (in the BINDING tab of the OBJECT palette). Because the default binding contains an asterisk with square brackets ([*]) and because the FLOWED option is selected for the content of the wrapping subform, the REPEAT SUBFORM FOR EACH DATA ITEM option is now available. Select this option for the form template. This defines that the number of subform outputs depends on the number of data nodes in the data stream.

8. Next, take a look at the default binding of the CARRID text field. The binding expression is CARRID, that is, without $record..., and is often called the relative binding of the form fields. The CARRID text field has a relative binding to the wrapping subform whose binding expression is $record.BOOKINGS. DATA[*]. Thus, the CARRID text field has a unique binding.

9. Note that the first subform now occupies less space in the template. Its actual size during the form output is now determined by the content. Navigate to PREVIEW PDF. The system now displays a list of all airline IDs similar to the one shown in Figure 5.36.

Repeating Subforms

You can have the system repeat subforms when they have a data binding to repeating data itself and when you have selected the FLOWED option for the content of the wrapping subform.

You can use the minimum, maximum, and initial counter to control the minimum or maximum number of instances of the subform. The initial counter defines how many instances are initially instanced. Therefore, a subform can be displayed five times, for example, although the data includes the corresponding node only three times.

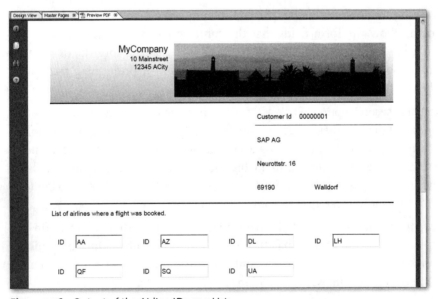

Figure 5.36 Output of the Airline IDs as a List

Subforms are further discussed in Chapter 7.

Data Binding to Repeating Data

You can implement a data binding to repeating data only once. Such binding expressions are indicated by [*]. For the example in this chapter, this means that you cannot output the list of the airline IDs another time. The data is used up, so to speak, and is no longer available for further data bindings.

You can easily check this by copying the AirlinesList subform (select it, open the context menu by right-clicking on it, and select the Copy entry) and inserting it again further below into the form template (open the context menu by right-clicking on it, select the Paste entry, and correct the position if required). In the preview, you can see that the second list displays only one empty text field.

5.5 Using Master Pages and Rich Text Fields

In the following section, we'll add a footer to the form template. The content of the footer is supposed to be a formatted text that is supposed to be maintained outside the form template. The FOOTER data node has already been provided for this in the interface and context of the form (see Section 4.3.3, "Structures," and Figure 5.5).

5.5.1 Customizing the Master Page

Master pages enable you to define a page background that is displayed on multiple form pages. To display the footer on all form pages, you must customize the master page as follows:

1. Navigate to the MASTER PAGES tab to go to the form design area for master pages. Check whether PAGE1 is selected. If it isn't, select it.

2. PAGE1 has a content area, which has a pink border in the MASTER PAGES view. It defines in which area of the design area form fields can be added to the form template. This is shown on the right in Figure 5.37.

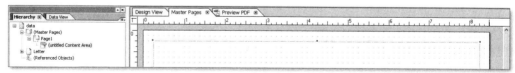

Figure 5.37 Master Pages

3. In the next step, we'll increase the space available in the bottom area of the master page. To do this, select the content area with the mouse. If required, you must move the master page upward using the scroll bars.

4. To have more space available on the page, you must decrease the content area. The content area provides the same object frame as any other form field. Move the bottom edge of the content area upward (see Figure 5.38).

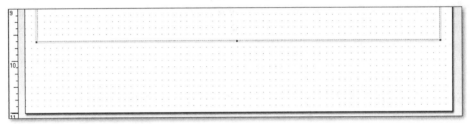

Figure 5.38 Bottom Area of the Master Page

5.5.2 Rich Text Fields

Now, add a text field, and edit its properties.

1. Drag and drop a text field from the STANDARD library to the area that you have previously created by decreasing the content area.

2. To edit the properties, first navigate to the LAYOUT palette, and set the position in CAPTIONS to NONE to hide the caption of the text field.

3. Then, select the OBJECT palette, and navigate to the FIELD tab. Here, set APPEARANCE to NONE to deactivate the border of the text field, and set the checkmark in ALLOW MULTIPLE LINES (see Figure 5.39).

4. Because the text in the footer is later transferred as it has been formatted, set the field format to RICH TEXT. The system displays a warning that the field and data formats do not correspond and that you're first supposed to eliminate the cause of this error.

5. To do this, navigate to the BINDING tab, where you can change the data format from PLAIN TEXT to XHTML (see Figure 5.40).

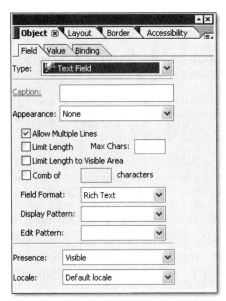

Figure 5.39 Field Tab for a Rich Text Field

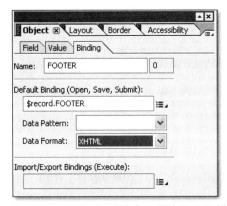

Figure 5.40 Binding Tab for a Rich Text Field

Text Fields and Formatted Text

Formatted text can be displayed by rich text fields. The text is transferred by the data and must be formatted according to an XHTML subset. Among other things, paragraphs and changes of the font style are supported.

You can find a list of the supported elements of the XML Forms Architecture Specification in Section 7.7.3.

6. Move the text field to the left of the content area, and enlarge the text field with the mouse until it is more or less as wide as the content area.

7. Also, enlarge it in such a way that a text with multiple lines easily fits into it. The system displays a message box, which you confirm by clicking OK.

8. Drag and drop the FOOTER node from the data view to the text field to create the default binding. Remember: The FOOTER node is a Smart Forms text module, the text of a text module is transferred in XHTML format.

9. If you used Adobe LiveCycle Designer to generate preview data, you should now refresh the data. To do this, you need a trick to retrieve the data for the footer:

   Add the FOOTER to the design view. Generate the preview data, and then delete the previously generated FOOTER text field from your form template again. The system doesn't generate preview data for the fields on the master pages. For this reason, a field for the generation of the preview data has been temporarily added to the design view.

10. Navigate to PREVIEW PDF to view the result, which should look like the one illustrated in Figure 5.41. You may have to scroll down to see this.

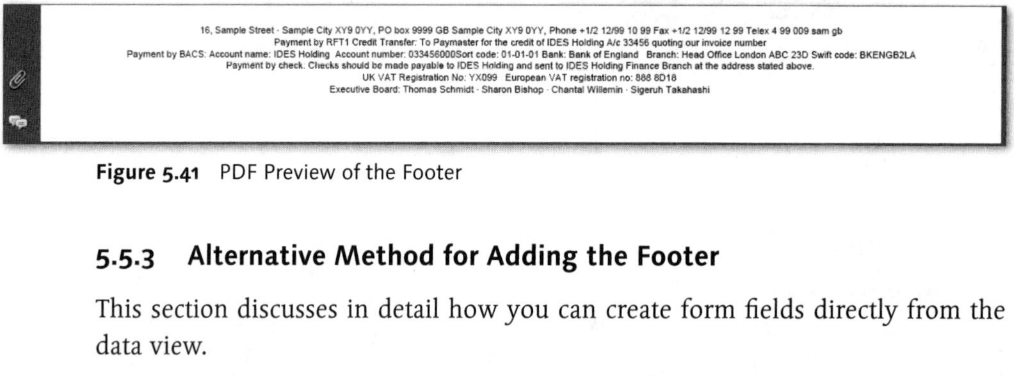

16, Sample Street · Sample City XY9 0YY, PO box 9999 GB Sample City XY9 0YY, Phone +1/2 12/99 10 99 Fax +1/2 12/99 12 99 Telex 4 99 009 sam gb
Payment by RFT1 Credit Transfer: To Paymaster for the credit of IDES Holding A/c 33456 quoting our invoice number
Payment by BACS: Account name: IDES Holding Account number: 033456000Sort code: 01-01-01 Bank: Bank of England Branch: Head Office London ABC 23D Swift code: BKENGB2LA
Payment by check. Checks should be made payable to IDES Holding and sent to IDES Holding Finance Branch at the address stated above.
UK VAT Registration No: YX099 European VAT registration no: 888 8D18
Executive Board: Thomas Schmidt · Sharon Bishop · Chantal Willemin · Sigeruh Takahashi

Figure 5.41 PDF Preview of the Footer

5.5.3 Alternative Method for Adding the Footer

This section discusses in detail how you can create form fields directly from the data view.

1. Delete the text field for the footer.

2. Now, drag and drop the footers from the data view to the master page. In this case, the system evaluates information from the schema and automatically configures the properties for the form fields.

3. Select the FOOTER node in the data view, and keep the left mouse button pressed. Drag and drop the FOOTER node to the area below the content area, and release the mouse button. Check the data format in the BINDING tab of the OBJECT pal-

ette for the text field. It has already been set to XHTML just as the field format has already been set to RICH TEXT (FIELD tab, see Figures 5.39 and 5.40).

4. Customize the appearance and captions as described and the position and size of the text field.

5.5.4   Activating Forms

Like all objects in the ABAP development, you must first activate the form before you can use it. To do this, click on the activation icon. The procedure is identical to the activation of an interface as described in Section 4.2.1, "ABAP Dictionary-Based Interface." In Chapter 6, "Form Output," you will use the created form template to create a print output.

5.6   Reusing Form Objects

Form objects enable you to reuse segments of a form template. If some of the segments are identical in multiple forms, or if you want to reuse script programs, you can use form objects.

For the method described in this section, the form objects are stored locally on the computer of the user. If other users are supposed to have access to these form objects, you must manually copy them.

Form objects can be grouped; this enables you to logically combine the form objects that are thematically linked. You can name these groups and display or hide them in the user interface of Adobe LiveCycle Designer as required.

The version of Adobe LiveCycle Designer delivered by SAP provides three additional libraries with form objects. These libraries are two libraries for Web Dynpro and one library for the ISR framework. The form objects of these libraries contain scripts for the integration with Web Dynpro or the ISR framework. When you use these two integrations, you must use the form objects from the respective library instead of the form fields from the STANDARD library to ensure correct processing.

> **Form Fragments in Adobe LiveCycle Designer**
>
> The form fragments in Adobe LiveCycle Designer are not yet available in this SAP environment. Form fragments externally manage parts of forms and integrate them with a form template through references.

Next, we'll create a library and store the address part of the form template in this library.

5.6.1 Creating Your Own Libraries

Begin creating a new group in the library.

1. To do this, click on the icon selected in Figure 5.42, and select the ADD GROUP... item in the menu that opens.

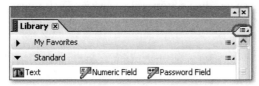

Figure 5.42 Menu for Managing Libraries

2. A dialog box appears where you must specify the name of the group. Enter the name "My Form Objects." Click the icon on the right-hand side of the "My Form Objects" library (it is identical to the icon that is selected in Figure 5.42), and select the group properties.

3. The system displays the dialog shown in Figure 5.43. Here, you can change the name of the group; LOCATION indicates the storage location for your form objects. You can also define what can be done with the form objects (add, remove, or modify).

Figure 5.43 Library Group Properties

5.6.2   Adding Form Objects

Form objects can consist of single form fields or subforms. Let's add the subform that contains the text fields for displaying the address as a form object to the previously created library.

1. There are two options to add the subform to the library:

    ▸ For the first option, you must select the subform in the design area and open the context menu by right-clicking on it. At the very bottom, this menu includes the ADD TO LIBRARY... menu item.

    ▸ For the second option, you must select the subform and keep the left mouse button pressed. Then, drag and drop the subform into the newly created library and release the mouse button.

2. In both cases, the system displays the same dialog, where you must enter the name, a description of the form object, and its usage. Finally, you must define to which library the form object is supposed to be added. Figure 5.44 shows an example of a possible input.

> **Note**
>
> In the hierarchy, there is no context menu to add an object to a library. Also, you cannot drag and drop an object from the hierarchy directly to a library.

Figure 5.44   Add Library Object Dialog

3. The library should now appear as illustrated in Figure 5.45.

Figure 5.45 Library with Your Own Group and Form Object

5.6.3 Using Form Objects

The following section uses an example to demonstrate using form objects.

1. Move the mouse to the newly added form object and wait a moment. The system then displays a note. This note is the description that you entered when adding the object to the library.

   Like form fields, you can also drag and drop add form objects from the STANDARD library to a form template.

2. Try this: Select the ADDRESS SUBFORM form object, and drag and drop it to the form template. Now, the system adds a new subform to the form template. This subform contains the same text fields with all previously set properties.

3. You can use the PREVIEW PDF option to see that the address data is now output twice.

5.7 Implicit Data Binding

So far, you have been introduced to so-called explicit binding. Here, the binding expressions for binding the data are explicitly specified (for example, $record. CUSTOMER.ID). An explicit binding also enables you to use relative binding expressions, for example, a relative data binding to the wrapping subform. You already used relative binding expressions in Section 5.3 for form fields. The CARRID field has a relative binding to the AIRLINE subform.

The following sections introduce an additional option to bind form fields to data structures. For implicit data bindings, the binding to the data is derived from the form hierarchy and the name of the form fields (and from the subforms). This requires that the form hierarchy has a structure that is similar to the data structure.

This can be best explained using an example: To do this, create a copy of the form template, and change the data binding from an explicit data binding to an implicit data binding. You can either use the PDF preview or refer to Section 6.1, "Print Program," to find out that the output for these two options is identical.

5.7.1 Creating Copies of Forms

To keep the original form template, create a copy of the already-created form template first. Proceed as follows:

1. Save the form layout if you haven't done that yet.
2. Navigate to the Form Builder start page (Transaction SFP).
3. In the start page, select FORM and enter "Z_IFBA_BOOK_FORM_01" as the name. Then, click on the button that is used to copy objects in the toolbar.
4. This opens the dialog shown in Figure 5.46. Enter "Z_IFBA_BOOK_FORM_01_ IMPL" into the COPY TO field, and click on the button with the green checkmark.

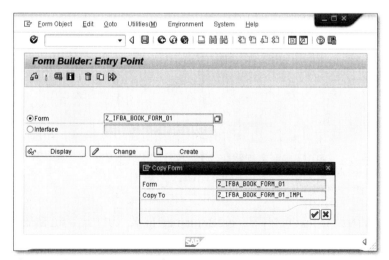

Figure 5.46 Copying a Form Object

5. In the next dialog, Create Object Dictionary Entry, create the copy of the form as a local object. At this point, you should have a look at Figure 4.21.

6. After having created the new form, return to the Form Builder start page. The name of the previously created form is already entered in the input field. Thus, you can start by clicking on the CHANGE button.

5.7.2 Implementing the Implicit Data Binding

Now let's change the data binding for the sample form from explicit to implicit.

1. First, compare the CUSTOMER data node and its child nodes (ID, NAME, etc.) with the Address subform and the form fields contained therein. Both have the same structure.

2. Then, rename the ADDRESS subform. To do this, select it in the form hierarchy, and press the [F2] key. Name it "CUSTOMER." Ensure that you spell it exactly as it is displayed in the data view.

3. Select the BINDING tab of the OBJECT palette for the subform, and change the default binding from NONE to NORMAL to activate implicit binding (see Figure 5.47).

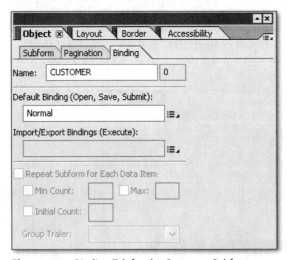

Figure 5.47 Binding Tab for the Customer Subform

The next step considers the text fields that are contained in the CUSTOMER subform.

1. First, rename the "CustomerId," "Name," "Street," "ZIP," and "City" fields to "ID," "NAME," "STREET," "POSTCODE," and "CITY." The data view defines how you must name the fields. Please note that case sensitivity is important here.

2. Then, set the DEFAULT BINDING for each text field to NORMAL.

3. For the list of the airlines, view the structure under the BOOKINGS data node (up to the CARRID node) in the data view (see Figure 5.5).

4. Return to the hierarchy, and rename the AirlinesList subform to BOOKINGS and the Airline subform to DATA.

   The text field already has the correct name, because you have added it to the form template via drag and drop.

5. For the BOOKINGS and DATA subforms and for the CARRID text field, sequentially set the default binding to NORMAL. Ignore the previous specifications of the default binding.

6. Finally, go to the master page, and set the default binding to NORMAL for the footer field (FOOTER).

7. In the BINDINGS of the REPORT palette, you can display the form fields grouped by their type of default binding. Select Fields with Normal Data Binding and the system displays all form fields. To check whether you have changed the setting for all form fields, you can select FIELDS WITH DATA BINDING BY REFERENCE. If you've considered all form fields, the system no longer displays any fields (see Figure 5.48).

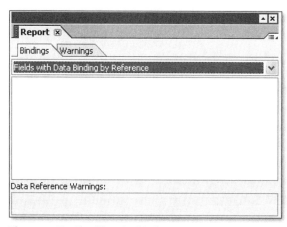

Figure 5.48 Checking the Bindings

8. Your form hierarchy should now look as illustrated in Figure 5.49.

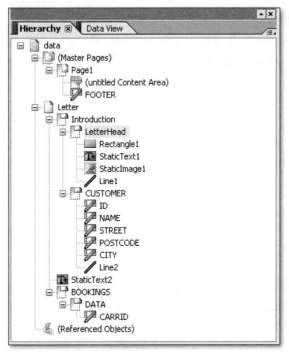

Figure 5.49 Hierarchy After Having Renamed the Fields

9. You can use the PDF preview to check whether the form is output in the same way as before the changes were made. If everything is correct, you won't see any difference.

10. Finally, activate this form template.

> **Implicit Binding to Data**
>
> For implicit binding (indicated by the Normal value for the default binding) the same applies as for explicit bindings to repeating data. Data that has been bound once is no longer available for the binding of additional fields.
>
> You can easily check this by copying the CUSTOMER subform and adding it to the form template for a second time. If you now navigate to the PDF preview, you can see that the second CUSTOMER subform is empty.

> **Implicit and Explicit Binding**
>
> Now that you are familiar with the two main binding types, we can provide the following recommendation: Don't use implicit and explicit binding in one form! We advise against it, because you must know exactly how these two interconnect. Among other things, the order in the hierarchy is relevant. It also significantly reduces the maintainability of the form template.
>
> However, with regard to comparing the performance of explicit and implicit data binding, note the following: During the generation of a print output or a PDF, the system must evaluate the data bindings.
>
> ▶ For explicit binding, the system always needs to process the complete binding expression for each binding, which requires additional time. You should therefore use relative binding expressions, because the system can evaluate them more easily.
>
> ▶ The same applies to implicit binding. Here too, it is often not necessary to evaluate complete binding expressions. However, note that for the implicit data binding the form fields have to be clearly assigned to the data, otherwise you may obtain unwanted results for the data binding and thus for the output.
>
> Therefore, the form hierarchy and the data structure should be as similar as possible to efficiently use implicit binding and obtain a clear result. If so, you should use implicit data binding. Alternatively, use explicit binding and relative binding expressions.

5.8   Useful Functions in Adobe LiveCycle Designer

This section discusses some useful functions of Adobe LiveCycle Designer.

5.8.1   Customizing the Toolbars

To have more space available for the design area, you should carefully consider how many toolbars you require and actually use. Simply hide the toolbars that you don't need, the use of palettes is preferable. If you want to follow this recommendation, deactivate all toolbars but the STANDARD toolbar.

You can also reduce the size of the buttons for the remaining STANDARD toolbars. To do this, right-click on the toolbar, and select the CUSTOMIZE... menu item in the menu that opens. In the next dialog (see Figure 5.50), remove the selection (green checkmark) for the LARGE BUTTONS option.

Figure 5.50 Customize Dialog in Adobe LiveCycle Designer

5.8.2 Field Editor

To simplify and accelerate the development of forms, version 8.0 of Adobe Live-Cycle Designer introduced the so-called field editor that you can activate via the VIEW • FIELD EDITOR menu path.

Figure 5.51 displays the field editor. It provides two details adjacent to the field, the name of the field and the type of field. You can change these two details here directly and don't have to navigate to the hierarchy to rename the fields. In addition, you can also use the field editor to call the context menu.

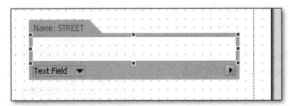

Figure 5.51 Field Editor

5.8.3 Spelling

Version 8.0 of Adobe LiveCycle Designer also introduced a spell check so that the system automatically checks the text for spelling mistakes when you enter text. If the system finds a spelling mistake, it underlines it with a red wave. This line is only visible if the respective text is ready for input.

You can trigger the check for the complete form template via the TOOLS • CHECK SPELLING... menu path anytime.

5.8.4 Managing Multiple Form Fields

Adobe LiveCycle Designer provides various functions to facilitate the processing of form templates with numerous form fields. You can navigate to the following functions via the Edit menu:

▶ **Lock Text**
The Lock Text option enables you to define that you must double-click on the text to begin editing the text. By default, it is sufficient to single-click on the text. You should select this option to avoid that you do not start the text editor by mistake.

▶ **Lock Static Objects**
With the Lock Static Objects option, you can avoid selecting static objects. In the created form template, for example, the letterhead only consists of static objects. After having completed the creation, you can lock these objects to prevent objects from being moved by mistake.

▶ **Lock Fields**
Like the option for locking static objects, you can use this option to lock the nonstatic objects. You should use this and the previous option depending on the requirements and task.

5.9 Summary

This chapter introduced the tool for creating form templates, Adobe LiveCycle Designer, and described its usage. You created a form template based on the context of Chapter 4 (and therefore based on the interface prepared there) with an example.

You also created a template for a print form. The explained method applies to the creation of both print forms and interactive PDF forms. In a print form, the text fields are used to output data. In an interactive PDF form, these fields are interactive and allow you to change their content.

Chapter 6 describes how you can fill the form template with data and generate a print output. To do this, it explains the creation of a so-called print program in detail.

This chapter describes how you can output a form and quickly analyze the cause of an error. It also details the translation of forms and a connection option to external form software via a certified interface.

6 Form Output

So far, you've learned how to create a form interface and a form. The form interface constitutes the connection between the print program and the form. It defines what parameters are expected at runtime and provides them for the form. The form context models the data of the interface and, if necessary, enriches it with texts, addresses, or graphics. Here, the data of the interface is arranged as it is logically required in the form. The context, and particularly its option to define conditions for different node types, makes it an efficient tool for defining form logic.

The form layout refers to the schema that is generated from the context, whereas the fields of this schema are arranged in the layout and formatted in accordance with their requirements. Here, the appearance of the form is specified through fonts and other design characteristics.

This chapter details how you can create a completed document on the basis of a form and enrich it with data. Because problems may occur during the form output, you are provided with the most important alternatives for analyzing errors and resolving them. The translation of forms is another important topic because many enterprises use different languages for corresponding with business partners. You will learn how to manage language-dependent layouts and how you can translate forms.

If you already use other form software within your systems and want to integrate them with the print programs of your SAP system, you are provided with a certified interface. This chapter presents the options of this interface and details how it can be used.

6.1 Print Program

The print program is an ABAP program and is responsible for data retrieval, the type of output, and the selection of forms. The complexity of data retrieval may vary and strongly depends on the respective application.

In this example, you only have to read data for a customer from the CUSTOMER table and flight connections with the respective information from the two tables, SBOOK and SPFLI. Because this chapter is supposed to focus on the interaction of print program and form, you don't require any complicated data logic; the principle is always identical. The sample program therefore includes a simple selection screen and some SELECT statements for database access.

6.1.1 Data Selection

Now, first create an ABAP program and implement the following steps (Transaction SE38).

1. Enter Z_IFBA_BOOK_PRINT as the program name and save it as a local object.
2. Listing 6.1 shows the first part of the program that defines the selection screen and reads the data from the database for the specified customer:

   ▶ The P_CUSTOM parameter expects the customer ID. Enter the Z_IFBA_BOOK_FORM_01 form for the P_FORM parameter, the default value corresponds to the form that you've already created.

   ▶ P_LANGU specifies the form language and defines — together with the country from P_CTRY — the formatting of the number and date fields.

   ▶ P_DATE expects a date.

   ▶ The first SELECT statement reads the customer information from the SCUSTOM table. Here, the customer ID of the selection screen is the access key.

   ▶ The second SELECT statement imports all bookings of the customer in a sorted manner.

   ▶ The third SELECT statement reads the flight connections for all bookings.

```
PROGRAM z_ifba_book_print.
TYPE-POOLS: abap.
```

```
PARAMETER: p_custom TYPE s_customer    DEFAULT 1,
           p_form   TYPE fpwbformname
                    DEFAULT 'Z_IFBA_BOOK_FORM_01',
           p_langu  TYPE spras          DEFAULT 'E',
           p_ctry   TYPE land1          DEFAULT 'US',
           p_date   TYPE sydatum.

DATA: gs_customer    TYPE          scustom,
      gt_bookings    TYPE          ty_bookings,
      gt_connections TYPE          ty_connections,
      gs_outputpar   TYPE          sfpoutputparams,
      gv_fmname      TYPE          rs381_fnam,
      gx_exc_api     TYPE REF TO   cx_fp_api,
      gv_err_string  TYPE          string,
      gs_docparams   TYPE          sfpdocparams.

* Select data.
SELECT SINGLE * FROM scustom INTO gs_customer
               WHERE id = p_custom.
IF sy-subrc <> 0.
*    Error handling. No data for customer found.
  EXIT.
ENDIF.
SELECT * FROM sbook INTO TABLE gt_bookings
        WHERE customid = p_custom
        ORDER BY PRIMARY KEY.
IF sy-subrc <> 0.
*    Error handling. No data for booking found.
  EXIT.
ENDIF.
SELECT * FROM spfli INTO TABLE gt_connections
        FOR ALL ENTRIES IN gt_bookings
        WHERE carrid = gt_bookings-carrid
          AND connid = gt_bookings-connid
        ORDER BY PRIMARY KEY.
IF sy-subrc <> 0.
*    Error handling. No flight connection information found.
  EXIT.
ENDIF.
```

Listing 6.1 Selecting Data

> **Note**
>
> Note that at this point not much effort has been invested in error handling. For example, if no data exists for the customer the program terminates without any notification. This should never occur in live programs.
>
> Good error handling often requires a lot of space compared to the actual coding. Because this book only focuses on the essential elements and the call of a form, minimum error handling is sufficient for demonstration purposes.

3. If you navigate to the texts in the program via the menu path GOTO • TEXT ELE-MENTS • SELECTION TEXTS, you can activate the Dictionary Reference checkbox. As a result, the texts are displayed in the selection screen at runtime.

4. To check this, activate and start the program. The result should then appear as shown in Figure 6.1.

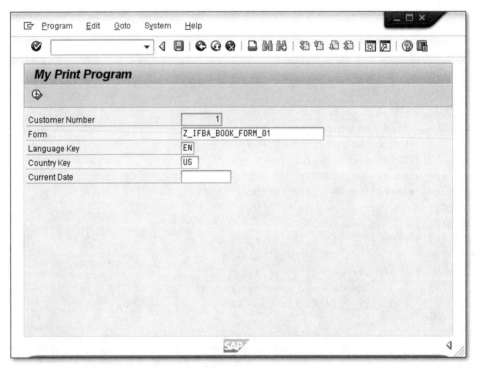

Figure 6.1 Completed Selection Screen of the Print Program

The application data required for the present form is now available in the global field, GS_CUSTOMER, or in the global tables, GT_BOOKINGS and GT_CONNECTIONS.

6.1.2   Determining the Generated Function Module

You can't directly address the form that you created as a form object. Instead, an ABAP function module is created from the form. This function module inherits the parameters of the form interface, which were defined there, including all properties (name, data type, optional, pass by value). In addition, it also includes the coding to communicate with the form runtime environment. You don't have to consider this because the form is simply a function module at runtime to which you transfer all required data of the form interface. The formatting of data and call to Adobe Document Services (ADS) runs automatically.

Because you can't simply use the name of the function module as the name of the form, a mapping exists between the two objects. The assigned name must be provided to you via the FP_FUNCTION_MODULE_NAME function module and the function module is generated upon the first call. If you change the form, this is determined upon calling the FP_FUNCTION_MODULE_NAME function module and regeneration takes place.

> **Never Use the Name of the Generated Function Module Directly!**
>
> The name of the generated function module is different in every system because it is not transported. If you transport your form from the development system to the test or live system, it has a different name in each system. Therefore, you should never address the form via a generated name directly, even if you know it in a system.
>
> In another system, this name almost always stands for another form. If the interface doesn't match, a runtime error is triggered. Note, however, that no error occurs for a compatible interface and a wrong form would be output.
>
> In addition, it is very likely that the function module doesn't exist in the target system at all. The generation is done by calling the FP_FUNCTION_MODULE_NAME function module.

Let's expand the program to determine the name of the generated function module.

1. Add the coding provided in Listing 6.2 directly to the coding provided in Listing 6.1.

```
* Retrieve name of generated function module.
TRY.
    CALL FUNCTION 'FP_FUNCTION_MODULE_NAME'
      EXPORTING
        i_name      = p_form
```

```
    IMPORTING
        e_funcname = gv_fmname.
  CATCH cx_fp_api_repository
        cx_fp_api_usage
        cx_fp_api_internal INTO gx_exc_api.
    gv_err_string = gx_exc_api->get_text( ).
    MESSAGE  gv_err_string type 'E'.
ENDTRY.
```

Listing 6.2 Determining the Generated Function Module

2. Transfer the name of the form to the FP_FUNCTION_MODOULE_NAME function module. The return is the name of the generated function module that you will call later on.

3. Note that class-based exceptions are used here, which you must catch. Certainly, the most critical error is that the desired form doesn't exist. The error-handling simple catches all errors in the same manner, outputs the error text, and terminates the program.

6.1.3   Opening a Print Job

Before you can call a form, you must consider the general output options first. This includes, for example, whether you want to print a form or send a completed PDF document.

The ABAP function module, FP_JOB_OPEN, must be called at the beginning of the form output and determines these settings.

1. Insert the call to the FP_JOB_OPEN function module at the end of the program. To do so, simply select the Pattern button in ABAP Editor.

2. Removing the comments of the inserted coding results in a pregenerated error handling. The function module includes a CHANGING parameter with the name IE_OUTPUTPARAMS. In this program, a GS_OUTPUTPAR variable has already been defined, which you can transfer.

3. Listing 6.3 shows the finished coding, which directly follows Listing 6.2.

```
* Start print job.
gs_outputpar-reqnew = abap_true.
CALL FUNCTION 'FP_JOB_OPEN'
  CHANGING
    ie_outputparams = gs_outputpar
```

```
    EXCEPTIONS
      cancel          = 1
      usage_error     = 2
      system_error    = 3
      internal_error  = 4
      OTHERS          = 5.
  IF sy-subrc <> 0.
    MESSAGE ID sy-msgid TYPE sy-msgty NUMBER sy-msgno
            WITH sy-msgv1 sy-msgv2 sy-msgv3 sy-msgv4.
  ENDIF.
```

Listing 6.3 Initializing the Form Output

The CHANGING parameter of the FP_JOB_OPEN function module is typed as the SFPOUTPUTPARAMS structure. From the ABAP Editor, you can navigate to the structure's definition in the Dictionary by double-clicking the structure name. Table 6.1 lists the most critical parameters of the SFPOUTPUTPARAMS structure.

Field Name	Meaning
NODIALOG	Suppresses the dialog box for the output
PREVIEW	Initially selects a print preview
GETPDF	Requests the return of a PDF document
GETPDL	Requests the return of a print data stream
GETXML	Requests the return of application data
CONNECTION	Connection to ADS
ADSTRLEVEL	Trace level of ADS
BUMODE	Bundling mode
DEST	Defines the output device (printer)
REQNEW	Creates a new spool request
REQIMM	Immediate output of the spool request
REGDEL	Deletes the spool request after the output has been implemented
REGFINAL	Completes the spool request
SPOOLID	Adds the output to this spool ID
COPIES	Number of copies

Table 6.1 Important Parameters of the SFPOUTPUTPARAMS Structure

Field Name	Meaning
PDLTYPE	Printer language for the return of the print data stream
XDCNAME	XDC file for the return of the print data stream
ARCMODE	Archiving mode
NOARMCH	No modification of the archiving mode
NOPREVIEW	No preview possible from the print dialog
NOPRINT	No print possible from the print dialog
NOARCHIVE	No archiving possible from the print dialog
XFP	Activates the XFP output
XFPTYPE	Type of the XFP output
XFPOUTDEV	Device of the XFP output

Table 6.1 Important Parameters of the SFPOUTPUTPARAMS Structure (Cont.)

You don't need these parameters for the initial tests. If you call the FP_JOB_OPEN function module with the initial parameter, IE_OUTPUTPARAMS, a print dialog appears in which you can make all of the settings for a print output or preview.

Numerous fields are prepopulated with meaningful values. For example, if you don't specify any values, the connection with the name ADS is always used for the connection to ADS. You can override this connection using the CONNECTION parameter, for example, if you connect different systems and test them against different versions. If you don't specify a printer in the DEST parameter, the system tries to read the value from your user defaults.

REQNEW is an important parameter. If you don't set this parameter, the system tries to attach the new documents to an existing spool request during print output. You must decide for each application whether this behavior is desired. For this test program, the creation of a new spool request is supposed to be enforced. Therefore, the parameter was set to ABAP_TRUE.

6.1.4 Calling the Generated Function Module

To add a form to the print job, proceed as follows:

1. Call the generated function module whose name has already been determined in Listing 6.2.

2. For the ABAP statement, CALL FUNCTION, you must remember to enter the GV_FMNAME variable as the function module and not enclose it in single quotes, otherwise the system would try to call a function module with the name GV_FMNAME, which presumably doesn't exist.

   If you enter the GV_FMNAME variable directly, this is equivalent to a dynamic call. The decision about which function module is called is not made until runtime and depends on the value of GV_FMNAME. Due to this dynamic call, it can't be checked whether all parameters are transferred correctly at development time.

3. But you can use a trick to program the correct call: Call the FP_FUNCTION_MODULE_NAME function module in the single test from Function Builder (Transaction SE37), enter Z_IFBA_BOOK_FORM_01 as the name of the form for the I_NAME parameter, and select EXECUTE (see Figure 6.2). If the function module has not been generated yet, this might take a few seconds. But the following call will be considerably faster.

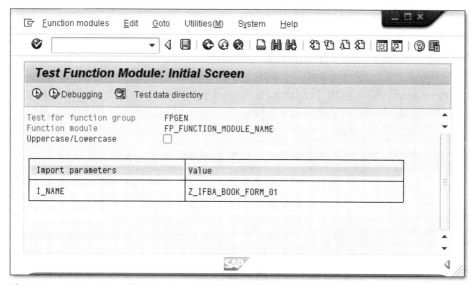

Figure 6.2 Determining the Generated Function Module

4. In the result screen (see Figure 6.3), you can see the assigned generated function module for the E_FUNCNAME parameter. In the present system, this is /1BCDWB/SM00000185; a different value might be displayed by your system, however.

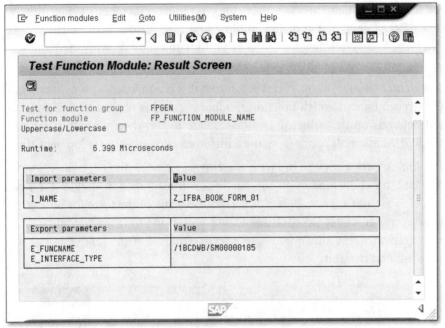

Figure 6.3 Name of the Generated Function Module

5. By entering the pattern for your function module, you can have your print program generate the call pattern. Thus, the available parameters of the interface are automatically inserted into the program call.

> **Note**
>
> Always call the generated function module dynamically. However, you must remember to remove the name again and to specify the call via the GV_FMNAME field.

6. You can recognize the interface of your form based on the parameters of the call. You must provide values for the parameters, CUSTOMER, BOOKINGS, and CONNECTIONS. The DATE parameter is optional because it was defined as such in the interface; the /1BCDWB/DOCPARAMS parameter requires the known structure, SFPDOCPARAMS, via which you can determine the form language, for example.

7. Listing 6.4 shows the completed call of the generated function module. Add the coding directly to the coding provided in Listing 6.3. You don't need the /1BCDWB/FORMOUTPUT return parameter with the FPFORMOUTPUT structure in this program because it provides information about the number of generated pages. Keep the error handling as plain as possible.

```
* Set language and country.
gs_docparams-langu   = p_langu.
gs_docparams-country = p_ctry.
* Call generated function module (form).
CALL FUNCTION gv_fmname
  EXPORTING
    /1bcdwb/docparams          = gs_docparams
    customer                   = gs_customer
    bookings                   = gt_bookings
    connections                = gt_connections
    date                       = p_date
* IMPORTING
*    /1BCDWB/FORMOUTPUT        =
  EXCEPTIONS
    usage_error         = 1
    system_error        = 2
    internal_error      = 3
    OTHERS              = 4.
IF sy-subrc <> 0.
  MESSAGE ID sy-msgid TYPE sy-msgty NUMBER sy-msgno
          WITH sy-msgv1 sy-msgv2 sy-msgv3 sy-msgv4.
ENDIF.
```

Listing 6.4 Calling the Generated Function Module

6.1.5   Closing the Print Job

The form output must be closed by all means—to do this, you are provided with the FP_JOB_CLOSE function module. Depending on the type of form output you select, this function module displays a print preview or, if applicable, concludes the spool request.

1. Add the call of the FP_JOB_CLOSE function module to your program and use the statement pattern again.

2. Listing 6.5 shows the finished coding, which you add directly to the coding from Listing 6.4.

```
* Close print job.
CALL FUNCTION 'FP_JOB_CLOSE'
* IMPORTING
*    E_RESULT              =
  EXCEPTIONS
    usage_error           = 1
```

```
    system_error        = 2
    internal_error      = 3
    OTHERS              = 4.
IF sy-subrc <> 0.
  MESSAGE ID sy-msgid TYPE sy-msgty NUMBER sy-msgno
          WITH sy-msgv1 sy-msgv2 sy-msgv3 sy-msgv4.
ENDIF.
```

Listing 6.5 Closing the Print Job

3. The E_RESULT return parameter with the SFPJOBOUTPUT structure is not required in this program. However, you can use information from this structure, for example, the number of forms or the number of the generated spool request.

6.1.6 Form Output

The program is now complete and contains all of the necessary elements for the form output. You could invest more effort in error handling, but you already have all of the elements required to print a form. The following note summarizes the basic structure of a print program.

> **Structure of a Print Program**
> - Data selection (see Listing 6.1)
> - Determining the generated function module (see Listing 6.2)
> - Opening the print jobs (see Listing 6.3)
> - Calling the generated function module (see Listing 6.4)
> - Closing the print job (see Listing 6.5)

Note that you can output multiple forms or the same form several times within a print job. To do this, simply call multiple generated function modules between the function modules, FP_JOB_OPEN and FP_JOB_CLOSE, for example, in a LOOP statement in ABAP. You can also call the FP_FUNCTION_MODULE_NAME function module several times for different forms. For performance reasons, you should generally implement the determination of a function module prior to opening the print job and not repeatedly within a loop.

1. After you've activated the program, you can start it. The selection screen (see Figure 6.1) appears and the default values have already been preselected for the first call. The customer number is 1, the language of the form output is English,

the country for formatting the date and number fields is United States, and the name defined for the form is Z_IFBA_BOOK_FORM_01. The date is optional and you can therefore call the form with or without the date.

2. If you select EXECUTE in the selection screen, a print dialog appears as illustrated in Figure 6.4.

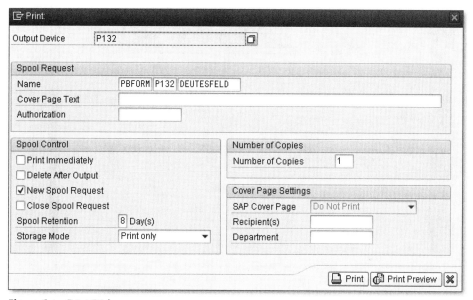

Figure 6.4 Print Dialog

3. If no output device is displayed, you can select it via the input help, if required. When calling the FP_JOB_OPEN function module, you can also provide GS_OUT-PAR-DEST with the name of the printer or alternatively define an output device in your user defaults.

4. In the lower left-hand part of the dialog, you can see that the NEW SPOOL REQUEST checkbox is activated under SPOOL CONTROL. This was set in Listing 6.3.

5. Select the PRINT PREVIEW button in the dialog. Now, all forms are processed internally; in this case, it is only one form. The ABAP Dictionary data, which you transferred in the interface, is converted into an XML data stream based on the context definition, and ADS is called on the Java stack for creating a PDF document. Figure 6.5 shows the PDF document for your form.

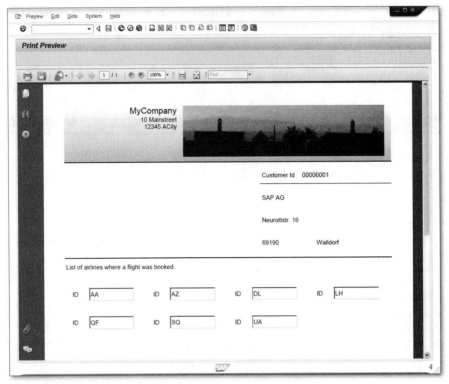

Figure 6.5 Print Preview of a Form

6. If you receive an error message, you should proceed as described in Section 6.5, "Error Analysis." If your system doesn't contain the data records for the flight-booking model, you can regenerate them via the ABAP program, SAPBC_DATA_ GENERATOR (start using Transaction SE38). The program automatically creates the entries in the required database tables.

7. Adobe Reader is required for displaying the PDF document. Different display options are available, for example, you can save the document or print it locally. However, the server-based print output option is more important. You can find this button in the application toolbar. If you select this button, the document is sent via the SAP spool system to the printer that you defined in your program or in the print dialog.

8. Printing via the SAP spool system creates a spool request. However, you can also print without the print preview by clicking the PRINT button in the print dialog (see Figure 6.4). Section 6.2, "Spool System," provides detailed information on spool requests.

You can customize the behavior in many ways using the parameters listed in Table 6.1, which you transfer when calling the FP_JOB_OPEN function module. For example, if you set NODIALOG to 'X,' then no print dialog is displayed. You can then use the PREVIEW parameter to define whether the preview is to be displayed ('X' means show preview). Provided that you don't want to display a print dialog, you should implicitly define an output device in the DEST field, otherwise the value is taken from your user defaults.

An Output Device must be Known at Runtime

If you haven't specified an output device in your user defaults and don't transfer an output device in the DEST parameter, the system asks for it. In this case, the print dialog opens even though you suppressed it via the NODIALOG parameter. Provided that no connection exists to the front end, for example, because your program runs in background mode, a runtime error occurs because not enough information is available for further processing.

You can also use your print program for other forms provided that they have the same interface. You can output the forms that you created in Chapter 4, "Interface and Form Context," without any changes to the print program.

6.2 Spool System

A spool request is necessary to print a completed form via the SAP system. A spool request can be sent to the printer either automatically or manually, and you can view the completed document once again on the system—before and after the output.

For a better understanding, create a spool request by calling the Z_IFBA_BOOK_ PRINT program and clicking on the PRINT button in the print dialog (see Figure 6.4). Make sure that you specify a valid printer; the requirements that must be met to use an output device for SAP Interactive Forms by Adobe are detailed later on. The checkboxes, in particular, PRINT IMMEDIATELY and NEW SPOOL REQUEST, should be selected as illustrated in Figure 6.4. As a result, a new spool request is created that is not printed immediately.

To display the spool requests, you are provided with different options for accessing the output controller. You can start Transaction SP01 and limit the selection by various criteria, for example, by the creator or the creation date of the spool request. You can also use Transaction SP02 as a direct access to your requests. You can access the list of your own spool request via the menu path SYSTEM • OWN SPOOL REQUESTS. As a result, a new mode is opened and a list of your requests is displayed in a new window. Figure 6.6 shows how this list can look.

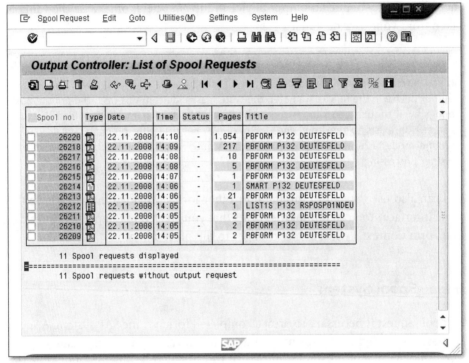

Figure 6.6 List of Spool Requests

There are different types of spool requests, which are identified by different icons. The requests that you created using SAP Interactive Forms by Adobe are identified by the Adobe Reader icon and PDF document is displayed as the tooltip.

To create an output request from the spool request, activate the checkbox of the corresponding spool number and select the PRINT DIRECTLY button. The document is then sent to the output device.

You can display the spool requests from this transaction both before and after the output. To do so, click on the PDF document icon or select the spool request and choose the DISPLAY CONTENTS button. A PART LIST opens that provides an overview of all documents contained in a spool request. You can print multiple documents in one spool request either by calling multiple generated function modules between the two function modules, `FP_JOB_OPEN` and `FP_JOB_CLOSE`, or by not setting the `REQNEW` parameter when calling `FP_JOB_OPEN`; the system then tries to attach the document to an existing spool request.

In the present system, Spool Request 26217 was created and contains five documents with two pages each. If you display the list of parts for this request, you obtain an overview as illustrated in Figure 6.7. You can display the list of parts by selecting a spool request (see Figure 6.6) and choosing the Display Contents button. The number of pages per form depends on the quantity of data in your system.

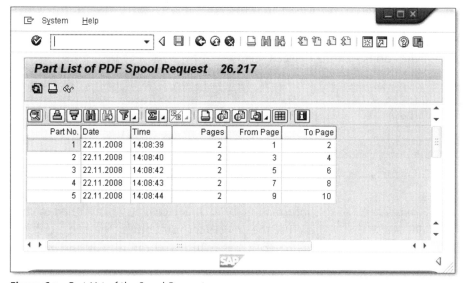

Figure 6.7 Part List of the Spool Request

If you double-click on a part number, the document in Figure 6.5 is displayed.

For more information on spool requests and output requests, call the application help via Transaction SP01. To do so, follow the menu path HELP • APPLICATION HELP.

6.3   Device Types for the Output

All printers that are provided for the output via the SAP system are managed through the spool administration, which is available via Transaction SPAD. An output device has different settings. The spool administration is not an integral part of this book; however, it is supposed to provide some specifics for the output via the SAP Interactive Forms by Adobe solution concerning output devices.

Basically, each output device is assigned to a device type; these device types, however, are required for other form solutions, such as SAPscript or SAP Smart Forms. For printing via ADS, they are not used directly, because the formatting is done on the Java stack. For more information on device types refer to the online documentation of Transaction SPAD, which you can reach by starting Transaction SPAD and following the HELP • APPLICATION HELP menu path.

However, ADS requires information about the printer for which formatting is requested. For this reason, the spool administration was extended by a mapping between the SAP device types and the printer information for ADS. The benefit here is that the information doesn't have to be defined for each output device, but only for the corresponding device types.

Device Types for Printing Using ADS
▶ PostScript
▶ PCL
▶ ZPL (for label printers)
▶ PDF (for printers that understand PDF directly)

You need a reference to this information for each device type you assigned to your output devices so that you can use the devices for print output via ADS. SAP provides an assignment for some device types, which you can display and enhance using the RSPO0022 program.

1. Start the RSPO0022 program using Transaction SE38 and click on the DISPLAY XDC ENTRIES button in the initial screen. The result should then appear as in Figure 6.8.

2. You can see, for example, that the POST2 device type was mapped to the PostScript printer language (*.ps*). However, this information is not always sufficient for formatting because many different PostScript printers exist, each providing different options. These differences are of particular concern regarding paper trays or additional fonts, which are provided via enhancements.

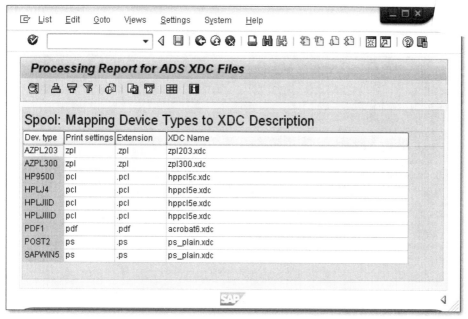

Figure 6.8 Assigning Device Types

For this reason, you must specify an assignment to an XML Device Configuration (XDC) file. These files comprise device descriptions, some of which have already been delivered.

3. The processing of the XDC files is done using the XDC Editor. You can find information on the installation of the XDC Editor in Section 3.6.5, "XDCs."

If you created new XDC files, you must assign them to an SAP device type, which is done using the RSPO0022 program.

1. In the initial screen, select CREATE/CHANGE XDC ENTRY and specify a device type and print settings.

2. A dialog box opens in which you select your XDC file. After confirming your selection, the system assigns the SAP device type and the XDC file (see Figure 6.9).

If you receive an error message stating "Cannot find PDL type for output device XYZ" (FPRUNX 113), this may be due to the fact that no XDC file has been assigned to the corresponding device type. For more information, see SAP Note 685571.

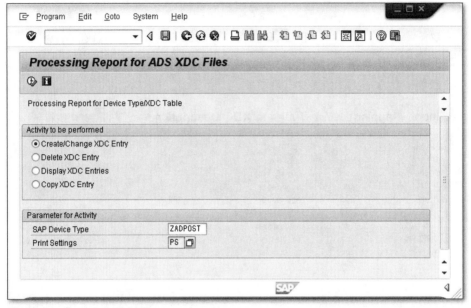

Figure 6.9 Assigning XDC Files

6.4 Special Output Scenarios

Additional options for output processing exist. So far, you've learned that a document can be displayed as a PDF in a preview or that a spool request can be created directly. In addition, you have many more options to influence document creation and process completed documents yourself. The following descriptions provide you with some valuable information.

6.4.1 Archiving

Frequently, statutory requirements necessitate the optical archiving of business documents. You can do this with SAP ArchiveLink interface, which enables integration with the archiving solutions.

To archive a completed PDF document, you only have to set the archiving mode accordingly using the ARCMODE parameter when calling the FP_JOB_OPEN function module. The following values exist (see Table 6.2):

ARCMODE Value	Meaning
1 or SPACE	Print only
2	Archive only
3	Print and archive

Table 6.2 Archiving Options

If you set this value to 1 or not at all in the program, only a print output is generated; if you set it to 2, the document is transferred to the archive and no print output is created. The value 3 means both—creating a print output and archiving the PDF document.

A PDF document requires an index so that it can be stored in the archive. This index can't be transferred when the FP_JOB_OPEN function module is called because a print job can contain multiple forms. Therefore, you must transfer such an index for each call of the generated function module.

The index is part of the /1BCDWB/DOCPARAMS parameter. The assigned structure, SFPDOCPARAMS, contains a DARATAB table of the TFPDARA type and is a table that includes archive indexes. According to this, multiple archive indexes can be transferred with each document, but usually only one entry is used. The row type of the table is TOA_DARA. At runtime, the completed PDF document is transferred to SAP ArchiveLink together with the archiving information. For more information on SAP ArchiveLink, refer to the online documentation (*http://help.sap.com/saphelp_nw70/helpdata/EN/5e/566039b85f9443e10000000a114084/frameset.htm*).

If you set the STORAGE MODE in the print dialog (see Figure 6.4), archiving is only possible when the application program transfers the indexes for the documents. If you want to prevent the user from changing the storage mode, you must set the NOARMCH parameter to 'X' when calling the FP_JOB_OPEN function module. This disables the selection list in the print dialog.

6.4.2   Returning Documents

Another interesting option is to return the created document to the application. Thus, the calling program assumes full control of further distribution—for example, no print preview is displayed or no print output is triggered. The application program receives the document in formatted form and can, for example, send it via email, store it in a repository, or provide it via a Web service.

The following sections briefly describe how you can request a PDF document and save it locally. To do this, you will copy and change the Z_IFBA_BOOK_PRINT program.

1. Copy the Z_IFBA_BOOK_PRINT program and rename the copy to Z_IFBA_BOOK_DOWNLOAD. Listing 6.6 shows the completed program for requesting the PDF and saving it locally.

```
PROGRAM z_ifba_book_download.
TYPE-POOLS: abap.
INCLUDE fp_utilities.
PARAMETER: p_custom TYPE s_customer    DEFAULT 1,
           p_form   TYPE fpwbformname
                    DEFAULT 'Z_IFBA_BOOK_FORM_01',
           p_langu  TYPE spras         DEFAULT 'E',
           p_ctry   TYPE land1         DEFAULT 'US',
           p_date   TYPE sydatum,
           p_pdf    TYPE localfile OBLIGATORY.
DATA: gs_customer     TYPE          scustom,
      gt_bookings     TYPE          ty_bookings,
      gt_connections  TYPE          ty_connections,
      gs_outputpar    TYPE          sfpoutputparams,
      gv_fmname       TYPE          rs38l_fnam,
      gx_exc_api      TYPE REF TO cx_fp_api,
      gv_err_string   TYPE          string,
      gs_docparams    TYPE          sfpdocparams,
      gs_formoutput   TYPE          fpformoutput.
AT SELECTION-SCREEN ON VALUE-REQUEST FOR p_pdf.
  PERFORM value_help_for_output_file USING 'PDF'
                                CHANGING p_pdf.
START-OF-SELECTION.
* Select data.
  SELECT SINGLE * FROM scustom INTO gs_customer
               WHERE id = p_custom.
  IF sy-subrc <> 0.
*   Error handling. No data for customer found.
    EXIT.
  ENDIF.
  SELECT * FROM sbook INTO TABLE gt_bookings
         WHERE customid = p_custom
         ORDER BY PRIMARY KEY.
  IF sy-subrc <> 0.
*   Error handling. No data for booking found.
    EXIT.
```

```
      ENDIF.
      SELECT * FROM spfli INTO TABLE gt_connections
             FOR ALL ENTRIES IN gt_bookings
             WHERE carrid = gt_bookings-carrid
               AND connid = gt_bookings-connid
             ORDER BY PRIMARY KEY.
    IF sy-subrc <> 0.
*     Error handling. No flight connection information found.
      EXIT.
    ENDIF.
* Retrieve name of generated function module.
    TRY.
        CALL FUNCTION 'FP_FUNCTION_MODULE_NAME'
          EXPORTING
            i_name      = p_form
          IMPORTING
            e_funcname = gv_fmname.
      CATCH cx_fp_api_repository
            cx_fp_api_usage
            cx_fp_api_internal INTO gx_exc_api.
        gv_err_string = gx_exc_api->get_text( ).
        MESSAGE  gv_err_string TYPE 'E'.
    ENDTRY.
* Request PDF document.
    gs_outputpar-nodialog = abap_true.
    gs_outputpar-getpdf   = abap_true.
    CALL FUNCTION 'FP_JOB_OPEN'
      CHANGING
        ie_outputparams = gs_outputpar
      EXCEPTIONS
        cancel          = 1
        usage_error     = 2
        system_error    = 3
        internal_error  = 4
        OTHERS          = 5.
    IF sy-subrc <> 0.
      MESSAGE ID sy-msgid TYPE sy-msgty NUMBER sy-msgno
              WITH sy-msgv1 sy-msgv2 sy-msgv3 sy-msgv4.
    ENDIF.
* Set language and country.
    gs_docparams-langu   = p_langu.
    gs_docparams-country = p_ctry.
* Call generated function module (form).
```

```
    CALL FUNCTION gv_fmname
      EXPORTING
        /1bcdwb/docparams   = gs_docparams
        customer            = gs_customer
        bookings            = gt_bookings
        connections         = gt_connections
        date                = p_date
      IMPORTING
        /1bcdwb/formoutput  = gs_formoutput "Returns PDF!
      EXCEPTIONS
        usage_error         = 1
        system_error        = 2
        internal_error      = 3
        OTHERS              = 4.
    IF sy-subrc <> 0.
      MESSAGE ID sy-msgid TYPE sy-msgty NUMBER sy-msgno
              WITH sy-msgv1 sy-msgv2 sy-msgv3 sy-msgv4.
    ENDIF.
*   Close print job.
    CALL FUNCTION 'FP_JOB_CLOSE'
*   IMPORTING
*     E_RESULT            =
      EXCEPTIONS
        usage_error         = 1
        system_error        = 2
        internal_error      = 3
        OTHERS              = 4.
    IF sy-subrc <> 0.
      MESSAGE ID sy-msgid TYPE sy-msgty NUMBER sy-msgno
              WITH sy-msgv1 sy-msgv2 sy-msgv3 sy-msgv4.
    ENDIF.
*   Save PDF document.
    PERFORM download_file USING gs_formoutput-pdf p_pdf.
```

Listing 6.6 Requesting a PDF Document

2. The basic difference is the call to the FP_JOB_OPEN function module; by setting the NODIALOG parameter you suppress the print dialog. To notify the system that you want to receive a PDF, you must set the GETPDF parameter to 'X'. Now, when the generated function module is called, the document in the PDF field of the /1BCDWB/FORMOUTPUT import parameter is returned. At the end of the program, save this document into the local file system.

3. For the input help and for saving, access the FP_UTILITIES include, which is used in many test programs for the form processing topic and provides useful routines, such as, uploading and downloading files.

4. When you start the program and enter a local file under File name in the selection screen, a PDF document is created and saved on your PC.

5. To create an interactive PDF document, you must set the FILLABLE field in the GS_DOCPARAMS parameter when calling the generated function module. Once you have done that, the fields of the PDF document become ready for input.

6. You can also request the document in another printer language by setting the GETPDL parameter. To do this, you must specify which printer language is to be created and which XDC files are to be used.

   You specify the printer language in the PDLTYPE field and the XDC file in the XDCNAME field, for example, *ps_plain.xdc*. The completed print data stream is returned in the /1BCDWB/FORMOUTPUT-PDL field after the generated function module has been called. You can also request both formats in one call.

6.5   Error Analysis

Errors can occur in the development phase of a form. Basically, there are two types of errors: Cancellations that prevent a form output or a generated document that is not structured as desired.

Because you work in a complex system landscape, it is important to have good error-analysis tools at hand. The following sections present a few simple examples of the importance of error-handling tools.

6.5.1   Trace and PDF with Additional Information

To gather additional information during document generation, ADS provides options to generate a trace or to enrich a PDF document with additional information. The trace contains detailed information about the process that is rather technical, but also enables you to draw conclusions about the error cause. The trace can be returned to the calling application or saved locally on your PC.

A PDF document can include file attachments that you can display and save in Adobe Reader. The PDF becomes a data container that contains all documents important for the output and analysis. Transaction SFP provides you with some setting options to create a PDF with additional information. For more information on this topic, refer to SAP Note 944221.

1. Start Transaction SFP and follow the UTILITIES • SETTINGS menu path. A dialog box as illustrated in Figure 6.10 appears.

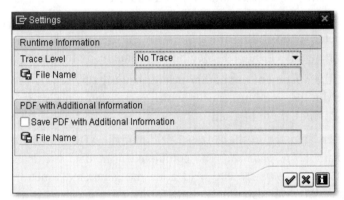

Figure 6.10   Settings for Error Analysis

2. In the upper half of the screen, you can request a trace, which you can store on your local PC. Different trace levels with increasing levels of detail are available.

   Select a level other than NO TRACE and the input field of the file name becomes ready for input. Enter a name for a text file to save the trace.

3. The most interesting option for error analysis is the aforementioned PDF with additional information. This PDF is created by ADS if you set the trace level to the highest value, Very detailed trace, in the selection list.

> **Note**
>
> The settings are maintained until you change them again or log off from the system. They also apply to any other session of your logon.

4. Now start the Z_IFBA_BOOK_PRINT print program and create a print preview. The PDF looks as usual, but now contains different file attachments (see Figure 6.11). You can display them by clicking on the PAPER CLIP icon on the left.

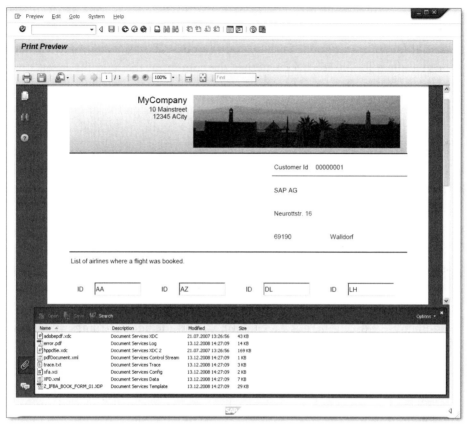

Figure 6.11 PDF with Additional Information

Meaning of the File Attachments

Some file attachments are listed that are useful for further error analysis. A lot of the information is only relevant for the support team and you don't have to know it in detail. Nevertheless, you should know the meaning of the individual files and which conclusions you can draw.

▶ Files with the extension *.xdc* are files for printer configuration, which were discussed in Section 6.3, "Device Types for the Output." Because a print preview has been requested in this example, both a file for the PDF (*adobepdf.xdc*) and for the print output (*hppcl5e.xdc*) is attached. Your system may also contain another XDC file depending on the printer selection.

Here, you can see whether the desired XDC file has been used at all. If, for example, you created your own XDC file, the list indicates whether ADS has used it for form creation. Basically, you can open all files using Adobe Reader or save them locally to check whether the content of the XDC file meets your expectations.

If problems occur for the print output, you should assign the original XDC file to the device type. As a result, however, your additionally defined fonts or paper trays are not available.

▶ The *xfa.xci* file contains some configurations. If you haven't changed the file or haven't created a *custom_xfa.xci* file with your own configuration, you don't have to consider it.

▶ The *trace.txt* file contains the trace with the maximum level of detail. Here, you can find information about the operating system and the version of ADS that is particularly important for the support team. Warning or possible errors that occur during document creation and information about the runtime duration can be found in this file.

▶ Another file existing here is called *error.pdf* and includes warnings and errors in readable form.

▶ The file attachment with the name *XFD.xml* contains application data that is transferred to ADS in XML format. If values are not displayed or displayed incorrectly in your form, you can check this file to determine whether the values are still correct here. The schema of the XML data stream corresponds to the context definition of your form. You can also use this file to create a preview of the form in Adobe LiveCycle Designer.

▶ The list of file attachments also contains the form template, which was used for document creation—in this example, *Z_IFBA_BOOK_FORM_01.XDP*. Here, you can see whether the correct form has been used.

▶ The *pdfDocument.xml* file contains the work instructions for ADS. You don't have to know the structure; nevertheless, the file comprises some information that can be useful for quick error analysis. Here, for example, the locale is transferred for which the document is to be formatted. It consists of the language and the country; for the present example, it is en_US.

If problems occur for the number formats or the date display in the completed document, you should check here to see if the correct locale has been used and examine the call in the print program. Language and country are transferred when calling the generated function module.

Saving the PDF Document with Additional Information

In case a problem occurs, you should always first try to generate a PDF with additional information. This allows for initial conclusions with regard to the error cause.

Such a PDF can only be displayed if you implement a print preview. In case of a print output without a PDF, it is useful to save the PDF after generation:

1. To do this, you should activate the SAVE PDF WITH ADDITIONAL INFORMATION checkbox in the lower part of the dialog box illustrated in Figure 6.10 and enter a file name for the PDF, for example, *C:\TEMP\INFO.PDF*. Make sure that the directory exists and use the input help, if required.

2. Press the ENTER key to close the window.

3. If you now create a print request without preview, you can find the PDF with additional information in the specified location.

Maybe you noticed in the dialog box shown in Figure 6.10 that the input field for the file name of the PDF document is always ready for input. The PDF with additional information is also created if a serious error occurs in the processing done by ADS.

6.5.2 Activating and Retrieving the Trace in the Print Program

You can activate and save or display the trace in the print program. To activate the trace, you must call the FP_JOB_OPEN function module, where you can find the ADSTRLEVEL field in the IE_OUTPUTPARAMS parameter. The values ranging from 00 to 04 correspond to the values of the dialog illustrated in Figure 6.10, where 00 is no trace and 04 means maximum level of detail.

The trace is provided in the calling application program and you can retrieve it after the call of the generated function module by calling the FP_GET_LAST_ADS_TRACE function module. This function module only contains E_ADSTRACE as a parameter and includes the trace of the last call of ADS.

6.5.3   More Detailed Error Messages

A T100 error message is created if a runtime error occurs. This error message is output dynamically in the programs in ABAP via the MESSAGE statement. For example, the errors can be triggered by the form processing, the spool interface, or ADS.

If the error message is triggered by ADS, its text is usually longer than can be output in the message and some information may not be displayed. This error text is available in the trace or in the PDF with additional information; you can also query the error text in the program. To do this, call the FP_GET_LAST_ADS_ERRSTR function module. If it provides a result, you can write the error text to the application log or display it to the user.

6.5.4   ICF Recorder

You can analyze errors relatively easy using the procedure described in Section 6.5.1, "Trace and PDF with Additional Information." However, if an error occurs during background processing, you need other options to root out the problem. Even if the error only occurs sporadically, for example, within a billing run, you should log the calls to ADS.

To do this, use the Internet Communication Framework (ICF) Recorder. The ICF Recorder can log both inbound and outbound requests. In this case, the ABAP stack of SAP NetWeaver calls ADS on a Java stack. Hence, the ABAP system acts as a client. Refer to SAP Note 724804 to obtain a detailed description on the usage options of the ICF Recorder.

The following sections describe how you can record outbound requests using the ICF Recorder.

1. To start the ICF Recorder, use Transaction SICF and select the [F8] key or the Execute button in the initial screen, MAINTAIN SERVICES.

2. In the next screen, follow the menu path CLIENT • RECORDER • ACTIVATE RECORDING. Now, you can log outbound requests.

   You can find a similar path under EDIT • RECORDER • ACTIVATE RECORDING, which is intended for inbound requests, however. So, you must make sure to activate the correct recorder.

3. Enter "*/adobedocumentservices/config*" in the CLIENT URL PATH field as illustrated in Figure 6.12.

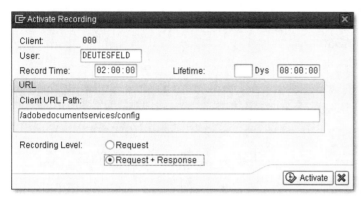

Figure 6.12 Settings for the ICF Recorder

4. Select the REQUEST + RESPONSE radio button to ensure that both the outbound request and the ADS response are logged.

5. Click the ACTIVATE button. The status bar should then display a message stating that the recording has been activated.

6. You can now start the Z_IFBA_BOOK_PRINT print program and create a print output as described in Section 6.1.6, "Form Output."

7. You can find the recordings of the ICF Recorder via the menu path CLIENT • RECORDER • DISPLAY RECORDING. In the following dialog box (see Figure 6.13), enter "*/adobedocumentservices/config*" as the REQUEST PATH. Click the EXECUTE button.

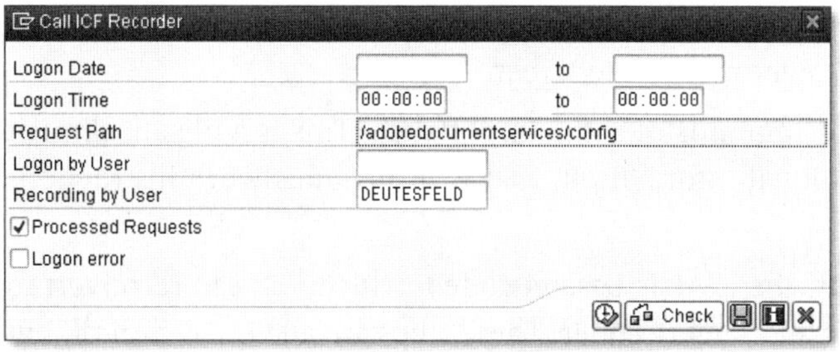

Figure 6.13 Display Options for the Recordings

8. You can see a list of recordings for the outbound requests (see Figure 6.14), including the date, time, and the user who called ADS.

9. The STATUS of the recording is an important field. In Figure 6.14, the status is OK (HTTP Code 200). An error code is displayed here if a problem occurs with the connection to ADS.

ICF Recordings								
Client Requests	Request Path	Stat	Date	Time	User Name	Status	Message ID	Session (Se
/adobedocumentservices/config	/adobedocumentservices/config	200 C	22.11.2008	14:28:41	DEUTESFELD		0A421591697949280090049900000000	1
	/adobedocumentservices/config	200 C	22.11.2008	14:28:48	DEUTESFELD		0A421591697949280910049B00000000	1
	/adobedocumentservices/config	200 C	22.11.2008	14:28:57	DEUTESFELD		0A421591697949280919049D00000000	1
	/adobedocumentservices/config		22.11.2008	14:29:05	DEUTESFELD		0A421591697949280921049F00000000	1
	/adobedocumentservices/config	200 C	22.11.2008	14:28:09	DEUTESFELD		0A4215916B91492808E91D8300000000	2
	/adobedocumentservices/config	200 C	22.11.2008	14:28:06	DEUTESFELD		0A4215916B91492808E61D8000000000	3
	/adobedocumentservices/config	200 C	22.11.2008	14:28:04	DEUTESFELD		0A4215916B91492808E41D7D0000000C	4
	/adobedocumentservices/config	200 C	22.11.2008	14:28:01	DEUTESFELD		0A4215916B91492808E11D7A00000000	5
	/adobedocumentservices/config	200 C	22.11.2008	14:27:58	DEUTESFELD		0A4215916B91492808DE1D770000000C	6
	/adobedocumentservices/config	200 C	22.11.2008	14:27:54	DEUTESFELD		0A4215916B91492808DA1D740000000C	7

Figure 6.14 List of ICF Recordings

However, the OK status doesn't indicate whether a request was processed successfully for a document processing. It only states that the communication between the ABAP and the Java stack worked properly from a technical point of view. This is a necessary prerequisite for a successful processing. Whether an individual document has been formatted correctly can only be determined in the response of the respective request.

The following sections detail how you can display recorded data and which information can be obtained.

1. To display a request, highlight it and select the Display option.

2. Select Request in the menu that opens. The request that was used to call ADS is then displayed in the lower part of the screen.

3. In this context, PDFDocument is of some importance. This is a file attachment from a PDF with additional information, that is, it includes work instructions for ADS.

   Due to transfer reasons, the XML is Base64-coded, which you can reconvert to the original XML using a Base64 decoder. These steps are all very technical, but in extreme cases this procedure can be useful or may even be the only option to analyze the error.

4. Whether additional sections such as XFD exist, depends on the respective call. The form runtime environment decides whether the data is transferred as part of the Web service communication or is provided using a reference.

5. Now you can display the response. To do this, select the Display button and then Response for the highlighted request.

   Depending on the scenario, one or more larger Base64-coded sections, such as PDLOut or PDFOut, may be displayed in the response, which contains the print output or the PDF in Base64-coded form. You can copy the sections and reconvert them to their original format to display the files.

6. If you scroll further down, you can see multiple sections that are marked with RpString (see Figure 6.15). The most important entry is RpString with the name, Results. It provides information about whether ADS was able to correctly process the request. In this case, the value is OK.

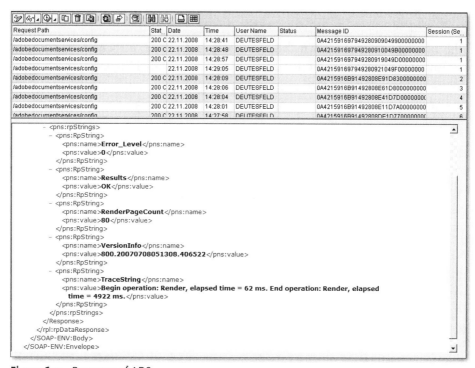

Figure 6.15 Response of ADS

If an error occurs, however, an error text is displayed here instead. Incidentally, this is the same error text that you determined using the FP_GET_LAST_ADS_ERR-STR function module (see Section 6.5.3, "More Detailed Error Messages") or contained in the error message of the ABAP message.

7. The RenderPageCount entry specifies the number of created pages, while VersionInfo indicates the version of ADS. TraceString includes more or less detailed information depending on the trace level, which is particularly important in case of an error.

Deactivating the ICF Recorder

After the analysis, remember to switch off the ICF Recorder again, otherwise the requests continue to be recorded and the system's performance decreases.

---

8. Exit the screen, including the list of recordings, and switch off the ICF Recorder via the menu path CLIENT • RECORDER • DEACTIVATE RECORDER. Again, enter "/adobedocumentservices/config" as the client URL path and select Deactivate.

9. A dialog box opens in which usually only one entry is displayed. You can see multiple entries here if other users have activated the ICF Recorder as well.

10. Select your entry and choose Deactivate. You can still display the recordings later on.

6.6   Performance Optimization

Frequently, performance is a critical topic for the output of documents. The processing speed is particularly important for a high volume of documents, such as for mass printing.

Most of the performance-critical SAP print programs run in the ABAP stack; therefore, in mass printing, a high volume of data must be transferred to the Java stack, where the documents are formatted by ADS. The finished documents (PDF or print formats) must then be sent to the ABAP stack again because the SAP spool system implements the output here.

Therefore, the performance is always a combination of the times for rendering the form and the times for the communication between the systems. The time required for the data transfer becomes particularly noticeable if you process multiple small documents. This is the case in many mass printing scenarios—numerous documents are generated that only comprise one or two pages. Depending on the complexity of the documents, the system conditions, and the network speed, it may be possible that the communication itself takes longer than the actual formatting of the documents.

6.6.1 Bundling Forms

You have the option to bundle multiple calls to ADS and transfer them collectively. This reduces the initial communication overhead and the initialization time. Bundling means that you collect the data of multiple forms in the form runtime environment and call ADS when a specific data volume has been reached. The data is collected in such a way that the system can assign it to the individual forms. A combination of different forms is also supported.

So, if you alternately output order confirmation, delivery note, and invoice in any sequence, the system ensures the correct assignment. The number of forms that are bundled in one call is dynamic and depends on the number of pages of the individual forms. The system tries to obtain an optimal bundle volume with regard to performance. Therefore, at the beginning of a print job, there is a learning phase during which statistics are gathered about the forms. The optimal volume can be determined after some calls have been made.

The benefit of bundling is that you have to do virtually nothing in your print programs:

▶ The most critical aspect is that the system requirements are met for bundling. Chapter 3, "Installation and Configuration," discussed this topic.

▶ Another important aspect is the method of how the print program calls forms. Remember that a print job is enclosed within the function modules FP_JOB_OPEN and FP_JOB_CLOSE. You can only bundle forms that are called within *one* such enclosure. However, bundling is not possible if a program only outputs one form per job, concludes the job, and reopens for the next form.

Therefore, you must ensure that the loop is within the function modules, FP_JOB_OPEN and FP_JOB_CLOSE, and that you don't reopen the spool job for each form.

The system provides bundling support for the following scenarios:

▶ Print output
▶ Archiving

▶ Print output and archiving

▶ PDF return

For returning the PDF, you must make some changes to the program, which are discussed later on. If you request the PDF using the GETPDF parameter, bundling is not implemented initially. Bundling switches off automatically when the print data stream is requested using the GETPDL parameter.

The print output and archiving scenarios and their combination are the most important ones for a mass output of documents. When you implement a print preview, the system automatically deactivates bundling. Bundling does not take place if you request an interactive PDF document.

6.6.2 Activating Bundling

If you activate the bundling in the FPCONNECT table as described in Chapter 3, you don't have to attend to the bundling any longer. Only in some cases, you have to consider some aspects.

You can also explicitly activate and deactivate bundling in every print program. For this reason, the BUMODE field is available in the IE_OUTPUTPARAMS parameter when the FP_JOB_OPEN function module is called.

Table 6.3 shows the possible values for the BUMODE parameter.

Value	Meaning
space	Setting is taken from the FPCONNECT table
M	Bundling
-	No bundling
X	Obsolete, do not use

Table 6.3 Possible Values of the BUMODE Parameter

If you don't specify a value, the setting in the FPCONNECT table (MBATCHING field) decides whether bundling is implemented or not. If you enter 'M' in the BUMODE field, this enables the bundling for the print program independent of the setting in the FPCONNECT table. However, you can also deactivate the bundling for individual print programs by entering '-' in the BUMODE field during the call.

6.6.3   Deactivating Bundling

Bundling is automatically deactivated for those scenarios for which bundling is not supported, for example, the print preview. But it may still be necessary to deactivate bundling. This may be due to the delayed processing of documents.

Normally, a call of the generated function module also entails the synchronous call to ADS. As a result, the document is created and the application receives some information. For example, the application learns whether the form could be created successfully and how many pages it contains. This would not be possible with bundling because a call of the generated function module only saves the data internally and the call to ADS is only carried out when another generated function module is called later on. This generated function module can even stand for another form type.

If the call of the generated function module was successful for the bundling, this only means that the call was marked for implementation. If an exception occurs, however, the entire processing of the last bundle was unsuccessful.

The number of return pages is a good orientation point. If the number of pages is zero, the form was marked for bundling. If the number of pages is returned after the call of a generated function module, then the entire bundle was created successfully and the number of pages indicates the total of all documents in the bundle. It is not possible to determine the number of pages of individual documents contained in the bundle. However, the overall number of pages of all documents is available and is provided in the spool system later on.

This sets some criteria for when you should deactivate the bundling in a print program:

▶ If the print program requires the number of pages of every document, you mustn't bundle the forms.

▶ If the processing status of the document must be recorded in real time, for example, for updates, bundling should be deactivated.

▶ If you have to assign occurring errors to exactly one document, it is recommended to use individual processing.

Bundling is particularly effective to improve performance for the generation of multiple small documents. For large documents, the benefits of bundling can hardly be noticed as fewer forms are bundled in a call. As of a specific size, the forms are automatically processed in single calls. This is automatically controlled by the form runtime environment.

6.6.4 Bundling Example

SAP provides the FP_CHECK_BATCH_SPOOL_OUTPUT sample program as an example for bundling and for testing purposes. The structure of the program is very similar to the Z_IFBA_BOOK_PRINT program and is also based on the flight data model.

When you take a look at the program in Transaction SE38, you can determine that two different forms are used for output: Initially, you specify the generated function modules for the forms, FP_TEST_03_TABLE and FP_TEST_02 (see Listing 6.7).

```
CALL FUNCTION 'FP_FUNCTION_MODULE_NAME'
  EXPORTING
    i_name     = 'FP_TEST_03_TABLE'
  IMPORTING
    e_funcname = fm_name_1.
CALL FUNCTION 'FP_FUNCTION_MODULE_NAME'
  EXPORTING
    i_name     = 'FP_TEST_02'
  IMPORTING
    e_funcname = fm_name_2.
```

Listing 6.7 Using Two Forms in the Print Job

The lines provided in Listing 6.8 open a new spool job, deactivate the immediate output (you don't want to send several thousands of pages directly to the printer), disable the print preview, and activate the bundling. If you set the MBATCHING field of the FPCONNECT table to 'X,' you don't require this line.

```
* Set output parameters and open spool job
  fp_outputparams-reqnew      = 'X'.
  fp_outputparams-reqimm      = ' '.
  fp_outputparams-nopreview   = 'X'.
  fp_outputparams-connection  = p_conn.
  fp_outputparams-bumode      = 'M'.
```

Listing 6.8 Setting the Parameters for Bundling

Prior to calling the first generated function module you can see that the program switches between two different form languages (see Listing 6.9). Section 6.7, "Translating Forms," describes how you can provide forms in multiple languages.

```
* change language and country
  help = index MOD 2.
  IF help = 0.
    fp_docparams-langu   = 'D'.
    fp_docparams-country = 'DE'.
  ELSE.
    fp_docparams-langu   = 'E'.
    fp_docparams-country = 'US'.
  ENDIF.
```

Listing 6.9 Switching between Two Form Languages

The FP_TEST_00 form is inserted at regular intervals at the end of the loop (see Listing 6.10).

```
help = index MOD 7.
IF help = 0.
  CALL FUNCTION fm_name_2
    EXPORTING
      /1bcdwb/docparams = fp_docparams
      mychar            = sy-uname
      mydate            = sy-datum
      mytime            = sy-uzeit
      mynum             = '042'
      myint             = index.
ENDIF.
```

Listing 6.10 Adding a Second Form to the Job

1. Now start the program. In the selection screen, you can specify a range of customer numbers. If you select a larger interval here, for example, 1 to 100 or 1,000, a spool request with many documents is created.

2. In case an error occurs during output, you can assume that your system is not configured for bundling. The necessary configuration steps are detailed in Chapter 3.

3. Display your spool requests when the program is complete. To do so, call Transaction SP02 or select SYSTEM • OWN SPOOL REQUESTS from the menu as described in Section 6.2.

4. Then, display the part list, which you already know from Figure 6.7. The part list looks similar to the part list of a print job without bundling (an example is shown in Figure 6.16); however, each part can now contain multiple documents.

Part No.	Date	Time	Pages	From Page	To Page
		Part List of PDF Spool Request 26.229			
1	22.11.2008	14:33:18	2	1	2
2	22.11.2008	14:33:22	5	3	7
3	22.11.2008	14:33:26	7	8	14
4	22.11.2008	14:33:26	2	15	16
5	22.11.2008	14:33:27	1	17	17
6	22.11.2008	14:33:27	2	18	19
7	22.11.2008	14:33:31	11	20	30
8	22.11.2008	14:33:36	15	31	45
9	22.11.2008	14:33:41	19	46	64
10	22.11.2008	14:33:45	17	65	81
11	22.11.2008	14:33:50	23	82	104
12	22.11.2008	14:33:56	31	105	135
13	22.11.2008	14:34:02	42	136	177
14	22.11.2008	14:34:08	40	178	217
15	22.11.2008	14:34:15	47	218	264
16	22.11.2008	14:34:23	60	265	324
17	22.11.2008	14:34:30	53	325	377
18	22.11.2008	14:34:38	80	378	457
19	22.11.2008	14:34:46	65	458	522
20	22.11.2008	14:34:55	98	523	620
21	22.11.2008	14:35:07	100	621	720
22	22.11.2008	14:35:18	125	721	845
23	22.11.2008	14:35:30	139	846	984
24	22.11.2008	14:35:44	161	985	1.145
25	22.11.2008	14:35:59	195	1.146	1.340
26	22.11.2008	14:36:15	177	1.341	1.517
27	22.11.2008	14:36:31	196	1.518	1.713
28	22.11.2008	14:36:47	199	1.714	1.912
29	22.11.2008	14:37:03	201	1.913	2.113
30	22.11.2008	14:37:13	92	2.114	2.205

Figure 6.16   Part List with Activated Bundling

When you take a look at the part list, you can see that the number of pages starts with a low value and increases with each part number. This is the aforementioned learning phase of the system, in which it tries to specify the optimal bundle volume for the forms involved. In this case, the optimum of approximately 200 pages per bundle was reached after some 20 calls (one call corresponds to one part).

5. You can display the individual documents by selecting a part and choosing the DISPLAY CONTENTS button. This may take some time if you carry out this process for a part for the first time, because the PDF is created for display upon request.

6. Provided that you want to experiment with the bundling, you can enhance your program with a DO loop and output the same form repeatedly. Alternatively, you can enhance the selection conditions and output data for multiple customers. You can also provide the bundling mode as a selection parameter and thus run the program with and without bundling. Here, you should consider the runtimes for both execution variants.

6.6.5 Bundling the PDF Return

The option to obtain a completed PDF document after the call of the generated function module has already been detailed in Section 6.4.2, "Returning Documents." Here, the GETPDF parameter was simply set to 'X' during the call of the FP_JOB_OPEN function module. Then, the PDF was available after the call of the generated function module.

This is not possible for activated bundling because not every call of the generated function module results in a call to ADS. When a bundle is completed, it contains the output of multiple forms. Because such a bundle can't be returned by the generated function module, a program that wants to activate the bundling for the PDF return must look different.

SAP delivers the FP_CHECK_BATCH_PDF_RETURN sample program for bundling the PDF return. You must explicitly activate this special bundling variant in the program by setting the GETPDF parameter to 'M'. You then must receive a table of PDF documents after each call of the generated function module. In most calls, this table is empty, but as soon as a bundle is completed, the table contains all PDF documents of the bundle. The name of the function module you must use to receive the table of PDF documents is called FP_GET_PDF_TABLE.

The Last Bundle Is Available Only at a Later Stage

Because a bundle may only be completed when the FP_JOB_CLOSE function module is called, you must also query the table of PDF documents after the call of this function module. Otherwise, the last bundle might be missing.

Set the bundling mode to 'M' when you start the program if, in your system, the FPCONNECT table contains no entry where MBATCHING equals 'X'. Double-click the individual PDF documents in the results list to select them.

6.7   Translating Forms

Because business documents usually have to be output in different languages, an option must be available to translate a created form. When you create a new form, it automatically obtains an original language. This is the language with which you are logged on to the SAP system at this point in time. Future extensions of the form should always be implemented in the original language. In Form Builder, the original language of the form is indicated under properties. If you try to change a form in another language the system notifies you accordingly.

Forms include a language-independent part and texts that are relevant for translation. The language-independent components comprise, for example, the interface used, the structure of the context, and the arrangement of the layout elements you created using Adobe LiveCycle Designer. Texts, however, are language-dependent—therefore, you are provided with an option to translate them into multiple languages.

The following sections describe how you can translate forms yourself.

1. Start Transaction SFP in the display mode for your form, for example, Z_IFBA_BOOK_FORM_01.

2. Follow the menu path GOTO • TRANSLATION. A dialog box opens where you enter the target language of the translation. For example, select DE for German.

3. Don't change the default for the source language (English). For further translations, it may be useful to select another source language (if the form has already been translated into other languages) depending on the language skills of the respective translator. Choose the Translate button.

4. In the following screen (see Figure 6.17), you are provided with three text categories:

   ▶ **<AD> PDF-Based Forms**
   AD stands for the form documentation. This entry is only displayed if documentation exists for the form.

   ▶ **<PDFB> PDF-Based Forms**
   PDFB identifies texts that you entered directly in the layout of the form using Adobe LiveCycle Designer.

   ▶ **<TLGS> Lockable Logical Objects (Short Texts)**
   TLGS identifies the short texts that you entered in the context.

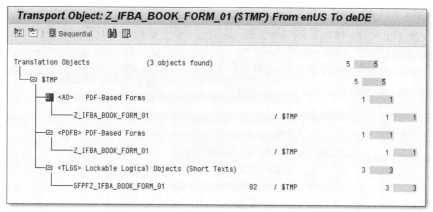

Figure 6.17 Starting Up the Translation of a Form

6.7.1 Translating Short Texts

The following sections describe the translation of short texts in a form.

1. Initially, double-click the entry for the short text, SFPFZ_IFBA_BOOK_FORM_01. In the following screen (see Figure 6.18) you can see three texts available for translation. If you return to this screen after the translation, the already-translated texts will be displayed here.

```
TLGS (..) From enUS To deDE: SFPFZ_IFBA_BOOK_FORM_01 02
 ▲  ▼   🗑 🖉 📋 📇 🖽   🗞 📄 📑 🔳

(No comment exists for object)

[0000010005TEXT]                     📝              (60)
My first form
Mein erstes Formular

[0000020005TEXT]                     📝              (60)
Business Connection
Geschäftsverbindung

[0000030005TEXT]                     📝              (60)
Date
Datum
```

Figure 6.18 Translating Short Texts

2. The text "My first form" is the short text you entered during creation of the form. Translate it to "Mein erstes Formular." Translate the texts "Date" or "Business Connection" into "Datum" and "Geschäftsverbindung."

3. Save the text prior to returning to the previous screen (see Figure 6.17).

4. You can check the translated texts by logging on to the system in German and displaying the context of the form. There, you can see the two texts, "Datum" and "Geschäftsverbindung", which you just entered. Under properties (Eigenschaften), you can find the text "Mein erstes Formular."

6.7.2 Translating Long Texts

This section describes how to handle long texts. Because all texts from the layout are saved in XML format, the translation is a bit more complex.

1. Double-click the Z_IFBA_BOOK_FORM_01 entry (see Figure 6.17).

2. The following screen (see Figure 6.19) displays an XML document in the upper area containing the texts of the original language. The target language is displayed in the lower area.

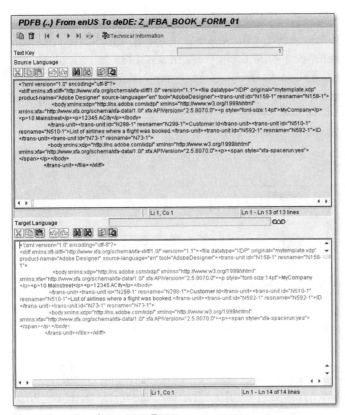

Figure 6.19 Translating Long Texts

If you call the translation of long texts for a form for the first time, the target language is still the primary. Therefore, select the COPY SOURCE TEXT button.

3. In the lower area, you can change the texts highlighted in blue. Because you copied the source language as a suggestion, the texts to be translated are located in the correct position and you can overwrite them with German texts. You may not and mustn't change the surrounding XML sections because the texts can't be assigned in the translated form any longer.

4. Save your entries when you've translated all texts. To check the translation, log on to the system in the target language and start Adobe LiveCycle Designer in Form Builder. The texts you just translated are now displayed.

6.7.3   Output of a Translated Form

After you've translated a form, you can call it at runtime. To do so, start the print program and enter the required language in the LANGU parameter when calling the generated function module. If the form is not available in the language selected, the system tries to find a replacement language. You can influence this process by filling the values, REPLANGU1, …, REPLANGU3, with replacement languages.

Provided that no replacement languages are set or that the form is not available in the requested languages, the system tries to output the form in the logon language.

Propagating Layout Changes

Provided that you extend the form in the original language after the translation has already been carried out, these changes are copied to the existing translations upon activation. The new texts are simply copied here. So when you call a form in the foreign language, the texts are displayed in the original language until you update the translation.

When you transport a form, this synchronization is done in the target system if other translations already exist there.

If you start the translation transaction after the layout has been changed, the system displays a mixture of languages. Texts that have already been translated exist in the target language. New texts, however, are copied from the original language and must still be replaced by their translations.

For the translation of forms you must note that longer texts may change the layout. So you should always provide sufficient space for fields and labels in the layout.

If the form is output in a language with a text flow from right to left (Hebrew and Arabic), the layout is not mirrored. But because the layout is uniform for all languages, in this case you must create a copy of the form in which the layout can be arranged as required.

6.8   XFP Output

If you need to connect another form solution to the SAP system, you can use the XFP interface. It may be necessary to use an external solution, for example, because another form solution is already in use or advanced printer control requirements exist.

Interfaces for external form providers are also available for the other two form solutions provided by SAP—SAPscript and SAP Smart Forms—which both have been on the market for quite a while. These interfaces include the Raw Data Interface (RDI) for SAPscript and the Smart Forms XSF interface, which works on an XML basis. The XFP interface for SAP Interactive Forms by Adobe is very similar to the XSF interface.

The primary aim of the XFP interface is to continue to use the existing application programs and to forward only the application data to the external software. The layout formatting is not implemented here directly—instead, this task is assumed by the form software. The external form software is responsible for the creation of documents based on the application data. Furthermore, it is also responsible for distributing the documents to the correct output devices.

The XFP interface involves an interface certified by SAP. You can obtain information on the certified partners of this interface in the Partner Information Center at *http://www.sap.com/ecosystem/customers/directories/SearchSolution.epx*.

There are two variants of the XFP data stream: The application data can be transferred with or without context evaluation.

▶ For the XFP variant with context evaluation, the application data of the interface is processed in the same way as if it was transferred to ADS. Here, only minor adaptations are made to the XML namespaces. The system is also provided with additional information so that the external software knows which output will be created.

▸ For the XFP variant without context evaluation, the application data of the interface is directly transferred into an XML format without considering the context. Graphics, addresses, or texts from the context are not consider here either.

Facts like the complexity of the application data and whether the external software can support the variant without context evaluation determine which XFP variant is more suitable for the respective scenario. The variant without context evaluation may be interesting for plain forms which hardly contain any logic in the context, because the XFP data stream can be created faster.

Further information on the XFP interface is available in the SAP online documentation for Transaction SFP. Follow the menu path HELP • APPLICATION HELP in the menu. On the help page, select SAP INTERACTIVE FORMS BY ADOBE • PDF-BASED PRINT FORMS • FORM OUTPUT • OUTPUT IN XFP FORMAT.

You can activate and control the XFP interface using parameters when calling the FP_JOB_OPEN function module:

▸ **XFP**
Use the XFP parameter and enter 'X' to activate the XFP output.

▸ **XFPTYPE**
You can control this variant of the XFP output (with or without context evaluation) using the XFPTYPE parameter. The initial value means with context evaluation; if you enter 'R', the application data is directly transferred in XML format.

▸ **XFPOUTDEV**
XFPOUTDEV is an optional parameter that controls the connection to the external system. This parameter is described in the following text.

The SAP spool system is used for the connection of the external system and the transfer of data. The form runtime environment utilizes the virtual output device, XFP, which must have the XFP device type. To use the XFP interface, you must create such an output device. If you select another name, you must transfer it via the XFPOUTDEV parameter. You must assign the XFP device type to the output device in any case, otherwise the data stream is not formatted correctly.

For an XFP output, the data is not transferred via the output device that is used by the application (DEST parameter). A spool request is not created for this printer, but for the XFP device that is used for each transfer to the external form software. You can create multiple virtual output devices and then distribute the data to the respective print programs depending on the scenario. The actual printer is provided in the XFP data stream together with other metainformation and is thus available to the external system.

> **Tip**
>
> You can obtain detailed information on the definition of output devices in the SAP Printing Guide. A link to this document can be found in XFP documentation.

The way data is received by the external system and which additional settings must be made, depends on the respective form software.

6.9 Summary

This chapter outlined the meaning and the tasks of the print program and its interaction with the form interface. The print program is responsible for data retrieval and for the output and print job control. Besides the data selection, the specification of the correct form is also important.

This chapter discussed different output scenarios, such as print preview, print output, archiving, or return of PDF documents. In this context, you gained an insight in the SAP spool system and the necessary device definitions for the use of printers using the SAP Interactive Forms by Adobe solution. Error analysis constituted another important topic. You learned how you can create a PDF with additional information or operate the ICF Recorder to log the communication between the SAP system and ADS. After that, you got to know the bundling for form output and its effects on performance. Another section dealt with the translation of forms. You learned how to translate your own forms to provide them in different languages. The final section introduced you to the XFP output. You can use this certified interface to connect third-party form software to the SAP system.

Chapter 7, "Advanced Form Template Creation," describes advanced techniques for layout design, such as tables.

This second chapter on the creation of forms addresses advanced form designers. Here, the example regarding the creation of form templates from Chapter 5, "Creating Form Templates," is further developed, and you are introduced to the basic principles of creating interactive forms.

7   Advanced Form Template Design

In Chapter 5, you created a first form template for the print output. In this context, you were introduced to the first form fields and used them to create a form template that outputs one page. The output itself was generated by a print program, which you developed in Chapter 6, "Form Output." You can continue to use this print program for the first part of this chapter.

The form template from Chapter 5 will be extended in this chapter, for example, by implementing tables and page breaks. Furthermore, you will move from the creation of form templates for print forms to the creation of form templates for interactive PDF forms. This chapter then lays the foundation for the creation of interactive PDF forms, as they are required in the following chapters, by introducing you to the implementation of script programs, providing notes on how to increase performance, and describing the creation of accessible PDF forms.

7.1   Advanced Techniques for Print Forms

In this section, we'll extend the form templates that were created in Chapter 5 using advanced techniques to output a list of flight bookings by means of tables, for example. This list has several pages, that is, you need to define page breaks. Another critical aspect of the output is the formatting of the individual data values. At the end of this chapter, we'll prepare a form template for duplex printing.

7.1.1 Preparations

First, prepare the form template from Chapter 5 for further usage. To keep the old form template, copy it, and then customize it. Proceed as follows:

1. Start Transaction SFP in the SAP GUI, and create a new form template with the name Z_IFBA_BOOK_FORM_02 by copying the form from Chapter 5 (Z_IFBA_BOOK_FORM_01).

2. Start editing the newly created form, and navigate to the layout view.

3. For the AIRLINESLIST subform, set the content from FLOWED to POSITIONED to facilitate the editing process for the next steps.

4. Then, delete the AIRLINE subform by selecting it in the hierarchy and pressing the DEL key.

5. Finally, increase the height of the subform to approximately 2 inches. You can check the size using the LAYOUT palette.

The preparations are now complete, and you can begin extending the form template.

Tip for Editing Subform Structures

To create more complex structures, such as nested subforms, tables, etc., it is often much easier to handle subforms with positioned content than subforms with flow content. By carefully switching the content type, you can facilitate the management of the form templates in Adobe LiveCycle Designer. Start with the subforms with positioned content and then proceed with switching to flowed content.

7.1.2 Floating Fields

Floating fields enable you to embed data (for example, a name, a date, or an amount of money) in a static text. This can be best explained using an example. To do this, extend the form template as follows:

1. First, select the static text above the subform for AIRLINESLIST in the hierarchy and rename it to "LetterText."

2. Then, navigate to Design View, and increase the static text until it more or less reaches the right border; leave some space in the vertical direction, too.

3. Move the AIRLINESLIST subform down until it no longer overlaps the static text.

4. Replace the text of the static text, LetterText, with the following: "List of airlines where a flight was booked. This list was also sent to the email address." The text field enlarges if the text exceeds the right border; you can use the [ENTER] key to jump to a new line.

5. Set the size of the font to twelve points.

6. Now, wrap the LetterText text in a subform, and name it "LetterTF."

7. Select the static text and place the mouse pointer directly after the word "address." Now, insert a so-called "floating" field into the static text by selecting the menu path INSERT • FLOATING FIELD.

8. Then, insert a space between the word "address" and the just inserted floating field.

9. Select the floating field in the form hierarchy (it is the text field in the LetterTF subform), and rename it to "EmailFloatingField."

Figure 7.1 shows a part of the form template and what it should look like. The system automatically inserted a text field into the form hierarchy. This represents the floating field in the form hierarchy and is thus invisible in the form template. In the text of the form template, the floating field is enclosed by curly brackets. The text reads: {EmailFloatingField}.

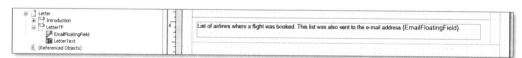

Figure 7.1   Floating Field

In the next step, you format the floating field as follows:

1. You can also format the text. To do this, navigate to the FONT palette, and set the font size to 14 Points and the style to BOLD.

2. Finally, define the data binding for the field. To do this, navigate to the BINDING tab of the OBJECT palette. Bind the field to the EMAIL node under the CUSTOMER structure.

3. Take a look at the output using the PDF preview (see Section 5.3.2, "Using Preview Data") or use the print program from Section 6.5.1, "Trace and PDF with Additional Information."

Figure 7.2 shows the result of the text output. The text format enables you to determine how the content of the EMAIL data node was inserted in the text.

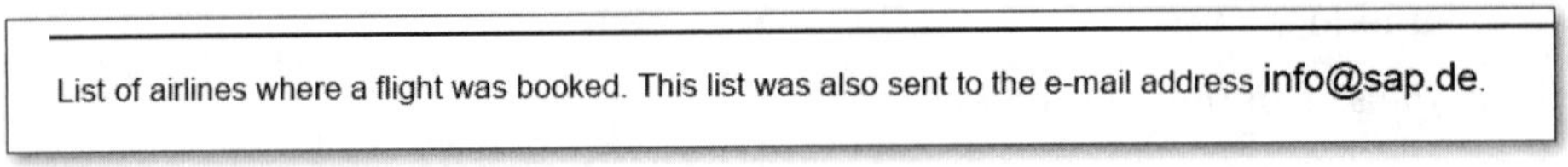

List of airlines where a flight was booked. This list was also sent to the e-mail address **info@sap.de**.

Figure 7.2 Floating Field for Output

7.1.3 Using Tables

Next, you're supposed to output the flight connections with the form. To do this, tables are available as structure elements for the creation of form templates.

First, view the structure under the BOOKINGS node in the data view. The data structure is a nested table that groups the data according to the IDs of the airlines. The data for the output is already provided in groups by the Z_IFBA_BOOK_PRINT print program, which was created in Section 6.1, "Print Program." The reason for this is that the sorting of data is not supported for the output as a PDF or in print languages.

Adding a Table to a Form

To insert a table, you can drag and drop form fields, or even complete structures, directly from the data view to the form template. Proceed as follows:

1. Check whether the AIRLINESLIST subform is visible in the DESIGN VIEW and whether the DESIGN VIEW is displayed.

2. Then, drag and drop the BOOKINGS node via from the data view to the AIRLINESLIST subform.

3. Confirm the dialog that indicates that there is not enough space available in the form to add the table. You will solve this problem in the next step.

> **Working with Tables in Adobe LiveCycle Designer**
>
> To better handle the creation and processing of tables, you should search for the key word "using tables" in the Adobe LiveCycle Designer Help or navigate the menu path USING LIVECYCLE DESIGNER • WORKING WITH FORM DESIGNS • USING TABLES • SELECTING, COPYING, MOVING, AND NAVIGATING and read the *Selecting, Copying, Moving, and Navigating* section. This section explains how you can select the entire table, rows, or columns using the mouse pointer.

By performing the previous steps, you added the table to the form template. The following description involves several steps to initially format the table.

1. Click in the cell for the ID column heading. Open the context menu, and select the EDIT TEXT... menu item.

2. Then, change the column heading from ID to AIRLINE ID, and set the style of the font to BOLD. Click in the cell below the AIRLINE ID column heading, and reduce the size of the cell (and therefore of the column) so that the column heading only just fits into the cell. To enlarge the first row for the table heading, click on the upper edge of the still selected cell using the mouse and drag it downward. This doesn't reduce the size of the cell but increases the size of the preceding row.

3. Select the cell for the GROUP column heading, specify CONNECTIONS as the new column heading, and set the style of the heading's font to BOLD.

4. Select the cell below the No. column heading, and reduce the cell to approximately two thirds of the original width. Also, decrease the width of the DATE column.

5. In the next steps, edit the FLTIME form field that displays the duration of the flight in the form. To do this, select it, and change the form field type to Date/Time Field. The reason for this is that—as described in Section 4.3.8, "Alternatives"—the duration is stored as a decimal value and is mapped through a conversion routine in the hours/minutes format.

6. Set the appearance to NONE. Then, deactivate the caption (in the LAYOUT palette). Finally, decrease the size of the field until it no longer exceeds the cell of the table.

7. Change the column heading of the CONNECTIONS column to DURATION. Select all column headings of the inner table while pressing the Ctrl key, and set the style of the font to BOLD.

8. Display the BORDER palette via the PALETTE • BORDER menu path. Again, select all column headings of the internal table, and navigate to the BORDER palette. Here, set the style from NONE to SOLID in the BACKGROUND FILL area, and select a light shade of grey as the color.

9. Perform the previous two steps for the two column headings of the external table, too.

The table in the form template should now appear as illustrated in Figure 7.3. The column headings have a gray background. The rows and cells in which data is included for the output have a white background.

Airline ID	Connections				
	No.	Date	Amount (for.currncy)	Curr.	Duration

Figure 7.3 Structure of the Table in the Form Template

Structure of Tables

The structure and the data binding of tables are described using the previously inserted table as an example. First, this section discusses the structure of the table in the hierarchy of the form template. This hierarchy is also shown in Figure 7.4.

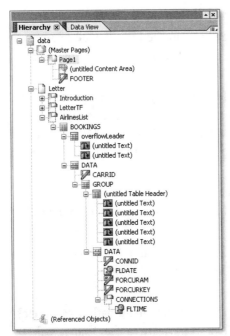

Figure 7.4 Hierarchy of the Form Template After Having Inserted the Table

In general, a table is displayed with one node for the table itself and two child nodes that map the header and a data row, respectively. This is displayed by the corresponding icons in the hierarchy. In the example, the table is mapped by the BOOKINGS node. Below it, the header of the first table is mapped by the overflow-Leader node. This table has two columns and therefore two static texts for the column headings. The name of the data row (also called the body row) is DATA. In the first column, there is a text field with the name CARRID that outputs the airline ID. The second column contains a new table. This table is thus a nested table. The second table is mapped by the GROUP node and, in turn, has an untitled header and a data row, DATA. The second table has five columns for the data output.

The structure of the table only contains one data row to describe the structure. The number of data rows that the table actually contains during the output depends on the data volume that was provided for the output.

Data Binding for Tables

This section uses the table for the flight bookings to explain the procedure of binding the data of a table.

▶ First, have a look at the BOOKINGS table node and its default binding (BINDING tab in the OBJECT palette). Due to the $record.BOOKINGS binding expression, the table has an explicit data binding to a data node. In most cases, the data structure has one node to which the table can be bound. In particular, this is the case if forms are created with Transaction SFP and if an ABAP Dictionary-based interface is used. However, you may also use tables where only the data row has a binding.

▶ Now have a look at the default binding of the DATA data row in the first table. This data row has a relative binding due to the DATA[*] expression. These expressions for subforms where detailed in Chapter 5. It is a binding expression that binds to repeating data. Accordingly, the REPEAT ROW FOR EACH DATA ITEM option is selected. In the form, this data row is therefore displayed as many times as the data node exists in the data stream.

▶ A relative binding expression for the individual fields of the data cells defines how the individual cells of the tables are filled. You can check this by viewing the default binding for the CARRID field. The expression is CARRID. Therefore, the value is defined in relation to the data node that is bound to the table row.

Tip for Problems with the Output of Tables

Problems with the output of tables, for example, where the data is not displayed at all or at the wrong position, are often caused by an incorrect data binding of the individual table rows. For problems with tables, you should always check the data binding of the table first.

To do this, first check the table element in the hierarchy and then the rows. Finally, check whether the cells have a relative binding to the row. Note that headers usually don't require a data binding. Thus, you can set the default binding for headers to None.

> ### Note for Tables with Empty Cells
>
> For tables where the data stream doesn't include the data nodes for empty fields, you must follow the instructions described in this section. Otherwise, table cells may be moved. You can easily recognize this because the binding expression for the cell contains the [*] string in this case.

7.1.4 Page Breaks

Before you extend the form template, you should have a look at the output now. You can use the Z_IFBA_BOOK_PRINT print program from Section 6.1, or call the PDF preview as described in Section 5.3.2. If everything functions correctly, your output should appear as shown in Figure 7.5.

List of airlines where a flight was booked. This list was also sent to the e-mail address info@sap.de.

Airline ID	Connections					
	No.	Date	Amount (for.currncy)	Curr.	Duration	
AA	0017	Jul 18, 2007	686.59	SGD	6:01	
	No.	Date	Amount (for.currncy)	Curr.	Duration	
	0555	Mar 28, 2007	166.50	EUR	2:05	
AZ	0790	May 23, 2007	1,312.90	CAD	13:35	
	0790	May 23, 2007	1,357.03	CHF	13:35	
DL	No.	Date	Amount (for.currncy)	Curr.	Duration	
	1984	Apr 23, 2007	380.65	USD	5:25	
	No.	Date	Amount (for.currncy)	Curr.	Duration	
	0400	May 26, 2007	371.84	GBP	7:24	
	0401	Aug 28, 2007	549.91	USD	7:15	
	0402	Apr 23, 2007	549.91	USD	7:35	
LH	0402	Aug 13, 2007	549.91	USD	7:35	
	2402	Jun 23, 2007	217.80	EUR	1:05	
	2402	Aug 18, 2007	435.60	EUR	1:05	
	2407	Apr 28, 2007	217.80	EUR	1:05	
	No.	Date	Amount (for.currncy)	Curr.	Duration	
	0005	Jun 22, 2007		USD	13:45	
QF	0005	Aug 17, 2007	866.97	USD	13:45	

Figure 7.5 Print Output After Having Inserted the Table

Note that the output still only consists of a single page. The table no longer fits on one page, because it has too many data rows. Let's correct this by implementing page breaks.

Extending the Form Template for the Usage of Page Breaks

If you have a look at the Subform tab in the Object palette for the Letter page and Airlineslist subform, you see that both have an absolute position (with X and Y coordinates) on the page or in the subform defined for the contained form fields. Because you cannot define the size of the table until the output is generated, you must change the setting for the form template from positioned to flowed. Proceed as follows:

1. First, select the Letter page in the hierarchy. In the Subform tab of the Object palette, change the content type from Positioned to Flowed.
2. Set the flow direction to Top to Bottom.
3. Check whether the Allow Page Breaks Within Content option is enabled.
4. Select the Airlineslist subform, and perform the same steps as for the Letter subform.

Due to this modification, the subforms are now aligned along the left border of the page and may have slightly moved to the left. The subforms directly adjoin each other at the top or bottom border. This is not relevant for this example.

> **Positioning of Flowed Form Fields**
>
> In those cases where this is not wanted and you want the form fields to have an absolute position, wrap them in a subform, and retain the Positioned option for the content. A flowed subform can contain the newly inserted subform without any problems.

Due to the previous modifications, the subforms can grow along with their content and, if required, span multiple pages after page breaks. The next step deals with the table:

1. Navigate to the Table tab in the Object palette for the BOOKINGS table.
2. Check whether the Allow Page Breaks Within Content option is already enabled.
3. Next, go to the Row tab for the data row of the BOOKINGS table. Here, the Allow Page Breaks Within Content option is not selected.

This means that page breaks are allowed within the table but only between the rows and not within the content of a row, that is, the internal table in our example. As a result, all connections of an airline must always be output as a block. If this block doesn't fit on the page as a whole, it is moved to the next page. You can check this by having a look at the output. Now, the system outputs multiple pages so that all connections are visible.

For this definition of page breaks, it is assumed that all connections of an airline fit on one page. You can modify the form template in such a way that the system also allows page breaks for the internal table.

1. Select the DATA data row of the BOOKINGS table.

2. Select the ALLOW PAGE BREAKS WITHIN CONTENT option in the ROW tab of the OBJECT palette.

3. Select the inner table, GROUP, and check whether the ALLOW PAGE BREAKS WITHIN CONTENT option is enabled in the CELL-TABLE tab.

Take another look at the output. For this book, we used the customer with the customer ID 1 so that the page break for the internal table occurs on the first page. Thus, the form template can manage lists of flight connections of any length. A disadvantage is that the airline ID is not repeated on the next page for page breaks within the internal table.

Finally, view the DATA data row of the GROUP table. For this row, the ALLOW PAGE BREAKS WITHIN CONTENT option is not selected. This option would only be relevant if the size of one of the form fields in the cells of the row would change, which would require a page break in the data row itself. A typical example for this case is a multiple line text field for which you don't know the number of lines in advance.

Tip for Form Templates with Layout Problems

If you have problems with the page breaks of your form, you should check whether all relevant subforms have flow content.

To do this, you must trace back the hierarchy from the form element that has the problem to the subform that displays the page. In this context, check whether the Flowed option is selected in the respective Subform tab of the Object palette.

For tables, check whether the Allow Page Breaks Within Content option is set correctly (that is, as described in this section) for the table and the data row(s).

Outputting the Page Numbering in the Form

The output of the sample form now spans several pages. In the next step, we'll extend the form template in such a way that the current page number and the total page count are output on each page. To do this, customize the master page as follows:

1. Navigate to the master page view, and move the visible part of the master page so that you can view the lower part.

2. Below the text field for the footer, add a new static text, and replace the text with ""Page /." Set the paragraph to CENTER. You can do this via the PARAGRAPH palette. Then, navigate to the Font palette, and set the font size to 12 Points.

3. Next, center the text on the page. To do this, select the text and follow the LAY-OUT • CENTER IN PAGE • HORIZONTALLY menu path.

4. Afterward, navigate to the edit mode for the text, and move the mouse pointer to the left of the slash. Use the INSERT • CURRENT PAGE NUMBER menu path to insert a placeholder for the current page number in the text.

5. Then, move the mouse pointer to the right of the slash, and follow the INSERT • NUMBER OF PAGES menu path to insert a placeholder for the total page count in the text.

6. Finally, rename the static text, "StaticText2," to "NumberofPages."

The bottom area of the master page should now appear as illustrated in Figure 7.6. Have a look at the form template output to view the result of the changes made to the master page.

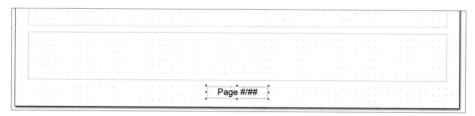

Figure 7.6 Bottom Area of the Master Page After Having Added the Output of the Page Numbering

7.1.5   Subform Set

You can use a subform set to group subforms and define the order in which the subforms are output. There are two types of subform sets that distinguish themselves as follows:

▶ **Normal subform sets**
  This type defines the output order for the creation of the form. This order is derived from the order of the subforms in the hierarchy.

▶ **Choice subform sets**
  For this type, you can define an expression to specify whether the subform is supposed to be output or not. The most common method is to define a data binding for the subforms and display or hide the subforms when the data is generated by adding or omitting a data node.

For the form interface used for this form template, DATE was set as an optional parameter. In Section 4.3.8, an alternative was inserted in the form context to use the system date if the DATE parameter is not transferred. To implement this for the form template creation, use a choice subform set.

In the following steps, we'll customize the form template in such a way that if a date was transferred, the respective date is output, and if no date was transferred, the system date is output.

1. Drag and drop the ALT_DATE node via from the data view to the ADDRESS subform and navigate to the hierarchy to view how the subform set is displayed. The subform set is mapped by a specific node in the hierarchy. This node has subforms and child nodes (see Figure 7.7).

2. Enlarge the ALT_DATE subform and the SYSTEM_DATE and DATE date fields. Then, provide more space for the caption of these two date fields.

3. Select the SYSTEM_DATE field, and change its caption to "Date of (SYS)." (SYS) enables you to later recognize what date was used for the output.

4. Select the DATE field, change its caption to "Date of," select the subform set in the ALT_DATE subform, and rename it to "DateAlternative."

5. Navigate to the SUBFORM SET tab of the OBJECT palette. As you can see, the SELECT ONE SUBFORM FROM ALTERNATIVES option is selected for the type. The tab contains another button, EDIT ALTERNATIVES.... Click on it.

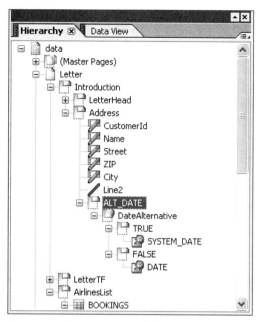

Figure 7.7 Representation of the Subform Set in the Hierarchy

6. This opens the dialog shown in Figure 7.8. In this dialog, you can see that the CHOOSE SUBFORM USING EXPRESSION option is selected and the data binding is defined. A relative binding to the wrapping subform was used.

   For both subforms, there is one area in which you can define the binding of the subform. In this example, the names for the data node and the subform are the same. In addition, you can specify an expression to further limit the choice for the two subforms. However, this is not required in the example shown here.

7. Select CANCEL to close the dialog. Then, navigate to the BINDING tab of the subform set. This tab contains the REPEAT SUBFORM SET FOR EACH DATA ITEM option that defines whether the system is supposed to evaluate the subform as many times as data nodes exist in the data stream. For our example, this option is not selected, because there is only one alternative in the data stream.

8. Now you can output the form and check which subform is used for the date output. You can use the Z_IFBA_BOOK_PRINT program to try both variants. The two variants distinguish themselves by whether the data is transferred as an optional parameter or not.

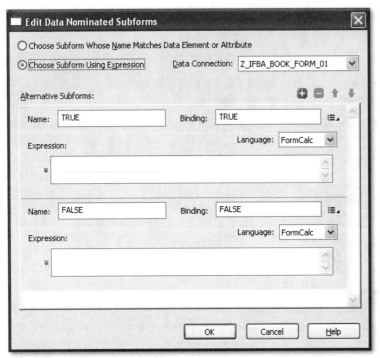

Figure 7.8 Dialog for Defining the Selection Criteria of the Subforms

---

Sections and Choice Sections in Tables

The subform set concept also exists for tables. For tables, the subform set is called Section and the choice subform set is the Choice Section. The usage is identical.

7.1.6 Using Patterns for Display Formatting

If you take a look at the current appearance of the form output, you will probably notice that the status date, the costs for a flight, and the flight duration are not output in the correct format in the form. By means of the developed sample form, you format one date, one number, and one time in the following sections, respectively. The corresponding pattern that is used is explained, too, and the general documentation describes the structure of the patterns in detail. The documentation is part of the XML Forms Architecture (XFA) specification (see Section 7.7.3, "XML Forms Architecture").

Formatting Date Fields

Let's first have a look at the SYSTEM_DATE and DATE date fields. The goal of the following formatting process for the output is to display the day of the week (spelled out) in front of the date.

1. Increase the size of the ALT_DATE subform so that there's more space available to the right of both date fields. This is necessary to have sufficient space for the formatted output of the date.

2. Next, enlarge the TRUE subform and then the SYSTEM_DATE date field until the space created in the previous step is also used.

3. Select the SYSTEM_DATE date field, and navigate to the FIELD tab of the OBJECT palette. Here, set the appearance to NONE.

4. This tab also includes the field to input the display pattern. Here, enter "EEEE, MMMM D, YYYY," or select it from the dropdown list (see Figure 7.9).

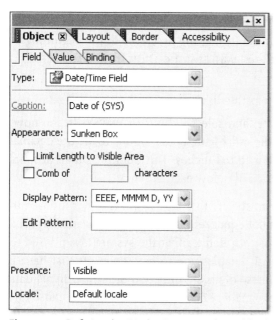

Figure 7.9   Defining the Display Pattern in the Field Tab

5. Perform the last two steps the same way for the DATE date field.

To output the spelled-out day of the week (for example, Monday), by definition the E must be used four times for the day-of-the-week pattern. The four Ms define that the month is also spelled out (for example, July). This is followed by the day of the month, which is mapped by a single D. The single D indicates that the day is output in one or two digits. The four Ys define that the year is output in four digits. Therefore, this pattern is supposed to output a date in the following format: "Wednesday, December 24, 2020."

Formatting Numeric Values

In the next step, we'll modify the FORCURAM field. This fields outputs the costs for a flight. It is a field that formats amounts according to the corresponding currency and is supposed to output them with the correct alignment. Note that in this context, Japanese currency, for example, has no decimal places and that there are Arabic currencies that have three decimal places. For all formats of amounts, the decimal points are supposed to be positioned below each other to have a uniform appearance in the form. This can be achieved as follows.

1. Select the FORCURAM field, and navigate to the CELL tab in the OBJECT palette.
2. You must use display patterns for the formatting described at the beginning of this section. To do this, deselect the LIMIT LEADING DIGITS and LIMIT TRAILING DIGITS options.
3. Then, enter the following pattern as the display pattern: "zzz,zzz,zz9.888."
4. Navigate to the PARAGRAPH palette, and select RADIX ALIGNMENT. In the now-active input field to the right of the radix icon, enter "0.3in" to set the decimal point's distance to the right border to 0.3 inches. This defines that all decimal points of the table rows are positioned below each other.

The output pattern uses the small z to specify that the system is only supposed to display a digit here if the digit does not equal zero. No leading zeros are supposed to be output. The 9 in the output pattern defines that the system is supposed to output a zero for the digits here. This enables you to map amounts that have a "0.xx" format. The 8 indicates that these digits are only output if the original data has a digit here, too. This is used for Japanese currency, for example, because this currency doesn't have decimal places and thus does not provide decimal places in the data. The comma is the thousands separator and the point the decimal point. Both are supposed to be output for the used pattern. Later, they are replaced by the correct signs according to the locale. For example, in Germany the decimal point is mapped by a comma and in the U.S. by a point.

Formatting Time Outputs

The third and last formatting type is the formatting of the flight duration.

1. Select the `FLTIME` field and navigate to the BINDING tab in the Object palette.
2. Set the date format to TIME.
3. Navigate to the FIELD tab, and select the HH:MM display pattern from the drop-down list, or enter it directly.
4. Navigate to the PARAGRAPH palette and select the right-aligned paragraph.

In this context, note that a time format was selected to map the flight duration, which means that the flight time is only supported up to 23:59 hours. A rather simple pattern can be used in this case. The two Hs indicate that the time is supposed to be output in a 24-hour format. The "MM" stands for the two-digit output of the minutes.

Display Formatting

Now it's time to have a look at the output. The form looks much more harmonic now (see Figure 7.10). You should always use display patterns to format the output, if possible.

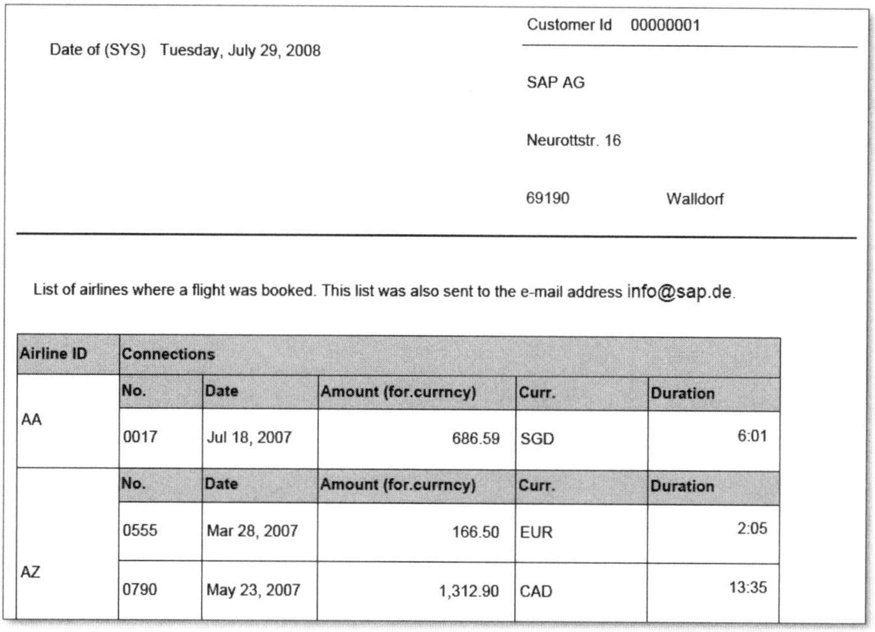

Customer Id 00000001

Date of (SYS) Tuesday, July 29, 2008

SAP AG

Neurottstr. 16

69190 Walldorf

List of airlines where a flight was booked. This list was also sent to the e-mail address info@sap.de.

Airline ID	Connections				
	No.	Date	Amount (for.currncy)	Curr.	Duration
AA	0017	Jul 18, 2007	686.59	SGD	6:01
	No.	Date	Amount (for.currncy)	Curr.	Duration
AZ	0555	Mar 28, 2007	166.50	EUR	2:05
	0790	May 23, 2007	1,312.90	CAD	13:35

Figure 7.10 Excerpt for the Formatted Output of Date, Amounts, and Times

This section introduced formatting using patterns by means of output formatting. However, there are two other cases where patterns are critical and allow for a generalization of the usage of patterns—displays and data patterns.

Display and Data Patterns

In the earlier example, you only used display patterns, which is sufficient for understanding the structure and usage of patterns. However, in more complex form scenarios, you can also use patterns to process data from the XML data stream underlying the form. So-called data patterns define how the system is supposed to interpret strings in the XML data stream. You specify the data patterns in the BINDING tab of the OBJECT palette.

For the example in this chapter, it was not necessary to define the data patterns, because the system automatically identified the data during the generation of the XML data stream thanks to the form field types and the corresponding mapping to a default pattern.

However, for interactive PDF forms, there are two other cases where patterns are critical. In this context, patterns are used to input data and to validate the input. This is described in Section 7.2.2, "From PDF–Based Print Forms to Interactive PDF Forms."

7.1.7   Form Output with Duplex Printing

The last modification of the form template is configuring for the support of duplex printing when the form is output on a duplex printer. To achieve this, you must use one page set and two master pages (one for the front and one for the back). To do this, you must extend the example of this chapter as follows:

1. Select the node (Master Pages) that is located directly under the DATA node in the hierarchy and rename it to "PageSet."

2. Click the right mouse button on the PAGESET node to display the context menu for the page set, and select the NEW MASTER PAGE menu item.

3. Copy the static text, "NumberofPages," of "Page1" by selecting it and following the EDIT • COPY menu path.

4. Paste the previously copied text to Page2. To do so, move Page2 until you can view the bottom area, then open the context menu below the content area with a right click to select the PASTE menu item.

5. Rename Page2 to "back" and Page1 to "front."

6. Move the static text, NUMBEROFPAGES, to the right on the front and to the left on the back. You can also set the paragraph for the NUMBEROFPAGES text on the front to right-aligned and on the back to left-aligned.

7. In addition, you can copy the FOOTER form field from the front to the back so that the footer is displayed on both the front and the back.

Up to now, you have only carried out preparations. In the next step, you actually configure the duplex printing.

1. Select the PAGESET node.

2. The PAGE SET tab of the Object palette includes the Printing dropdown list. Here, select the PRINT ON BOTH SIDES option. Confirm the dialog that indicates that this is only supported for PDFs with Adobe Reader/Adobe Acrobat 8.0 and later.

3. Select the front, and navigate to the Pagination tab in the Object palette. Select the ODD (FRONT) PAGES option for the ODD/EVEN field. For the back, select the EVEN (BACK) PAGES option for the ODD/EVEN field (same procedure).

To test whether the last actions were successful, you must output the form on a printer that allows for duplex printing. However, the PDF preview or print view also enables you to recognize whether the pages were correctly assigned.

Complex Simplex and Duplex Printing Scenarios

This example considered a very simple duplex printing scenario. You can also use several page sets and combine them via the tray control. To select the page sets, you need conditional page breaks.

The Adobe LiveCycle Designer Help provides more information on this if you search for the key word "page set." You can also refer to SAP Note 1122142.

7.1.8 Output of the Completed Form Template

By outputting the form with duplex printing, you have completed the creation of a PDF-based print form. Figure 7.11 displays the form template for comparison. You can compare it with your form template and use it as a reference for the positioning of the form fields and the structure of the hierarchy.

For a better overview of the output, Figure 7.12 shows the first page of a sample output.

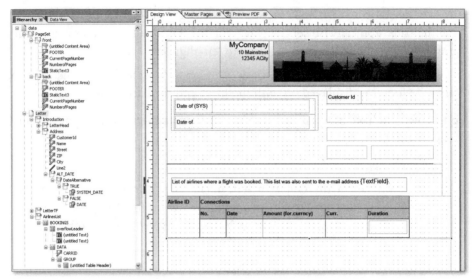

Figure 7.11 Completed Form Template

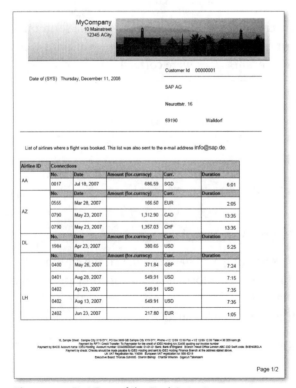

Figure 7.12 First Page of the Final Output

7.2 Interactive PDF Forms

Whereas the creation of print outputs was the primary focus of the previous sections, the following sections now concentrate on the creation of interactive PDF forms. These are required for Chapter 8, "Integration with Web Dynpro ABAP," Chapter 9, "Internal Service Requests," Chapter 10, "ABAP PDF Object," and Chapter 11, "Offline Scenarios via Web Services." The behavior of the already-known form fields in interactive PDF forms is described first. The following sections then introduce additional form fields and so-called dynamic properties.

7.2.1 Preparations

You must first prepare a new form object to reproduce the individual sections. To quickly check it, use the PDF preview. To do this, create a print program, and then specify the preview data for the form.

Creating a New Form

For the first steps for the interactive PDF forms, you need a simple interface that only consists of one table. You are supposed to use the customer table from the flight-booking application here. Proceed as follows to create the interface (Section 4.2.1, "ABAP Dictionary-Based Interface," provides a detailed description of the procedure):

1. Start Transaction SFP, and create a new interface with the name `Z_IFBA_BOOK_DDIC_02`.
2. Add a parameter to the interface. Enter `CUSTOMERS` as the name, `TYPE` as the type, and `TY_CUSTOMERS` as the type name. The parameter is not optional and the values are not passed.
3. Finally, save and activate the interface.

Next, create a new form. Proceed as follows (Section 4.3, "Context of a Form," provides a detailed description of the procedure):

1. Create a new form with the name `Z_IFBA_BOOK_FORM_03` in the start screen of Transaction SFP.
2. Add the `CUSTOMERS` interface parameter to the context.
3. Deactivate all of the fields but `ID` and `NAME`.

4. Save the form.

At a later stage, you must not forget to activate it after saving. However, this is not required at this point, because you are just creating the form.

Print Program to Generate Preview Data

Now you need a print program to test the form in the print view or to generate test data. Section 6.1 describes how you create a print program in detail. Create the print program for this chapter as follows:

1. Start Transaction SE38, and create a new program with the name Z_IFBA_BOOK_ INTERACTIVE.

2. Use the ABAP programming code in Listing 7.1.

3. Save and activate the program.

4. Now, create the preview data as described in Section 6.5.1. The usage of preview data is described in Section 5.3.2.

Note that in this context the print program in Listing 7.1 creates a dynamic, interactive PDF form for the preview. To do this, the two fields, fillable and dynamic, are set in docparams. These two code lines are bold in Listing 7.1.

```
PROGRAM z_ifba_book_interactive.
PARAMETERS: p_form  TYPE fpwbformname
                    DEFAULT 'Z_IFBA_BOOK_FORM_03',
            p_langu TYPE spras      DEFAULT 'E',
            p_ctry  TYPE land1      DEFAULT 'US'.
DATA: gt_customers  TYPE          ty_customers,
      gs_outputpar  TYPE          sfpoutputparams,
      gv_fmname     TYPE          rs381_fnam,
      gx_exc_api    TYPE REF TO cx_fp_api,
      gv_err_string TYPE          string,
      gs_docparams  TYPE          sfpdocparams.

SELECT * FROM scustom INTO TABLE gt_customers
    UP TO 10 ROWS
        ORDER BY PRIMARY KEY.
* Retrieve name of generated function module.
TRY.
    CALL FUNCTION 'FP_FUNCTION_MODULE_NAME'
      EXPORTING
        i_name     = p_form
```

```
      IMPORTING
        e_funcname = gv_fmname.
  CATCH cx_fp_api_repository
        cx_fp_api_usage
        cx_fp_api_internal INTO gx_exc_api.
    gv_err_string = gx_exc_api->get_text( ).
    MESSAGE  gv_err_string TYPE 'E'.
ENDTRY.
* Start print job.
gs_outputpar-reqnew = abap_true.
CALL FUNCTION 'FP_JOB_OPEN'
  CHANGING
    ie_outputparams = gs_outputpar
  EXCEPTIONS
    cancel          = 1
    usage_error     = 2
    system_error    = 3
    internal_error  = 4
    OTHERS          = 5.
IF sy-subrc <> 0.
  MESSAGE ID sy-msgid TYPE sy-msgty NUMBER sy-msgno
        WITH sy-msgv1 sy-msgv2 sy-msgv3 sy-msgv4.
ENDIF.
* Set language and country.
gs_docparams-langu    = p_langu.
gs_docparams-country  = p_ctry.
gs_docparams-fillable = abap_true.
gs_docparams-dynamic  = abap_true.
* Call generated function module (form).
CALL FUNCTION gv_fmname
  EXPORTING
    /1bcdwb/docparams        = gs_docparams
    customers                = gt_customers
* IMPORTING
*   /1BCDWB/FORMOUTPUT       =
  EXCEPTIONS
    usage_error              = 1
    system_error             = 2
    internal_error           = 3
    OTHERS                   = 4.
IF sy-subrc <> 0.
  MESSAGE ID sy-msgid TYPE sy-msgty NUMBER sy-msgno
        WITH sy-msgv1 sy-msgv2 sy-msgv3 sy-msgv4.
```

```
ENDIF.
* Close print job.
CALL FUNCTION 'FP_JOB_CLOSE'
* IMPORTING
*    E_RESULT              =
 EXCEPTIONS
    usage_error           = 1
    system_error          = 2
    internal_error        = 3
    OTHERS                = 4.
IF sy-subrc <> 0.
  MESSAGE ID sy-msgid TYPE sy-msgty NUMBER sy-msgno
          WITH sy-msgv1 sy-msgv2 sy-msgv3 sy-msgv4.
ENDIF.
```

Listing 7.1 Print Program for the Interactive PDF Form

Preparing the PDF Preview

To use the PDF preview, define the properties of the PDF preview. Proceed as follows:

1. Start Transaction SFP, select the previously created form, Z_IFBA_BOOK_FORM_03, and then navigate to the form editing functions (in Change Mode).

2. Here, go to the Layout tab to display the form in Adobe LiveCycle Designer.

3. Follow the EDIT • FORM PROPERTIES... menu path, and navigate to the DEFAULTS tab of the dialog that opens.

The following three steps define the properties of the PDF form for the preview. Like the print program, the PDF preview is supposed to display a dynamic, interactive PDF form. In addition, you can specify the preview data. Figure 7.13 shows the FORM PROPERTIES dialog and the corresponding tab.

1. Set the PREVIEW TYPE to INTERACTIVE FORM.

2. For the XDP PREVIEW FORMAT, select the ACROBAT 8 (DYNAMIC) XML FORM entry.

3. For the DATA FILE, select the file that you created in the previous section when generating the preview data.

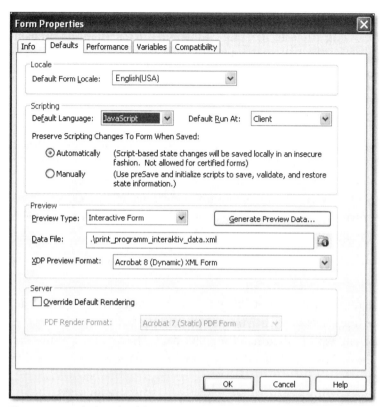

Figure 7.13 Defaults Tab of the Form Properties Dialog

PDF Preview of Interactive PDF Forms

No usage rights are added for the generation of a PDF document in Adobe LiveCycle Designer. If you use the PDF preview to test interactive PDF forms, the system displays a warning that the input cannot be stored (see Section 2.2.1, "Comparing Adobe Reader and Acrobat Professional"). You can select the Don't Show Again option to not to have to confirm this dialog for each test.

Copying the Form Template for Reuse in Multiple Examples

At this point, you can copy the previously created form; the procedure was described in Section 5.7.1, "Creating Copies of the Forms." This enables you to distribute the following examples across several forms for test purposes, for example, you can create a new form after each section according to your requirements by copying the empty form. Now, create a copy of the Z_IFBA_BOOK_FORM_03 form, and assign the following name to it: Z_IFBA_BOOK_FORM_03_EMPTY. The preparations are now complete. The following sections introduce the different aspects of interactive PDF forms in detail.

7.2.2 From PDF-Based Print Forms to Interactive PDF Forms

In Chapter 5 and during the course of this chapter, you created a print form. Everything that you have learned about the form creation so far also applies to the creation of interactive PDF forms. This section discusses those fields that also have an interactive behavior. These include text fields, decimal fields, and date/time fields. These form fields are used to describe the editable status of form fields and to extend the usage of patterns to input and validation.

Text Fields

In interactive PDF forms, text fields enable you to enter a text. The text can either have one or more lines. The fact that you don't know the text length in advance is the most important aspect when handling text fields. Have a look at the first example, which shows how this is handled when no preparations were made during the form template creation.

1. Start Transaction SFP, open the Z_IFBA_BOOK_FORM_03 form in change mode, and navigate to the Layout tab.

2. Drag and drop a text field from the STANDARD library to the upper left of the form template.

3. Then, call the PDF preview, and enter a text that exceeds the text field.

4. Exit the text fields either by clicking next to the field or pressing the TAB key.

Examine the result (see Figure 7.14). Because the text doesn't fit into the text field, the system displays a plus sign in the lower right-hand corner of the text field. The following sections detail four different options to handle this case.

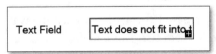

Figure 7.14 Display of Text Fields with Exceeding Text

1. Return to the Design View and select the text field.

2. Increase the width of the text field so that you can enter more text.

3. Then, navigate to the FIELD tab of the OBJECT palette.

4. Here, select the LIMIT LENGTH TO VISIBLE AREA option (see Figure 7.15).

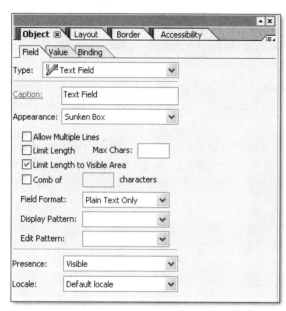

Figure 7.15   Field Tab for a Text Field

5. Check the behavior of the text field in the PDF preview.

Now you can only enter as much text as fits into the text field. This procedure limits the length of the text to the visible area but has the disadvantage that you don't know the number of characters.

It is therefore better to define the number of characters that can be entered, because the data is supposed to be processed and thus usually subject to length restrictions. Proceed as follows:

1. Return to the Design View and select the text field.

2. Deselect the LIMIT LENGTH TO VISIBLE AREA option and select the LIMIT LENGTH option instead. Enter "30" into the MAX. CHARS input field, for example.

3. Check the behavior in the PDF preview. The number of possible characters is limited to a maximum of 30. The text field does not accept further input.

So far, we have only discussed how to limit the input. Alternatively, the system can automatically adapt the font size or enlarge the text field. Let's first have a look at how to adapt the font size in the following example:

1. Navigate to the Design View, and add another text field to the form template.

2. Select the new text field, and enable the ALLOW MULTIPLE LINES option.

3. Increase the width and the height of the text field so that you can enter more text. If the *Expand to Fit* message is displayed, confirm it. You already selected the option in the previous step.

4. Navigate to the PARAGRAPH palette and select ALIGN TOP for the caption and the value. Then, navigate to the FONT palette. Here, select that you only want to edit the value properties.

5. Enter "0" into the size input field to activate the automatic determination of the font size. This value is not provided in the dropdown list (see Figure 7.16).

Figure 7.16 Font Palette with Font Size 0

6. Go to the PDF preview to check the behavior.

If you enter more text than fits into the text field, the system automatically decreases the font size. The advantage of this is that the complete text is always visible. However, it only makes sense to select this option for large, multiple-line text fields; otherwise the font quickly becomes too small and illegible.

The options detailed so far don't affect the layout of the form. The following procedure, however, uses so-called *resizable text fields* and thus affects the layout. The following description shows how you can add such text fields to the form template.

1. Add a third text field to the form template.

2. Select it, and activate the ALLOW MULTIPLE LINES option in the FIELD tab of the OBJECT palette.

3. In the Design View, increase the width and the height so that you can enter more text.

4. Navigate to the PARAGRAPH palette and select ALIGN TOP for the caption and the value.

5. Go to the PDF preview to check the behavior.

If you now enter a multiple-line text that doesn't fit into the text field, a scrollbar appears on the right of the text field when you enter the text (see Figure 7.17). When you exit the field, the scrollbar disappears, and the system no longer displays the entire text. The plus sign (+) is displayed again to indicate that the entire text is not visible.

Figure 7.17 Scrollbars in a Text Field During the Input

To have the system display the entire text, you must define that the height of the text field is allowed to change. The text field then becomes a resizable text field.

1. To do this, select the third text field and navigate to the PARAGRAPH palette.

2. Here, select the EXPAND TO FIT option below the input field for the height to define that the system may adapt the height of the field after text has been entered (see Figure 7.18).

3. Check the behavior in the PDF preview.

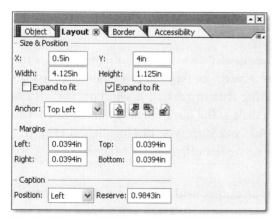

Figure 7.18 Layout Palette with the EXPAND TO FIT Option Selected

Let's have a look at a case where more text is entered than fits into the field. During the input, the scrollbar is displayed, but the size of the text field is adapted accordingly after you have exited it. If you delete lines at a later stage, the system decreases the size of the text field again. However, the size of the text field never falls below the values that you specified during the creation of the form template, because this defines the minimum height of the text field.

> **Using Resizable Text Fields**
>
> You must use resizable text fields in a subform hierarchy that has flow content. Otherwise, the form may become illegible due to overlapping form fields. For the sake of simplicity, the example didn't discuss these aspects. This concept is described in Section 7.1.4, "Page Breaks."

Editable State of Form Fields

All text fields that you previously added to the interactive PDF form were automatically ready for input. However, this is not wanted in all cases. The form may contain areas that have been filled with data in advance that are not supposed to be modified by the user because it is for information only. An example for this may be a customer ID that has been assigned by the system and is not supposed to be changed by the customer.

This section discusses the following three editable states that assume a critical role:

▶ **User Entered — Optional**
For this option, the input for the form field is optional, that is, it is not relevant for the further processing of the form whether data has been entered or not.

▶ **User Entered — Required**
This option defines that the user must enter data into this form field for further processing. The form processor receives a message in three cases. If the user exits the form field without entering data or making a selection, the system outputs a message in the form of a dialog. The form can only be submitted if all required fields are populated. In Adobe Reader, you can highlight form fields, that is, form fields that require input are indicated by a red frame.

▶ **Read Only**
This option defines that this is just an output field. The user of the form cannot change the value or selection.

The following example is supposed to illustrate a case where input is required. To do this, define the ready-for-input status for a text field as follows:

1. Select the initially added text field.

2. Navigate to the VALUE tab of the OBJECT palette.

3. For TYPE, select the USER ENTERED – REQUIRED entry.

4. In the EMPTY MESSAGE input field that is displayed after having selected the option in the previous step, enter the text "Please fill in field." (See Figure 7.19).

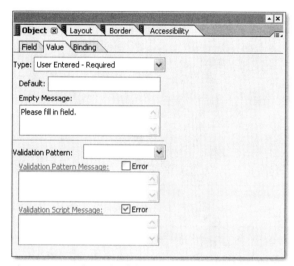

Figure 7.19 Value Tab of the Object Palette for the Text Field

5. For fields that require input, you must specify a data binding. Therefore, define the data binding for the text field by dragging and dropping the NAME node under DATA from the data view to the text field.

   You can ignore that the data binding contains [*] in the binding expression (due to the repeating data in the table structure). Only the first data value is output.

6. Now, call the PDF preview.

7. Select HIGHLIGHT FIELDS in the upper-right corner of Adobe Reader (see Figure 7.20). This highlights all form fields that are ready for input in grey-blue, and the text field that requires an input is indicated by a red frame.

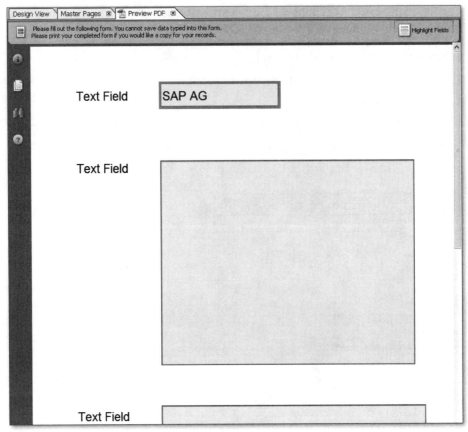

Figure 7.20 Marking of Interactive and Required Form Fields

8. In the last step, delete the content of the first text field and exit the text field by clicking next to it or pressing the [TAB] key. A dialog box opens that displays the previously specified error message.

> **Defining the Editable State of Form Fields**
>
> For interactive PDF forms, you should define the editable status for all form fields so that the user can only modify the content of those fields for which this is intended. This aspect is not relevant for the print output, because all form fields are always inactive here.

Decimal Field

For the print output, a decimal field was used to output the costs for the flights. For interactive PDF forms, the decimal fields are used to enter numeric values. Because decimal fields always require the input of a numeric value, you cannot use all characters. For example, the letter A doesn't make sense for numbers and thus cannot be entered. In addition, the decimal fields provide an easy option to limit the number of leading and trailing digits. This is illustrated in the following example.

1. Drag and drop a decimal field from the STANDARD library to the form template.
2. Select the decimal field and navigate to the FIELD tab of the OBJECT palette.
3. Select Limit Leading Digits and enter "3" into the input field.
4. Select Limit Trailing Digits and enter "2" into the input field.
5. Check the behavior by navigating to the PDF preview and entering various values.

You can check that you can only enter digits and, for example, a minus sign at the beginning, or a comma, but no characters. If decimal places are not allowed (due to limiting the number of trailing digits to zero), it is because the system doesn't accept decimal points.

Using Decimal Fields and Numeric Fields

In addition to decimal fields, numeric fields are also available. You should use decimal fields because the integrated support for leading and trailing digits facilitates the creation of form templates.

Date/Time Field

The date/time field that is used for the print output can be used for a formatted output and for the input of a date or time. There are two options to enter a date: either directly with the keyboard or with the mouse using a so-called datepicker (see Figure 7.21).

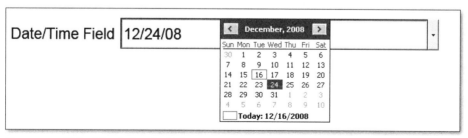

Figure 7.21 Datepicker to Input a Date

The following example illustrates this:

1. Drag and drop a date/time field from the STANDARD library to the form template.
2. Check whether the data format in the BINDING tab of the OBJECT palette is set to Date.
3. Set the display pattern in the FIELD tab to EEEE, MMMM D, YYYY.
4. Enlarge the date field until the complete date can be displayed.
5. Navigate to the PDF preview.

You should first try to enter the date directly into the field using the keyboard. If you correctly enter the date, it is displayed in the long form. You probably noticed that it was quite difficult to enter the date directly. The reason for this is that no explicit input pattern has been specified—the default pattern is MM/DD/YY. Try again to enter a date.

It is considerably easier to use the datepicker. When you click into the date field, the system displays a button on the right (see Figure 7.21). By clicking on this button, the calendar window opens, and you can select a day by clicking on it or go from month to month in the upper half of the calendar window.

In the context of the direct entry of data, you were introduced to the edit patterns. Using the previously added date field as an example, the following sections discuss these patterns in detail.

Patterns

So far, you know of two types of patterns: display and data patterns. For interactive PDF forms, however, there are two additional patterns: the edit and the validation pattern.

Edit and Validation Pattern

Edit and validation patterns are used to increase the quality of the input data. They enable you to validate the input directly when the user processes the form and to have the user correct the input, if required. Therefore, you should use them whenever possible (for example, for email addresses, telephone numbers, customer names, etc.).

The use of edit and validation patterns is explained in the following sections using the previously added date field as an example. The procedure is the same for all form field types.

Using Edit Patterns

To test the usage of edit patterns, navigate to the PDF preview, and enter "01/01/2008" into the date field. Because the date is not spelled out after you enter it, you know that the entry was not accepted. No message is output here. This is further discussed in Section 7.2.2. First, you're supposed to facilitate the entry using another edit pattern. Proceed as follows:

1. Return to the Design View and select the date field.

2. In the FIELD tab of the OBJECT palette, enter the "M/D/YYYY" edit pattern.

   To facilitate the input, the system is supposed to accept the one-digit input of the day and month. In the M/D/YYYY edit pattern, the single M or D represents the one- or two-digit input of the month or day. If you use MM (or DD), the user has to always enter the month or day with two digits, for example, 12/24/2020.

3. Check the PDF preview to see if the previously defined edit pattern is accepted.

For example, enter "12/24/20." This input is not accepted by the edit pattern because it expects you to enter a four-digit year. Because the short version for years is often used in dates, you must modify the edit pattern so that it accepts both alternatives—the two-digit and the four-digit input for the year. Proceed as follows:

1. Return to the Design View.

2. Select the date field and navigate to the Field tab of the Object palette.

3. Enter "M/D/YY|M/D/YYYY" for the edit pattern.

   By using the vertical slash in edit patterns, you can define two or more alternative patterns. The order is important here. The complete pattern is read from left to right and the first pattern that can be successfully implemented cancels the processing.

   In this example, the difference between these two alternatives is the two- or four-digit year, mapped accordingly by YY or YYYY in the edit pattern.

4. Return to the PDF preview and enter dates with different formats to see what happens.

Using Validation Patterns

The next problem that you must solve is the missing message that should be displayed when the date has been entered with the wrong format. For this, you use a validation pattern. Validation patterns are a comfortable way to check whether the correct input format was used for the input. A correct format also implies that no nonexisting days or months are used for the date. You can check this by simply entering "13" for the month: The system won't display a message.

To solve this problem, customize the form template as follows:

1. Return to the Design View and select the date field if it is no longer selected.

2. Then, navigate to the VALUE tab of the OBJECT palette.

3. Here, enter "M/D/YY|M/D/YYYY" in the VALIDATION PATTERN input field. It is the same pattern as the edit pattern and also uses the alternative of two- or four-digit years.

4. Then, enter the following text into the VALIDATION PATTERN MESSAGE input field (see Figure 7.22): "Please enter a valid date using one of the following patterns M/D/YY or M/D/YYYY."

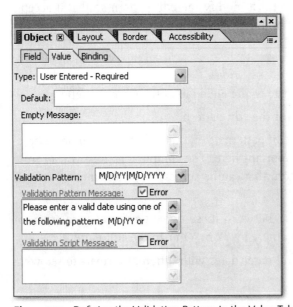

Figure 7.22 Defining the Validation Pattern in the Value Tab

5. Finally, select the ERROR option (located directly above the input field for the message) to define that it is an error if the validation of the input fails. This affects further processing.

6. Navigate to the PDF preview, and enter a date with an invalid month or day (for example, "12/32/20"). You receive a dialog (see Figure 7.23) that displays the text that you defined in the example. The problem of the missing message is now solved.

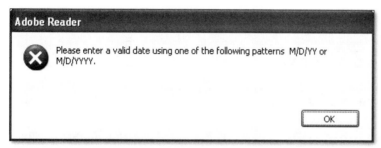

Adobe Reader

Please enter a valid date using one of the following patterns M/D/YY or M/D/YYYY.

OK

Figure 7.23 Message for Failed Validation

Complex Display Patterns

To complement the example, let's take a closer look at the display patterns again. You are already familiar with the definition of alternatives. Now you can use this knowledge in the following sections to output a text if no values exists for the date field. Proceed as follows:

1. Return to the Design View and select the date field.

2. Navigate to the FIELD tab of the OBJECT palette.

3. Here, enter the following new display pattern: "null{,M/D/YYYY or M/D/YY'}|date{EEEE, MMMM D, YYYY}."

4. Return to the PDF preview.

The new display pattern uses so-called *pattern categories*:

1. On one hand, the date category is used for the date pattern.

2. On the other hand, the special category, null, is used to process null values (nonexisting values).

3. Further categories are num for number patterns and time for time patterns.

In the curly brackets, the pattern for the category is specified. In the example, the string itself is used as the display pattern for null values. The string doesn't contain formatting symbols. Therefore, the text is displayed in the date field (see Figure 7.24). If a value exists, it is formatted according to the date pattern. The previously defined display pattern is used.

Date/Time Field M/D/YY or M/D/YYYY

Figure 7.24 Display of the Date Field in the Case of Missing Values

The XFA describes patterns in more detail. For more information on this specification, refer to Section 7.7.3.

7.2.3   Form Fields of Interactive PDF Forms

In addition to the already-described form fields that can be used for the print output and for interactive PDF forms, there are several form fields that are specific for use in interactive PDF forms. They can also be used for the print output but are not functional there. Instead, they display the current status. For example, they display the selected list item for dropdown lists or display whether a checkbox is selected or not.

The following sections discuss password fields, buttons, image fields, checkboxes, radio buttons, dropdown lists, and list boxes successively. They are added to the template to enable you to test their behavior. Figure 7.25 illustrates what the form fields mentioned earlier look like in an interactive PDF form.

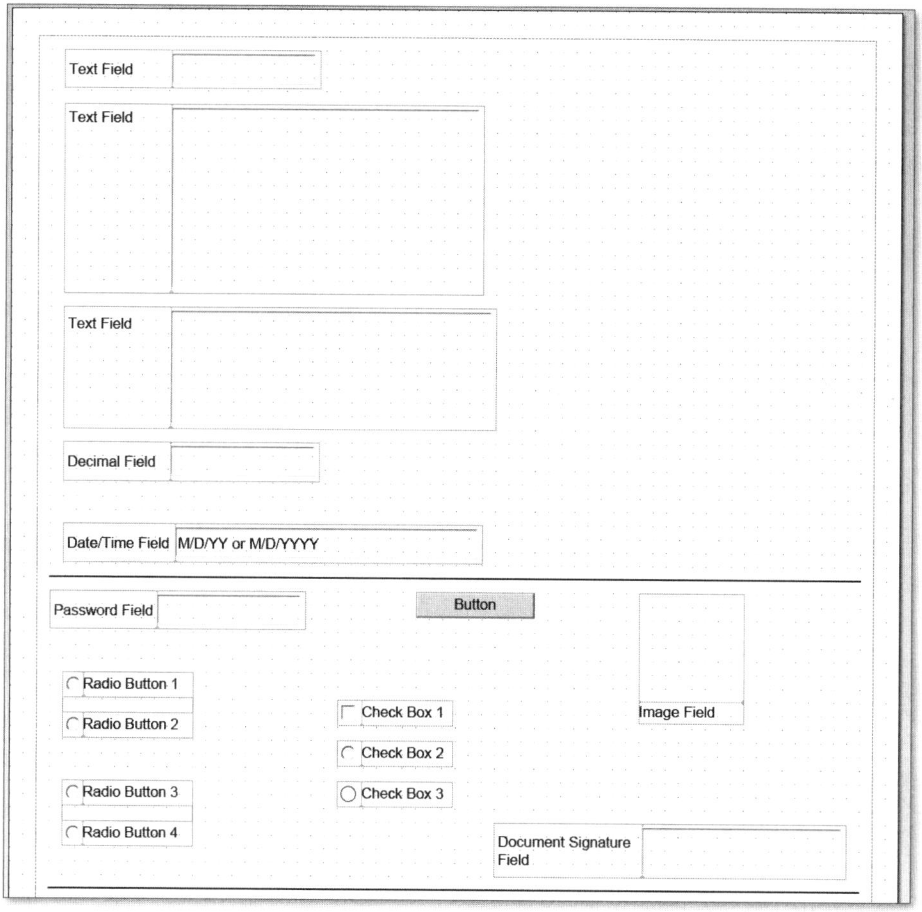

Figure 7.25 Overview of the Interactive Form Fields

Password Field

Password fields enable you to enter a text without displaying the characters and numbers on the screen.

1. Drag and drop a password field from the STANDARD library to the form template.

2. Navigate to the FIELD tab of the OBJECT palette.

3. Here, you can define which character or sign is supposed to be displayed for the entered characters or numbers. To do this, you must specify the character in the PASSWORD DISPLAY CHARACTER input field.

In the PDF preview, you can enter a text into the password field. The system only displays the previously defined display character instead of the characters and numbers entered. The entered password cannot be read on the screen, but it is provided as clear text in the data. If a password is supposed to be encrypted, the encryption must be implemented by a script program.

Buttons

Buttons are a common part of user interfaces. If you click on them, an action is triggered. For this example, the action is supposed to be the submission of an interactive PDF form as an email attachment. This can be achieved as follows:

1. Add a button to the form template.
2. Then, select the button and navigate to the FIELD tab.
3. Set the CONTROL TYPE to SUBMIT. An additional tab is displayed in the OBJECT palette.

By default, the control type is set to NORMAL. In this case, the action must be implemented via script programming (see Section 7.3.1, "Initial Script Program"). These two special cases—the call of a Web service and the submission to a URL— are supported by a specific control type; the process of calling a Web service (EXECUTE control type) is described in detail in Chapter 11. This section only deals with the submission.

To define the exact activities for the submission, proceed as follows:

1. Navigate to the SUBMIT tab.
2. Enter the following text into the SUBMIT TO URL input field: "mailto:<your_email_address>." Replace <your_email_address> with your actual email address (see Figure 7.26).
3. Select PDF for SUBMIT AS. This defines that the system is supposed to submit the PDF itself. All other options are not discussed in this section.
4. To test the submission of the PDF, you must use the print program to generate the PDF, because this process requires usage rights. By clicking on the button, your email program is started and a window opens where you can edit a new email. The PDF is already attached to this new email. Thus, the email program is responsible for the actual submission.

Figure 7.26 Submit Tab for the Button

5. At this point, have another look at the required input and the validation patterns. Delete the content of the first text field for which the input is required, and then click on the button to submit the PDF. The system displays the message that indicates that at least one form field that requires input is not filled. In addition, this field is highlighted with a red frame. The email cannot be submitted until all required form fields are filled.

6. Enter text into the form field so that you can test the validation pattern for the date field at a later stage.

7. Enter an incorrect date (for example, 1/2/3) into the date field. A message is displayed that reads that the date is not correct.

8. Then, click on the button to submit the PDF. The dialog is displayed again to inform you prior to the submission that the date field is filled incorrectly. After having confirmed the dialog, the system displays another dialog that indicates that the submission has been cancelled. The reason is that you defined that it is regarded as an error if the validation with the pattern fails for the validation pattern.

Image Field

Image fields are different from static images in that they are interactive and thus enable you to upload an image to the PDF form. You can also define a data binding here. A data binding enables you to provide image data via the XML data stream. If you want to contain the image data to the XML data stream, you must set the image field to READ-ONLY, as described in Section 7.3.5.

You can add an image field to the form template for testing purposes. The following file formats are supported: Windows Bitmap (BMP), Joint Picture Experts Group (JPG), Graphic Interchange Format (GIF), Portable Network Graphics (PNG), and some variants of the Tagged Image File (TIF) format. You can find those in the Adobe LiveCycle Designer Help using the key words "image fields overview."

Checkboxes

You can use checkboxes to provide options in interactive PDF forms, for example, a checkbox in a form for renting a car. The user can then select or deselect these options. In addition to the car itself, the requester can use checkboxes to select an insurance category and a GPS device.

Three definitions must be examined for using checkboxes:

▶ **States**
In the FIELD tab of the OBJECT palette, you can define whether the checkbox should have two (ON/OFF) or three (ON/OFF/NEUTRAL) states.

▶ **Value for the states**
In the BINDING tab, you specify the data value for the states.

▶ **Appearance and check style**
The appearance and check style of the checkbox are again defined in the FIELD tab. For appearance, you are provided with the following options: Sunken Circle, Sunken Square, Solid Circle, and Solid Square. For the check style, you can choose between Default, Check, Circle, Cross, Diamond, Square, and Star.

At this point, test the behavior of the checkboxes by adding three checkboxes to the form template, for example, and selecting different combinations of the appearance and check style. You should also use a checkbox with three states and check in the PDF preview how the neutral state is mapped. In contrast to the On state, the icon (for example, Check) is mapped in gray instead of black.

Radio Button

Generally, radio buttons behave the same way as checkboxes. However, there's one difference: Radio buttons are combined in so-called *radio button groups*. Exactly one radio button can be selected for one radio button group. For this reason, radio button groups are also often referred to as *exclusion groups*. However, multiple radio button groups can be used in one form.

The use of radio button groups is illustrated using the following example:

1. Navigate to the Design View and add four radio buttons to the form template.

2. In the HIERARCHY palette, you can see that all four radio buttons of a radio button list (this is the name of the exclusion group) were added.

3. Right-click on the third radio button in the hierarchy (or design view) to display its context menu for the page set, and select the WRAP IN NEW RADIO BUTTON GROUP menu item to create a new exclusion group.

4. Drag and drop the last added (fourth) radio button in the hierarchy to the second exclusion group. The black bar indicates where you would add the radio button if you released the mouse button (see Figure 7.27).

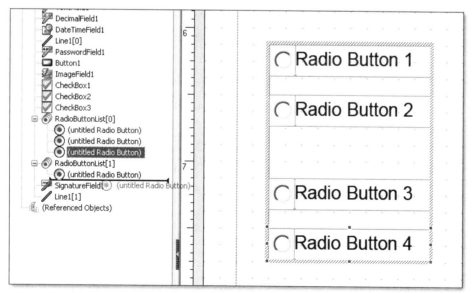

Figure 7.27 Moving the Fourth Radio Button

In the PDF preview, you can make sure that the user can only select a single option in both exclusion groups. To use radio buttons, you must specify the data values for the individual options in the Binding of the Object palette.

Document Signature Field

Document signature fields enable you to prevent further entries to the form fields and identify the user that signed the PDF form by means of their certificate. When processing a signed document, you can check whether the document has been modified since the last signature and which certificate was used for the signature. The certificates must be assigned to the users by the application itself.

If you have a certificate, you can reproduce the following example. Here, you need to use the print program again, because the corresponding usage right is required for the digital signature.

1. Add a signature field to the form template.

2. Navigate to the SIGNATURE tab of the OBJECT palette and select the LOCK FIELDS AFTER SIGNING option.

3. In the dropdown list, select ALL FIELDS IN DOCUMENT.

You can test the document signature field in the PDF preview.

▶ Once you have signed the document, the system locks all input fields.

▶ After having deleted the signature via the CLEAR SIGNATURE menu item in the context menu of the signature field, the form fields are ready for input again.

▶ You can define the list of the form fields that are supposed to be locked by using collections. This is illustrated in the Adobe LiveCycle Designer Help under the key word "collections."

Section 10.4, "Processing an Interactive PDF Document," analyzes the usage of signature fields and the validation of the signature in more detail.

> **Note on the Usage of Document Signatures**
>
> SAP Note 834573 states that you need at least Adobe Reader 8.1 to use document signatures. Another point is the size of the PDF files when you use document signatures. With each document signature, the size of the PDF file increases, because additional information on the state of the PDF at the time of the signature must be added. This cannot be avoided for the document signature function and thus needs to be considered for the usage.

Dropdown List and List Box

Let's finally have a look at the dropdown list and the list box. Both provide a list of entries the user can select from. For dropdown lists, the user can only view the list during the selection and can only select one entry. In contrast, for list boxes, list a part of or the entire list is visible and you can define whether multiple entries can be selected or not. However, the direct input of a value is only enabled by dropdown lists. To test this, supplement the form template as follows:

1. Navigate to the Design View.
2. Add a dropdown list to the form template.
3. Add a list box to the right of the dropdown list.
4. Select the dropdown list and navigate to the FIELD tab of the OBJECT palette.
5. Here, select the ALLOW CUSTOM ENTRY option.

For the test, the most important thing is missing: the list of the entries. Both the dropdown list and the list box enable you to compile these list entries in the Field and Binding tabs (both belong to the Object palette). An entry in the list consists of the text of the list entry that is displayed in the PDF form and the input value that is used in the data model.

The definition of the list entries in the form template has the disadvantage that the lists must be maintained twice if the entries are not known in advance or if the entries frequently change, that is, they must be maintained in Customizing and in the form template. For these cases, a better approach is to transfer list entries through data when generating the PDF form. This is enabled by so-called *dynamic properties*.

7.2.4 Dynamic Properties

Dynamic properties enable you to dynamically define a form template at runtime instead of during the time of creation. These properties include list entries of dropdown lists and list boxes, captions of form fields, validation messages and tool tips, and user-defined screen reader text for the input/output help (see Section 7.6, "Introduction to Accessible PDF Forms"). The properties are defined via bindings to data nodes. How this works is described next.

Activation of the Dynamic Properties

To use dynamic properties, you must first activate them.

1. To do this, follow the TOOLS • OPTIONS... menu path and navigate to the DATA BINDING area.

2. The DYNAMIC PROPERTIES area contains the SHOW DYNAMIC PROPERTIES option (see Figure 7.28). Select this option.

3. If you want to, you can define a color for the label of the input fields of Adobe LiveCycle Designer (the default setting is green).

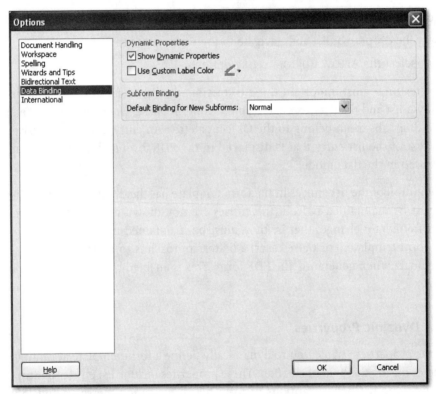

Figure 7.28 Data Binding Options

Dynamic Population of Dropdown Lists

Similar to hyperlinks, the system underlines properties of form fields that can be defined by dynamic properties and maps them in green. Figure 7.29 illustrates this for the CAPTION and the LIST ITEMS of the dropdown list. In addition, the figure displays a little chain icon after the LIST ITEMS field. This is visible after a dynamic property has been defined, for example, the list entries in this case.

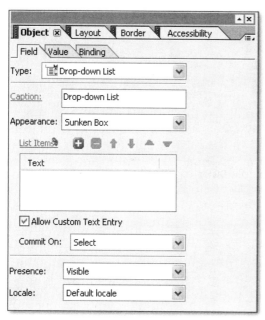

Figure 7.29 Caption and List Items as Dynamic Properties

To define the list entries for the dropdown list, proceed as follows:

1. Select the dropdown list and navigate to the FIELD tab of the OBJECT palette.

2. Click on LIST ITEMS to open the DYNAMIC PROPERTIES dialog.

3. Similar to the procedure for defining the data binding manually (see Section 5.3.1, "Defining the Data Binding"), define the binding for the items to the repeating node, DATA, under CUSTOMERS.

4. Then, you implement a binding of the item text and the item value as NAME and ID. This is relative to the binding of the items. Figure 7.30 illustrates what the dialog for the definition of the dynamic properties should look like after you have performed the preceding steps.

5. In the data view, nodes that are bound by a dynamic property are indicated by a specific icon. This icon is shown in Figure 7.31.

Figure 7.30 Dynamic Properties for the List Items Dialog

Figure 7.31 Indicator in the Data View for Nodes
That Are Bound by Dynamic Properties

6. The procedure of defining list entries for list boxes is identical to the procedure for dropdown lists. Therefore, perform the same steps for the list box.

7. You can check in the PDF preview which entries were used to populate the list and how the selected entry is displayed (see Figure 7.32). For the DROP-DOWN LIST, the selected entry is mapped in an input field. For the LIST BOX, the selected entries are highlighted by a blue background.

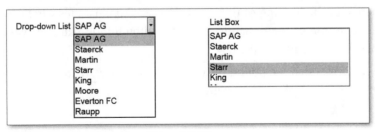

Figure 7.32 Open Dropdown List and List Box

Dynamic Captions and Texts

In addition to the dynamic population of the list entries of dropdown lists and list boxes, the dynamic properties also enable you to provide captions, texts, and messages. The following section describes this procedure using the caption as an example:

1. Select a form field and navigate to the FIELD tab of the OBJECT palette.
2. Click on CAPTION to open the dialog that is shown in Figure 7.33.

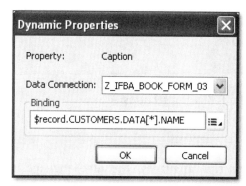

Figure 7.33 Dynamic Properties for the Caption Dialog

3. In this dialog, you can define the Binding for the caption text the same way as for normal data bindings.

For the transfer of fields, no fields are provided in the context that is based on the example for the interactive forms. To check the functionality for this example, you can bind the caption to the CUSTOMERS • DATA • NAME node. This works without problems in the example. However, in real-life scenarios, you should not bind captions to a repeating data node, because every caption should be uniquely bound to one data node.

7.3 Using Script Programs

In some cases, the desired functionality cannot be defined in a graphical interactive way due to its complexity. Some examples include validations that go beyond the mere use of patterns, complex calculations based on data and user entries, and the dynamic behavior of interactive PDF forms, such as displaying and hiding form fields or adding or deleting table rows. Therefore, form creation also supports the programming of script programs.

The following sections use examples to introduce you to using script programs in interactive PDF forms. Figure 7.39 illustrates the form template that you will develop in this section. You can also use script programs for print forms. Chapter 11 provides additional examples that make extended use of script programs.

The documentation mentioned in Section 7.7.2, "Adobe Designer Scripting Reference" and Section 7.7.3, "XML Forms Architecture," describes this topic in more detail. It contains more examples and the names of the properties that are used in the following script programs.

7.3.1 First Script Program

The basic principles and the usage of script programs can be illustrated with a simple example, which we'll look at in the following sections.

Script Languages and Events

You can create script programs in two script languages. The first language is JavaScript, which is commonly known. The second language is called FormCalc, which is a script language developed by Adobe. The use of FormCalc is somewhat easier if you want to carry out calculations, particularly on the basis of table structures. The advantage of JavaScript is its popularity.

The execution of script programs is always triggered by an event. For example, by clicking on a button, the `click` event is triggered. Another example is the `docReady` event. It occurs after all preparations and required processes have been completed. The difference between these two examples is that the `click` event requires a user interaction whereas the `docReady` event requires no interaction at all. Therefore, events can be divided into two groups: *interaction events* and *system events*.

This book uses JavaScript as the script language, again, due to its popularity. It is expected that you are familiar with its basic principles. Forms provided by SAP mostly use FormCalc. Section 7.7.3 contains more information on FormCalc.

Preparations

To reproduce the description, you need a new form template. Proceed as follows:

1. Start Transaction SFP.

2. Create a new form template, Z_IFBA_BOOK_FORM_04, by copying the back-up copy (Z_IFBA_BOOK_FORM_03_EMPTY) that you created in Section 7.2.1, "Preparations."

3. Start editing the new form template by navigating to the Layout tab in Form Builder. Then, call the dialog for defining the form properties via the EDIT • FORM PROPERTIES… menu path.

   In this dialog (see Figure 7.34), you set two default values to simplify the procedure of creating new script programs for the following examples.

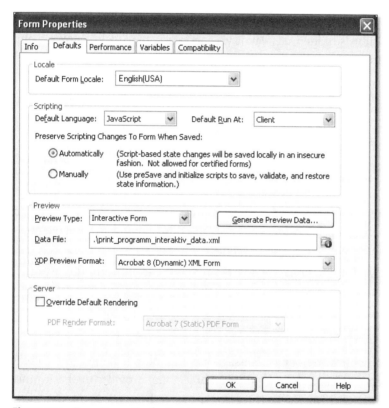

Figure 7.34 Form Properties for Scripting

4. Click on the DEFAULTS tab in the dialog.

5. In the SCRIPTING area, set the DEFAULT LANGUAGE to JAVASCRIPT.

6. Then, check whether DEFAULT RUN AT is set to CLIENT.

This way, you have defined that all new script programs are, by default, created in JavaScript and that the script programs are displayed in Adobe Reader (client) so that you can easily test them. The alternatives are to have the system run the script programs at the server (SERVER option) or to combine both types (Client and Server option).

Script Editor

First, create a script program that is called when you click a particular button.

1. Add a new button to the form template.

2. If the script editor is hidden, display it via the PALETTES • SCRIPT EDITOR menu path (see Figure 7.35).

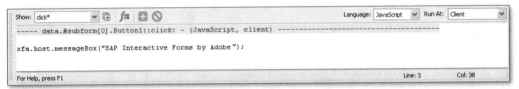

Figure 7.35 Script Editor with Script Program for the Example

3. Enlarge the area for the script editor by keeping the mouse button pressed and moving the border at the bottom of the script editor downward to have more space available for entering script programs.

4. Open the SHOW dropdown list, and select the `click` event from the list of all available events.

5. Go to the input field and enter the following programming code:

```
xfa.host.messageBox("SAP Interactive Forms by Adobe");
```

The `messageBox` function opens a message box that outputs a text (the parameter). The `xfa.host` expression identifies an object that provides the basic functions and properties. The `currentPage` property indicates the currently displayed page. When entering the program code you probably noticed that a selection area was displayed after the point (.) for supporting completion of the code. This box provides all available functions and properties, including a short description (see Figure 7.36).

6. Test the form in the PDF preview. After you have clicked on the button, the system opens a message box that displays the text *SAP Interactive Forms by Adobe*. To proceed, you must confirm the dialog by clicking OK.

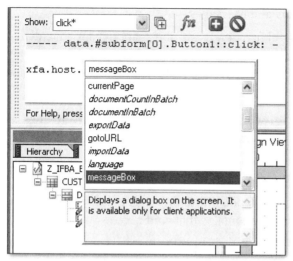

Figure 7.36 Completion of Script Code

7.3.2 Tips for Debugging Script Programs

Before describing further examples, the following sections provide some useful tips for debugging script programs, because when testing script programs, it is often difficult to determine at which point the execution of the script program was aborted. For example, the execution of the script program may be aborted due to a syntax error.

Using the Message Box

Using the message box enables you to easily define whether a script was executed up to a specific line of the script program or not. Simply add the program code of the previous example to your script program. If the system displays the dialog during the execution, you know that the script program has been executed up to that point.

In addition, you can also output the values of variables. If you replace the script program from the previous example with Listing 7.2, the message box outputs the value of a variable.

```
var i = 10;
xfa.host.messageBox(
  "SAP Interactive Forms by Adobe : i = " + i);
```

Listing 7.2 Message Box for the Output of a Variable Value

315

Displaying the Console for Errors and Messages

As of Adobe Reader 8, a very useful function is available that can be used to debug scripts: the console of the JavaScript debugger. For the development of interactive PDF forms, only the console is relevant. It outputs messages when errors occur during the execution of the script.

1. First, you must activate the console. You can do this in the basic settings of Adobe Reader via the EDIT • PREFERENCES... menu path.

2. The JavaScript category contains the JAVASCRIPT DEBUGGER area. Here, select the SHOW CONSOLE ON ERRORS AND MESSAGES option.

3. To test this function, add a third program line to the script program of the `click` event for the button. This line only contains the word `test`.

4. Then, navigate to the PDF preview, and click on the button. The console opens and the system displays a message that the `test` symbol is not defined (see Figure 7.37). In the bottom right corner of the dialog, there is the "trash can" icon. You can use it to delete the content of the console between the individual test runs.

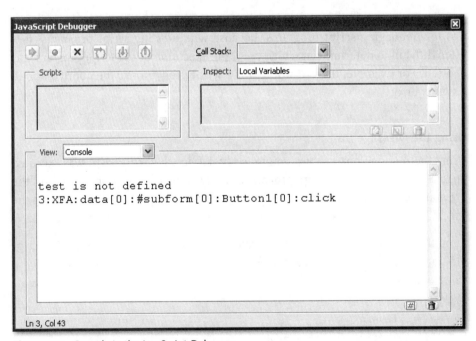

Figure 7.37 Console in the JavaScript Debugger

Using the Console with Adobe Reader 8

As of Adobe Reader Version 8, you can also use coding to show the console. To do this, use the `console.show()` statement. You can then output a text in the console using the `console.println("<text>")` statement.

7.3.3   Calculations via Script Programs

To facilitate the input, you can have interactive PDF forms carry out calculations automatically. For example, for travel expenses, the form can automatically add the costs for individual items, such as flight tickets, hotels, and so on, and display the total for the user. Therefore, the user doesn't have to add the costs manually, and the result is immediately available.

Let's reproduce this case with the following example. To do this, extend the form template as follows:

1. Add three decimal fields to the form template. Arrange the fields below each other.

2. Modify the caption of the form fields as follows (from top to bottom): Value1, Value2, and SUM. Then, select the third decimal field.

3. Navigate to the Value tab of the Object palette, and set the Type to Calculated – Read Only.

4. Then, go to the script editor, and select the `calculate` event for Show to enter a script program for calculations.

5. Enter Listing 7.3.

```
var value1 = parseInt(DecimalField1.rawValue);
var value2 = parseInt(DecimalField2.rawValue);
this.rawValue = value1 + value2;
```

Listing 7.3 Sum for a Calculated Form Field

First, the script program reads the value from the first input field (`rawValue` property). The field itself is referenced in the hierarchy through its name (`DecimalField1`). For decimal fields, a string is returned for the input value. Thus, the string is additionally converted into an integer. The same is carried out for the second decimal field. Finally, the two entries are added and set as the new value for the third decimal field. This is also the field for which the `calculate` event was called. It can be referenced with `this`.

317

6. Navigate to the PDF preview, and check to see if the entered values are added.

> **Naming Variables in JavaScript**
>
> When naming variables, don't use names of properties (for example, `value`), because the property will be used instead of the variable from the script program. You should always add a prefix or postfix to the variable, for example, `aValue` instead of `value`, to avoid this problem.

7.3.4 Input Validation via Script Programs

In those cases where validation patterns are no longer sufficient, you can use script programs to implement validations. The validation for whether an input value is within a specific interval, for example, greater than 10 and less than 20, cannot be mapped by patterns. Thus, the validation for this example must be carried out by a script program. The example can be implemented as follows:

1. Add another decimal field to the form template.
2. Navigate to the VALUE tab of the OBJECT palette.
3. Enter the following text for the VALIDATION SCRIPT MESSAGE: "The entered value must be greater than 10 and less than 20."
4. Select Error to define that it is regarded as an error if the validation fails.
5. Navigate to the script editor and select the `validate` event.
6. Enter Listing 7.4 as the script program.

```
aValue = parseInt(this.rawValue);
(aValue > 10 && aValue < 20);
```

Listing 7.4 Input Validation via Script Program

In Listing 7.4, the input value of the current field (`this`) is read first, and the returned string is converted into an integer as described in the last example. The last line contains a logical expression that implements the interval limits. The system evaluates this expression either as true or false.

7. If the condition is false, the system displays the previously defined error message. You can check this in the PDF preview.

7.3.5 Controlling the Ready-for-Input Status and Visibility of Form Fields

Another very critical function that can be implemented via script programs is the dynamic modification of the editable status of form fields. In the same context, you also frequently need the option to display or hide form fields or complete subforms. Some examples include forms that are supposed to dynamically adapt the forms after a payment method or marital status has been selected to reduce the input options for the user to a minimum. An additional example where the editable status is often modified via script programs is the image field. The implementation of this example is illustrated next:

1. Add four buttons to the form template. Arrange the buttons in a 2×2 matrix.

2. Add a text field to the right of the buttons.

3. Enter "Read-only" and "Editable" as captions for the two buttons at the top. Enter "Invisible" and "Visible" as captions for the two buttons at the bottom.

4. Select the two upper buttons and add one line from the program code of Listing 7.5 to the `click` event. The comments in Listing 7.5 facilitate the selection of the correct program line. Carry out the same process for the two buttons at the bottom as well.

```
// Set form field to read only
TextField1.access ="readOnly";
// Set form field to editable
TextField1.access ="open";
// Exclude form field from layout ("hidden") and
// hence make it invisible
// "invisble" also makes form fields invisible but
// it still occupies space in the layout
TextField1.presence ="hidden";
// Set form field visible
TextField1.presence ="visible";
```

Listing 7.5 Program Lines for Controlling the Ready-for-input Status and Visibility

The programming code in Listing 7.5 assumes that the text field in your example also has the name `TextField1`. You can check this in the hierarchy. If this is not the case, you must change either the name of the text field or the reference in the program code.

5. You can modify the status of the text field in the PDF preview by clicking on the respective buttons. This example requires that the PDF is a dynamic PDF form.

7.3.6 Dynamic Tables

The next example discusses dynamic tables. Dynamic tables enable you to add new table rows, delete existing rows, or change the order of rows at runtime. Some examples of using this function include order forms that display the details of an order as a table, and work reports that contain information on individual tasks and required material. In both examples, the content of the table varies from case to case and is not specified until the form is used.

Using Dynamic Tables

If you want to use dynamic tables via integration or a framework, you must check to see if the framework also supports dynamic tables.

For subforms, the so-called *instance manager* is used for the implementation of dynamic tables. Tables are technically based on subforms. Therefore, this description not only applies to tables but also to subforms. The instance manager provides three functions:

- Creating a new instance (`addInstance`)
- Deleting an instance (`removeInstance`)
- Changing the order of the instances (`moveInstance`)

To use these functions, the table rows or subforms must be bound to repeating data and dynamic PDF forms must be generated. The following section describes the creation of an example to test these functions.

1. Add a table to the form template by dragging and dropping the CUSTOMERS data table from the data view to the design view.

2. Decrease the width of the two table columns add an additional column by selecting the right column and following the TABLE • INSERT • COLUMNS TO THE RIGHT menu path.

3. Increase the width of the previously added column by selecting its right border using the mouse and moving it to the right while keeping the mouse button pressed.

4. In the cell of the data row of the third column, insert a subform to the far right by dragging and dropping a subform from the Standard library to the table cell. During this process, the static text is replaced by the subform.

5. Check whether the content of the subform is set to Flowed and whether the flow direction is set to Western Text.

6. The subform is required to insert two buttons in the subform in this step. Enter "Add" as the caption for the left button and "Remove" as the caption for the right button.

7. Supplement the `click` event of the left button with the script program from Listing 7.6 to enable the user to add rows. To do this, click on the button, navigate to the script editor, display the script for the `click` event, and add the coding.

```
var anInstanceManager =
  this.parent.parent.instanceManager;
var newInstance = anInstanceManager.addInstance(1);
var aToIndex = this.parent.parent.index + 1;
var aFromIndex = newInstance.index;
    anInstanceManager.moveInstance(aFromIndex, aToIndex);
```

Listing 7.6 Adding a Table Row

The script program first specifies the instance manager (`instanceManager`) for the individual table rows. To do this, the system navigates twice from the button (`this`) to the parent node in the form hierarchy (`parent`). The first parent node is the subform, whose parent node is the table row. Then, the system calls the `addInstance` method with the parameter value 1 to generate a new instance and merge it with the data (parameter value 1). The system always adds new instances to the end of a table. The `index` property therefore defines in which row the button was clicked and which index the newly added row has. The `moveInstance` method can then move the instance from the old to the new position.

Dynamic Tables and Calculations

If the table contains calculations, the following function call must be used to trigger the new calculation: `xfa.form.recalculate(1)`.

8. Analogous to the previous step, add Listing 7.7 to the `click` event of the right button to enable the user to delete rows.

```
this.parent.parent.instanceManager.removeInstance(
                          this.parent.parent.index);
```

Listing 7.7 Removing a Table Row

As in Listing 7.6, the instance manager for the table row is determined and the `removeInstance` method is called in Listing 7.7. This method includes a parameter that maps the index of the instances (rows) that are supposed to be removed. `this.parent.parent.index` identifies the index of the row that contained the button that was clicked.

Navigate to the PDF preview. The table has been filled with some rows in advance; two buttons exist for each row (see Figure 7.38):

▸ The ADD button adds a new table row directly after the row that contained the button that was clicked.

▸ The REMOVE button deletes the row that contains the button that was clicked.

Dynamic Table		
Cust. No.	Customer name	
00000001	SAP AG	Add Remove
00000004	Staerck	Add Remove
00000005	Martin	Add Remove
00000006	Starr	Add Remove
00000007	King	Add Remove
00000008	Moore	Add Remove
00000009	Everton FC	Add Remove
00000010	Raupp	Add Remove

Figure 7.38 Dynamic Table with Buttons to Add or Remove Table Rows

The example doesn't include error handling, for example, querying the minimum and maximum number of rows. The instance manager provides two properties, `occur.min` and `occur.max`, to determine the allowed minimum and maximum number of rows, respectively. The `count` property of the instance manager returns the current number of instances.

7.3.7   Access to Data Nodes and Form Fields

The last script example discusses the access to data nodes and form fields, which are often accessed when you implement calculations or validations. Accessing data nodes enables you to use data that is contained in the PDF form but is not bound to any form field and is thus not visible to the user. Supplement the form template as follows:

1. Add a button to the form template. Position it above the table. This is necessary because no flowed layout has been defined. If the table was supposed to be above the button, the button would be positioned below the table.
2. Change the Caption of the button to "Access D + F."
3. Navigate to the script editor while the button is selected, and have the system display the `click` event.
4. Enter the script program from Listing 7.8.

   The script program first uses the `resolveNodes` method to reference all data nodes that have been identified by the parameter in a list. Then, a `for` loop reads the value (`value`) for each data node and compiles a string from those values. The second part repeats these steps. The only difference is that the references to form fields are defined in a table and that `rawValue` accesses the values of the form fields.

```
//accessing data nodes
var theFields = xfa.resolveNodes(
        "xfa.datasets.data.data.CUSTOMERS.DATA[*].NAME");
var aString = "";
for (var i = 0; i < theFields.length; i++) {
  aString = aString + theFields.item(i).value;
  if (i<theFields.length-1) { aString = aString + ", ";}
}
// Accessing form fields
var theFields = xfa.resolveNodes(
                "xfa.form.data.CUSTOMERS.DATA[*].NAME");
aString = aString + "\n";
for (var i = 0; i < theFields.length; i++) {
  aString = aString + theFields.item(i).rawValue;
  if (i<theFields.length-1) { aString = aString + ", ";}
}
xfa.host.messageBox(aString);
```

Listing 7.8 Script Program for Accessing Data Nodes and Form Fields

---

Using resolveNode and resolveNodes

The two methods, resolveNode and resolveNodes, enable you to define references to one or more data nodes or form fields. You can use them if unknown subforms or form fields are supposed to be referenced for repeating data.

To do this, you need so-called Scripting Object Model (SOM) expressions. These expressions begin with xfa.datasets.data. for the access to data and with xfa.form. for access to form fields. In both cases, this is followed by the name of the data structure's root node, and a path in the data hierarchy is specified for the data nodes and a path in the form hierarchy for the form fields. You can use the data view or hierarchy if you want to specify a path, because they graphically map the hierarchy. Listing 7.8 contains an example of these two cases.

---

5. Then, navigate to the PDF preview, and click on the Access D + F button to test the script program. A dialog box opens that outputs a text with two lines. Both lines should be identical. The text of the first line was determined from the underlying data of the form. The second text line shows the same result; however, in this case the text was determined from the values of the form fields.

Finally, Figure 7.39 displays the complete form template as a reference for the arrangement and captions of the individual form fields.

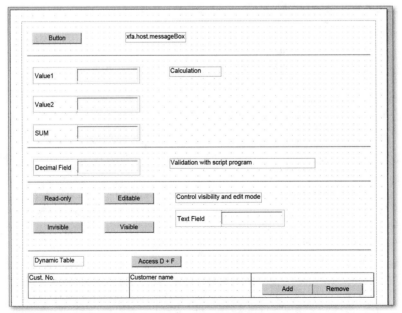

Figure 7.39 Form Template for the Script Programs as a Reference

7.4   Using Barcodes

Using barcodes is rather easy, because barcodes behave as normal form fields and can be dragged and dropped into a form template. You can define the value that is supposed to be encoded to the barcode using data bindings. The supported barcodes are provided separately in the BARCODES library (see Figure 7.40).

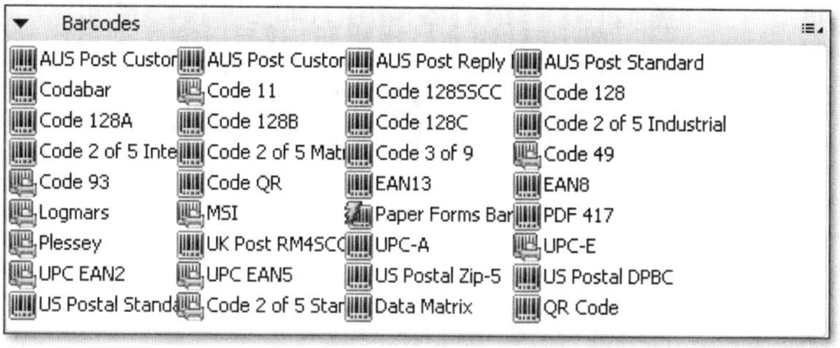

Figure 7.40 Supported Barcodes in the Barcodes Library

7.4.1   Properties of Barcodes

These are two barcode categories:

▶ **1D barcode**
  For one-dimensional barcodes, the encoded value is output in one dimension (usually, horizontally). These barcodes generally have a checksum, because no redundancy is integrated into the barcode pattern itself.

▶ **2D barcode**
  For this barcode category, the encoded value is output in two dimensions, that is, horizontally and vertically. Due to the two-dimensional output, you can use the redundancy to correct errors. The data matrix, QR, and PDF 417 barcodes are 2D barcodes.

The differences are illustrated in Figure 7.41.

Also of importance is whether a barcode is only directly supported by Zebra label printers or whether the barcode can also be output in PDF forms and to other printers. This is indicated in the BARCODES library by a specific printer icon (see Figure 7.40). For PDFs or outputs to other printers, only a gray rectangle is provided. An example of a barcode that can only be output to a Zebra label printer is the CODE 11 barcode. CODE 128 is a barcode that can also be output in PDF forms and to other printers.

Figure 7.41 1D Barcode (Code 128) and 2D Barcode (PDF 417)

> **Using the Paper Form Barcode**
>
> The paper form barcode is a specific barcode that enables you to encode the underlying data of a form. During the interaction with the PDF form, the system continuously updates the paper form barcode to display the current state. If the paper form barcode is printed and scanned, it contains the data that had been entered in the form prior to printing.
>
> You can use this barcode, for example, to print a form after having completed it and then sign the printed form manually. For further processing, the paper form barcode can be scanned so that the system can decode the data. In this scenario, you don't have to manually enter the data again.
>
> Paper form barcodes are not fully supported by the Adobe Document Services (ADS) version used in this book and therefore not described here. For information on when to expect a full support, refer to your SAP contact.

7.4.2 Notes on the Output of Barcodes with Zebra Label Printers

You must consider the following two points when you create forms that can be output to Zebra label printers:

▶ You must define a specific paper type for the page. This paper type must match the label format. To do this, you must select the master page, and then select the Custom value for the Paper Type in the Master Pages tab of the Object palette. You can enter the size of the labels into the Height and Width input fields.

▸ Zebra label printers support 200 and 300 Dots per Inch (DPI). For output to a printer, you must configure the correct device type (see Section 6.3, "Device Types for the Output").

7.5 Tips for Increasing Performance

The creation of form templates is a complex process where the way in which the template is created may considerably affect performance. This section provides tips that you should consider when creating form templates, or that can support you in analyzing the performance of existing form templates.

7.5.1 Merging Static Texts

If you use multiple adjacent static texts in one form template, you should merge these static texts. This is especially the case if a normal PDF is imported for the creation of a form template. In this case, numerous texts from the original are mapped as single static texts.

To solve this problem, the context menu of the hierarchy or the design view contains the MERGE SELECTED TEXT OBJECTS menu item if multiple static texts are selected simultaneously. By using this function several times, you can reduce the number of static texts and thus increase output performance.

7.5.2 Resolution of Used Images

If you use images (company logos, for example), you should use an external application to reduce them to the proper size. It is also possible to use the original images in Adobe LiveCycle Designer for the output; however, this has the following disadvantages:

▸ The image is added to the form template in its original size. This increases the size of the form template and thus the PDF file.

▸ It involves additional effort to correct the scaling.

These two aspects can be prevented by adapting the image.

7.5.3 Ensuring Correct Data Bindings

When a form output is generated, the system must evaluate all data bindings. It is therefore important to only define required data bindings. Some examples of unnecessary data bindings include headings in tables, which only use static texts but have the Normal default binding. The same applies to subforms. Here, you must ensure that you don't combine the implicit and explicit binding for nested subforms and that no subform with the Normal default binding is accidently included.

In addition to avoiding unnecessary data bindings, using relative data bindings also increases performance. Relative binding expressions were introduced in Section 5.3, "Data Bindings for Form Fields."

7.5.4 Nesting Depth of Subforms

The number of the subforms used in one form template affects processing time, because each subform must be processed separately. Therefore, you shouldn't use unnecessary subforms in form templates.

The content and the data binding of the subform indicate whether or not this is required. A subform is not required if it contains only one subform and if the data binding is set to None. However, you must check every case.

7.5.5 Gradient Fills for PostScript Level 2

Gradient fills (gradients) are not supported by PostScript Level 2 and must be simulated for the output. This affects the size of the generated PostScript output and the required processing time. Therefore, if you need to use PostScript Level 2, you shouldn't use gradient fills.

7.5.6 Using Script Programs

It is quite easy to use complex calculations and loops in the supported script languages. However, because they affect the output time, you should consider whether the calculations need to be carried out in the form or whether you can increase performance by carrying them out during the data formatting in the print program.

Long running script programs can cause delays for interactive PDF forms, for example, when you open script programs that are located in the `initialize`, form:ready, layout:ready or doc:ready, event, or when you interact with PDF forms. In the latter case, the script programs are usually located in the click, enter, exit, or change event.

If there are considerable delays, check the events mentioned previously. A tip for selecting the script language: Compared with JavaScript, FormCalc usually has a higher performance when it comes to calculations on the basis of table-like structures.

7.5.7 Limiting the Volume of Transferred Data for the Form Output

The data volume that is used for the generation of the output affects the overall duration of the generation process for the output. It is therefore important to only transfer the data required via a context.

To do this, let's have a look at the data view. If there are multiple data nodes that are not bound to a form field, you should view the context, for example, with Transaction SFP if you used Form Builder to create the form template (see Section 4.3.3, "Structures").

If you used an implicit data binding, this information cannot be taken from the data view that easily. In this case, you must compare the structure in the hierarchy with the data view. Remember: The implicit data binding requires a structure that is as similar as possible in terms of structure and names (see Section 5.7, "Implicit Data Binding").

7.5.8 Using Fonts

The number of fonts used affects the size of PDF files or print language outputs— if the font is not supported by the printer hardware itself. You should use as few fonts as possible in a form.

7.6 Introduction to Accessible PDF Forms

Accessible PDF documents must have a so-called *tag structure* to enable access to the content of a document together with tools that are often referred to as screen readers. On one hand, the tag structure includes details on the contained elements; on the other hand, it provides information on the structural relationship between these elements. The system needs to generate the tag structure during the creation of the PDF document.

You can easily check whether a PDF document has a tag structure by following the FILE • PROPERTIES menu path. The dialog that opens, Document Properties, contains a note, Tagged PDF: Yes, in the ADVANCED area of the Description tab if the PDF has a tag structure.

Adobe Reader and Adobe Acrobat already provide a tool that reads the document content out loud. You can select it via the VIEW • READ OUT LOUD • ACTIVATE READ OUT LOUD menu path. The same menu can also be used to have the system read only the current page or to the end of the document. You can also pause or stop this option via this menu.

To externally access the tag structure using additional screen readers, Adobe Reader supports the Microsoft® Active Accessibility® (MSAA) interface. You can use the JAWS® screen reader by Freedom Scientific®, for example.

> **Generation of Accessible PDF Forms for Print Outputs**
>
> To display a PDF form in the print view, the system reads the corresponding setting of the SAP GUI to define whether a tag structure should be generated or not. When a PDF form is archived or returned, the system always generates the tag structure.

7.6.1 Creating Accessible PDF Forms

Adobe LiveCyle Designer provides a palette solely for the text definition that is supposed to be output by the screen reader. This is the ACCESSIBILITY palette (see Figure 7.42). If this palette is hidden in Adobe LiveCycle Designer, you can use the PALETTES • ACCESSIBILITY menu path to display it.

You can use the SCREEN READER PRECEDENCE dropdown list to define which text is output for a form field by the screen reader. In addition to the NONE option for no output, the following four options are available:

▶ **Custom Text**
Using the CUSTOM TEXT option, you can enter a specific text, which is not displayed in the form.

▶ **Tool Tip**
This is a specific text that is also displayed in the form when the mouse pointer is positioned on a particular field for a few seconds.

▶ **Caption**

If you use this option, the caption of a form field is output.

▶ **Name**

If this option is selected, the system outputs the (technical) name from the form hierarchy.

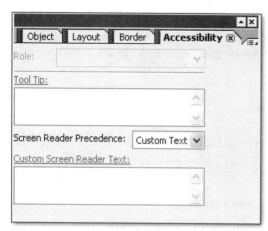

Figure 7.42 Accessibility Palette

For the last two options, the screen reader determines the text from the form template. For the first two options, you must enter the text in the ACCESSIBILITY palette. To do this, you are provided with the two input fields, TOOL TIP and CUSTOM SCREEN READER TEXT. Both texts can also be made available via the underlying data of the form. To do this, you can define the data binding and a binding expression via the dynamic properties.

7.6.2 Tips for Creating Accessible PDF Forms

When creating form templates, you must take into account the following aspects:

▶ All form fields should be provided with a caption.

▶ For the captions, you should use the caption option available for form fields.

▶ You shouldn't use abbreviations, such as "pcs." for "pieces," in texts, because the screen reader tries to read out loud "pcs." otherwise.

▶ How the form fields are arranged is important. You should therefore use the grid or the subforms with the FLOWED option for the content.

▶ You can view the order of form fields via the VIEW • TAB ORDER menu path.

▶ You shouldn't use colors and effects to provide additional information.

▶ You should provide descriptive text for all images.

> **The Structure of the Forms Must Support the Accessibility**
>
> In addition to the practical tips, it is also important to consider the structure of the form. The structure of the PDF forms needs to be designed for accessibility. That means that the structure must be rather simple. If the structure of a form is too complex to be understood by the user, even the best technology is no longer helpful.

7.7 Additional Information

This book cannot describe all of the relevant topics for the creation of form templates in detail. This section provides a list of additional information sources.

7.7.1 Additional Information on the Internet

There's a wide range of additional information sources available on the Internet:

▶ The SAP Community Network should be mentioned first. There is a complete area for SAP Interactive Forms by Adobe (at *https://www.sdn.sap.com/irj/sdn/ adobe*). In addition, there are numerous blogs on specific topics regarding the creation of forms. A separate forum publishes questions about the creation of forms and frameworks, which are answered by the community. You can find this forum at *https://www.sdn.sap.com/irj/sdn/forum?forumID=155*.

▶ You can also access further information on the Adobe website. The pages on Adobe Developer Connection contain a separate area for Adobe LiveCycle Designer. The URL is *http://www.adobe.com/devnet/livecycle/*.

▶ Adobe also provides general information on the partnership between SAP and Adobe Systems (*http://www.adobe.com/enterprise/partners/sap.html*).

The following sections list information sources and describe the information provided on these Internet pages. Various chapters in this book also refer to these URLs.

7.7.2 Adobe Designer Scripting Reference

You can find a more detailed introduction to the usage of script programs for the creation of forms at *http://www.adobe.com/devnet/livecycle/articles/lc_designer_scripting_basics. html*.

7.7.3 XFA

XFA describes the underlying technology of the PDF-based and interactive PDF forms. It includes references for the following four areas:

▸ *Part 2: XFA Grammar Specifications* contains the template reference. For the properties of the form fields, you can find the names that are relevant to the creation of scripts here (such as the `presence` property that controls the visibility of the form fields).

▸ *Part 3: Other XFA-Related References* contains the FormCalc specification and a lot of additional information on the FormCalc script language.

▸ *Part 3: Other XFA-Related References* also includes the picture clause specification. It describes in detail how you create, display, and edit data and validation patterns.

▸ The last part that should be mentioned is the Rich Text Reference. It provides detailed information on how you must format the XHTML text for rich text fields.

You can find the XFA at *http://partners.adobe.com/public/developer/xml/index_arch. html*. The release of SAP Interactive Forms by Adobe described in this book is based on version 2.5.

> **Note**
>
> The document on the XFA is a specification of the underlying technology, which is mainly implemented by Adobe LiveCycle Designer and ADS. If you use elements that cannot be accessed via the user interface of Adobe LiveCycle Designer, you should carefully check whether you're specific requirements can be implemented at all. For Version 2.5, you must also consider that you need at least Adobe Reader 8 and ADS for SAP NetWeaver 7.0 SP 15.

7.7.4   Acrobat JavaScript Reference

When creating interactive PDF forms, you can also use objects and functions that are defined in Acrobat JavaScript. Regardless of the name, they also function in Adobe Reader. You can find the following two documents at *http://www.adobe.com/devnet/acrobat/javascript.html*:

- *JavaScript for Acrobat API Reference*
- *Developing Acrobat Applications Using JavaScript*

The reference details the available options, and the second document describes the usage by means of examples.

> **Note**
>
> The functions that are described in the two Acrobat JavaScript references are only available for interactive PDF forms but not for PDF-based print forms!

7.8   Summary

This chapter first introduced you to the advanced topics of the creation of print outputs by extending the form template from Chapter 5. It then moved toward interactive PDF forms by transferring the knowledge about print forms to interactive forms. The chapter also introduced the form fields that are specifically used for interactive PDF forms. The creation of script programs, tips for increasing performance, and the introduction to the creation of accessible PDF forms finally complemented the advanced topics.

This laid the foundation for the next chapters, which introduce interactive PDF forms in even more detail.

This chapter details the integration of SAP Interactive Forms by Adobe with Web Dynpro ABAP. Many of the scenarios described here can also be used in Web Dynpro Java without a lot of adaptations, because Web Dynpro ABAP and Web Dynpro Java have the same programming model (except for platform-specific modifications).

8   Integration with Web Dynpro ABAP

This chapter provides you with an overview of the options for integrating Adobe with Web Dynpro ABAP. The first part of this chapter details the structure of a component in Web Dynpro ABAP based on a plain Hello World example (see Section 8.1, "Web Dynpro ABAP"). This is followed by a presentation of the individual scenarios of SAP Interactive Forms by Adobe in Web Dynpro ABAP (see Section 8.2, "Scenarios for the Adobe Integration"), with a particular focus on the InteractiveForm User Interface (UI) element (see Section 8.3, "The Interactive-Form UI Element").

Chapter 4, "Interface and Form Context," introduced form templates, which you can also use in Web Dynpro ABAP. Section 8.4, "Interaction with Form Builder," outlines the creation and integration of form templates with your Web Dynpro application. The information and techniques provided in the first sections of this chapter form the basis for Section 8.5, "Implementing the Scenarios Using Web Dynpro ABAP," where you'll learn step-by-step instructions on how to implement individual scenarios of the Adobe integration using Web Dynpro ABAP.

8.1   Web Dynpro ABAP

Web Dynpro is SAP's latest user interface technology. It is a technology that is independent of the client and the platform:

▸ Client independence means that an application that was developed with Web Dynpro can be run via different clients (web browsers, SAP NetWeaver Business Client).

► Platform independence, however, relates to the programming model and the architecture of Web Dynpro. At present, Web Dynpro has been implemented on two platforms by SAP—on SAP NetWeaver ABAP and Java stack. Applications that have been created for one of the platforms can be ported to the other.

Web Dynpro for the Java platform was first delivered with SAP NetWeaver 6.40. Web Dynpro ABAP followed with release 7.0.

8.1.1 Initial Overview

The Web Dynpro component is the core object of every Web Dynpro application. It is a new Workbench object and can be created and manipulated using Transaction SE80 (just like reports or classes, for example). A separate transaction for Web Dynpro—similar to Transaction SE38 for reports or Transaction SE24 for classes—doesn't exist. The environment, integrated with Transaction SE80 for developing Web Dynpro components, is called Web Dynpro Explorer.

A Web Dynpro component is a normal Workbench object and has a development class assigned to it. Hence, it can be transported into other systems.

The architecture of Web Dynpro is based on the established Model View Controller (MVC) approach, that is, data, layout, and program logic can be separated from each other. The data storage (in the model) is carried out via the context.

The context is a hierarchical structure that can be freely defined by the application developer. This structure consists of nodes, which, in turn, can have attributes. A node may comprise zero, one or more elements at runtime—similar to the rows of an internal table. You can establish a simple recursion between nodes, for example, to map trees with an indefinite depth. The area in which you can define the context is called the Context Editor.

The program logic is defined in controllers. Basic object-oriented programming for a controller includes attributes, methods, and events. Depending on the controller type, specific attributes and methods are predefined by Web Dynpro. Therefore, the constructor of a controller is called wdDoInit, whereas wd_this is the name of the attribute that indicates its attributes and methods.

A Web Dynpro component consists of various subobjects, which, in turn, are used for different tasks. According to the MVC approach, these subobjects each contain a controller and a context. The most important subobjects with their respective controllers are listed in the following:

▶ **View** (includes ViewController)
You can use the view to design the layout of a screen, that is, add UI elements and specify their properties. Properties have additional settings; the most important ones are listed in the following:

  ▶ The data type (Boolean, string, enumeration type, and so on).

  ▶ Whether the property can (or even must) be bound to a context attribute or a context node. This way, a connection is established between the view and the model. By modifying the data in the model you can change the content and the appearance of the UI elements dynamically at runtime.

  ▶ Whether the property contains text or data. If it contains text, the text is automatically stored in the Online Text Repository (OTR).

The layout of a view consists of UI elements that can be arranged in a hierarchical structure. However, specific (simple) rules apply here. For example, the grouping of UI elements is implemented using containers. This is a UI element that, in turn, can contain other UI elements. The area in which you can define the layout of a view is called the ViewDesigner.

A component can have any number of views; however, it is not recommended to use more than 15 due to performance reasons.

▶ **Window** (includes WindowController)
A view can't be displayed in the screen directly. This is always done via a window. Therefore, you embed a view into a window to display it. In addition, you can define a hierarchical structure of views by embedding one view of a window inside another. You can also define which views you can navigate by connecting them using outbound and inbound plugs. In a way, a window represents the views of a component to the user. A component can have several windows. However, this usually only makes sense if you want to define additional pop-up windows. The area in which you can define the structure of a window is called the WindowEditor.

A Web Dynpro component can comprise several controllers. These include:

▶ **ComponentController** (part of each component)
The ComponentController is a central controller that exists in every Web Dynpro component. Data that you would like to share with all other controllers

can be stored here centrally. The first option concerns the storage of the data in the context. You can access it from another controller via context mapping. The second option concerns the storage of data directly in the attributes of the controller. As soon as you select an attribute as `public`, you can access it from every other controller.

▶ **CustomController**
This is a controller to which you can outsource data (similar to the Component-Controller) that is supposed to be shared by other controllers. This structure has been created to enable the application developer to group shared data logically. This means that you don't have to store all shared data in the ComponentController. The ComponentController is a specially configured CustomController.

▶ **InterfaceController**
In the InterfaceController, you can view all context nodes, methods, and events of the ComponentController that can be used by other Web Dynpro components. You can define them in the ComponentController using the properties, `interface` or `public`.

▶ **ConfigController**
This is a special controller that can be used for the configuration of a Web Dynpro component. For further information on the configuration topic, refer to the online help for Web Dynpro. In this chapter, no configuration is carried out.

A Web Dynpro application package consists of a Web Dynpro application and a Web Dynpro component. A Web Dynpro application is a Workbench object, too. A user never sees a window of a component directly, but indirectly via a Web Dynpro application. As a result, a Web Dynpro application package refers to the window of a component. In addition, you can also specify other properties, for example, parameters or the help linking.

It is also useful to subdivide larger Web Dynpro application packages into multiple Web Dynpro components. This is either done through direct embedding of the component or using a ComponentInterface.

Each Web Dynpro component implements a ComponentInterface, which is also a Workbench object. When you create a component using the Web Dynpro Explorer, you automatically generate a ComponentInterface of the same name, which is implemented by the Web Dynpro component.

In addition, you can also create a ComponentInterface as a single object using the Web Dynpro Explorer and implement it in any number of Web Dynpro components. A ComponentInterface contains an InterfaceController and a window. The definitions made here are also available in all external implementing components. This enables you to use a simple form of polymorphism between different Web Dynpro components.

If a component uses a ComponentInterface (not implemented, but referenced), you must specify at runtime which component is actually supposed to be used. The component then must implement this ComponentInterface.

Each component can also have an assistance class. This is an ordinary ABAP objects class to which you can outsource source code for better tool support. In this context, the assistance class acts as the interaction layer, that is, UI-based services are implemented there. In smaller applications it can also assume the role of the business logic. The assistance class must inherit from `CL_WD_COMPONENT_ASSISTANCE`.

> **Note**
>
> Internet Explorer 6 and 7 were used as the browser and Windows XP Professional as the operating system for all examples provided in this chapter.
>
> It is also possible to use Firefox (as of SAP NetWeaver 7.0 SP 15).
>
> Throughout this chapter, Adobe Reader Version 8.0 was used and Adobe Reader 7.09 was used for testing purposes.
>
> The examples, which can be downloaded from the website dedicated to this book, were created on an SAP ERP system with version SAP ECC 6.0 EhP3, and SAP NetWeaver 7.0 SP 16 was used as the basis. However, none of the examples requires the additional functions provided by SAP ERP. They can also run on a pure SAP NetWeaver system. Before testing the examples, you should load the flight data model first.

8.1.2 Step by Step: Hello World

Prior to getting started on the Adobe integration examples, let's look at the concepts detailed in Section 8.1.1, "Initial Overview," based on a simple example. The aim is to use a practical example so that you can understand the other examples in this chapter without having any previous knowledge of Web Dynpro ABAP.

As shown in Figure 8.1, a Web Dynpro component is created in the Web Dynpro Explorer using Transaction SE80.

1. Therefore, start Transaction SE80 and select the WEB-DYNPRO COMP./INTF. Entry.

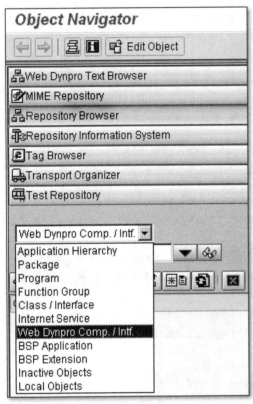

Figure 8.1 Selecting the Category in Transaction SE80

2. Enter the name of the Web Dynpro component to be created and press the ENTER key. In this example, the name of the Web Dynpro component is ZADB_HELLO_WORLD.

3. If the component doesn't exist yet, the system automatically asks if a component is to be created. To confirm, click the YES button (see Figure 8.2).

4. Another dialog opens in which you can enter a descriptive text for the component. Here, the text is "Example: "Hello World" (see Figure 8.3). The system automatically creates a window. You can specify the name in the WINDOW NAME field.

Figure 8.2 Newly Created Component After Entering the Name of the Web Dynpro Component and Pressing ENTER

Depending on the support package level of your system and the release, you can also specify the name of a view in this dialog. This view is also automatically created by the system and embedded in the window.

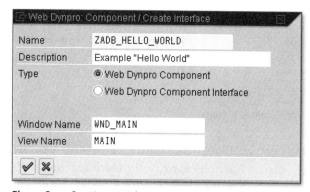

Figure 8.3 Creating a Web Dynpro Component

5. To confirm the dialog, click on the button with the green checkmark. The system then creates the Web Dynpro component. Because it is a Workbench object, you are prompted to select a package to assign the Web Dynpro component to.

6. Each Web Dynpro component contains a ComponentInterface via which other components can use released functions of this component. For this reason, a second dialog opens in which you must select the ComponentInterface package. Select the same package as for the component. This is not mandatory, but useful, because you usually want to transport both objects together later on. If you select a package whose objects are transported, you must select a transport request for the component and the ComponentInterface, respectively.

7. Then, the component and its subobjects—the window and, if applicable, the view—are displayed in the tree of the Web Dynpro Explorer.

If the automatic creation of a view wasn't provided in the dialog for creating the component due to the low support package level of your system, then you must create a new view. To do so, right-click the name of the component and select the corresponding entry from the context menu that appears (see Figure 8.4).

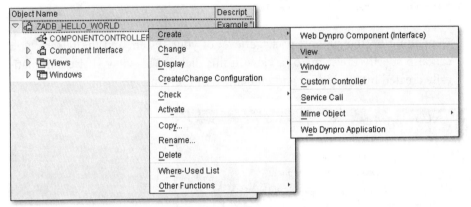

Figure 8.4 Creating a New View via the Context Menu

8. Then, a dialog opens in which you enter the name of the view and a description, if required. Confirm the dialog. The new view is displayed together with the ViewDesigner to show its layout in the correct area of the Web Dynpro Explorer. The ViewDesigner is divided into three different areas:

▶ The upper-right area of the ViewDesigner provides the hierarchical structure of the layout. Currently, it only includes an empty container called ROOTUIELEMENTCONTAINER.

▶ The lower right area shows the properties of this container.

▶ The left-hand side shows a layout preview displaying the still-empty container. The layout preview can be hidden and shown using the respective buttons in the toolbar.

9. Now is a good time to save your work. To do so, click on the button with the SAVE icon in the SAP GUI toolbar.

To output the text "Hello World," you must add a suitable UI element to the view, because the container only defines an area where other UI elements can be placed inside.

1. As shown in Figure 8.5, right-click the ROOTUIELEMENTCONTAINER entry in the upper-right area of the ViewDesigner. In the context menu, select the INSERT ELEMENT entry.

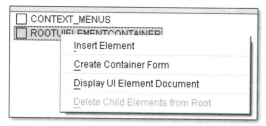

Figure 8.5 Inserting a New UI Element

2. Another dialog opens in which you can further specify the new UI element. For the text output, you need a TextView UI element. Select this UI element from the lower dropdown list (see Figure 8.6). In the view, the UI element also requires a unique name as the identifier. Specify such a name, for example, SOME_TEXT.

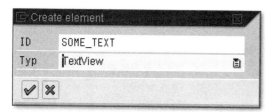

Figure 8.6 Creating a UI Element

3. Confirm the dialog. The new UI element now appears as a subelement of ROO-TUIELEMENTCONTAINER in the ViewDesigner (see Figure 8.7).

4. Enter the string, "Hello World," in the TEXT property of the SOME_TEXT Text-View. After you've pressed the ENTER key, the text appears in the layout preview in the middle of the screen (see Figure 8.8).

5. If, depending on the support package level of the system, you were not provided with the option that the view is automatically generated during the creation of the component, you must embed it manually in the window. To do so, navigate to the window by double-clicking its name in the tree of the Web Dynpro Explorer. The right-hand side switches from ViewDesigner to WindowEditor.

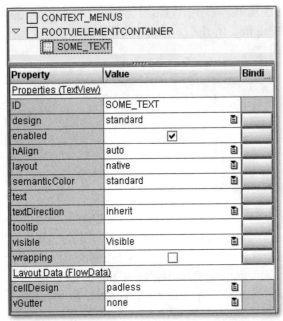

Figure 8.7 TextView as a Sub-element of ROOTUIELEMENTCONTAINER

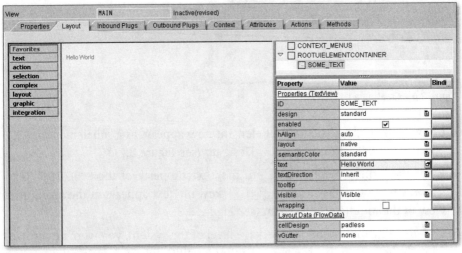

Figure 8.8 Layout Preview

6. Drag and drop the view from the tree of the Web Dynpro Explorer to the root node of the window structure displayed on the right-hand side. You can also select the view by choosing the EMBED VIEW entry from the context menu of the WND_MAIN window in the window structure. The result should then appear as shown in Figure 8.9.

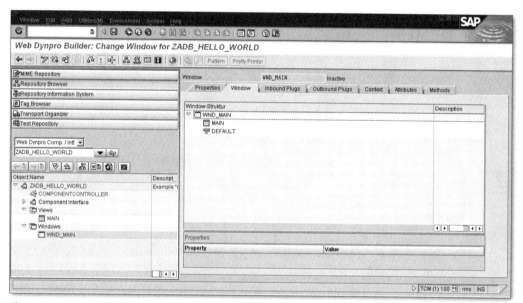

Figure 8.9 MAIN View Embedded in the WND_MAIN Window

7. Activate the component by right-clicking its name in the tree of the Web Dynpro Explorer and selecting the appropriate menu entry. You may have to switch to the display mode for the window to prevent locking yourself out.

8. Now, create a new Web Dynpro application with the name of the component using the context menu path, CREATE • WEB DYNPRO APPLICATION.

9. The name of the component is suggested as the name of the application in the dialog that now appears. This is fine because both are different Workbench objects and may have the same name due to the different type. Retain the default value of the name and enter an optional description. Confirm the dialog.

10. The system prompts you again to select a package. Select the same package as for the component. If the package can be transported, you must specify a transport request. Then, the application is displayed in the Web Dynpro Explorer as illustrated in Figure 8.10.

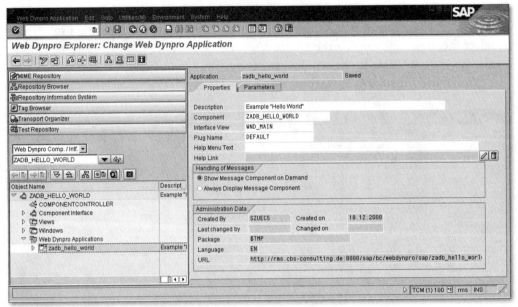

Figure 8.10 Application After the Creation in the Web Dynpro Explorer

11. To start the application, press the F8 key or select the Test entry from the context menu of the application in the tree of the Web Dynpro Explorer. The browser is started automatically and the Web Dynpro application is executed therein. Depending on the setting of your system, you may have to log on again.

12. You then see the "Hello World" text in your default browser (see Figure 8.11).

Figure 8.11 "Hello World" in the Web Browser

8.2   Scenarios for Adobe Integration

SAP provides three basic scenarios for Adobe integration. They are created in such a way that they can be combined freely and therefore cover virtually all kinds of application cases. This section provides you with an overview of how you can use these scenarios by means of Web Dynpro. For more information on the individual scenarios, refer to Chapter 2, "Use of SAP Interactive Forms by Adobe."

8.2.1   Print Scenario

In the print scenario, the system either displays a Portable Document Format (PDF) file or automatically creates a noninteractive PDF form that is based on a form template. Because every PDF form is also a PDF file it is displayed within the Web Dynpro application package using Adobe Reader. You can find the example shown in Figure 8.12 in the Web Dynpro component, `ZADB_DISPLAY_PDF`, for testing purposes. You can start it using the application of the same name.

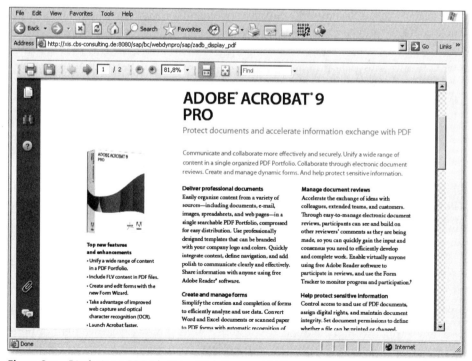

Figure 8.12   Displaying a PDF File Using Web Dynpro ABAP

Caution: Differences in Terminology!

In Chapter 4, "Interface and Form Context," Chapter 5, "Creating Form Templates," and Chapter 6, "Form Output," you learned how to create a PDF form based on a PDF form template and input data. The same mechanisms are used internally by the Web Dynpro runtime to automatically create a PDF form at runtime according to your specifications.

Within this chapter, the following linguistic simplifications are therefore used to prevent confusions: If the terms, form and form template, are used, they always stand for PDF form and PDF form template. Furthermore, the term PDF form is used instead of PDF file if the focus is on the display or modification of data.

Particularly in Chapter 4, which is about Form Builder, the term form is used instead of form template. This abbreviated term is alright from the Form Builder viewpoint because it exclusively deals with form templates. The term form is used consistently within this transaction.

In Web Dynpro, however, you must differentiate between design-time object and runtime object. For this reason, within Web Dynpro, the forms created in Form Builder are called form templates. Therefore, the corresponding property in the InteractiveForm UI element is called templateSource. The runtime object, that is, the object the users can view in Adobe Reader and in which they can enter their data, is called form. The data contained in the form is called form data.

A form in which a user enters data or can trigger actions on the server is an interactive form. Here, it is insignificant whether the application suppresses the input depending on the situation—for example, in the display mode. Every PDF form is also a PDF file, which is displayed in Adobe Reader. If the focus is on the file character of a form, for example, for the download or upload, the term PDF file is used.

8.2.2 Online Scenario

In the online scenario, the user is provided with a PDF form that is ready for input. Therefore, the user can directly fill out the fields in the form and have the inputs checked by the server. This is basically an alternative UI in which the user works with a PDF-based view that is equivalent to the paper form.

Similar to the print scenario, the PDF form is directly embedded in the application in Web Dynpro ABAP using Adobe Reader. This way, the Web Dynpro application package can navigate between different PDF forms, for example.

You, as an application developer, are provided with some very convenient options to implement the online scenario. For example, it is usually sufficient to specify the name of a form template and to supply the data in the Web Dynpro context according to its structure in the form interface. The creation of the PDF form and the return transport of the user's inputs are automatically carried out by the Web Dynpro runtime.

You can find an example of a simple Web Dynpro application package that shows the online scenario in ZADB_ONLINE_EXAMPLE (see Figure 8.13). The input field in Adobe Reader and the readOnly input field in the browser below Adobe Reader both bind to the same context attribute. After entering a value in Adobe Reader, this value is also displayed in the readOnly input field. The source code in your application can access the entered data or prepopulate the fields via the connection to the Web Dynpro context. You can obtain more detailed information on this scenario in Section 8.5.2, "Online Scenario."

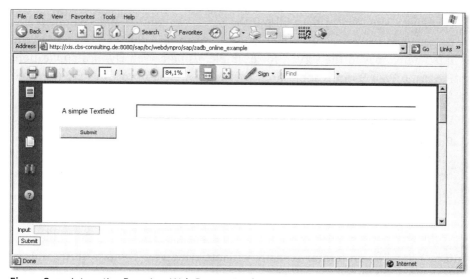

Figure 8.13 Interactive Form in a Web Dynpro Application

8.2.3   Offline Scenario

In the offline scenario, and similar to the online scenario, the PDF form is ready for input. However, Adobe Reader is not embedded in a Web Dynpro application in the browser, but runs in a standalone mode. As a result, you don't need a permanent connection to the server. In a typical offline scenario, the user downloads the PDF form from a server to his computer, fills it out offline, and sends the filled-out copy back to the server as soon as he is online again. The following lists some real-life examples implementing Web Dynpro:

- A request form for a government agency that can be filled out by a citizen. The offline character of this scenario involves that the citizen receives a (printable) copy and that the government agency doesn't have to set up a user account on the system for every single citizen. With Web Dynpro, you create an application for downloading, uploading, and (optionally) reviewing the form. After the upload, the Web Dynpro application package triggers follow-up processes for processing the request.

- In a key account scenario, the key account manager has stored some blank PDF forms on his notebook so he can open them when he visits a customer. At the customer's site, he can then fill out the forms as required and save them as a copy. When the key account manager returns to the office, he can upload the filled-out copies to the server, for example, using a Web Dynpro application. From the Web Dynpro application package, follow-up processes are triggered for processing the data further.

  In contrast to a pure offline scenario, you can use Web Dynpro to create a mixed offline/online scenario. The key account manager would then work with the online scenario while he's in the office and with the offline scenario when he's with a customer or at home. The online scenario could also be implemented using a pure Web Dynpro UI.

You can find an example for a simple Web Dynpro application package that shows the offline scenario in `ZADB_OFFLINE_EXAMPLE`. For more details on the implementation of the different offline scenario variants using Web Dynpro ABAP, refer to Section 10.1.1, "Offline Scenario."

8.3   The InteractiveForm UI Element

The use of the `InteractiveForm` UI element is the core of the Adobe integration with Web Dynpro ABAP. This UI element enables you to map all of the scenarios presented in Section 8.2. For this reason, the UI element is comprised of several properties (see Figure 8.14). The most important of these are:

▶ **enabled**
Indicates that a PDF form is ready for input. The capacity to enter data is already set on the server. Using this property, you can toggle between the print scenario and the online scenario.

▶ **readOnly**
Indicates that the PDF form is ready for input in the online scenario. To ensure that this property functions, switch on the online scenario by means of the `enabled` property. The capacity to enter data is set in the client. In contrast to switching the `enabled` property, this has the following benefits:

   ▶ It provides a higher performance because the server doesn't have to create a new PDF form.

   ▶ Adobe Reader doesn't lose its current scroll status by loading a new PDF form.

▶ **dataSource**
Specifies the context node that the displayed form data is stored on, provided that a form template has been specified. Therefore, this special context node is also called the `dataSource` node.

▶ **templateSource**
If you use a form template, you can enter its name here. `dataSource` and `templateSource` are always paired. It doesn't make any sense to only specify one of them because the system automatically creates the PDF form based on the form data and the form template.

▶ **pdfSource**
Binds to the context attribute on which the PDF file is stored. This property is particularly significant for the print and the offline scenario. In the online scenario, it enables you to store the form as a PDF file on the server.

It primarily depends on the scenario if and how these properties must be set. Section 8.4 and Section 8.5 each include examples that provide more detailed information.

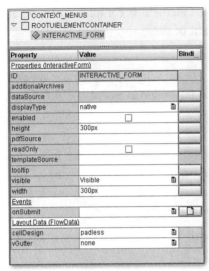

Figure 8.14 InteractiveForm UI Element

8.4 Interaction with Form Builder

The ViewDesigner in Web Dynpro provides direct access to Form Builder (Transaction SFP). Therefore, you can conveniently navigate from the InteractiveForm UI element to the used form template and adjust changes to both objects, if necessary. For more detailed information on form templates and the use of Transaction SFP, refer to Chapters 4 and 5.

8.4.1 Using Form Templates

A form template can simply be used by entering its name in the templateSource property of the InteractiveForm UI element or by selecting the connected input help.

Provided that the entered form template exists and that the dataSource property has not been bound yet, the system immediately provides you with the option to create a tree of nodes and attributes in the context that is equivalent to the form interface and to bind the dataSource property to the root of this tree. The system attempts to give the generated node the same name as the form template. It is possible that the name will be shortened to comply with the name-length restrictions in the context. If a node of the same name already exists, an appropriate sequential number is appended to the name of the new node.

Using a Form Interface in ViewDesigner

You can find an example of an existing form template in the Web Dynpro component, ZADB_DISPLAY_EXIST_TEMPL. It is a quasi Web Dynpro equivalent to the SAP example report, FP_EXAMPLE_01. The report creates—based on the form template of the same name—a form that includes flight-booking data.

The following list provides a step-by-step guide on how the existing form template, FP_EXAMPLE_01, was integrated with the Web Dynpro component:

1. Create a new Web Dynpro component, including a view.

2. Navigate to the view and create an InteractiveForm UI element there.

   At first, neither templateSource nor dataSource of the InteractiveForm UI element are filled or bound.

3. You can select the already-existing form template FP_EXAMPLE_01 via the input help of the templateSource property (see Figure 8.15).

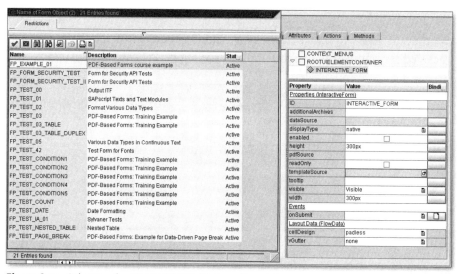

Figure 8.15 Selecting the FP_EXAMPLE_01 Form Template

4. A dialog opens in which the system offers to automatically create the context nodes. Select Yes to confirm.

5. Then, the system fills the `templateSource` and binds the `dataSource` to the newly-created context node (see Figure 8.16).

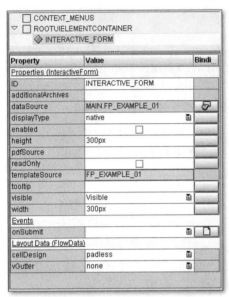

Figure 8.16 Automatically Bound Properties, dataSource and templateSource

6. `dataSource` binds to the `FP_EXAMPLE_01` node generated by the system, which received the name of the form template (see Figure 8.17) by the system.

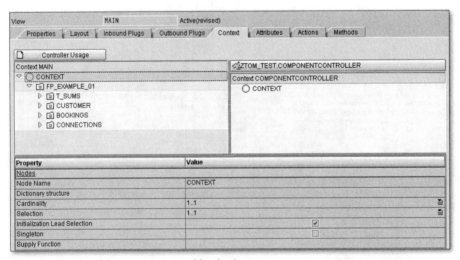

Figure 8.17 Part of the Context Created by the System

7. You can find the source code for populating the context nodes generated from the form template in the `wdDoInit` method (see Listing 8.1). It is implemented similar to the SAP example report, `FP_EXAMPLE_01`. This allows you to compare the two implementations.

```
METHOD wddoinit.
  DATA:
    ls_customer          TYPE scustom,
    lt_bookings          TYPE ty_bookings,
    lt_connections       TYPE ty_connections,
    lt_sums              TYPE TABLE OF sbook,
    lr_form_node         TYPE REF TO if_wd_context_node,
    lr_customer_node     TYPE REF TO if_wd_context_node,
    lr_connections_node  TYPE REF TO if_wd_context_node,
    lr_bookings_node     TYPE REF TO if_wd_context_node,
    lr_t_sums_node       TYPE REF TO if_wd_context_node,
    ls_sums              LIKE LINE OF lt_sums.

  FIELD-SYMBOLS:
    <booking> LIKE LINE OF lt_bookings.

* get the data of the invoice from the database
  SELECT SINGLE * FROM SCUSTOM INTO ls_customer
              WHERE ID = '38'.
  CHECK sy-subrc = 0.
  SELECT * FROM sbook INTO TABLE lt_bookings
          WHERE customid = ls_customer-id
            AND carrid   = 'LH'
          ORDER BY PRIMARY KEY.
  IF lt_bookings[] IS NOT INITIAL.
    SELECT * FROM spfli INTO TABLE lt_connections
            FOR ALL ENTRIES IN lt_bookings
            WHERE carrid = lt_bookings-carrid
              AND connid = lt_bookings-connid
            ORDER BY PRIMARY KEY.
  ENDIF.

* currency key dependant summary
  LOOP AT lt_bookings ASSIGNING <booking>.
    ls_sums-forcuram  = <booking>-forcuram.
    ls_sums-forcurkey = <booking>-forcurkey.
    COLLECT ls_sums INTO lt_sums.
  ENDLOOP.
```

```
* bind the selected values their respective context nodes
  lr_form_node        = wd_context->get_child_node(
                          wd_this->wdctx_fp_example_01 ).
  lr_customer_node    = lr_form_node->get_child_node(
                          wd_this->wdctx_customer ).
  lr_connections_node = lr_form_node->get_child_node(
                          wd_this->wdctx_connections ).
  lr_bookings_node    = lr_form_node->get_child_node(
                          wd_this->wdctx_bookings ).
  lr_t_sums_node      = lr_form_node->get_child_node(
                          wd_this->wdctx_t_sums ).

  lr_customer_node->bind_structure( ls_customer ).
  lr_connections_node->bind_table( lt_connections ).
  lr_bookings_node->bind_table( lt_bookings ).
  lr_t_sums_node->bind_table( lt_sums ).
ENDMETHOD.
```

Listing 8.1 wdDoInit Method

You can also create a completely new form template from the ViewDesigner.

1. Define the structure of the new form interface in the context—in this example, this is the DATA_SOURCE node with the 1:1 cardinality and with a VALUE attribute of the STRING type (see Figure 8.18).

2. Enter the name of the new form template in the templateSource property of the InteractiveForm UI element and confirm your entry by pressing the ENTER key.

3. Then, a dialog opens in which you can either use an already-existing form interface or have the system generate a new one via a subtree of the context. Because a new interface is supposed to be created, enter its name, ZADB_DIS-PLAY_NEW_TEMPL, and click on the CONTEXT button (see Figure 8.19).

4. Then, click on the DATA_SOURCE node in the CONTEXTVIEWER that opens. Its structure will be used for the new form interface (see Figure 8.20). Confirm your selection by clicking on the button with the green checkmark.

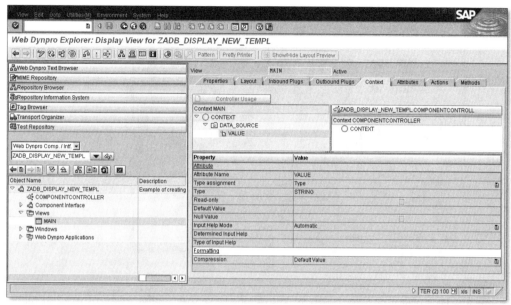

Figure 8.18 Form Interface

Figure 8.19 Specify New Form Interface

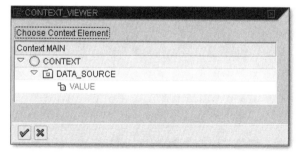

Figure 8.20 Selecting the Root Node of the New Form Interface in the CONTEXTVIEWER

5. The system then automatically creates a new form interface and subsequently a form template (see Figure 8.21).

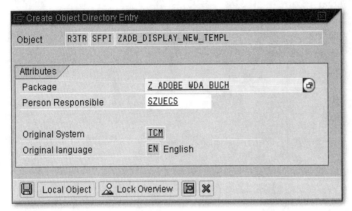

Figure 8.21 Create Object Directory Entry

6. Form Builder opens where you can process the newly created form template. For print forms, you should first change the LAYOUT TYPE to STANDARD LAYOUT. You can find this setting in the PROPERTIES tab of Form Builder (see Figure 8.22).

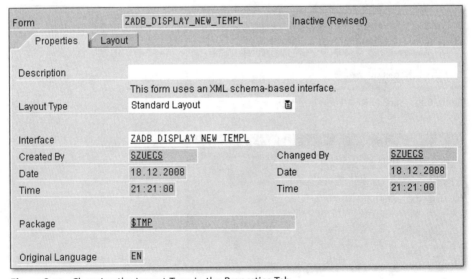

Figure 8.22 Changing the Layout Type in the Properties Tab

7. Switch to the LAYOUT tab. Drag and drop the VALUE attribute from the DATA VIEW palette to the work area of Form Builder—the system creates the binding automatically and correctly (see Figure 8.23). Remember to select Activate before you return to the ViewDesigner, otherwise the ViewDesigner doesn't recognize the new form template.

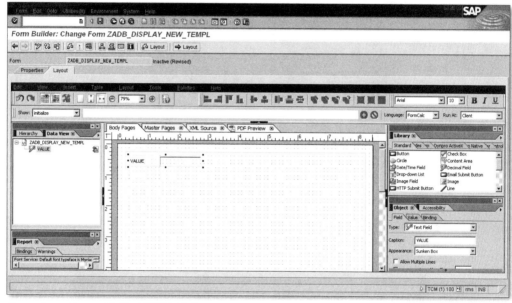

Figure 8.23 Form with the VALUE Attribute

8. After returning to the ViewDesigner, the system automatically binds the `data-Source` property to the previously selected context node (see Figure 8.24).

9. It is recommended to set the width of the `InteractiveForm` UI element to 100% and the height to 500 pixels (provided that the screen size is big enough) after you've created the form template. The corresponding properties are called `width` and `height`.

10. Before testing the application, you must fill the VALUE context attribute. The source code in Listing 8.2 implements this in the supply function, `S_DATA_SOURCE`, of the `DATA_SOURCE` node.

```
METHOD s_data_source.
  DATA:
    ls_data_source TYPE wd_this->element_data_source.
```

```
  ls_data_source-value = '42'.
  node->bind_structure( new_item = ls_data_source ).
ENDMETHOD.
```

Listing 8.2 S_DATA_SOURCE Supply Function

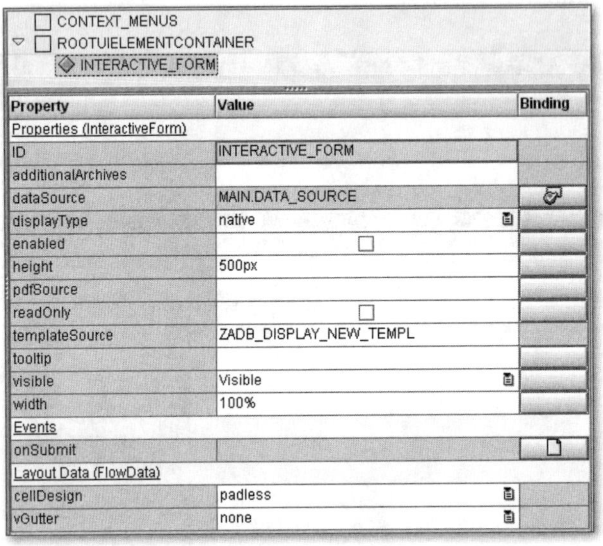

Property	Value	Binding
☐ CONTEXT_MENUS		
▽ ☐ ROOTUIELEMENTCONTAINER		
◇ INTERACTIVE_FORM		
Properties (InteractiveForm)		
ID	INTERACTIVE_FORM	
additionalArchives		
dataSource	MAIN.DATA_SOURCE	🖘
displayType	native	
enabled	☐	
height	500px	
pdfSource		
readOnly	☐	
templateSource	ZADB_DISPLAY_NEW_TEMPL	
tooltip		
visible	Visible	
width	100%	
Events		
onSubmit		☐
Layout Data (FlowData)		
cellDesign	padless	
vGutter	none	

Figure 8.24 Automatically Bound DATASOURCE Property

Web Dynpro ABAP supports DDIC and XML-based form interfaces for form templates. Form templates that are based on an SAP Smart Forms interface can't be used.

The additional features of DDIC interfaces, which were covered in Chapter 4, are only supported in the print scenario. In the online and offline scenarios, the 1:1 conversion between form data and context data is mandatory. As a result, you can't use any calculating or data-limiting functions. This is due to the fact that user entries must be reconverted from the form into the Web Dynpro context.

The relationship between the Web Dynpro context, the interface of a form, and the form itself is illustrated in Figure 8.25. As you can see, Web Dynpro uses the context to access the form template or the PDF form that was automatically created by the Web Dynpro runtime via the form interface. In the print scenario, the arrows only go in one direction: from the Web Dynpro context to the PDF form.

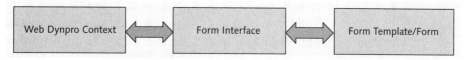

Figure 8.25 Relationships Between the Web Dynpro CONTEXT, FORM INTERFACE, and FORM TEMPLATE/FORM

Adjusting Changes to the Form Interface

If the form interface was changed, you should also change the context of the Web Dynpro views that use the forms involved. Therefore, Web Dynpro ABAP provides the option to update the context from the definition of the interface. A prerequisite is that the form template has been specified via the `templateSource` property in the `InteractiveForm` UI element. If the `dataSource` property is bound, the context node behind it is updated; otherwise a new context node is created.

The adjustment is implemented via the context menu in the `InteractiveForm` UI element of the ViewDesigner. Figure 8.26 shows the menu entry GENERATE CONTEXT.

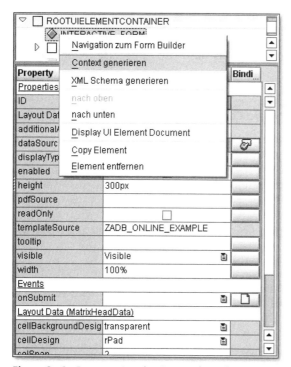

Figure 8.26 Regenerating the Context from the Form Interface

At present, you don't necessarily have to adjust the context to the changed form interface if the change was additive. In this case, the new interface fields or nodes aren't provided with data by Web Dynpro and are thus empty in the form. For interactive forms, these new fields must not be ready for input.

But then, the extension of a form template serves a specific purpose. Usually, the additional fields are supposed to be filled from all applications involved. To avoid the cumbersome regeneration of the context, you should define the design from the outset. To do so, proceed as follows:

► Use a data structuring that is as useful as possible. Even if your table currently only has one entry, you shouldn't make it "flatter" than it actually is. Treat yourself with a real table node with a 0:N cardinality and have Web Dynpro set the leadSelection automatically. Then, it is always positioned as the first entry. Thus, your table node acts like a structure, while ensuring extensibility without any structure adjustment.

► Benefit from the option to define a DDIC structure for a context node. This way, you don't have to adjust the node any longer if a new field was added. Simply add the field to your DDIC structure. It is then automatically available as an attribute in the context node.

► In ABAP, and therefore in Web Dynpro ABAP, you must use uppercase spelling. In an XML-based form interface, you must also use uppercase letters for the name of the data nodes.

Adjusting Changes to the Web Dynpro Context

Changes to the Web Dynpro context must be transferred to the form template in the following cases:

► Changing the data type of an attribute, for example, from STRING to MATNR

► Adding or deleting an attribute

► Changing the properties of a node (for example, converting a structure into a table)

► Adding or deleting a node

In these cases, you must also adjust the form interface.

If it is an interface generated by the ViewDesigner, and if you navigate to the form template from the ViewDesigner, the system notifies you that the two definitions no longer match (see Figure 8.27). You then have the option of having the system update the form interface.

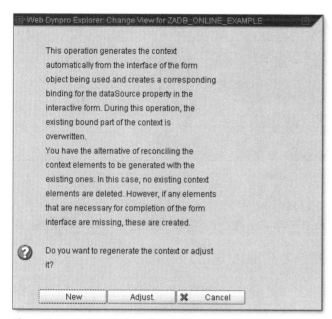

This operation generates the context automatically from the interface of the form object being used and creates a corresponding binding for the dataSource property in the interactive form. During this operation, the existing bound part of the context is overwritten.
You have the alternative of reconciling the context elements to be generated with the existing ones. In this case, no existing context elements are deleted. However, if any elements that are necessary for completion of the form interface are missing, these are created.

Do you want to regenerate the context or adjust it?

New | Adjust. | ✖ Cancel

Figure 8.27 Automatic Interface Adjustment

You can also update the interface manually anytime. To do so, right-click the `Inter-activeForm` UI element in the ViewDesigner and select the Generate XML Schema entry (see Figure 8.28). The adjustment of an interface may also affect other forms. The system provides a corresponding warning (see Figure 8.29).

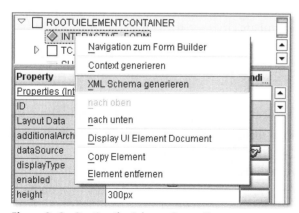

Figure 8.28 Starting the Schema Generation

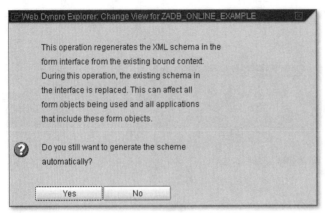

Figure 8.29 System Warning

The regeneration of an XML-based interface is only possible if the interface has been created using the ViewDesigner. The logic for the adjustment was implemented in SAP NetWeaver 7.0 SP 12 and completed with SP 14. Refer to the corresponding SAP notes if you have a system with a lower support package level.

You will come across the previously presented type of adjustment whenever you implement a field extension in a project and want to display the value of this field in the PDF form, for example. Here, you should note that you can append the additional field to the context node without any modifications (via an enhancement of the node or possibly via an append structure for the node's DDIC structure); the necessary form interface/form template change, however, is only possible with modifications.

The best approach is to copy the form template provided by SAP (including its interface) to the customer namespace. Then, overwrite the value of the `template-Source` property using an implicit enhancement at the end of the `wdDoModifyView` method.

8.4.2 The pdfOnly Case

The pdfOnly case is a special case in which it is your responsibility to generate a PDF form on the basis of a form template and data. If it is an interactive form, you are also responsible for the data extraction. For this reason, only the `pdfSource` property is bound to the context in this case. `templateSource` and `dataSource` are not used. In the online scenario, this approach only functions in combination with the Active Component Framework (ACF) integration (see Section 8.5.2). Therefore, the `pdfSource` property contains an ACF-enabled PDF form.

8.5   Implementing Scenarios Using Web Dynpro ABAP

In this section, we'll implement different scenarios of the Adobe integration by means of Web Dynpro ABAP with the help of examples. First, we'll discuss two rather comprehensive variants of the print scenario. Then, we'll look at the implementation of online and offline scenarios.

8.5.1   Print Scenario

The print scenario can be implemented in two different ways: On one hand, you can display an already-existing PDF file and, on the other hand, the Web Dynpro runtime can automatically create a PDF form based on a form template and data via ADS. In both cases, the file is presented to a user via the `InteractiveForm` UI element.

Displaying a PDF File

To implement this scenario, transfer a PDF file that is located in the MIME Repository or in a database table to a context attribute of type `XSTRING`. Then, bind the `pdfSource` property of the `InteractiveForm` UI element to this context attribute.

You can use the code shown in Listing 8.3 to access a file in the MIME Repository:

```
DATA:
  lr_mime_repository TYPE REF TO if_mr_api,
  content            TYPE XSTRING.

CONSTANTS:
  url TYPE STRING VALUE '/SAP/BC/Web Dynpro/SAP/ZADB_DISPLAY_PDF/
acrobatpro_datasheet.pdf'.

lr_mime_repository =
  cl_mime_repository_api=>get_api( ).
lr_mime_repository->get(
  EXPORTING
    i_url = url
  IMPORTING
    e_content = content ).
wd_context->set_attribute(
  NAME  = 'PDF'
  VALUE = content ).
```

Listing 8.3 Loading a PDF File from the MIME Repository

The `wdDoInit` method of the view is a good location to load the already-existing PDF file in this example. If the file is used by multiple views, you should use the same method of the ComponentController or a CustomController. You can also use a load-on-demand by moving the source code to an action handler.

With regards to Listing 8.3, the path provided in the `URL` constant points to the file in the MIME Repository. The file itself is located within the `ZADB_DISPLAY_PDF` component. You can recognize this by the components of the path, which are described as follows:

▶ **/SAP/BC/Web Dynpro**
Path to the Web Dynpro component

▶ **/SAP/ZADB_DISPLAY_PDF/**
Name of the Web Dynpro component

Components without a namespace always receive the name prefix, `/SAP/`. If you use a custom namespace, it changes from `/SAP/` to `/CBSGMBH/`, for example, for component `/CBSGMBH/MY_WDA_COMPONENT` (see Figure 8.30).

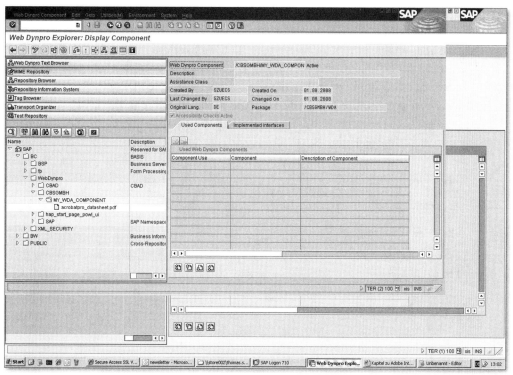

Figure 8.30 Available Folder Structure per Namespace for MIME Objects from the Web Dynpro Components

These are all of the steps required. The PDF file is displayed after executing the application. You can find the example in the Web Dynpro component, ZADB_DISPLAY_PDF.

Caution: Pitfall!

In early support packages of SAP NetWeaver 7.0, the default value of the `enabled` property of the `InteractiveForm` UI element is set to `true`. Later on, this was changed in the ViewDesigner to better support the print scenario. Therefore, you should always check to see if the `enabled` property is switched off. Only then is the print scenario active.

The Application Program Interface (API) of the `InteractiveForm` UI element by means of the `CL_WD_INTERACTIVE_FORM` class has not been changed by SAP so as to not jeopardize the functionality of existing Web Dynpro applications. There, the default value is still set to `true`. If you make use of dynamic programming with the `InteractiveForm` UI element, you must consider this.

Because the `pdfSource` property is bound to a context attribute in this scenario, its value can be changed—even at runtime. This way, you can create an application that enables the user to navigate between different PDF files. You can find an example of this in the Web Dynpro component, `ZADB_DISPLAY_PDF_NAV`. The corresponding application has the same name. Multiple PDF files are provided in a context node of the 0:N cardinality and made available in the `DropdownByIndex` UI element for selection by the user using the `LeadSelection` of the connected context node (see Figure 8.31).

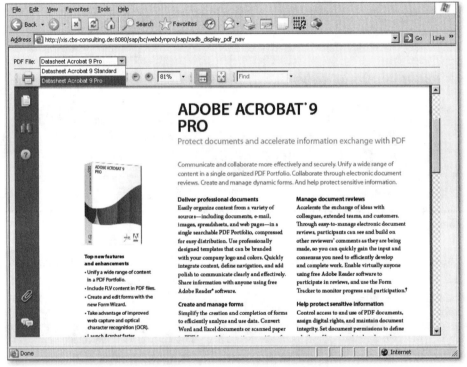

Figure 8.31 Switching Between Different PDF Files Using a Dropdown List

Displaying a PDF Form According to a Form Template

This variant of the print scenario is based on a form template. A PDF form is generated based on it containing data stored in the context. The resulting PDF form is then displayed by the system. All of this is done automatically by the Web Dynpro runtime.

Section 8.4 already detailed how you can define a form template in the `Interac-tiveForm` UI element or generate a new form template from the ViewDesigner. This information is sufficient to allow you to display a PDF form. For this reason, you only have to load the corresponding data into the context structure to which the `dataSource` property binds. This functions in the same way as if you worked with Web Dynpro—for example, by means of a supply function or direct population from other methods of the View Controller.

This is where you can benefit from the use of a form template: Layout and data are separated. This way, you can use different form templates while reusing the same data structures and program logic. A classic example is the rollout of a solution in different regions, for example, from the United States to Japan. Here, the pure translation of texts in the form template is usually not sufficient.

Using DDIC Interfaces versus XML-based Form Interfaces

Up to this point, form templates and their use in Web Dynpro ABAP have only been considered from the integration point of view. The following sections take a look at the technical background. You already know from the previous chapters of this book that each form template has an interface. This interface can either be an SAP Smart Forms, DDIC, or XML-based interface. Web Dynpro ABAP supports both DDIC and XML-based interfaces. SAP recommends using the XML-based interface for new form templates. Legacy SAP Smart Forms–based interfaces are not supported.

Despite the many benefits of the XML-based interface, which will be detailed in the course of this chapter, users often select the "outdated" DDIC interface—particularly for the print scenario. Compared to the XML-based interface, it enables the use of additional functions, for example, the display of addresses that you would otherwise have to implement yourself. In addition, old forms often use the DDIC interface.

With regard to the integration with Web Dynpro, you won't see any difference between the two interface types at first glance. An equivalent context is generated for equivalent interfaces. Among other aspects, this enables you to change a form interface from DDIC to XML later on without having to change the Web Dynpro components involved.

> **Note**
>
> Form templates that you create using the ViewDesigner always have an XML-based interface. In addition, they are protected against external changes, for example, by means of Transaction SFP. Such forms are intended as ad hoc forms that are mostly used in a single Web Dynpro component. This can be very useful.
>
> If you don't want this dependency, create the form template externally using Transaction SFP. However, an automatic adjustment from the Web Dynpro context is no longer possible then.

pdfSource Property in the Print Scenario with Form Templates

One property of the `InteractiveForm` UI element, which has not been considered in detail so far, is important for the print scenario with form templates. It is the `pdfSource` property, which was mentioned in the "Displaying a PDF File" section. If you bind this property to a context attribute of the type `XSTRING`, you are provided with the currently displayed PDF form in the next roundtrip.

Note that the transfer of the PDF form to the context requires some time per roundtrip. Therefore, you shouldn't bind the property to the context if you don't need the PDF form. The same applies to the online scenario that is described in more detail in the following section.

8.5.2 Online Scenario

In the online scenario, a PDF form is ready for input in the browser. Furthermore, you are provided with several additional functions, for example, the value help from Web Dynpro ABAP as an input support. But before you can start to use interactive forms in Web Dynpro ABAP, let's look at the basic technologies for interactive forms.

Basic Technologies for Interactive Forms in the Online Scenario

In the online scenario, interactive forms are based on either of two completely different technologies: ACF or Zero Client Installation (ZCI). They indicate the type of embedding and the control of Adobe Reader in the browser. As a developer, but particularly as an architect, you should know both variants to make the right decision for your project.

▶ **ACF**

ACF is a technology that is used to integrate ActiveX controls or Java applets selected by SAP with Web Dynpro. It is a wrapper around the actual ActiveX control or Java applet. It provides a defined interface to the calling framework (Web Dynpro). ACF is not only used for Adobe integration, but also for other UI elements such as `Network`, `Gantt` and `OfficeControl`.

An ActiveX wrapper is used in the case of Adobe Reader. This reveals a disadvantage of this solution: Its use is limited to Internet Explorer. An ACF-based Adobe integration can't function in Firefox, for example. Another disadvantage of the ActiveX solution is that such a control must be installed on the client PC and maintained by an administrator. This, in turn, incurs a higher total cost of ownership (TCO).

However, the ACF integration has one advantage: You can use almost any PDF form template here because it doesn't require any special adjustments compared to the ZCI integration.

▶ **ZCI**

The ZCI integration is the successor technology of the ACF integration and has been available to customers since SAP NetWeaver 7.0 SP 10. In contrast to the ACF approach, there is no wrapper around Adobe Reader, but Adobe Reader is controlled per JavaScript via a special API provided by Adobe. As a result, this solution functions in all browsers supported by SAP. Therefore, as of SP 15, not only Internet Explorer, but Firefox is also supported for Adobe integration (see SAP Note 1098009).

Unfortunately, not every form template is suitable for the ZCI integration. To use ZCI, you must first insert the ZCI script into the form template. This can be done either via the menu path UTILITIES • INSERT WEB DYNPRO SCRIPT (see Figure 8.32) or via the `FP_ZCI_UPDATE` report for several form templates at one go.

The ZCI script is constantly developed further by Adobe, which is why there are different versions. Each version is bound to a specific release and therefore to a specific support package of SAP NetWeaver. So if you import a support package, you may have to adapt the ZCI script for all form templates you use. From a technical point of view, this constitutes a modification of the form templates provided by SAP.

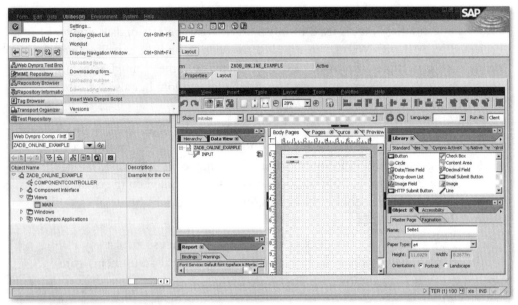

Figure 8.32 Inserting the ZCI Script via the Menu

For your developer PC the basic rule applies that different versions of Adobe LiveCycle Designer also entail different versions of the ZCI script. Newly created form templates receive the ZCI script that is currently installed on your computer. Ensure that it matches the support package level of the SAP system.

Also note that you must adjust the ZCI script on the PCs of the project members after an update of the ZCI script on ADS. Otherwise, an obsolete ZCI script is inserted into new forms. Then, you would have to replace it using the ZCI conversion report, FP_ZCI_UPDATE.

In addition to the ZCI script, there are different versions of the respective controls which must correspond to the version of the ZCI script. The ZCI conversion report is used to update them.

Important Notes

Up to SAP NetWeaver 7.0 SP 15, there are some serious errors and deficiencies within the ZCI integration. Therefore, you should install SP 16 or higher if you want to use the online scenario. SP 12 is sufficient for initial tests. However, you must expect several errors, for example, when locking the form against input and when using pop-up windows, and deficiencies, such as the lack of input/output conversion.

With Enhancement Package 1 of SAP NetWeaver 7.0, there is an automatic update of the ZCI script. Here, the form template doesn't have to contain a ZCI script any longer. It is automatically added and updated by ADS at runtime. Therefore, version problems due to obsolete form templates are a thing of the past.

If you use 7.0 EhP1, for example, within the framework of an EhP of SAP R/3, you should note that ADS runs on the Java platform. The automatic update of the ZCI script is not included in SAP's allowed combination of ABAP 7.0 EhP1 and Java 7.0. For this reason, you would have to install Java 7.0 EhP1.

Problematic Aspects of the Interactive Online Scenario

There are several problematic aspects that you should consider if you want to use the online scenario:

▶ Adobe Reader is a separate UI environment. This is required for the offline scenario—in the online scenario, however, it constrains the full integration with Web Dynpro. For example, within Adobe Reader some Web Dynpro features don't function, such as error navigation and personalization. Developers are not provided with the wide range of UI elements to create highly interactive applications to the degree provided by Web Dynpro. The structuring of data by means of a `Tree` UI element is not possible either.

▶ Forms that have been created for the offline scenario are usually not suitable for the online scenario. This is due to the fact that forms in offline scenarios usually contain additional data (for example, summarized in dropdown lists), which may result in large forms. This in turn is not suitable for an online scenario in which all form data is continuously exchanged with the server. Here, you would only create fields with small value sets as dropdown lists and include a value help for cases with many entries. Overall this would result in better performance. However, this is not suitable to fill out a form offline due to the missing server connection.

▶ Adobe Reader fully occupies the intended area in the browser. A mixing with Web Dynpro UI elements is not possible. Up to SAP NetWeaver 7.0 SP 11, it was possible to specify the height and width of this area in fixed sizes only (for example, pixel) that is, it was impossible to automatically adjust the size of the form to the size of the browser.

▶ Web Dynpro only supports some features of the PDF standard and Adobe Reader. It will always be a technology that must implement support for new functions of ADS, the PDF standard, and Adobe Reader before you as the application developer can use them from Web Dynpro. SAP strives to do so; however, the PDF standard alone is too extensive to implement completely.

For example, digital signatures and job profiles are currently not supported in Web Dynpro ABAP. In addition, only a subset of the controls available in Adobe LiveCycle Designer is released for use in Web Dynpro. SAP has not even implemented a series of controls in the xACF and ZCI libraries that have been developed by Adobe specifically for Web Dynpro.

▶ You can't display multiple interactive forms in the browser at the same time, for example, to compare the content of two forms. However, this is enabled for noninteractive forms, that is, for forms that have been created according to the print scenario.

▶ Whereas you can apply a consistent corporate design to Web Dynpro without changing the application, this is not possible for a form template. It can only have a single design. If the corporate design is changed, you must adjust every form template concerned.

▶ Problem effects observed in the browser (for example, no data transfer after a roundtrip) can't always be traced back to a problem with the Adobe integration because Adobe Reader has a high error tolerance. For this reason, Adobe Reader does not always display an error message for problems.

▶ Forms of the online scenario created by the Web Dynpro runtime always constitute a dynamic PDF. Adobe specifies a maximum of twelve pages, which shouldn't be exceeded due to performance reasons. More information is available on the Adobe website at *http://www.adobe.com/devnet/livecycle/articles/ DynamicInteractiveFormPerformance.pdf*.

▶ Up to Release SAP NetWeaver 7.0, ZCI-based forms must already contain the source code for communication with the Web Dynpro framework—the ZCI script. As of Release 7.0 EhP1, the script for creating the PDF form is automatically added by ADS. So, if you use SAP NetWeaver 7.0, you must pay special attention to the use of the correct ZCI script and always keep it up to date. This can be very tedious or even impossible.

▶ It is a technical challenge to integrate an ActiveX control with a browser that interacts with its environment via a JavaScript framework, which must not lose its contents between roundtrips, and is supposed to be performant. The alternative is to use the two technologies and their strengths directly, for example, Web Dynpro for online scenarios and SAP Interactive Forms by Adobe for offline scenarios.

- ▶ Client certificates are not supported by the ZCI integration at present. If you must use client certificates, you can only revert to the ACF integration (which has not been and will not be further developed by SAP) or exchange the interactive form embedded in Web Dynpro with a pure Web Dynpro application package.

- ▶ HTTPS is supported by the ZCI integration as of Adobe Reader 8.1. If you use an older version of Adobe Reader, you must revert to the unsecure HTTP variant or to the ACF integration. For this reason, it is always advisable to schedule the rollout of the latest Adobe Reader version recommended by SAP at the start of a project.

Due to the numerous problems and the unsteady integration of two technologies (browser and Adobe Reader) you should use the online scenario with special care. However, there are also some good usage options, which are presented in the following.

Reasonable Usage of the Online Scenario

Typically, the scenario is used in two areas:

- ▶ For entering data in simple forms, for example, paper. The permanent connection to the server for the online scenario enables the immediate check of entries, the support of value helps, and the possible start of follow-up processes.

- ▶ For the online review of small forms from the offline scenario.

The implementation of the two scenarios is discussed in the course of this chapter, whereas the review of offline forms is included in Section 8.5.3.

It is useful to answer some questions prior to the use of the online scenario. Some of these questions result from the list of problematic aspects of the use of the online scenario. The following checklist should help you with your projects:

- ▶ Check whether an implementation using Web Dynpro (or another technology) without interactive forms would be more reasonable. In a pure online scenario, it usually makes no sense to embed an Adobe form in a Web Dynpro environment because the maintenance and development effort resulting from the combination of the two technologies is usually higher than if you focused on only one technology.

- Decide whether the entries in the browser are supposed to be made via Adobe Reader or Web Dynpro. This means that there should be virtually no dependencies between the UI logic outside and inside Adobe Reader. Such dependencies can arise if you position the same input field both within Adobe Reader and outside Adobe Reader in a Web Dynpro application package, for example, to provide users with the option to enter data either in the form or in the Web Dynpro environment. This usually results in problems because the sequence for transferring changes between Adobe Reader and Web Dynpro is undefined.

  This also applies to interconnected input fields. For example, you should never provide the `City` field in the form and the `Country` field in the Web Dynpro environment with ready-for-input status. This would be hard to understand for the user. The best solution is to establish groups of logically related fields and to implement them completely in one of the two technologies.

- ZCI is used as the integration technology right from the start of the project because the ACF integration is no longer developed by SAP.

- All project members use the same version of Adobe LiveCycle Designer.

- The same version of ZCI is stored on ADS as on the project members' PCs.

- The latest and, in particular, the same ZCI script is used in all form templates right from the outset. After an update of the ZCI script (in all used form templates, on all PCs and ADS) the business scenarios concerned are retested.

- No new support package is imported during the project or else the ZCI script must be updated in the form templates already created. Furthermore, you must carry out the same additional actions as described in the previous item.

- The used form templates only have a manageable number of fields. The resulting PDF form has a maximum of twelve pages because Adobe has set this limit for dynamic PDFs due to performance issues.

- The form is primarily developed for the online scenario and not for the offline scenario. This is a typical (unconscious) error when converting an existing paper form into a form template for the online scenario. This includes, for example, that dropdown lists are used sparingly and may only contain a small, manageable number of entries (less than or equal to seven). Otherwise, you should add a value help to the `Text Field` control. Dropdown lists of any size can cause performance problems.

- The page size remains Letter or DIN A4 only in exceptional cases, such as displaying an existing paper form. In all other cases, the size of the form is adapted so that its content is just enclosed. This way, you can avoid unnecessary scroll-bars within Adobe Reader and increase the initial magnification of the form. This improves the readability and usability of the form considerably. The worst thing that can happen is that the user must select a suitable form magnification by means of Adobe Reader's zoom function after the form has been loaded.

For converted paper forms, you should also check whether Letter or DIN A4 is a useful format. Because the user works online, you can split a large form into many small forms and interlink them using a wizard created by means of Web Dynpro UI elements. For example, consider a program for filling out an annual tax declaration: Here, you are guided through the individual sections of the form step by step.

▶ At the beginning of the project you must check whether the support of client certificates is necessary because they are not currently supported by the ZCI integration.

▶ Because Adobe Reader sets up a separate communication channel to the server without using the communication object of the browser, no communication is possible via a VPN connection created this way.

▶ Always use the latest version of Adobe Reader recommended by SAP. This way, you can prevent problems for the support of HTTPS, for example. Schedule the rollout of a possible Adobe Reader update.

If you consider these rules, there is nothing to prevent a successful use of the online scenario.

Updating the ZCI Script

Because version problems of the script occur in every project, the following sections describe how you can detect and resolve them. The first question to ask is how do you determine the version of the ZCI script?

1. To do so, start Form Builder (Transaction SFP) and open the form template concerned.

2. Go to the Layout view and select the Hierarchy palette there.

3. You can find the included ZCI script under (Variables). It has the name, Containerfoundation_JS; click on it.

4. The beginning of the file should now appear in the Script area. There you'll find the version information. In Figure 8.33, the version number is 802.20070

810081039.413428.411870. The area directly after the first dot is important: It includes the date and enables you to determine the up-to-dateness of the script. The structure of the date is year/month/day—in this case August 10, 2007. If the script area is not displayed, you can expand it using the blue slider.

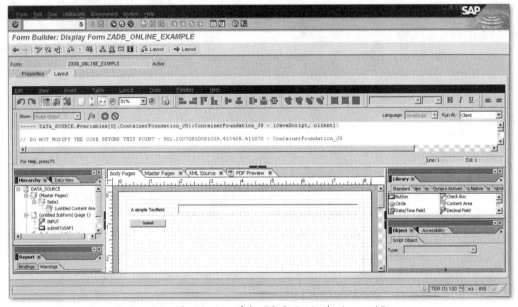

Figure 8.33 Determining the Version of the ZCI Script in the Layout View

The next question is whether the determined version is obsolete, just right, or too new. Here, the rule applies that up to SP 16 the version mentioned is the correct version. You need a more recent version of the ZCI scripts for higher support package versions or after downloading SAP Notes 1229392, 1227102, and 1180004.

If the ZCI script is obsolete, you have two options to update it:

▸ Via Transaction SFP_ZCI_UPDATE for several forms
▸ Using Form Builder (Transaction SFP) for exactly one form

In the former case, the new ZCI script must be available on ADS. For more information, refer to SAP Note 956074. In the latter case, the ZCI script must be available in different directories on your computer. Let's look at this case more closely.

1. The ZCI script is located in subdirectories of the Adobe LiveCycle Designer directory together with the controls and sorted by language. For version 8.0, for example, the path is *C:\Programs\Adobe\Designer 8.0*. The subdirectories are called *DE*, *EN*, etc.

   Each of these subdirectories includes a *Templates* subdirectory. The ZCI script should at least be found in the subdirectories, *Web Dynpro* and *Custom*. The corresponding file is called *Web DynproInteractiveForm.tds* and can be opened with a text editor. You can find the version entry within the file.

2. For an update, this file must be replaced consistently in all subdirectories for all languages used. For later versions of the file refer to the respective SAP notes (for example, SAP Note 956074).

3. Once you have restarted Adobe LiveCycle Designer, the new version of the file is used. If this doesn't work, delete the cache directory of Adobe LiveCycle Designer under *C:\Documents and Settings\<developer>\Application data\Adobe\ Designer*. You must replace the *<developer>* path component with the name of the current Windows user.

The following sections present different techniques that will be used in a real online example later on.

Processing Input Fields

In the first and most simple example, you are to create an interactive PDF form that "only" contains one single input field and a button for sending the input to the server. The text entered in the form is displayed in a Web Dynpro input field for verification outside the form after the SEND button has been activated. You can find an example in the Web Dynpro component, ZADB_ONLINE_INPUT_FIELD.

Carry out the following steps to create such a component:

1. Create a new Web Dynpro component using Transaction SE80. The component should contain a view (MAIN) and a window (WND_MAIN).

2. In the context of the view, create a DATA_SOURCE node with the cardinality 1:1 and with a VALUE context attribute of the type STRING (see Figure 8.34).

379

3. Use the following UI elements in the layout of the view:

- an `Inputfield` with `Label`
- an optional `Button`
- an `InteractiveForm` UI element

4. Bind the `value` property of the `Inputfield` to the `VALUE` context attribute.

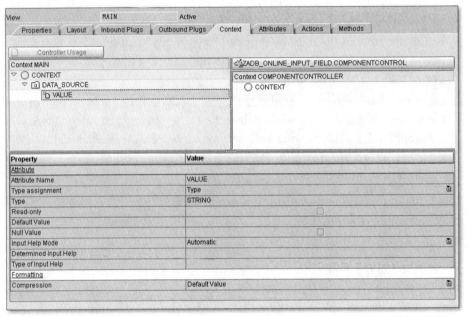

Figure 8.34 Context of the View

5. Activate the `enabled` property for the `InteractiveForm` UI element so that the PDF form becomes interactive.

6. Next, create a new form template from the ViewDesigner as described in Section 8.4.1, "Using Form Templates." In this form template, a text field binds to the `VALUE` attribute from the data view of Form Builder.

7. Because you want to create a ZCI-based interactive PDF form, you first have to set the layout type in the PROPERTIES tab to ZCI LAYOUT (see Figure 8.35).

8. Add a SEND button from the WEB DYNPRO NATIVE library (see Figure 8.36). If the ZCI script is not yet displayed in the HIERARCHY palette, you can add it to the form template later on.

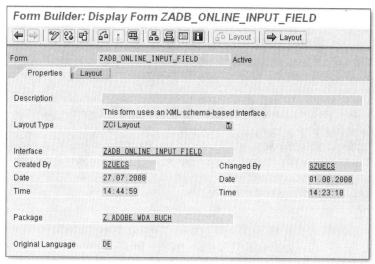

Figure 8.35 Layout Type Manually Set to ZCI Layout

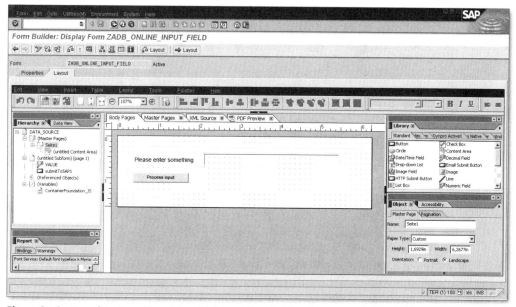

Figure 8.36 Complete Form Template with Bound Text Field and a Send Button

---

Two Web Dynpro Tabs in Form Builder

There are two Web Dynpro libraries in Form Builder: WEB DYNPRO ACTIVEX and WEB DYNPRO NATIVE. The ActiveX library contains controls for the use in ACF-based form templates. The Native library contains the controls intended for ZCI-based form templates.

A form template must use the controls of the corresponding library depending on the layout type. Otherwise, the interactive form won't function properly. Unfortunately, the system doesn't display an error message if an incorrect control is used. For example, if you use the wrong SEND button you can still activate the form template without any problems. No error message is provided at runtime either. A click on the button triggers absolutely nothing—a frequent source of error whose cause is not obvious. So it is your responsibility to ensure that the right controls are used.

9. Return to the ViewDesigner in Web Dynpro after the new form template and form interface have been activated. The `dataSource` property of the `InteractiveForm` UI element was automatically bound by the system (see Figure 8.37).

Property	Value		Binding
Properties (InteractiveForm)			
ID	INTERACTIVE_FORM		
Layout Data	MatrixHeadData	▣	
additionalArchives			
dataSource	MAIN.DATA_SOURCE		☞
displayType	native	▣	
enabled	☑		
height	400px		
pdfSource			
readOnly	☐		
templateSource	ZADB_ONLINE_INPUT_FIELD		
tooltip			
visible	Visible	▣	
width	100%		
Events			
onSubmit		▣	
Layout Data (MatrixHeadData)			
cellBackgroundDesign	transparent	▣	
cellDesign	rPad	▣	
colSpan	1		

Figure 8.37 Automatically Bound dataSource Property

10. If you created a `Button` UI element above the `InteractiveForm` UI element, it is only active in the web browser if you assigned an action to its `onSubmit` event. Because the action is to do nothing but trigger a roundtrip to the server, it is sufficient to create an action without source code. The transfer of the entries from the PDF form to the input field is done automatically because they both bind to the same context attribute.

For the example created just now, `Inputfield`, the `readOnly` property should only be set to prevent accidental inputs. The user is supposed to make the entries only in the PDF form. You can also use a `TextView` UI element. However, in this case the user would not recognize that a specific area contains information or is supposed to receive information.

11. Create a Web Dynpro application package as the last step for the Web Dynpro component and start it. After you've entered a text and clicked on one of the two buttons, the browser should then appear as illustrated in Figure 8.38. After you've entered "to appear above" in the PDF form and clicked one of the two buttons, the input appears in `Inputfield` above the PDF form.

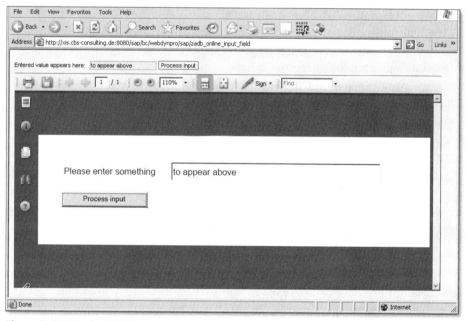

Figure 8.38 Finished PDF Form

In this example, it is not important whether you click the SEND button in the PDF form or the Web Dynpro button outside the form. In both cases, you trigger a roundtrip to the server and your entries are transferred from the form into the Web Dynpro context. This, in turn, means that you could omit the SEND button in the form. Then, it would be closer to a real paper form.

Due to its simplicity, this example is perfectly suited to consider some what-if situations:

▶ For example, change the capacity to enter data for the two input fields via the properties, `readOnly` and `enabled`. What happens if both input fields are ready for input at the same time? (This is undefined.)

▶ Can you use existing form templates that were created using Form Builder? (Yes.)

▶ What happens if you omit the ZCI script? (Depending on the support package level of the system, the text field is no longer ready for input or the form "gets stuck" upon sending it.)

▶ What happens if you use the Send button from the wrong library in Form Builder? (The text field is ready for input, but clicking on the Send button has no effect.)

▶ Can you retroactively change the layout type from ZCI to another value? (That is not possible retroactively. A conversion in the other direction is possible using the ZCI update report that was presented earlier.)

You can also experiment with this example in other browsers or Adobe Reader versions if you have the chance. If a complex example does not function in a project, this simple example may help you to exclude these and similar infrastructure problems.

One decisive what-if question has not been considered yet. This involves the option to use already-existing form templates with a DDIC interface. In principle, these form templates can also be used for interactive forms in Web Dynpro ABAP. However, the DDIC interface may not carry out any operations for the inbound data (conversions, limiting or extending user input, and so on).

Because no option exists for application developers to define the re-transformation of an input from the form into the Web Dynpro context, the input of a user would probably not be processed. As long as you stick to this rule, you can also use the form template with DDIC interface as interactive forms.

This feature was not intended originally. Form templates with DDIC interface were supposed to be used only as pure print forms. Upon request of the users, this option has been retroactively provided. For this reason, it is not sufficient to switch on the `enabled` property for a form template with DDIC interface to make the resulting form interactive.

Existing Web Dynpro applications with print forms that have a DDIC interface could become interactive. For those, the value of the `enabled` property was irrelevant prior to the implementation of this feature; they've never been ready for input. Therefore, a method handler was assigned to the `InteractiveForm` UI element. You may know the method handler from other Web Dynpro UI elements, such as `OfficeControl`, `BIApplicationFrame`, or `Table`. A method handler enables the Web Dynpro developer to call additional functions on a UI element, which can't be mapped via a property or for which SAP didn't want to introduce a new property due to the special role of the feature.

In this case, the latter applies. The additional property that can be addressed using the method handler is called `legacyEditingEnabled`. It is a Boolean value that is switched off by default. The method handler includes a set and a get method to change or read the current value. You can access the method handler only via the UI element. For this reason, you should position the respective code in the `wdDoModifyView` method of the view on which the `InteractiveForm` UI element can be found.

You can use the code shown in Listing 8.4 to access the method handler and set `legacyEditingEnabled` to true.

```
METHOD wddomodifyview.
  DATA:
    lr_interactive_form TYPE REF TO
      cl_wd_interactive_form,
    lr_method_handler   TYPE REF TO
      if_wd_iactive_form_method_hndl.

* make sure that it's only done once
  CHECK first_time = abap_true.

* get the InteractiveForm ui element
  lr_interactive_form ?= view->get_element(
                           'INTERACTIVE_FORM' ).

* get the method handler of the InteractiveForm
* ui element
  lr_method_handler ?=
    lr_interactive_form->_method_handler.

* set legacyEditingEnabled to true
  lr_method_handler->set_legacy_editing_enabled(
                       abap_true ).
ENDMETHOD.
```

Listing 8.4 Setting legacyEditingEnabled in wdDoModifyView

Now, the interactive form with the DDIC interface is ready for input. You can find the corresponding example in the Web Dynpro component, `ZADB_ONLINE_INPFLD_DDIC`.

Integrating ACF-Based Forms

Now that the ZCI integration has been described in great detail, only one aspect remains to be discussed—the integration of ACF-based form templates. Because SAP doesn't develop new features for such form templates and because ACF form templates have the disadvantages previously discussed, you should always use the ZCI integration for new form templates.

Before ZCI was developed, customers used ACF and went live with their projects. Because a retroactive changeover to ZCI is not required as long as the conditions remain unchanged (e.g., system, user requirements) or a changeover is not yet worthwhile, you will still come across ACF-based form templates. Therefore, the following briefly discusses ACF integration.

You must implement the following when using ACF form templates:

▸ Set the layout type of the form template to XACF LAYOUT

▸ Use the controls from the ACTIVEX palette of Form Builder

▸ Don't add any ZCI script to the form

▸ Change the `displayType` from NATIVE (ZCI) to ACTIVEX (ACF) in the `InteractiveForm` UI element

In more recent support packages, the `displayType` property is automatically set to NATIVE after inserting an `InteractiveForm` UI element so that a useful default value is specified for the ZCI form templates. Note that the default value in the `CL_WD_INTERACTIVE_FORM` class is still set to ACTIVEX due to the necessary downward compatibility.

> **Caution: Pitfall!**
> There are numerous pitfalls for the creation of interactive PDF forms. The following is a checklist. The ZCI-based form becomes interactive only if all of these points are met.
> ▸ The `enabled` property is activated.
> ▸ The `readOnly` property is not activated.
> ▸ The `displayType` property has the NATIVE value. (Note: In older support packages the default value is ACTIVEX.)

- For a DDIC form template, `legacyEditingEnabled` was activated using the method handler.
- The layout type of the form template is ZCI OR XACF.
- The controls from the correct Web Dynpro palette in Form Builder were used.
- The ZCI script is available and up to date.

Connecting Value Help

This section discusses a convenient function that is indispensable when running an average business application in the SAP environment—value help. The design of the value help connection ensures that the user can use the same scope of input help types for an interactive form as is available in Web Dynpro. You can set the type of value help in the corresponding context attribute as usual. The connection of the Object Value Selector (OVS) or a freely programmed value help is also fully identical.

Refer to the Web Dynpro online help for more information on the integration of value helps with Web Dynpro ABAP. There you'll find a comprehensive description of the options available. In addition, you'll find an implementation of all these options in an interactive PDF form in the Web Dynpro component, `ZADB_ONLINE_VALUE_HELP`.

What's new is the connection of the value help to the Web Dynpro context by means of Form Builder. Here, you must note that the availability of a value help must already be specified in Form Builder via a corresponding control at design time. For a Web Dynpro `Inputfield` this is done only at runtime. This means that the value help button is always visible in interactive forms—even if no value help is defined in the context attribute at runtime.

The other effect is that the value help button occupies space in the form. If a table field is supposed to receive a value help button, this button is always visible for all rows of this column. In Web Dynpro it is only visible if you click or put the focus on `Inputfield`, for example, through tabbing. Therefore, interactive forms with a value help don't correspond to a paper form. Here, you must make a compromise between the detailed mapping of a paper form and user friendliness.

But how do you actually integrate a value help with an interactive form?

1. Create a Web Dynpro component with a simple interactive form according to the description in the "Processing Input Fields" section.

2. Use a data element that already contains a value help, for example, S_CARR_ID (the airline), as the type of the context attribute that is assigned to the Text-field in the PDF form. This way, the Web Dynpro runtime environment knows which value help to display. The value selected by the user is automatically populated to the context attribute.

3. A trigger is required in the PDF form to display the value help. For this reason, the WEB DYNPRO NATIVE library contains the Value Help control (see Figure 8.39). Drag and drop this control next to the Text Field.

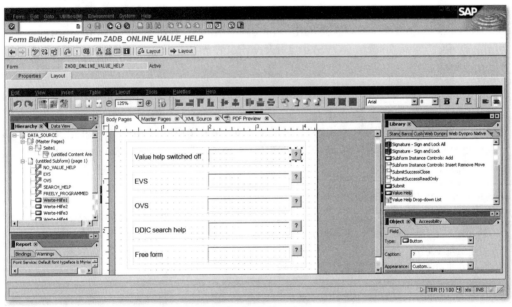

Figure 8.39 VALUE HELP Button in the Form Template

Caution: Pitfall!

The Value Help Drop-Down List control is available in addition to the Value Help control. This value help is displayed as a dropdown list. Unfortunately, only the OVS can be displayed this way. All other value sets resulting from value helps can't be provided as a dropdown list by the user (more than one result field, too large data quantity, filter options available via the value help, and so on).

If this was the case, you could also use a dropdown list directly. The alternative of opening an empty dropdown list with a subsequent value help dialog for the other value help types doesn't make sense from a usability standpoint. For these reasons, Web Dynpro ABAP doesn't support this control.

4. If you execute your application now, you will see that nothing happens. The reason is that the Value Help button doesn't know which Text Field it belongs to. Because the layout and the data are separated also in a form template, the Value Help button contains a data binding instead of a reference to another control.

   This data binding can't be set via the object properties, but must be entered manually in the button's script. To do so, click on the Value Help button and open the script area in Form Builder.

5. Then, enter the value of the binding in the row below the comment. The result for the binding to the NO_VALUE_HELP attribute is:

   ```
   var fieldName = "NO_VALUE_HELP";
   ```

   Figure 8.40 illustrates this.

Figure 8.40 Data Path Sent to the Server via the VALUE HELP Button

You may notice that this is not a classic binding, but rather some kind of pointer or reference that is sent to the server when the button is activated. The Value Help button uses the script of the click event to send the data path to the server for which the value help is to be called.

The Web Dynpro runtime on the server maps this data path from the PDF form back to a path in the context. It then determines the value help to be shown and displays it as a pop-up window. If no value help is available, a message is displayed.

Web Dynpro ABAP supports the connection of a value help to ZCI form templates as of SAP NetWeaver 7.0 SP 12. SAP Note 1029721 describes the necessary adaptations.

> **Caution: Pitfall!**
>
> If you forget to set the data path in the script, no error message is displayed either in Form Builder or at runtime. Clicking the Value Help button doesn't trigger any reaction of the system.
>
> If the path can't be mapped in the Web Dynpro context, a short dump is triggered at runtime. In the ViewDesigner, no error message is sent at design time.
>
> If you change a form interface, you should check to see if the script of the Value Help buttons must be adapted.

Using Dropdown Lists

As of SAP NetWeaver 7.0 SP 10 or with SAP Note 983699, application developers have the option to integrate dropdown lists with their ZCI form template whose entries are automatically set by the system. Up to that point, values in dropdown lists had to be included in the form template at design time.

Like for the Web Dynpro UI element, DropdownByKey, the entries of a dropdown list in a ZCI form template are taken from the ValueSet of the context attribute to which the dropdown list binds. If the type of the context attribute includes a domain with fixed values, these are automatically used. The NodeInfo of a context node provides the option to set a ValueSet dynamically at runtime via the SET_ATTRIBUTE_VALUE_SET method.

The following example illustrates the use of a dropdown list in an interactive PDF form. You can find the example in the Web Dynpro component, ZADB_ONLINE_DROPDOWN.

1. Create a Web Dynpro component with a view and a window.

2. In the view, create a DATA_SOURCE node with the cardinality 1:1 and with a CLASS attribute of type S_CLASS (see Figure 8.41). This data element already contains a domain with three fixed values for the cabin classes on an airplane (first, business, economy). These values are supposed to be displayed as a dropdown list in an interactive form later on.

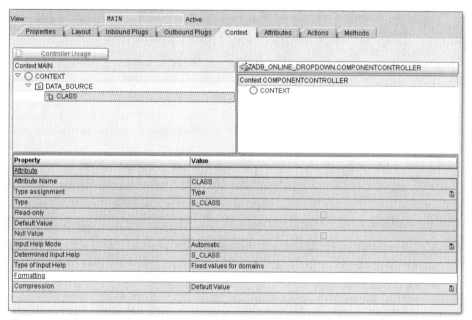

Figure 8.41 The Context Editor Automatically Recognizes that the Context Attribute CLASS has Fixed Values

3. Set the layout of RootUIElementContainer to RowLayout. In the view, create a DropdownByKey with Label and a Button with a dummy Action for triggering a roundtrip. The selectedKey property of DropdownByKey should bind to the CLASS context attribute (see Figure 8.42).

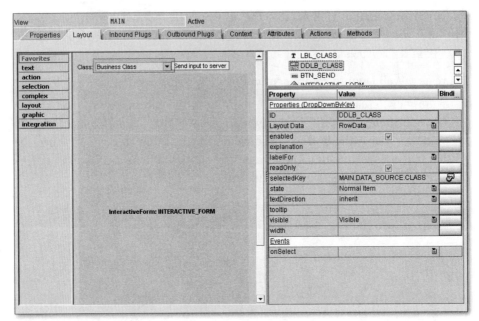

Figure 8.42 DROPDOWNBYKEY UI Element Binds Directly to the CLASS Context Attribute

Create a Web Dynpro application package for the component. Now, you have already created a functioning dropdown list in an application using the onboard means of Web Dynpro. Use this option as a countercheck to the dropdown list in the interactive PDF form later on.

4. Once the Web Dynpro dropdown list functions, create an `InteractiveForm` UI element on the view in the next step. Set its `LayoutData` to `RowHeadData` so that it appears in a new row.

5. Bind the `dataSource` property to the `DATA_SOURCE` context node.

6. Create a new ZCI-based form template by entering the name of a new form template in the `templateSource` property and using the context node. Form Builder displays the `CLASS` attribute as a dropdown list in the DATA VIEW palette (see Figure 8.43).

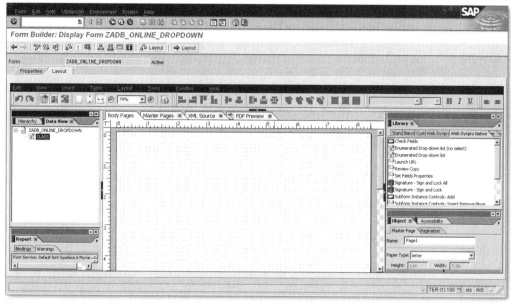

Figure 8.43 Form Builder Displays the CLASS Attribute as a Dropdown List

> **Caution: Pitfall!**
>
> Even if a dropdown list is already displayed for the CLASS attribute in the DATA VIEW, you must not drag and drop the attribute to the form template.
>
> Although Adobe LiveCycle Designer automatically creates a dropdown list in the empty form template, this dropdown list is still an ordinary dropdown list and not a ZCI-based dropdown list from the WEB DYNPRO NATIVE library. It doesn't provide the option to automatically assign a value set from the Web Dynpro context.

7. In the WEB DYNPRO NATIVE library, you are provided with three different drop-down lists:

   ▸ NUMBERED DROP-DOWN LIST

   ▸ NUMBERED DROP-DOWN LIST (NO SELECTION)

   ▸ VALUE HELP DROP-DOWN LIST

   Only the two types of numbered dropdown lists are real dropdown lists, that is, they represent the ValueSet of a context attribute. For more information on the VALUE HELP DROP-DOWN LIST see "Connecting the Value Help" in Section 8.5.2.

8. The difference between the two actual dropdown lists is that you don't have to select an entry for NUMBERED DROP-DOWN LIST (NO SELECTION). This is mapped in the context with the initial value of the context attribute.

Because the user has to select first class, business class, or economy for a flight booking in the present example, choose the NUMBERED DROP-DOWN LIST and drag and drop it to the form template. The data binding is also done by drag and drop. To do this, drag the CLASS attribute from the data view to the previously created dropdown list.

9. Then, change the text of the dropdown list to "Class," adjust the size of the form template, and add a Send button. The intermediate result should appear as illustrated in Figure 8.44.

> **Caution: Pitfall!**
>
> In Adobe LiveCycle Designer 7.1, you must also specify a binding path for the items of the dropdowns. This can be done via a special dialog in the BINDING tab that is called via the SPECIFY ITEM VALUE link. In the displayed path, $record.sap-vhlist.REPLACE_THIS. item[*], you must replace REPLACE_THIS with the name of the attribute (see Figure 8.45). In Adobe LiveCycle Designer 8, this is no longer required (see Figure 8.46).

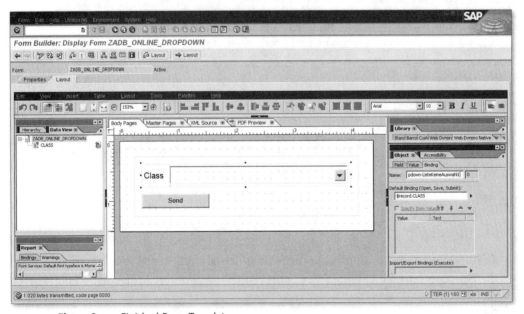

Figure 8.44 Finished Form Template

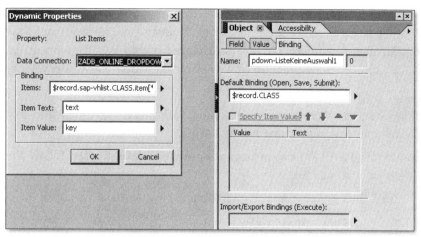

Figure 8.45 Dynamic Properties—Adobe LiveCycle Designer 7.1

Figure 8.46 Dynamic Properties—Adobe LiveCycle Designer 8

10. Activate the form template and the form interface. But first, check to see if you have removed all of the pitfalls for interactive forms (ZCI script available, ZCI layout type) and return to the ViewDesigner in Web Dynpro.

11. Activate the `enabled` property for the `InteractiveForm` UI element.

12. Activate the view and test the application. The interactive form should now be displayed in the browser. If the dropdown list is changed within the form, and if a roundtrip is triggered, the change should be displayed in the `DropdownByKey` UI element.

In the next section, let's take a look at the form data. You can export the data from the PDF form using a function from the Adobe Reader menu. Unfortunately, the Adobe Reader menu is not visible if it is displayed within Web Dynpro in the browser. The corresponding function isn't available via the Adobe Reader toolbar either.

1. Therefore, start the Web Dynpro application package and save the form as a PDF file on your computer using Adobe Reader.

2. Then, open the PDF file in a separate window. In Adobe Reader, follow the menu path DOCUMENT • FORMS • EXPORT DATA...

3. Save the XML file on your computer and double-click on the file to open it.

4. Below the XML Node, `<sap-vhlist>`, you'll find the items existing in the drop-down list (see Figure 8.47). If a second context node, FOO, was available, which would also include a ValueSet, an XML node, FOO, with an equivalent substructure would appear parallel to the XML node, CLASS. The XML node, CLASS, directly below the XML node, DATA_SOURCE, contains the input of the user.

```xml
<?xml version="1.0" encoding="UTF-8" ?>
- <DATA_SOURCE>
    <CLASS />
  - <sap-vhlist>
    - <CLASS>
      - <item>
          <key>C</key>
          <text>Business Class</text>
        </item>
      - <item>
          <key>Y</key>
          <text>Economy Class</text>
        </item>
      - <item>
          <key>F</key>
          <text>First Class</text>
        </item>
      </CLASS>
    </sap-vhlist>
  </DATA_SOURCE>
```

Figure 8.47 Form Data Exported from the PDF Form

This XML is exchanged between Adobe Reader and the server in each roundtrip. So, you can draw the following two conclusions:

▶ Because the value quantities are constantly transported back and forth, dropdown lists can have a decisive influence on the performance of an interactive form. Make sure that you use as few entries as possible in a dropdown list and utilize an input help for larger value quantities.

▶ There is no dynamic reload of the items of the dropdown list. All values of all dropdown lists are always available in the data XML.

Regarding the performance for the generation of an interactive PDF form via ADS, this process is considerably decelerated on the server as of a specific number of entries per dropdown list. Depending on the ADS version used and hardware, an upper limit of 50 entries should not be exceeded (see SAP Note 1013227 for Web Dynpro Java; with regard to the upper limit, this also applies to Web Dynpro ABAP, although the `sap.valuesetlimit.maxondemand` parameter doesn't exist on the ABAP stack).

Integrating Tables

Not all forms just consist of individual fields. Frequently, users must enter similar data whose number is not specified in advance—just consider the items of a sales order, for example. The representation of such data is done row by row in a table.

This option is also available in SAP Interactive Forms by Adobe. In combination with Web Dynpro, the data of the table originates from the context of the view in which the `InteractiveForm` UI element is located. In the next section, we'll create a corresponding example. You can find the result in the Web Dynpro component, `ZADB_ONLINE_TABLE`.

1. Create a new Web Dynpro component with a view, a window, and an appropriate application. In the context of the view, create a `DATA_SOURCE` node with the cardinality 1:1 and with a `SCARR` subnode of type `SCARR` (the database table; see Figure 8.48).

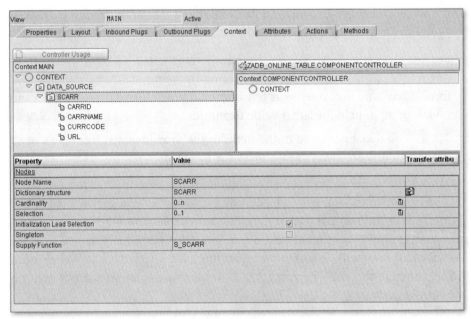

Figure 8.48 Context With the SCARR Node of the SCARR Type (List of Airlines)

2. This node is populated with the content of the database table later on. To do this, create a supply function, S_SCARR, and populate the node as shown in Listing 8.5:

```
METHOD s_scarr.
  DATA:
    lt_scarr TYPE wd_this->elements_scarr.

* get the list of carriers from database
  SELECT * FROM scarr INTO TABLE lt_scarr UP TO 13 ROWS.

* bind all the elements
  node->bind_table( new_items = lt_scarr ).
ENDMETHOD.
```

Listing 8.5 S_SCARR Supply Function

3. As in the previous example, you should first check to see if the implementation can be done using pure Web Dynpro means. To do that, create a `Table` UI element in the view and bind the `dataSource` property to the `SCARR` node.

4. Then, use the table wizard to generate the columns of each table containing an `Inputfield` as the `CellEditor`.

5. Activate the `readOnly` property for the table because the user is supposed to enter his data in the `InteractiveForm` UI element later on. The table is used to check the inputs in the PDF form only (see Figure 8.49).

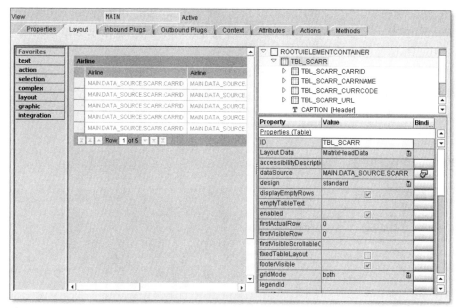

Figure 8.49 Using a Web Dynpro Table for Displaying the List of Airlines

6. Now, activate all items and start the application you previously created. The table should be populated with the list of airlines in the browser (see Figure 8.50).

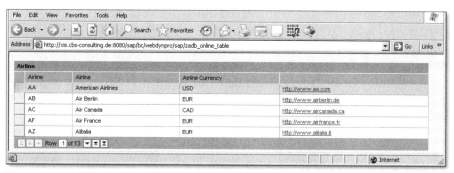

Figure 8.50 Table Containing the List of Airlines

399

If the application works and the table is displayed in the browser, your next task is to create a form template with an equivalent table.

1. To do so, create an `InteractiveForm` UI element in the view.

2. Generate a new ZCI-based form template from the ViewDesigner just as in the previous examples.

3. Again, use the `DATA_SOURCE` node as the root node for the interface of your form template. If you switch to Form Builder, you should see the table and its fields in the DATA VIEW palette.

   You should notice immediately that a `DATA` node was added between `SCARR` and the table fields (see Figure 8.51). This extra node is necessary whenever a 0:N or 1:N context node is used by Web Dynpro. It symbolizes the table row; in Web Dynpro this is a context element.

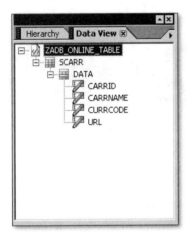

Figure 8.51 Converted Structure of the SCARR Context Node in the Data View Palette

4. The easiest way to generate the table is to drag and drop the table node from the data view to the form template. Here, a column, including a column header, is automatically created for each attribute (see Figure 8.52). For each respective table column, the system automatically selects an editor suitable for the attribute type and establishes the corresponding binding.

   Provided that a dropdown list is generated automatically, you must replace it with a corresponding dropdown list from the WEB DYNPRO NATIVE library. For more information on this topic, please refer to "Using Dropdown Lists" in Section 8.5.2.

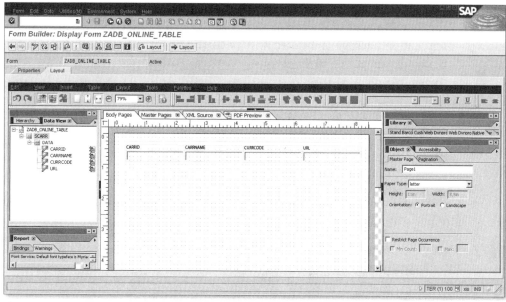

Figure 8.52 Table Generated via Dragging and Dropping the SCARR Node from the Data View

5. Then, add a SEND button above the table so that the data entries can be sent to the server (see Figure 8.53).

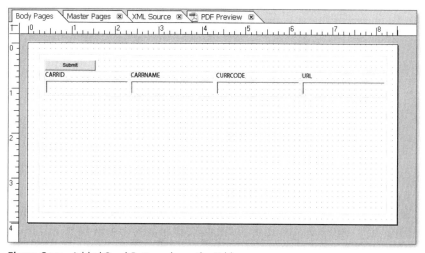

Figure 8.53 Added Send Button above the Table

6. Make all other necessary ZCI settings. Activate the form template and return to the ViewDesigner in Web Dynpro. Activate the view and start the Web Dynpro application package associated with the component. The system displays the ready-for-input table in the form.

Change a field of the table displayed in the form, for example, change the URL of Air Berlin from ".de" to ".com" (see Figure 8.54).

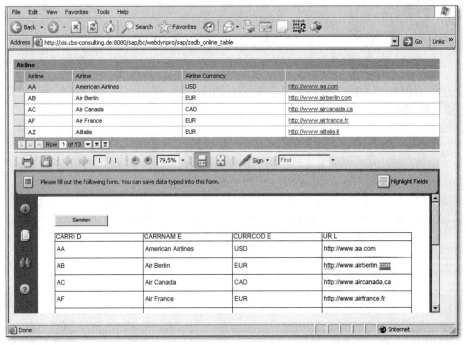

Figure 8.54 Ready-for-Input Table

7. If you click on the SEND button, the change is sent to the server. It then appears in the superordinate Web Dynpro table.

The form data of the PDF form that is available as XML is also interesting in this example. Extract the data analog to the dropdown list example (see "Using Dropdown Lists" in Section 8.5.2). As shown in Figure 8.55, the data XML always contains all of the table rows. Because the data XML is always sent back and forth between the server and Adobe Reader, you should do the following:

```
<?xml version="1.0" encoding="UTF-8" ?>
<DATA_SOURCE>
 - <SCARR>
  - <DATA>
     <CARRID>AA</CARRID>
     <CARRNAME>American Airlines</CARRNAME>
     <CURRCODE>USD</CURRCODE>
     <URL>http://www.aa.com</URL>
     <MANDT>100</MANDT>
   </DATA>
  - <DATA>
     <CARRID>AB</CARRID>
     <CARRNAME>Air Berlin</CARRNAME>
     <CURRCODE>EUR</CURRCODE>
     <URL>http://www.airberlin.com</URL>
     <MANDT>100</MANDT>
   </DATA>
```

Figure 8.55 Excerpt of the Data XML of the Table Example

▶ Avoid tables with a high number of rows due to performance reasons

▶ Limit the number of columns to the required minimum

With regard to the table rows, different aspects exist for interactive forms (in contrast to static print forms), which are discussed in more detail in the following sections.

Adding or Deleting Table Rows from the Form

Adding or deleting table rows from the form is not easy. Although you can add new table rows to a table or delete existing ones via a script in the form at runtime, you still have to consistently transfer this change to the server.

The Web Dynpro runtime receives the data from Adobe Reader and examines it to see if one or more context attributes should be updated. For table-like data, this examination is done row by row. If a row is missing in the received data, the attribute values of the subsequent rows overwrite their former preceding rows. The last row (corresponding to the last Web Dynpro context element) is not deleted or changed. Its content is available twice.

If, however, the received data contains an additional row, the update of the attribute values of the last table row in the appropriate context node will fail because no corresponding context element has been created. This results in a RABAX (short dump).

A solution for the deletion problem is to use a hidden column with a deletion indicator. If it is set, you can delete the unnecessary row from the context node through coding, for example, in the `wdDoBeforeAction` method.

There are two possible solutions to the problem of adding rows:

▶ On one hand, you can always provide a specific number of empty context elements in the context node of the table, which the user can fill. Once all of these context elements are filled, you can generate new ones on the server.

▶ On the other hand, you can completely omit the script in the form and generate new rows via the server. To do this, create a `Group` UI element around the `InteractiveForm` UI element. Insert a `Toolbar` in the `Group` and place an "Add row" `ToolbarButton` there (see Figure 8.56). You can find an example in the Web Dynpro component, `ZADB_ONLINE_TABLE_DYN`.

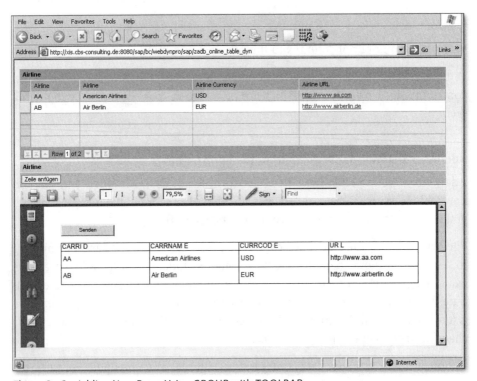

Figure 8.56 Adding New Rows Using GROUP with TOOLBAR

The same procedure is also an alternative for solving the deletion problem. Note that a user can't decide which row to delete using the button outside the form. Here, you need a separate selection column in your table that you must evaluate on the server.

Caution: Performance Pitfall!

According to the SAP support team, performance and memory problems can occur when table rows are dynamically added to or deleted from a PDF form.

Also, refer to the information and recommendations provided by Adobe regarding the performance of dynamic interactive forms. It is available on the Adobe website at *http://www.adobe.com/devnet/livecycle/articles/DynamicInteractiveFormPerformance.pdf*.

In this context, you should also consider omitting the PDF form in your online scenario and creating the form directly in Web Dynpro using only the Table UI element. Another case in which such a step makes sense is discussed in "Can You Use LeadSelection and Selection in a PDF Form?" in Section 8.5.2.

The Table Content is Larger Than the Page

If a table is larger than the page height specified in Form Builder, the table is cut off at the end of the page. You can avoid this by activating the Flowed property for the page. The disadvantage of this procedure is that the elements can't be positioned on the page any longer.

To prevent this problem, you can use the numerous binding options in Form Builder to distribute the table to multiple pages. In the table example presented, you could insert a 0:N context node between DATA_SOURCE and SCARR for the current page.

To keep this example as simple as possible, in the ZADB_ONLINE_TABLE sample table the number of selected airlines was restricted to 13 so that the page size is not exceeded.

Can You Use LeadSelection and Selection in a PDF Form?

The short answer is: The two Web Dynpro concepts are not directly supported for interactive PDF forms that are embedded in Web Dynpro.

The long answer is that you can reproduce this functionality in a form using two hidden Boolean attributes and scripts. However, it would go beyond the scope of this chapter to implement and document an example. But the techniques presented here should enable you to create such an application.

> **Caution: Complexity Pitfall!**
>
> When defining the implementation of such complex requirements, you should think twice about the technology to be used. It is recommended avoiding the implementation of such complicated and complex requirements within an interactive PDF form. Instead, consider fulfilling your requirements via onboard means of Web Dynpro. There you can create a plain master/detailed navigation via LeadSelection (for example, to display the list of available flight connections of a selected airline) with just a few clicks and without having to write any source code.
>
> For complex master/detailed scenarios you also need to write source code in Web Dynpro, for example, to recover entered detail data if LeadSelection of the master node is changed at the same time.
>
> Implementing such a requirement by means of an interactive PDF form is questionable due to the incurring development costs and the resulting TCO. Here, the use of Web Dynpro is the more cost-efficient alternative.

onSubmit Event

In all of the previous examples, a SEND button was positioned on the PDF form. It was used to send the entered data to the server. The InteractiveForm UI element contains an onSubmit event that is triggered as soon as you click the SEND button on the PDF form.

The following example discusses the behavior of the button, the sending of data to the server, and triggering of the event in detail. The example is kept simple intentionally: A counter is increased by one each time the event is triggered.

1. Create a new Web Dynpro component with a view, a window, and an appropriate application.

2. In the view, place an Inputfield UI element along with a Label (displays the current counter reading) and a Button to trigger roundtrips to the server. Bind the value property of the Inputfield to a COUNTER context attribute of type I and set the Inputfield to readOnly.

3. Create an `InteractiveForm` UI element. Bind the `dataSource` property to a new context node with the `VALUE` attribute of the `STRING` type.

4. Create a new ZCI-based form template from the ViewDesigner. On the form template, place a `Text Field` that binds to the `VALUE` attribute from the DATA VIEW palette.

5. Add a SEND button to the form template.

6. The Web Dynpro Native library contains other buttons in addition to the Send button. However, they are not supported by Web Dynpro ABAP (SAP Note 1098009). To illustrate the side effects of using the wrong button, add the Check Box button to the form. Form Builder automatically labels the button with Check (see Figure 8.57).

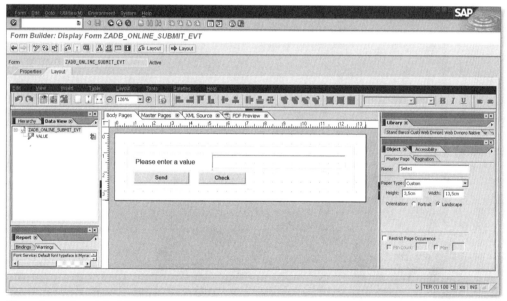

Figure 8.57 Completed Form

7. Activate the form template and return to the ViewDesigner in Web Dynpro.

8. Create a new `ON_SUBMIT` action and bind it to the `onSubmit` event of the `InteractiveForm` UI element. The counter should increase by one within the action. This is done using Listing 8.6.

```
METHOD onactionon_submit.
  DATA:
    counter TYPE I.

* increase the counter by 1
  wd_context->get_attribute(
    EXPORTING
      name = 'COUNTER'
    IMPORTING
      value = counter ).
  ADD 1 TO counter.
  wd_context->set_attribute(
    name  = 'COUNTER'
    value = counter ).
ENDMETHOD.
```

Listing 8.6 Action Handler of the ON_SUBMIT Action

9. Activate the Web Dynpro component and start the application you created previously (see Figure 8.58).

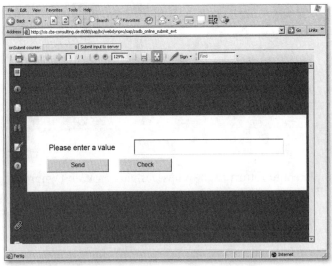

Figure 8.58 Completed Application for Examining the Behavior of the ONSUBMIT Event

By means of this application, you can examine the behavior of the `onSubmit` event of the `InteractiveForm` UI element. The behavior is as follows:

- Clicking the Web Dynpro button doesn't trigger the `onSubmit` event. This is because in Web Dynpro only one event can be triggered within a roundtrip and so only the action of this event can be processed. Therefore, the `onAction` event of the button is used. As described in the previous sections, the data change to the form is transferred to the server and is available in the action handler of the button event.

- Only if the request is submitted from within the PDF form to the server is the `onSubmit` event of `InteractiveForm` UI element triggered. This can be done by clicking on SEND or CHECK.

- There is no difference between SEND and CHECK because the Check Box control behind CHECK is not supported by Web Dynpro ABAP. The SEND button is the only control supported by Web Dynpro ABAP that you can use to send data to the server.

- Triggering the `onSubmit` event is independent of a data change in the form. The `onSubmit` event is triggered for each click of the `Send` button.

Hiding the Toolbar of Adobe Reader

In the online scenario the Adobe Reader toolbars may be irrelevant if the user doesn't use the functions provided there in the context of the particular application. However, they occupy a certain space in Adobe Reader.

Due to this requirement, SAP has developed an option so you can hide these toolbars. The method handler of the `InteractiveForm` UI element provides two corresponding methods — `SET_HIDE_TOOLBARS` for setting the visibility and `GET_HIDE_TOOLBARS` for reading a previously made setting.

> **Caution: Pitfall!**
>
> A user can display (and hide) the toolbars anytime using the F8 key. So don't assume that the toolbars are inaccessible. The result is that the `GET_HIDE_TOOLBARS` method only returns the last value set by you or the default value, but not the current visibility state of the toolbars in Adobe Reader.

The following example details how you can hide toolbars in Adobe Reader. You can find it in the Web Dynpro component, `ZADB_ONLINE_HIDE_TOOLBAR`.

1. Create a new Web Dynpro component. Here, you can use and copy the input field example for implementing the online scenario. It is the simplest example to add this new feature.

2. In the `wdDoModifyView` method of the view, add the source code shown in Listing 8.7:

```
METHOD wddomodifyview.
  DATA:
    lr_interactive_form TYPE REF TO
      cl_wd_interactive_form.

* make sure that it's only done once
  CHECK first_time = abap_true.

* get the InteractiveForm ui element
  lr_interactive_form ?= view->get_element(
                         'INTERACTIVE_FORM' ).

* get the method handler of the InteractiveForm
* ui element
  wd_this->m_method_handler ?=
    lr_interactive_form->_method_handler.

* set hideToolbars to true
  wd_this->m_method_handler->set_hide_toolbars( abap_true ).
ENDMETHOD.
```

Listing 8.7 wdDoModifyView Method

3. To activate the source code, you must create a new M_METHOD_HANDLER attribute of the IF_WD_IACTIVE_FORM_METHOD_HNDL type in the ATTRIBUTES tab of the view. This is the interface of the method handler.

   In contrast to the DDIC variant for the input field example, the method handler is now stored in the view for testing purposes to toggle the visibility of the toolbars according to the display of Adobe Reader. Provided that you don't want to implement this test, you can also define the method handler as a local variable in the source code of `wdDoModifyView`.

4. To test the toolbar toggle functionality, create a new Button UI element, TOGGLE_TOOLBAR, in the view and define a new action in the `onAction` event. Within

the action handler, the system first reads the status of the toolbar visibility that is available on the server; then it changes the status and defines the changed value by calling the method handler.

The source code of the `ON_TOGGLE_TOOLBAR` action handler shows the individual steps (see Listing 8.8).

```
METHOD onactionon_toggle_toolbar.
  DATA:
    hide_toolbars TYPE abap_bool.

* get the current value of the hideToolbars
  hide_toolbars =
    wd_this->m_method_handler->get_hide_toolbars( ).

* toggle the boolean
  IF hide_toolbars = abap_true.
    hide_toolbars = abap_false.
  ELSE.
    hide_toolbars = abap_true.
  ENDIF.

* save the new value
  wd_this->m_method_handler->set_hide_toolbars(
    hide_toolbars ).
ENDMETHOD.
```

Listing 8.8 Action Handler for the ON_TOGGLE_TOOLBAR Action

5. Activate the Web Dynpro component, create a new Web Dynpro application for the component, and start it.

You can observe the following effects:

▶ Initially, the toolbar is deactivated properly.

▶ You can show the toolbar again by pressing the F8 key.

▶ A click on the Web Dynpro button for toggling the toolbar neither shows the toolbar nor hides a toolbar that was displayed using the F8 key. Nothing happens at all.

The toolbar is only visible in the roundtrip when the `InteractiveForm` UI element becomes visible.

> **Caution: Pitfall!**
>
> To link the effect of SET_HIDE_TOOLBARS with a regeneration of the PDF form in the Web Dynpro runtime is more accurate than linking a change to the visibility of the InteractiveForm UI element. At present, the visibility of the toolbars in Adobe Reader is only influenced with the generation of a PDF file.
>
> However, the PDF generation is still implemented under more circumstances than the change of the visibility of the InteractiveForm UI element, to which the setting of SET_HIDE_TOOLBARS also applies:
>
> ▶ You also bind the pdfSource property.
> ▶ You toggle between print and online scenario by changing the enabled property.
>
> Therefore, it is recommended to call SET_HIDE_TOOLBARS once and then make no more changes. This way, you can avoid troubleshooting for side effects.

Try the following to check the two aspects mentioned in the previous box:

▶ Bind the pdfSource property to a new context attribute of type XSTRING. Display its content by means of a second InteractiveForm UI element, in which you only bind the pdfSource property to the same context attribute. Nothing happens after the first switch. This indicates that the population of the XSTRING type context attribute always lags one roundtrip behind the pdfSource property with the PDF file. The effect becomes even clearer if you use a ToggleButton instead of a Button for toggling the visibility of the toolbars.

▶ Create a ToggleButton in the view and bind its checked property to a new ENABLED context attribute of type WDY_BOOLEAN with 'X' as the default value. Also, bind the enabled property of the InteractiveForm UI element to this context attribute.

The sample component, ZADB_ONLINE_HIDE_TOOLBARS, also contains these two cases to illustrate the side effects of the downstream change of the visibility of toolbars in Adobe Reader.

Using Attachments in the Online Scenario

Contrary to the information provided in SAP Note 1080205, attachments are not supported for the online scenario in Web Dynpro ABAP—not even as of SAP NetWeaver 7.0 SP 14 or 7.10 SP 4. SAP Note 1080203 clarifies this. The reason is the poor performance of this feature, because in the online scenario data in Adobe

Reader is continuously exchanged with the server. This also applies to attachments that are directly defined in the PDF form.

Attachments may lead to performance problems due to the data volume to be processed. Frequently, you don't just attach a small text file of only a few kilobytes to the PDF form, but also design drawings or other documents, for example.

If you want to support attachments, you should send them to the server in Web Dynpro via the `FileUpload` UI element and outside Adobe Reader. For example, you can use a table to indicate which files are already available on the server. If users want to take the form with them (i.e., for usage in an offline scenario), you can generate a new PDF file for them on the server using the PDF object API and attach the previously uploaded files.

In Section 8.5.3, "Offline Scenario," you can find detailed information of how you can provide a PDF file to users.

Example: Contact Management Using an Interactive Form

In this section, we'll put into practice the information obtained in the previous sections about the implementation of the online scenario. Naturally, the example is more complex and longer than the previous examples. However, it provides the opportunity to experience the different aspects of Web Dynpro ABAP in combination with the online scenario of the Adobe integration. This example could also be implemented in a real-life customer project (with some minor cosmetic enhancements).

You can find the example in the Web Dynpro component, `ZADB_ONLINE_CONTACT_MGMT`. The corresponding PDF form template and its form interface have the same name.

Scenario Description

The fictitious enterprise, Dual Use Goods Inc., is present at many trade shows to canvass customers. By the end of each day, the employees have gathered a lot of business cards. In addition, the enterprise provides paper contact forms that are filled out by potential customers. This data must then be entered into the enterprise's SAP Customer Relationship Management (CRM) system. This data entry occupies employees who would otherwise be available for consulting tasks.

To accelerate the input of the numerous business cards and contact forms, the enterprise created an Adobe form that looks like an average business card. It replaces the web application in the enterprise's CRM system that has been used by the employees up to now.

The computer is freely accessible at the booth and potential customers can enter their data themselves. The benefit of this approach is that the completion of a paper form and the associated manual or Optical Character Recognition (OCR)–supported input of data into the CRM system are omitted.

A business card always contains the following basic data:

▶ Name of the company

▶ Name of the contact partner

▶ Function of the contact partner within the company

▶ Address of the contact partner in the company

For the sake of simplicity, the following restrictions apply:

▶ Only the first two out of the four possible lines are to be used for the company name.

▶ For the name of the contact partner, only the first and the last name are used. In addition, you can specify the title (e.g., Mr., Mrs.). German is specified as the correspondence language.

▶ For the address of the company, you only consider the fields, street, house number, ZIP code, and city. Germany is specified as the country.

▶ In addition to the address, you can enter the telephone number, fax number, and email address as communication data.

After the form has been submitted, the system implements the following:

▶ The entered company is created as a business partner in the prospect role provided that no company of the same name already exists in the system.

▶ The address of the company is created if it doesn't exist yet.

▶ The contact partner is created as a business partner in the contact role provided that no business partner of the same name already exists in the system.

▶ The "Has Contact Person" relationship is created between the contact and the prospect. The previously created address is assigned to the relationship as the standard address. All additional communication data is assigned to the relationship.

This example can be continued by populating additional fields. In addition, you could automatically assign an employee responsible for the new company. Or you could trigger a workflow process to integrate the company with the processes.

1. In the first step, create the interface to the form. It must contain all fields that can be entered by the user. Ideally, you do this within the Web Dynpro component in the context of the view because you can easily structure the data there (see Figure 8.59). The completed context contains the structured composition fields of the business card, typed with Business Application Programming Interface (BAPI) structures.

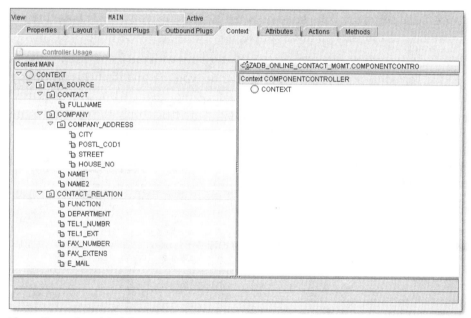

Figure 8.59 Completed Context

2. In SAP CRM, business partners are saved in the BUT000 tables and addresses of organizations in the ADRC table. There are also several dependent tables with detail data. The BAPI_BUPA_CREATE_FROM_DATA function module is available for the creation of a business partner (including the address). This function module has its own structures for data transfer whose field names are partly different from the database tables. For this reason, instead of the database tables the structures from the call of the function module are specified in the context nodes as follows:

- ▶ CONTACT with BAPIBUS1006_CENTRAL_PERSON

- ▶ COMPANY with BAPIBUS1006_CENTRAL_ORGAN

- ▶ COMPANY_ADDRESS with BAPIBUS1006_ADDRESS

- ▶ CONTACT_RELATION with BAPIBUS1006002_CENTRAL

3. Now, add the InteractiveForm UI element to the view. After you've bound the dataSource property to the top-level node of the previously created node hierarchy in the context and set the enabled property, enter the name of the interface to be created in the templateSource property.

4. Press the ENTER key. Then, create a new form interface as described in Section 8.4.1 and select the same node from the context that you already bound to the dataSource property. In this example, it is the DATA_SOURCE node.

5. The system creates a new form template together with the interface and switches to Form Builder. As shown in Figure 8.60, you can find the fields previously created in the context on the left-hand side. Although the DDIC structures used by the context node contain considerably more fields, only the used fields are transferred.

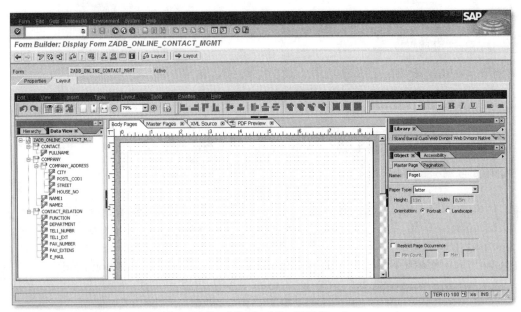

Figure 8.60 Form Builder with Used Fields of the BAPI Structures

6. Now, drag and drop the individual attributes from the DATA VIEW palette to the form template area. Remember the structure of a real business card when you arrange the text fields. Bear in mind that you must display the fields for the function and the department as dropdown lists. Use the corresponding dropdown list from the Web Dynpro Native library.

7. Also, specify the height and width of the form so that all fields are enclosed and no unnecessary space is wasted on the right-hand side and at the bottom. The aim is that the user doesn't have to scroll in the interactive form. Figure 8.61 shows the result.

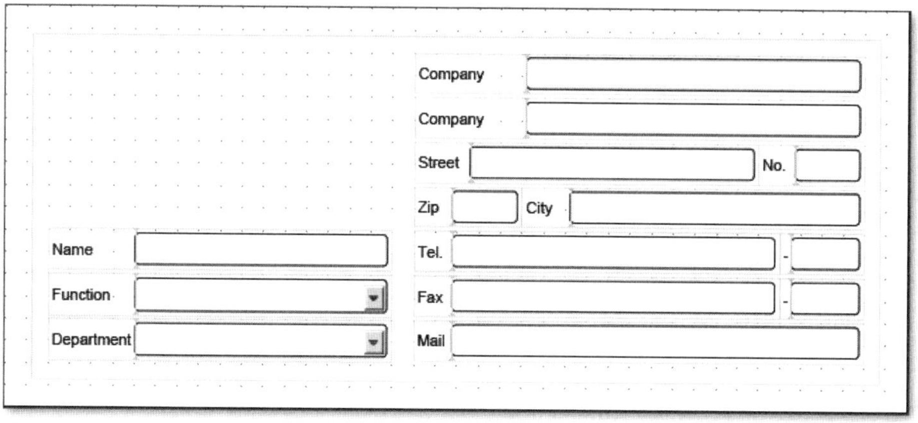

Figure 8.61 Fields Arranged in the Form

8. To improve user acceptance, you could specify a color for the controls. You can change the appearance of a control by selecting the control and choosing the USER-DEFINED... entry from the APPEARANCE DROPDOWN list in the Field subarea of the OBJECT tab. A dialog opens in which you can, for example, round off the corners or specify a background color.

9. Activate the form template and the corresponding interface, and return to the ViewDesigner. Remember to remove the ZCI pitfalls.

10. Because the form has no Send button, create a Button UI element above the InteractiveForm UI element to send the entries to the server and to trigger further processing of the contact data. To do this, create a new ON_SEND action for the onAction event of the Button.

11. You must also create a ValueSet for the dropdown lists because the individual characteristic values of the function and department are not available as fixed

values on the domain. They are each stored in a separate database table. The source code in Listing 8.9 from the `wdDoInit` method of the view adds the entries to the respective context attributes.

```
METHOD wddoinit.
  DATA:
    lr_node_info TYPE REF TO if_wd_context_node_info,
    lt_value_set TYPE wdr_context_attr_value_list.

* get the contact relation node info in order to fill
* fixed values
  lr_node_info = wd_context->get_node_info( ).
  lr_node_info = lr_node_info->get_child_node(
                   wd_this->wdctx_data_source ).
  lr_node_info = lr_node_info->get_child_node(
                   wd_this->wdctx_contact_relation ).

* fill the values of possible functions
  SELECT pafkt AS value bez30 AS text FROM tb913
       INTO TABLE lt_value_set
       WHERE spras = sy-langu.
  lr_node_info->set_attribute_value_set(
    EXPORTING
      name      = 'FUNCTION'
      value_set = lt_value_set ).

* fill the values of possible departments
  CLEAR lt_value_set[].
  SELECT abtnr AS value bez20 AS text FROM tb911
       INTO TABLE lt_value_set
       WHERE spras = sy-langu.
  lr_node_info->set_attribute_value_set(
    EXPORTING
      name      = 'DEPARTMENT'
      value_set = lt_value_set ).
ENDMETHOD.
```

Listing 8.9 wdDoInit Method

12. Activate the Web Dynpro component and create a new Web Dynpro application for the component.

13. You now have an interactive form whose input is sent to the server. Execute the Web Dynpro application to test the form. For example, you can set a breakpoint in the action handler of the ON_SEND action to see for yourself whether your inputs are sent to the server and transferred to the corresponding context attribute. Have the system display the context of your view in the new ABAP Debugger.

14. If everything functions correctly, you can implement the BAPI call in the action handler of the ON_SEND action. Read the input of the user from the respective context node. The types have already been selected at the beginning in accordance with the BAPI calls so that it is rather simple to implement this step. The source code in Listing 8.10 shows the necessary calls.

```
METHOD onactionon_send.
  DATA:
    lr_data_source         TYPE REF TO if_wd_context_node,
    lr_contact             TYPE REF TO if_wd_context_node,
    lr_company             TYPE REF TO if_wd_context_node,
    lr_company_address     TYPE REF TO if_wd_context_node,
    lr_contact_relation    TYPE REF TO if_wd_context_node,
    lv_company             TYPE bu_partner,
    lv_contact             TYPE bu_partner,
    lt_return              TYPE bapiret2_tab,
    ls_centraldata         TYPE bapibus1006_central,
    ls_company_org_data    TYPE bapibus1006_central_organ,
    ls_company_address     TYPE bapibus1006_address,
    ls_contact_data        TYPE bapibus1006_central_person,
    ls_contact_relation_data
                           TYPE bapibus1006002_central,
    lv_company_address_guid
                           TYPE guid,
    lv_company_address_guid2
                           TYPE bu_address_guid_bapi.

  DATA:
    lr_api_controller      TYPE REF TO if_wd_controller,
    lr_message_manager     TYPE REF TO
                           if_wd_message_manager.

  FIELD-SYMBOLS:
    <return> LIKE LINE OF lt_return.
```

```
* get all the context data that contain the data
  lr_data_source      = wd_context->get_child_node(
    wd_this->wdctx_data_source ).
  lr_contact          = lr_data_source->get_child_node(
    wd_this->wdctx_contact ).
  lr_company          = lr_data_source->get_child_node(
    wd_this->wdctx_company ).
  lr_company_address  = lr_company->get_child_node(
    wd_this->wdctx_company_address ).
  lr_contact_relation = lr_data_source->get_child_node(
    wd_this->wdctx_contact_relation ).

* get all the structures with their values out of the
* nodes
  lr_company->get_static_attributes(
    IMPORTING
      static_attributes = ls_company_org_data ).
  lr_company_address->get_static_attributes(
    IMPORTING
      static_attributes = ls_company_address ).
  lr_contact->get_static_attributes(
    IMPORTING
      static_attributes = ls_contact_data ).
  lr_contact_relation->get_static_attributes(
    IMPORTING
      static_attributes = ls_contact_relation_data ).

* add the country to the address, which always DE here
  ls_company_address-country = 'DE'.

* create the company
  CALL FUNCTION 'BAPI_BUPA_CREATE_FROM_DATA'
    EXPORTING
      partnercategory        = '2' "organisation
      centraldata            = ls_centraldata
      centraldataorganization = ls_company_org_data
      addressdata            = ls_company_address
      duplicate_message_type = 'W'
      accept_error           = 'X'
    IMPORTING
      businesspartner        = lv_company
    TABLES
      return                 = lt_return.
```

```
    LOOP AT lt_return ASSIGNING <return>
        WHERE type CA 'AXE'.
      CALL FUNCTION 'BAPI_TRANSACTION_ROLLBACK'.
      display_messages( lt_return ).
      RETURN.
    ENDLOOP.

* add role prospect to it
  CLEAR lt_return[].
  CALL FUNCTION 'BAPI_BUPA_ROLE_ADD_2'
    EXPORTING
      businesspartner              = lv_company
      businesspartnerrolecategory = 'BUP002'
      businesspartnerrole          = 'BUP002'
    TABLES
      return                       = lt_return.
  LOOP AT lt_return ASSIGNING <return>
        WHERE type CA 'AXE'.
      CALL FUNCTION 'BAPI_TRANSACTION_ROLLBACK'.
      display_messages( lt_return ).
      RETURN.
    ENDLOOP.

* create the contact
  SPLIT ls_contact_data-fullname AT ' '
        INTO ls_contact_data-firstname
             ls_contact_data-lastname.
  CALL FUNCTION 'BAPI_BUPA_CREATE_FROM_DATA'
    EXPORTING
      partnercategory       = '1' "person
      centraldata           = ls_centraldata
      centraldataperson     = ls_contact_data
      duplicate_message_type = 'W'
      accept_error          = 'X'
    IMPORTING
      businesspartner       = lv_contact
    TABLES
      return                = lt_return.
  LOOP AT lt_return ASSIGNING <return>
        WHERE type CA 'AXE'.
      CALL FUNCTION 'BAPI_TRANSACTION_ROLLBACK'.
      display_messages( lt_return ).
      RETURN.
    ENDLOOP.
```

```
* add role contact to the contact
  CLEAR lt_return[].
  CALL FUNCTION 'BAPI_BUPA_ROLE_ADD_2'
    EXPORTING
      businesspartner               = lv_contact
      businesspartnerrolecategory = 'BUP001'
      businesspartnerrole           = 'BUP001'
    TABLES
      return                        = lt_return.
  LOOP AT lt_return ASSIGNING <return>
      WHERE type CA 'AXE'.
    CALL FUNCTION 'BAPI_TRANSACTION_ROLLBACK'.
    display_messages( lt_return ).
    RETURN.
  ENDLOOP.

* get the previously created address of the company
  CALL FUNCTION 'BAPI_BUPA_ADDRESSES_GET'
    EXPORTING
      businesspartner     = lv_company
    IMPORTING
      standardaddressguid = lv_company_address_guid
    TABLES
      return              = lt_return.
  LOOP AT lt_return ASSIGNING <return>
      WHERE type CA 'AXE'.
    CALL FUNCTION 'BAPI_TRANSACTION_ROLLBACK'.
    display_messages( lt_return ).
    RETURN.
  ENDLOOP.

* create the contact relation between the company and the
* contact
  lv_company_address_guid2 = lv_company_address_guid.
  CALL FUNCTION 'BAPI_BUPR_CONTP_CREATE'
    EXPORTING
      businesspartner = lv_company
      contactperson   = lv_contact
      addressguid     = lv_company_address_guid2
      centraldata     = ls_contact_relation_data
    TABLES
      return          = lt_return.
```

```
    LOOP AT lt_return ASSIGNING <return>
        WHERE type CA 'AXE'.
      CALL FUNCTION 'BAPI_TRANSACTION_ROLLBACK'.
      display_messages( lt_return ).
      RETURN.
    ENDLOOP.

* commit the changes
    CALL FUNCTION 'BAPI_TRANSACTION_COMMIT'.

* display a success message
    lr_api_controller ?= wd_this->wd_get_api( ).
    lr_message_manager =
      lr_api_controller->get_message_manager( ).
    CALL METHOD lr_message_manager->report_success
      EXPORTING
        message_text =
      'Your contact data have been saved successfully.'.

* clear all fields so that the next person can continue
    lr_data_source->invalidate( ).
ENDMETHOD.
```

Listing 8.10 ActionHandler of the ON_SEND Action

15. Create the DISPLAY_MESSAGES method on the view to display messages from the BAPI function module. The method receives the IT_RETURN importing parameter of the BAPIRET2_TAB type. Listing 8.11 shows the source code for displaying the messages.

```
METHOD display_messages.
  DATA:
    lo_api_controller      TYPE REF TO if_wd_controller,
    lo_message_manager     TYPE REF TO
                             if_wd_message_manager.

  FIELD-SYMBOLS:
    <return> LIKE LINE OF it_return.

* get message manager
  lo_api_controller ?= wd_this->wd_get_api( ).
  lo_message_manager =
    lo_api_controller->get_message_manager( ).
```

```
* report the messages
  LOOP AT it_return ASSIGNING <return>.
    CALL METHOD lo_message_manager->report_t100_message
      EXPORTING
        msgid = <return>-id
        msgno = <return>-number
        msgty = <return>-type
        p1    = <return>-message_v1
        p2    = <return>-message_v2
        p3    = <return>-message_v3
        p4    = <return>-message_v4.
  ENDLOOP.
ENDMETHOD.
```

Listing 8.11 DISPLAY_MESSAGES Method

This message is called if a message of the E, X, or A type occurs after a BAPI call, that is, if an error occurs. Any further processing is cancelled and a rollback using the BAPI_TRANSACTION_ROLLBACK function module is implemented.

A success message is displayed at the end of processing. Then, all input fields of the form are reset. This way, the next future contact partner of an interested company can enter his data at the booth terminal.

This example can also be enhanced with additional features. For example, you can add a second Button UI element to the view that checks the entries of the user without posting them directly in the system.

The following figures show the inputs of a PDF form that is embedded in the Web Dynpro application package and data created in the system later on.

1. The user enters his contact data in the business card (see Figure 8.62).

2. A success message is displayed in the top-left corner after clicking on the Web Dynpro button to send the data. The fields are cleared for the entries of the next user (see Figure 8.63).

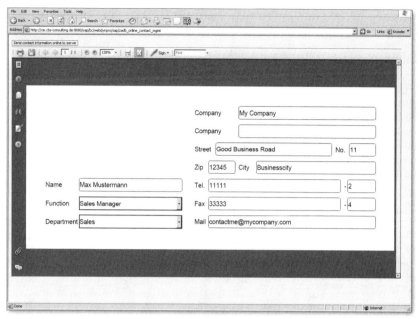

Figure 8.62 Entered Contact Data of the Contact Partner

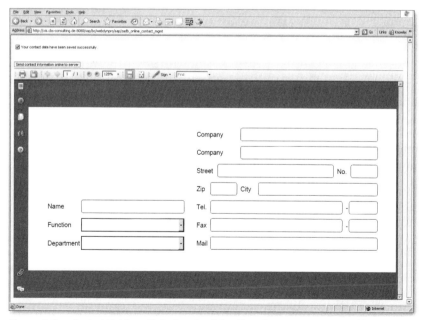

Figure 8.63 Posted Entries—Data Inputs of the Next Contact Person Possible

3. In the business partner master record, the prospect is created as an organization using the data from the business card (see Figure 8.64).

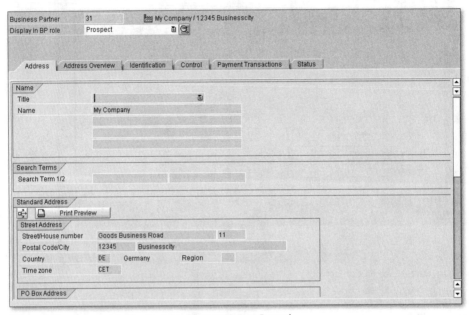

Figure 8.64 Prospect in the Business Partner Master Record

4. In addition, the system creates an address and assigns it to the prospect (see Figure 8.65).

5. The system also creates a contact partner and generates a contact relation between the prospect and the contact (see Figure 8.66).

This example illustrates how simple it is to implement a functioning online scenario using the Adobe integration with Web Dynpro ABAP for a real-life situation. Indeed, the application is not restricted to pure online processing. For example, users can save the (empty or partially completed) form on a memory stick, fill it out offline, and submit it via email or web upload. These and similar offline scenarios are discussed in the following section.

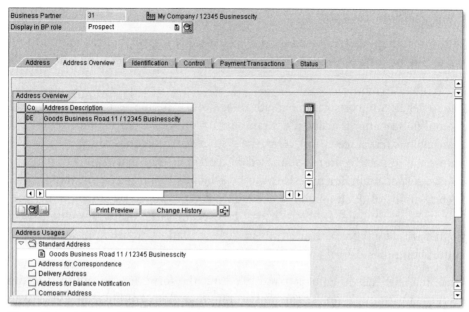

Figure 8.65 Address of the Business Partner

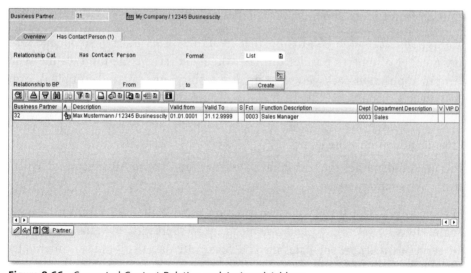

Figure 8.66 Generated Contact Relation and Assigned Address

8.5.3 Offline Scenario

In contrast to the online scenario, the offline scenario provides the option to fill out an Adobe form outside the browser and without a network connection to the server.

The lower license costs can be an advantage of the offline scenario compared to the online scenario. Usually, users can download forms from the intranet (or the Internet in external scenarios). Here, the system doesn't require any named user—unless the respective user is supposed to receive a form that is already partially filled out specifically for him. This can be achieved by means of integrating with Web Dynpro ABAP although it's not required very often. (We'll look at the corresponding techniques in the course of this section.) The offline scenario is very popular for any type of request, for instance, vacation, transfer, insurance, agricultural subsidies.

Once the user has downloaded and filled out the form, he can return it to the server via various channels. The most common options are uploading via a web application (for example, on the website on which the form was downloaded) or submission via email. This section details the implementation of the download and upload of a form in different application cases by means of Web Dynpro ABAP.

At this point, it is important to note that an offline form can be filled out and sent any number of times. Consider this fact when you receive the form via the Web Dynpro application package (avoid duplicate entry) or update the original form (avoid version conflicts).

Providing a Form to the Users

This section describes the options available in Web Dynpro ABAP to provide files to the users for download.

In the first phase of the offline scenario, you provide the PDF form to the user. The options range from a plain download up to sophisticated variants in which the server partially prepopulates the PDF form with data that has been entered by a user in previously implemented business steps.

LinkToURL

The LinkToURL UI element is one of the most convenient ways to provide a file to a user. The file is stored on a web server. The URL that indicates the storage location is entered in the `reference` property. This value can be dynamized through the context binding. A textual description in the `text` property is presented as a web link to the user. This link is executed by the browser.

SAP NetWeaver can also be used as the web server. In this case, you are provided with a number of options (from the simple Internet Communication framework (ICF) server to access to the Knowledge Warehouse).

You can find an example of the `LinkToURL` UI element in the Web Dynpro component, `ZADB_LINK_TO_URL`. It was implemented in the simplest possible way. The PDF file that contains the form was embedded in the component. The `LinkToURL` UI element points to the file (see Figure 8.67). Source code is not required.

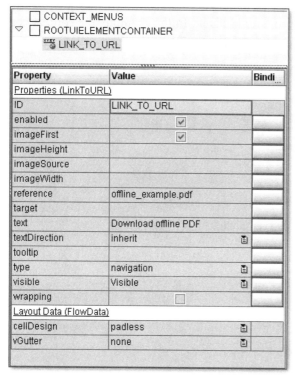

Figure 8.67 LINKTOURL UI Element

FileDownload

For the `FileDownload` UI element, you must provide the data in the roundtrip in which the `FileDownload` UI element is displayed (before the user clicks on it).

This way, a PDF form can be generated based on parameters of a previous step, for example. The name of the file is entered in the `fileName` property. You must select the APPLICATION/PDF value for a PDF file as the MIME type in the `mimeType` property. The file itself is kept in the context and connected via the `data` property. Here, the context attribute should be of the `XSTRING` type. The `FileDownload` UI element is presented as a link to the user. The corresponding text is defined in the `text` property.

The first example that you can find in the Web Dynpro component, `ZADB_FILE_DOWNLOAD`, illustrates how you must activate a `FileDownload` UI element so that the user can download a file. Its functionality is identical to the `LinkToURL` example and enables you to compare the two approaches. In contrast to the `LinkToURL` UI element, for the `FileDownload` UI element you must first load the file into the context attribute that the `data` property binds to. In the example, the context has a `PDF` attribute of the `XSTRING` type (see Figure 8.68).

The context attribute is populated in the `wdDoInit` method of the view according to the procedure described in Section 8.5.1, "Print Scenario" (see Listing 8.12).

```
METHOD wddoinit.
  DATA:
    lr_mime_repository TYPE REF TO if_mr_api,
    content            TYPE XSTRING.

  CONSTANTS:
    url TYPE STRING VALUE
'/SAP/BC/Web Dynpro/SAP/ZADB_FILE_DOWNLOAD/offline_example.pdf'.

  lr_mime_repository = cl_mime_repository_api=>get_api( ).
  lr_mime_repository->get(
    EXPORTING
      i_url = url
    IMPORTING
      e_content = content ).
  wd_context->set_attribute(
    name = 'PDF'
    value = content ).
ENDMETHOD.
```

Listing 8.12 wdDoInit Method

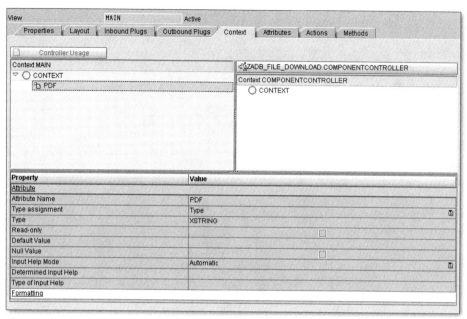

Figure 8.68 PDF File is Loaded into the PDF Context Attribute Later On

Compared to the `LinkToURL` UI element, this example doesn't provide any additional benefit. Instead, it requires more effort to implement it. A `LinkToURL` UI element would have been sufficient here.

For this reason, the PDF form is pre-populated with a value in the next example. To do this, extend the application with an `Inputfield` and a `Button` labeled with CHECK INPUT. If a user wants to continue his work offline, he can have the system generate a PDF form that includes his current entries and can be filled out offline using the CONVERT TO PDF button. The completely generated PDF file can then be provided to the user via the `FileDownload` UI element.

You can find an example in the Web Dynpro component, `ZADB_FILE_DOWNLOAD_ GENPDF`. Figure 8.69 shows the layout of the MAIN view of the component.

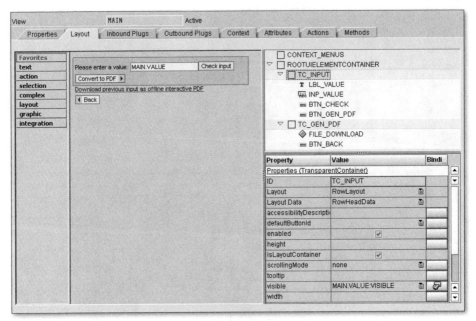

Figure 8.69 Layout of the MAIN View of the Sample Component

The view includes two `TransparentContainer` elements that are visible alternately. The user can activate the buttons, CONVERT TO PDF and BACK, to toggle between the content of the two containers. The `Inputfield` and the `FileDownload` UI element must not be visible at the same time because the current input must be converted into a PDF form prior to the download. Otherwise, the PDF form would only contain the input previously sent to the server.

The use of a supply function for generating a PDF is not a solution either. Although the file would be generated by the supply function in the roundtrip in which the PDF form would be retrieved for the first time, another change to the value in the `Inputfield` and a subsequent click on the `FileDownload` UI element would not result in another PDF generation.

The context of the view contains a VALUE attribute of the STRING type for the entered value and a PDF attribute of the XSTRING type for the generated PDF form. The `visible` property of the `TC_INPUT` `TransparentContainer` binds to the `visible` property of the VALUE context attribute (see Figure 8.70). For `TC_GEN_PDF`, it is the same property in the PDF context attribute.

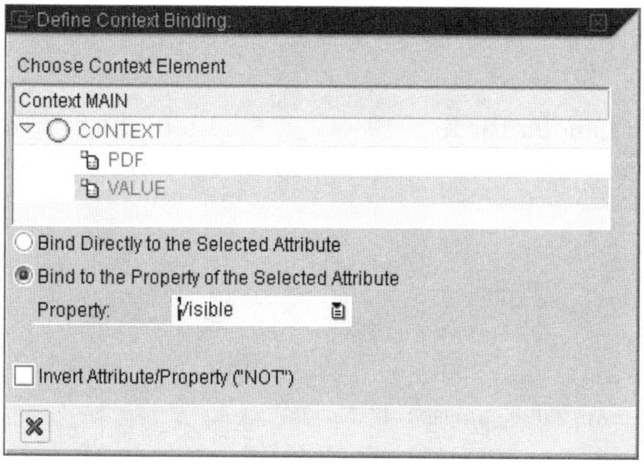

Figure 8.70 TC_INPUT.VISIBLE Binds to VALUE: VISIBLE

Note

If you want to follow this example in a system whose support package level is lower than SP 13, you are not provided with the additional properties of context attributes used here. In this case, you must create additional context attributes of the WDY_BOOLEAN type to control the visibility of the two TransparentContainer elements. Alternatively, you can also use two views instead of only one and toggle between them. Then, you would have to move the VALUE attribute to a new context node that would be mapped in the two views using the ComponentController.

Because the visible property is enabled by default, you must ensure that the area for the PDF form download is not visible initially. This is done in the wdDoInit method of the view using the coding shown in Listing 8.13.

```
METHOD wddoinit.
* make the download area invisible initially
  wd_context->set_attribute_property(
    EXPORTING
      attribute_name = 'PDF'
      property = if_wd_context_element=>e_property-visible
      value = abap_false ).
ENDMETHOD.
```

Listing 8.13 wdDoInit Method

A separate action is assigned to each of the onAction events of the two Web Dynpro buttons. Because the BTN_CHECK button is only used to send data to the server, its action handler doesn't have any source code. The action is also assigned to the onEnter event of the Inputfield UI elements so that a user can also trigger a roundtrip by pressing the [ENTER] key.

In the ONACTIOON_GEN_PDF action handler for the BTN_GEN_PDF button, the source code shown in Listing 8.14 converts the user's input into a PDF file for the File-Download UI element.

```
METHOD onactionon_gen_pdf.
  DATA:
    value             TYPE STRING,
    fm_name           TYPE rs38l_fnam,
    lt_params         TYPE abap_func_parmbind_tab,
    param             LIKE LINE OF lt_params,
    lt_exceptions     TYPE abap_func_excpbind_tab,
    exception         LIKE LINE OF lt_exceptions,
    pdf_ref           TYPE REF TO fpformoutput,
    fp_docparams      TYPE sfpdocparams,
    fp_formoutput     TYPE fpformoutput,
    fp_outputparams   TYPE sfpoutputparams,
    adserrstr         TYPE STRING,
    pdf               TYPE XSTRING,
    lr_api_controller TYPE REF TO if_wd_controller,
    lr_message_manager TYPE REF TO if_wd_message_manager.

* get the current value of the user's input
  wd_context->get_attribute(
    EXPORTING
      name = 'VALUE'
    IMPORTING
      value = value ).


* generate the PDF
* => get the name of the generated function module
  CALL FUNCTION 'FP_FUNCTION_MODULE_NAME'
    EXPORTING
      i_name     = 'ZADB_OFFLINE_EXAMPLE'
    IMPORTING
      e_funcname = fm_name.

* set doc params so that the pdf will be interactive
  fp_docparams-fillable = abap_true.
  param-name = '/1BCDWB/DOCPARAMS'.
  param-kind = abap_func_exporting.
```

```
      GET REFERENCE OF fp_docparams INTO param-value.
      INSERT param INTO TABLE lt_params.

*   add the value parameter
      param-name = 'VALUE'.
      param-kind = abap_func_exporting.
      GET REFERENCE OF value INTO param-value.
      INSERT param INTO TABLE lt_params.

*   add the formoutput exporting parameter
      param-name = '/1BCDWB/FORMOUTPUT'.
      param-kind = abap_func_importing.
      GET REFERENCE OF fp_formoutput INTO param-value.
      INSERT param INTO TABLE lt_params.

*   add the exception
      exception-name = 'OTHERS'.
      exception-value = 10.
      INSERT exception INTO TABLE lt_exceptions.

*   set output parameters and open spool job
      fp_outputparams-nodialog   = 'X'.
      fp_outputparams-getpdf      = 'X'.
      CALL FUNCTION 'FP_JOB_OPEN'
        CHANGING
          ie_outputparams = fp_outputparams.

*   dynamic call of the generated function module
      CALL FUNCTION fm_name
        PARAMETER-TABLE
          lt_params
        EXCEPTION-TABLE
          lt_exceptions.
      IF sy-subrc <> 0.
*       there was an error; check, if it was an ADS related
*       problem
        CALL FUNCTION 'FP_GET_LAST_ADS_ERRSTR'
          IMPORTING
            e_adserrstr = adserrstr.

*       get message manager
        lr_api_controller ?= wd_this->wd_get_api( ).
        CALL METHOD lr_api_controller->get_message_manager
```

```
        RECEIVING
          message_manager = lr_message_manager.

*     report error message returned by ADS
      CALL METHOD lr_message_manager->report_error_message
        EXPORTING
          message_text = adserrstr.

*     abort PDF creation
      RETURN.
    ENDIF.

*   close spool job
    CALL FUNCTION 'FP_JOB_CLOSE'.

*   get the pdf
    READ TABLE lt_params
        WITH KEY name = '/1BCDWB/FORMOUTPUT'
        INTO param.
    pdf_ref ?= param-value.
    pdf = pdf_ref->pdf.

*   save the pdf to context
    wd_context->set_attribute(
      EXPORTING
        name = 'PDF'
        value = pdf ).

*   hide the input area
    wd_context->set_attribute_property(
      EXPORTING
        attribute_name = 'VALUE'
        property = if_wd_context_element=>e_property-visible
        value = abap_false ).

*   display the download area
    wd_context->set_attribute_property(
      EXPORTING
        attribute_name = 'PDF'
        property = if_wd_context_element=>e_property-visible
        value = abap_true ).
ENDMETHOD.
```

Listing 8.14 Action Handler of the ON_GEN_PDF Action

Listing 8.14 is comprised of three areas:

1. Reading the current value of the user input
2. Generating the PDF form from the form template with the user's entry as input
3. Changing the visibility of the two areas so that the download areas become visible and the input area invisible

The function module generated by the system is used to generate the PDF form because the form contains a DDIC interface. The completed PDF form is made interactive in the DocParams by setting the `fillable = abap_true` field. The OutputParams (`FP_OUTPUTPARAMS` variable) are set in such a way that no dialog is displayed and a PDF form is returned.

Instead of the fully dynamic call using `parameter-` and `exception-table`, you can also enter the parameters and exceptions directly and only keep the name of the function module variable. However, if you need to supply different form interfaces generically, feel free use this source code for implementing such a requirement.

All that remains now is the source code of the action handler of the `ON_BACK` action of the `BTN_BACK` button. It toggles between the two areas (see Listing 8.15).

```
METHOD onactionon_back.
* display the input area
  wd_context->set_attribute_property(
    EXPORTING
      attribute_name = 'VALUE'
      property = if_wd_context_element=>e_property-visible
      value = abap_true ).

* hide the download area
  wd_context->set_attribute_property(
    EXPORTING
      attribute_name = 'PDF'
      property = if_wd_context_element=>e_property-visible
      value = abap_false ).
ENDMETHOD.
```

Listing 8.15 Action Handler of the ON_BACK Action

The preceding example created two minor weak spots from a usability standpoint:

▶ The user must first click on a button and then on a link to receive the file. It would be better to have the link visible permanently. As soon as the user clicks on it the PDF form would have to be generated immediately.

▶ To avoid having the `FileDownload` link visible all of the time and the user receiving a possibly outdated PDF form, he must toggle between the mode for input and the mode for form download.

For these reasons, the next example utilizes the option of load-on-demand via a supply function to generate a PDF file for each row of a table and provide the PDF file to the user. The example uses the `SPFLI` table. You can find the example in the Web Dynpro component, `ZADB_FILE_DOWNLOAD_MULTI`.

1. The component contains a `MAIN` view that includes the flight connection table. The table was generated from the context using the table wizard. The context contains a 0:N node of the `SPFLI` type for receiving data from the database table of the same name. In addition, it contains a `PDF` subnode with the `PDF` attribute of the `XSTRING` type in which the PDF form of the current table row is then generated on demand. This task is assumed by the `S_PDF` supply function that is assigned to the node (see Figure 8.71).

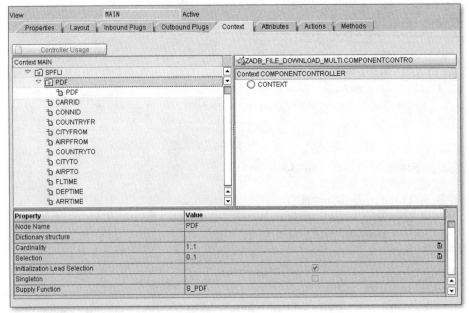

Figure 8.71 Structure of the Context of the Load-on-Demand Example

438

2. After you've generated the table in the ViewDesigner using the table wizard, you need to manually add another column, `TBLCOL_PDF`. The `FileDownload` UI element is the `CellEditor` of this column, which binds to the previously mentioned `PDF` context attribute. In addition, select a PDF icon as `imageSource` using the property's value help and define the file name in `fileName` (here, *flugbuchung.pdf*, see Figure 8.72).

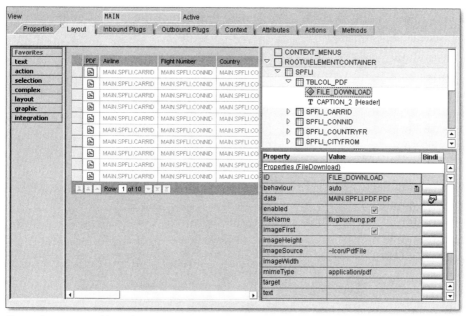

Figure 8.72 First Table Column with FILEDOWNLOAD UI Element

3. The example contains a total of two supply functions—one for determining the flight connections and another one for generating the PDF form. The supply function for populating the `SPFLI` node includes the content shown in Listing 8.16. It is called automatically by the Web Dynpro runtime as soon as the table is displayed for the first time.

```
METHOD s_spfli.
  DATA:
    lt_spfli TYPE wd_this->Elements_spfli.

  SELECT * FROM spfli INTI TABLE lt_spfli.
```

```
* bind all the elements
  node->bind_table( new_items = lt_spfli ).
ENDMETHOD.
```

Listing 8.16 S_SPFLI Supply Function

4. As soon as the user clicks on the PDF icon of the `FileDownload` UI element, the Web Dynpro runtime accesses the `PDF` attribute of the `PDF` subnode in this table row. The result is that the `S_PDF` supply function of the context node is called (see Listing 8.17).

```
METHOD s_pdf.
  DATA:
    value               TYPE STRING,
    fm_name             TYPE rs38l_fnam,
    lt_params           TYPE abap_func_parmbind_tab,
    param               LIKE LINE OF lt_params,
    lt_exceptions       TYPE abap_func_excpbind_tab,
    exception           LIKE LINE OF lt_exceptions,
    pdf_ref             TYPE REF TO fpformoutput,
    fp_docparams        TYPE sfpdocparams,
    fp_formoutput       TYPE fpformoutput,
    fp_outputparams     TYPE sfpoutputparams,
    adserrstr           TYPE STRING,
    pdf                 TYPE XSTRING,
    lr_api_controller   TYPE REF TO if_wd_controller,
    lr_message_manager  TYPE REF TO if_wd_message_manager,
    spfli               TYPE spfli,
    ls_pdf              TYPE wd_this->element_pdf.

* get the data of the parent spfli entry for which we
* were asked to supply the pdf
  parent_element->get_static_attributes(
    IMPORTING
      static_attributes = spfli ).

* generate the PDF
* => get the name of the generated function module
  CALL FUNCTION 'FP_FUNCTION_MODULE_NAME'
    EXPORTING
      i_name     = 'ZADB_FILE_DOWNLOAD_MULTI'
    IMPORTING
      e_funcname = fm_name.
```

```
* set doc params so that the pdf will be interactive
  fp_docparams-fillable = abap_true.
  param-name = '/1BCDWB/DOCPARAMS'.
  param-kind = abap_func_exporting.
  GET REFERENCE OF fp_docparams INTO param-value.
  INSERT param INTO TABLE lt_params.

* add the SPFLI parameter
  param-name = 'SPFLI'.
  param-kind = abap_func_exporting.
  GET REFERENCE OF spfli INTO param-value.
  INSERT param INTO TABLE lt_params.

* add the formoutput exporting parameter
  param-name = '/1BCDWB/FORMOUTPUT'.
  param-kind = abap_func_importing.
  GET REFERENCE OF fp_formoutput INTO param-value.
  INSERT param INTO TABLE lt_params.

* add the exception
  exception-name = 'OTHERS'.
  exception-value = 10.
  INSERT exception INTO TABLE lt_exceptions.

* set output parameters and open spool job
  fp_outputparams-nodialog  = 'X'.
  fp_outputparams-getpdf    = 'X'.
  CALL FUNCTION 'FP_JOB_OPEN'
    CHANGING
      ie_outputparams = fp_outputparams.

* dynamic call of the generated function module
  CALL FUNCTION fm_name
    PARAMETER-TABLE
      lt_params
    EXCEPTION-TABLE
      lt_exceptions.
  IF sy-subrc <> 0.
*    messages don't work inside of supply functions!
*    there was an error; check, if it was an ADS related
*    problem
*    CALL FUNCTION 'FP_GET_LAST_ADS_ERRSTR'
*      IMPORTING
```

```
*          e_adserrstr = adserrstr.
*
**    get message manager
*     lr_api_controller ?= wd_this->wd_get_api( ).
*     CALL METHOD lr_api_controller->get_message_manager
*       RECEIVING
*         message_manager = lr_message_manager.
*
**    report error message returned by ADS
*     CALL METHOD lr_message_manager->report_error_message
*       EXPORTING
*         message_text = adserrstr.

*    abort PDF creation Ð Web Dynpro runtime will trigger
*    a RABAX due to the missing file
     RETURN.
   ENDIF.

* close spool job
   CALL FUNCTION 'FP_JOB_CLOSE'.

* get the pdf
   READ TABLE lt_params
       WITH KEY name = '/1BCDWB/FORMOUTPUT'
       INTO param.
   pdf_ref ?= param-value.
   ls_pdf-pdf = pdf_ref->pdf.

* bind a single element
   node->bind_structure( new_item = ls_pdf ).
ENDMETHOD.
```

Listing 8.17 S_PDF Supply Function

Similar to the previous example, this generation of a PDF form is structured as follows:

1. **Reading the data displayed in the PDF form**
   Here, it is the current SPFLI row.

2. **Generating the PDF form from the form template with the previously read data as input**
   Note that in a supply function you can't react to errors by, for example, displaying a message. Therefore, the corresponding source code is commented out.

3. **Processing the generated PDF form**
   Here, it is written in the PDF attribute of the newly created context element.

The form template was created using Transaction SFP in a previous step. It contains not only the data of the flight connection, but fields from the SCUSTOM database table so that a user could book a flight by filling out the form (see Figure 8.73).

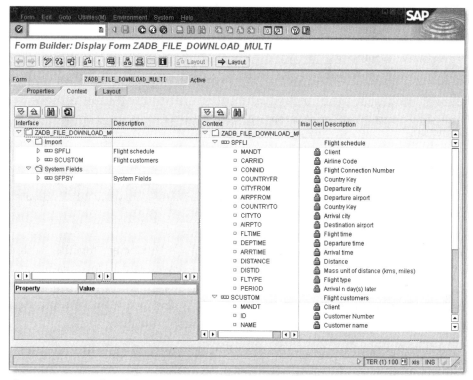

Figure 8.73 DDIC-based Form Template with Fields from the SCUSTOM Database Table

During the generation of the PDF form, the system could fill out some of the fields, for example, name, title, or even address, based on the data of the user (see Figure 8.74).

The flight book form also contains a signature field for the digital signature.

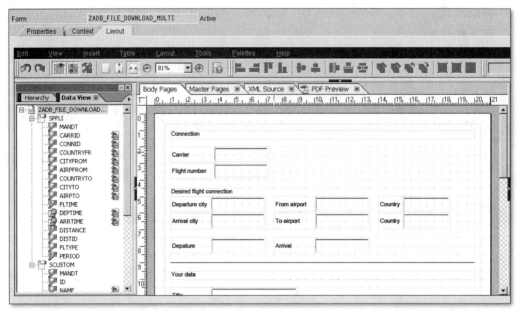

Figure 8.74 Structure of a Complete Form with a Mix of Fields Filled by the System and by the User

> **Note**
>
> Observe any legal requirements for using digital signatures before you put this example into practice.

This example discussed the use of the `FileDownload` UI element together with a supply function. As a result, a PDF form was only generated via a load-on-demand approach if requested by the user. The input data for a specific PDF form is always constant because the data of a flight connection is already known. In contrast to the previous example, this enabled the use of a supply function.

However, the disadvantage of this example is the use of a supply function. Here, a whole range of operations is not allowed, for example, no message is output if something goes wrong (for example, ADS is not available). You can neither update the context attribute of another node nor dynamically set the file name. The reason for the latter is that when the Web Dynpro runtime determines the name of the file during the view rendering process, it is undefined, whether or not the system has already accessed the context node that triggers the supply function.

Therefore, you are provided with another download mechanism called `AttachFileToResponse`, which is discussed in the following section.

AttachFileToResponse

`AttachFileToResponse` is not a UI element, but a static method of the class, `CL_WD_RUNTIME_SERVICES`. It can be called by every action handler (and other methods) and enables the developer to display a "file download dialog box" for one or more files.

In contrast to the `FileDownload` UI element, the file content doesn't have to be specified prior to the triggering action. The file can be generated or selected in a targeted manner depending on the current inputs of the user. This is the most flexible way to provide users with a file. You can find an example that provides a good overview of the available options in this method in SAP's Web Dynpro component, `WDR_TEST_EVENTS`, in the Button section.

Regarding Adobe integration, the `ZADB_FILE_DOWNLOAD_GENPDF` example is improved in the following example. Here, a special download view was set up because the form could not be generated on the fly by clicking on the `FileDownload` UI element. This problem needs to be resolved. You can find this example in the Web Dynpro component, `ZADB_ATTACH_FILE_TO_RESP`. The layout consists of an `Inputfield` with `Label` and a `Button`. When you click on the `GET_PDF` button, the system is supposed to generate a PDF form with the current input and provide it to the user for processing or saving.

In the action handler, the PDF form is generated in the same way as detailed in the `FileDownload` UI element example. The following call at the end of the source code is new (see Listing 8.18). It causes the system to display a FILE DOWNLOAD dialog in the browser that provides the generated PDF form as *myOfflinePdf.pdf* (see Figure 8.75).

```
* transfer the pdf to the user
  cl_wd_runtime_services=>attach_file_to_response(
    i_filename     = 'myOfflinePdf.pdf'
    i_content      = pdf
    i_mime_type    = 'application/pdf' ).
```

Listing 8.18 Calling AttachFileToResponse

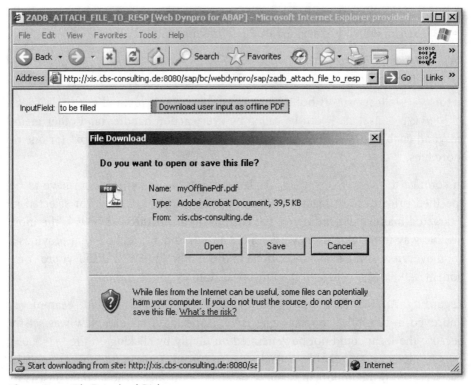

Figure 8.75 File Download Dialog

Furthermore, this method contains the optional parameters, I_IN_NEW_WINDOW and I_INPLACE. If I_INPLACE is set to ABAP_TRUE, then the file is immediately displayed in the browser window. The I_IN_NEW_WINDOW parameter controls whether the current or a new browser window is used.

The benefits of AttachFileToResponse are obvious: The application runs smoother, it enables direct storage of the file, and it is easier to implement from a developer's standpoint.

For this example of generating a PDF form from the input of the user, AttachFileToResponse is the best choice.

Enabling Users to Send the Form to the Server

In the subject area of form upload, you are provided with many options ranging from email dispatch to a web application for checking in the PDF file. This section describes how to upload a PDF form that was filled out offline using a web application implemented with Web Dynpro ABAP. Basically, there are two different cases: a pure upload with input confirmation and an upload with subsequent online review of the PDF form.

Upload with Input Confirmation

This first option of PDF upload uses—just like the subsequent case—a `FileUpload` UI element to send the file to the server via the browser. The upload process consists of the following steps:

1. Upload of the PDF form via a `FileUpload` UI element

2. On the server:

   ▶ Check the incoming PDF form (for duplicate entry, version of the form, authorization, and so on)

   ▶ If everything is OK, extract the data from the form using the PDF object API to ADS (see Chapter 10, "ABAP PDF Object") and trigger the data processing

   ▶ Inform the user about the confirmation or rejection of the file by displaying an appropriate message or a specially designed screen

You can find an example in the Web Dynpro component, `ZADB_OFFLINE_BASIC`. The component consists of the following three views:

▶ `DOWNLOAD_PDF`
For downloading the PDF form to fill out. In a real-life application this step is omitted because the user either obtains the file via a separate application or receives it by other means.

▶ `UPLOAD_PDF`
For uploading the filled-out PDF form

▶ `REVIEW_VALUE`
For confirming the inputs of the user that the system extracted from the PDF form

All three views are interlinked via outbound and inbound plugs so that the user can carry out all of the steps sequentially; in the `WND_MAIN` window, the views are interlinked via navigation links (see Figure 8.76).

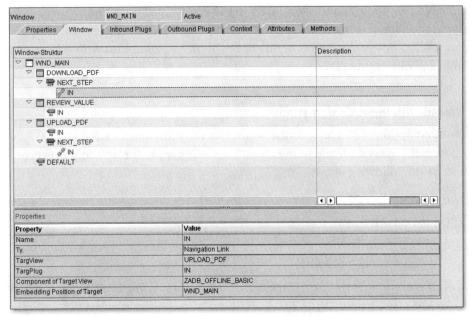

Figure 8.76 WND_MAIN Window

▶ The DOWNLOAD_PDF view contains a download option for the PDF form according to the example of the LinkToURL UI element. An additional button enables you to navigate to the UPLOAD_PDF view.

▶ The FileUpload UI element is located on the UPLOAD_PDF view. Because the file is required in the next REVIEW_VALUE view, the data property of this UI element binds to a CONTENT attribute of the PDF_FILE node that is mapped to the node of the same name at ComponentController. The PDF file specified in FileUpload is sent to the server via a Button UI element with the Upload label , put in the CONTENT context attribute, and navigated to the REVIEW_VALUE view.

▶ The user's input is extracted from the PDF form in the inbound plug of the REVIEW_VALUE view. The user confirms the correct upload in the view and triggers data processing. For this reason, ADS is accessed via the PDF object. Chapter 10 provides detailed information on the use of this interface.

The system then parses the returned XML data (you surely remember the form data from Section 8.5.2) using the iXML functionality available in SAP NetWeaver and determines the input of the user from the XML (see Listing 8.19).

```
METHOD handlein.
  TYPE-POOLS:
    ixml.

  DATA:
    lr_fp                   TYPE REF TO if_fp,
    lr_pdf_object           TYPE REF TO if_fp_pdf_object,
    lr_pdf_file_node        TYPE REF TO
                              if_wd_context_node,
    pdf                     TYPE XSTRING,
    form_data               TYPE XSTRING,
    lr_ixml                 TYPE REF TO if_ixml,
    lr_ixml_stream_factory  TYPE REF TO
                              if_ixml_stream_factory,
    lr_ixml_istream         TYPE REF TO if_ixml_istream,
    lr_ixml_document        TYPE REF TO if_ixml_document,
    lr_ixml_parser          TYPE REF TO if_ixml_parser,
    lr_ixml_element         TYPE REF TO if_ixml_element,
    value                   TYPE STRING,
    lr_api_controller       TYPE REF TO if_wd_controller,
    lr_message_manager      TYPE REF TO
                              if_wd_message_manager,
    lr_fp_exc               TYPE REF TO cx_fp_runtime,
    message_text            TYPE STRING.

* extract the data from the pdf
  TRY.
*   get a reference to form processing interface
    lr_fp = cl_fp=>get_reference( ).

*   create a pdf object Ð it will be used to extract the
*   data
    lr_pdf_object = lr_fp->create_pdf_object( ).

*   get the pdf from the context and put it into the pdf
*   object
    lr_pdf_file_node = wd_context->get_child_node(
      wd_this->wdctx_pdf_file ).
    lr_pdf_file_node->get_attribute(
      EXPORTING
        name = 'CONTENT'
      IMPORTING
        value = pdf ).
```

449

```
    lr_pdf_object->set_document( pdfdata = pdf ).

*   set the task to be extracting the data of the pdf
    lr_pdf_object->set_task_extractdata( ).

*   execute the data extraction task
    lr_pdf_object->execute( ).

*   get the data from pdf as xml
    lr_pdf_object->get_data(
      IMPORTING
        formdata = form_data ).

*   extract the value from the xml
    lr_ixml               = cl_ixml=>create( ).
    lr_ixml_stream_factory =
      lr_ixml->create_stream_factory( ).
    lr_ixml_istream =
      lr_ixml_stream_factory->create_istream_xstring(
        form_data ).
    lr_ixml_document = lr_ixml->create_document( ).
    lr_ixml_parser   = lr_ixml->create_parser(
                          stream_factory =
                                  lr_ixml_stream_factory
                          istream  = lr_ixml_istream
                          document = lr_ixml_document ).
    lr_ixml_parser->parse( ).

    lr_ixml_element = lr_ixml_document->find_from_name(
                          'VALUE' ).
    IF lr_ixml_element IS BOUND.
      value = lr_ixml_element->get_value( ).
      wd_context->set_attribute(
        name  = 'VALUE'
        value = value ).
    ENDIF.
    CATCH cx_fp_runtime INTO lr_fp_exc.
*     get message manager
      lr_api_controller ?= wd_this->wd_get_api( ).
      lr_message_manager =
        lr_api_controller->get_message_manager( ).
```

```
*        report message
         message_text = lr_fp_exc->get_text( ).
         lr_message_manager->report_error_message(
           message_text = message_text ).
   ENDTRY.
ENDMETHOD.
```

Listing 8.19 Extraction of the User's Input in the Inbound Plug

In this example, the PDF form contains a VALUE Textfield. The current value of this Textfield is copied to a context attribute called VALUE of the STRING type. An Inputfield UI element set to readOnly displays this value later on.

Below the Inputfield, you can find a Button that the user can use to confirm that his input has been extracted correctly. In a real-life application, the input would then be processed further. Clicking on the button deactivates it so that further processing can't be triggered more than once (see Figure 8.77).

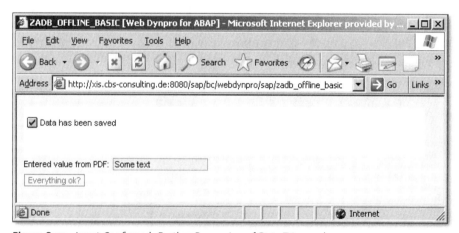

Figure 8.77 Input Confirmed, Further Processing of Data Triggered

Upload with Online Review of the PDF Form

Interactive PDF forms in the online scenario that don't utilize pure online features, for example, a value help, can also be used as interactive PDF forms in the offline scenario. This is a very convenient option for users because they can save the intermediate result of their work. For example, information that is temporarily not available can be entered offline at a later point in time. Due to its simplicity, the business card example falls into this category as well.

However, the integration of such an offline step requires downloading from and uploading to the server. After the upload, the user can further process the PDF form in the online scenario. You can either confirm that all inputs have been made or carry out a new offline step. In case of a confirmation, the system triggers the further processing of data.

You can find an example in the Web Dynpro component, ZADB_OFFLINE_ADVANCED. It is a further development of the ZADB_OFFLINE_BASIC component of the previous example for which the REVIEW_VALUE view was renamed to REVIEW_PDF and extended. The best way to follow this example is to copy and use the example of the previous section.

You don't have to rename the REVIEW_VALUE view—if you must rename it, embed the view in the WND_MAIN window. Also, modify the navigation links. In the following example, the REVIEW_PDF view is used according to the existing example.

Create an InteractiveForm UI element on the REVIEW_PDF view. Bind the existing form template of your offline form from the previous example. The ViewDesigner gives you the option to generate the context node for the form data—this is the ZADB_OFFLINE_EXAMPLE node—and automatically bind the dataSource property to it (see Figure 8.78). Make use of this option.

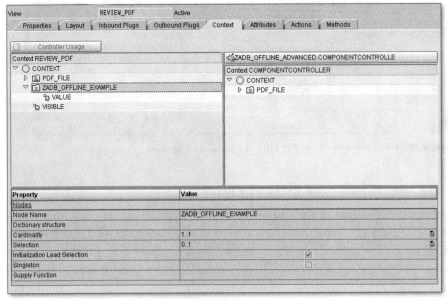

Figure 8.78 Generated Node from the Form Interface

Bear in mind that you are using an interface form from the online scenario. For this reason, you must convert the form template into a ZCI-based form template if you haven't done so yet. Then, bind the `pdfSource` property to the `CONTENT` attribute of the PDF node. This attribute contains the PDF form uploaded by the user.

Within the Web Dynpro runtime, the following happens during the first-time display:

- The system recognizes that a PDF form is located in the `CONTENT` context attribute. This form is displayed. If the node that the `dataSource` property binds to already contains data, this data is ignored. The user can *only* view his uploaded PDF form.

- Now the user can process the PDF form in the online scenario as usual. Changes are sent to the `dataSource` node on the server. The PDF form is updated in the `CONTENT` attribute so that it always contains the current input of the user.

In the subsequent rendering process of the application, the Web Dynpro runtime no longer uses the `pdfSource` property. This means that you can change the content of the `dataSource` node later on. You don't have to update the PDF form behind the `pdfSource` property because this is done automatically by the Web Dynpro runtime from now on.

The benefit of this procedure is that you as the developer don't have to program the extraction of the data from the PDF form yourself. This is all done automatically by the Adobe integration with Web Dynpro ABAP.

> **Caution: Pitfall!**
>
> For this procedure, the `InteractiveForm` UI element must appear for the first time. If the `InteractiveForm` UI element is already visible before the PDF form is put in the context attribute behind the `pdfSource` property, the PDF form is ignored. Instead, the system displays the form data from the `dataSource` node and generates a new PDF form based on this data via ADS. Your PDF form in `pdfSource` is then overwritten.
>
> The extraction of data is not carried out immediately, but is implemented by Adobe Reader in the browser. Adobe Reader receives the PDF form and only sends the form data to the server later on. This means that the data from the PDF form is not available until the subsequent roundtrip in the context.

This service functionality for the offline scenario is only enabled when both `pdfSource` and `dataSource` are bound and defined in the `templateSource` of a form template.

> **Caution: Another Pitfall!**
>
> Whenever you use the properties, `dataSource`, `templateSource`, and `pdfSource`, at the same time in an `InteractiveForm` UI element, you must keep this offline case in mind. Because, if you switch the `visible` property off and on again, the `Interactive-Form` UI element becomes visible and `pdfSource` has priority over `dataSource`.

Activate the component and create a Web Dynpro application. The example is now complete.

Comparing the Two Upload Procedures

The aim of this section is to differentiate the two procedures and point out their advantages and disadvantages.

The major advantage of the first example is that it is a pure offline procedure. For example, it doesn't require any ZCI script in the form template, which could become obsolete over time. After the upload of the PDF form, the user views his input in an input screen that was created in Web Dynpro. Just as in the second example, he could continue his work here and use the advanced features of Web Dynpro, such as personalization, master/detailed navigation, and high level of interaction and productivity thanks to more than 50 different UI elements.

The disadvantage of the first example is the change of the UI technology which is the advantage of the second scenario. The user always works with the same interactive form that he's already familiar with. He doesn't have to deal with the two different UI technologies.

This advantage has its price: The PDF form must be an interactive PDF form that can still be filled out offline. To bridge this divide is difficult because an online user wants to have value helps directly from the server and a high performance for the roundtrips, while an offline user selects his data from long dropdown lists and has no performance problems due to the lack of server roundtrips despite the large dropdown lists.

An optional solution for this tradeoff is the creation of separate online and offline forms with nearly identical appearances. In this case, however, you can't use the service function of Web Dynpro for displaying the PDF form after its upload. The data would have to be extracted separately and provided in the `dataSource` node.

If the processing of data is not supported, that is, if a completely filled-out PDF form is expected on the server, the system can display this form as a print form. To do so, simply deactivate the `enabled` property for the `InteractiveForm` UI element.

The following recommendations are based on practical experience:

▶ If it is an online application in which the users are supposed to have the option to work offline, most SAP applications are too complex to fully implement this by means of a PDF form. Focus on a specific aspect of the application and think about what data you want to include in the offline form. This can be an activity report that is filled out by the employee in-between customer visits in the course of the day, for example.

▶ Provided that it is a pure offline application (for example, a request form), you should use the first scenario and consider that you can omit the review step in a user interface that was created using Web Dynpro if the user receives a confirmation in the follow-up process. If the PDF form contained an incorrect input and the system determined this during the upload, the user can be notified accordingly via a corresponding message. In addition, it is beneficial for the user if he corrects incorrect entries in his PDF form directly: He can access it any time and compare the confirmation, which is then received, with the content of his PDF form.

▶ The second scenario is only suitable for simple forms because performance problems may occur. Consider the restrictions of the online scenario with regard to the maximum number of pages, dropdown lists, and tables with too many entries.

8.5.4 Specialized Topics

This section provides information on the use of digital signatures in the Adobe integration with Web Dynpro ABAP, the controls supported in Form Builder, a list of other interesting information sources, and important SAP Notes.

▶ **Digital signature**
This procedure for signing PDF files or form content is not directly supported by Web Dynpro ABAP. This means that you can only use it in the offline and print scenario, whereas in the print scenario you must generate the PDF file yourself and place it in the `pdfSource` of the `InteractiveForm` UI element.

▶ **Supported ACF and ZCI controls**
At present, Web Dynpro ABAP doesn't support all controls provided by Adobe LiveCycle Designer under ZCI or ACF. You can find a list of supported controls in SAP Note 1098009.

▶ **Where can you obtain further information?**
On one hand, the SAP Developer Network (SDN) includes an excellent forum for Web Dynpro ABAP with a link to the Wiki area. On the other hand, the continuously updated and comprehensive online help for Web Dynpro ABAP provides detailed information for Adobe integration and for programming Web Dynpro ABAP.

▶ **Important SAP Notes**
The notes listed in Table 8.1 have either been referred to in this chapter or are significant for Adobe integration in the context of Web Dynpro ABAP. They are sorted by their number in descending order so that the latest notes (for the latest support packages) are listed first. Some notes are independent of a specific support package because they contain general information and recommendations. You can recognize them by their title.

SAP Note	Title
1229392	Adobe: Errors in Adobe Integration
1227102	Adobe: Rabax if Only the pdfSource is Bound
1180004	Adobe: Handling Incorrect Inputs and Conversion Exits
1151340	Error during the XML Schema Generation in Web Dynpro ABAP
1113704	Adobe: User Parameter for Alternative ADS Destination
1098009	Restrictions for Web Dynpro ABAP
1090486	Adobe: Additional Features in DDIC-based Print Forms
1084367	Corrections/Improvements in the Adobe Integration DT for SP 14
1029721	Adobe: Support of Input Helps
1013227	Dropdown List Boxes in ZCI-enabled Interactive Forms
983699	Additional Features for Adobe Integration
980437	Toolbar Can't be Hidden for InteractiveForm

Table 8.1 Important SAP Notes for Web Dynpro ABAP and SAP Interactive Forms by Adobe

SAP Note	Title
962956	Adobe: Interactive DDIC Forms
956074	Using the Update Function for Forms
856882	Adobe: Making the DDIC Mode Partially Ready for Input

Table 8.1 Important SAP Notes for Web Dynpro ABAP and SAP Interactive Forms by Adobe (Cont.)

8.6 Summary

This chapter described how you can integrate SAP Interactive Forms by Adobe with Web Dynpro ABAP. Based on the three basic scenarios, real-life examples, and numerous step-by-step instructions you can implement these scenarios in your own projects.

The Internal Service Request (ISR) enables you to map request scenarios for internal processes that are used to process service requests. In this context, the interactive Adobe form serves as a flexible, modifiable request form.

9   Internal Service Request

This chapter describes the Internal Service Request (ISR), which integrates the interactive Adobe form as a flexible request form. After introducing you to the technical principles of the ISR and the basic conditions for some business request scenarios (see Section 9.1, "Introduction"), this chapter analyzes a scenario provided within SAP ERP (see Section 9.2, "Scenarios in SAP NetWeaver Portal"). Section 9.3, "Getting Started—Creating a Plain Scenario," explains what you must consider when creating and setting up a scenario. Sections 9.4, "Customizing and Programming a Scenario," 9.6, "Form Process Logic," and 9.7, "ISR Architecture" introduce and discuss the necessary Customizing settings and program-related enhancement options to refine the request scenario. Section 9.5, "Request Forms as Adobe Forms," explains how you can define the Adobe form in the ISR context.

In addition to Customizing and the program-related ISR details, this chapter focuses on the options provided by the ISR using examples and practical tips. After reading this chapter, you should have a better understanding of the options provided by the ISR framework and be able to implement specific form-based request scenarios according to your requirements.

The ISR and ISR Scenario Concepts

An ISR scenario comprises all settings in an SAP ERP system (for example, SAP ERP 6.0) that are required to map a service request for an internal process.

9.1   Introduction

This section describes the business background and the technical framework for using ISR scenarios within SAP ERP and the required system conditions. It also provides an overview of the ISR framework and names the critical basic concepts.

9.1.1   Concepts in the ISR Framework

The ISR serves to initialize an internal process in which a service defined by the user is processed. The service request enables occasional users to request any service in SAP NetWeaver Portal via an online request form and have the system process the related internal process. The applicant can implement this without having specific knowledge of the SAP ERP system. The main task here is to provide an input screen as a form to the user that is user friendly. This can be ensured via interactive Adobe forms. Due to the free and flexible design options provided by Form Designer, you can y design the form for any ISR scenario.

Online Form

ISR only supports online forms. That means that the user must populate and submit the form in the portal; the offline mode is generally not supported.

The following sections describe the ISR framework and the related essential concepts in detail.

Internal Process

An internal process that is appropriate for service requests is usually used and reused by multiple users. Such processes often require the execution of sometimes complex transactions for specialists or changes to protected data. For example, it makes sense to use a service request to request a system user with a password and the required authorizations for a particular system.

Due to the complexity of such transactions and the data security–critical or business-critical relevance of the data, or for efficiency reasons, such transactions are usually processed in small, central administrative units that provide the required specialized knowledge. However, a complex internal process may also require the involvement of several departments and may include one or more approval steps. The main components of the structure of the roles involved in such processes usually remain the same, regardless of the requester.

The applicant ⎩
because the occasional u⎫
the required access permissions t⎩ ,
ever, the user necessarily has the auth⎩
left to the occasional user to ensure the succ⎫
telephone, or in written form) using more or les⎫
process instructions.

Short Description of Service Requests

By completing and submitting the request form in SAP NetWeaver Portal, the SAP ERP system generates a notification for which a processor can be found via the SAP Business Workflow module. The processor can perform activities (for example, sending emails, carrying out transactions) directly from the notification. The request forms and the resulting workflow can be individually adapted to the service request that is supposed to be implemented and the situation in the respective enterprise.

You can quickly and easily set up your own ISR scenarios. By integrating the Controlling component, you can immediately bill the business costs of the request to the cost object. You can also influence the process and form anytime by means of Business Add-Ins (BAdIs).

Technical Roles

In the context of ISR, various technical roles are involved in the service request process:

- **Applicant**
  If required, the applicant completes and submits the interactive Adobe form to request a service. He tracks the service request status.

- **Approver**
  The approver approves or rejects the service request.

- **Processor**
  The processor ensures that one or more business transactions are carried out in SAP ERP that are necessary for the implementation of the service request.

- **Administrator**
  The administrator is responsible for the business scenario. He manages the scenario-specific Customizing and the related ABAP programming.

this also includes mapping, the requested process but also the integration of SAP interactive Forms by Adobe as the input screen for the applicant.

In addition to the mandatory input fields, the Adobe form delivers process-specific information and assistance to simplify the request creation. Scenario-specific pre-definitions for input fields, default values, input helps, online data checks, and various events make it easier to complete the form and ensure—when the request is made—a high data quality for the transactions that are carried out during the process. You can also design the functions and form layout specifically and dynamically for each user.

Plain scenarios require fewer Customizing settings and less programming effort than complex scenarios. However, it is critical that the request form can be easily understood and deployed by occasional users. This can be ensured with an ISR, regardless of the level of complexity.

9.1.2 Prerequisites

To use ISRs with interactive Adobe forms, you must use at least SAP ERP 5.0. The ISR Adobe forms in SAP ERP 5.0 are still based on ACF technology. As of SAP ERP 5.0, you're provided with the ISR interface in Web Dynpro Java. To use interactive Adobe forms, you also need version 6.0.2 or higher of Adobe Reader and at least SAP NetWeaver 6.40. In addition, you need SAP NetWeaver Portal to use all ISR functions. The recommended layout types for Adobe forms is the ZCI Layout (see Section 9.5.1, "Specific Properties," and Section 8.5.2, "Online Scenario").

As of SAP ERP 6.0 SP 8, the ISR's user interface is also in Web Dynpro ABAP. Besides the functions of the Web Dynpro Java interface, this interface provides some additional functions. Here, the technical prerequisites are SAP NetWeaver 7.0 SP 10 and Adobe Reader 7.08 or higher. You should always use the most current version of Adobe Reader.

You can find some sample scenarios of the ISR in SAP NetWeaver Portal in various business packages, such as Manager Self-Services (MSS), Business Unit Analyst (BUA), and Employee Self-Services (ESS).

To carry out a service request, the applicant requires various authorizations in the SAP ERP system. Typical error messages due to missing authorizations when starting or submitting a form include:

- **You are not authorized to display users** (01 495)
  This error message is displayed when the authorization for the S_USER_GRP authorization object is missing.

- **You have no authorization for the notification type...** (Q0 151)
  This error message is displayed when the authorization for the B_NOTIF authorization object is missing.

- **An error occurred while processing the notification...** (IM 277) (Q0 151)
  This error message is displayed when the authorization for the I_QMEL authorization object is missing.

- **No authorization for this action** (SBDS 106)
  This error message is displayed when the authorization for the S_BDS_DS authorization object is missing.

All descriptions in this chapter are based on the functions provided by SAP ERP 6.0; therefore, releases older than SAP ERP 5.0 are not covered in the following sections. The technical solution of the ISR using Web Dynpro ABAP is discussed, but the structurally nearly identical user interface in Web Dynpro Java is not.

9.1.3 What can be Configured and Where can It be Programmed?

As you'll see in the following sections of this chapter, the comprehensive design flexibility of service requests assumes a critical role for the ISR. Numerous settings are configured via Customizing, and numerous BAdI interfaces are provided for further adaptations if you want to use your own ABAP programming. Their implementations are called by the ISR framework when the service request is made and processed.

Figure 9.1 provides an overview of the Customizing settings and the interfaces and illustrates the corresponding relationships. The diagram focuses on the process from the request creation to its implementation by the processor. The ISR Customizing settings are indicated in dark gray, notification settings in medium gray, BAdIs are indicated in light gray, and functions modules or ABAP classes in black. The scenario Customizing is the frame around the entire service request. The following sections describe the different components in greater detail.

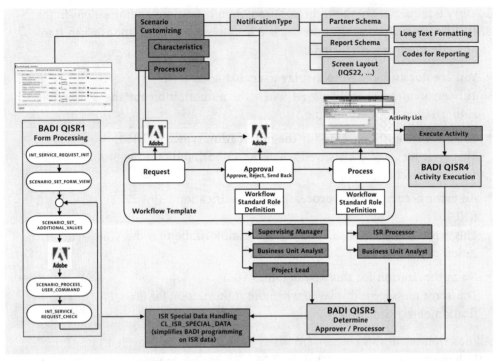

Figure 9.1 Schematic Diagram of the Interdependencies or Assignments of Customizing and BAdI Interfaces

9.2 SAP NetWeaver Portal Scenarios

This section provides an overview of the already-delivered scenarios with interactive Adobe forms and uses a sample implementation of an ISR scenario to illustrate the purpose and use of the framework. In the context of the sample scenario, this section describes the main ISR functions and demonstrates the integration options with the portal.

This chapter only provides an overview of the topic and does not provide a comprehensive description of the functions of the ISR. You can find detailed information on more specific functions in Section 9.4, Section 9.5, and Section 9.6.

9.2.1 Grouping of the Provided Scenarios

SAP ERP provides a lot of scenarios that are usually designed as application examples and thus as a template for customer-specific scenarios. The corresponding Adobe form, in particular, is often customized due to the requirements of customer-specific designs of the layout. Nevertheless, the provided scenarios are fully functional.

The scenarios can be grouped into the following business subject areas:

▶ Requests for creating or changing master data from SAP ERP, for example, equipment, cost center, internal order, profit center, WBS element, statistical key figures, etc.

▶ Requests for changing postings in financial accounting

▶ Requests for changing the budget

▶ Requests for new cost reports

▶ Planned value entry in the context of Express Planning

▶ Requests for changing HR master data of employees

▶ HCM Processes and Forms

▶ Forms for information or confirmations of specific regulations

▶ Forms for tax declarations (public sector)

▶ Notifications

9.2.2   Calling the Request Form in the Portal

The ISR scenario groups mentioned in Section 9.2.1, "Grouping of the Provided Scenarios," differ with respect to their business background and the way they can be started. In general, there are three ways the forms of the ISR can be made available to the user in SAP NetWeaver Portal:

▶ **Direct call of the request form as a service link (via URL)**
The request form is started in an iView via a service link (see the *Create Cost Center* example in Section 9.2.3, "Applicant Role"). You can find generic iViews of the ISR in the portal via the menu path PORTAL CONTENT • ERP COMMON PARTS.

▶ **Indirect call via the ISR Launchpad**
The request form is started in the context of another application via a generated button using the ISR Launchpad. The request includes the business context of the application from which it is called (see the *Create Cost Center* example in Section 9.2.3). This enables the surrounding application to fill out some of the form in advance. Similar to the service link, you can start the request form in a new browser window by clicking on the selection button. Direct communication between the ISR application and the surrounding application is not possible.

▶ **Integrated with a specific application**
Technically, the request form is integrated with another Web Dynpro component. In this case, the Web Dynpro components can exchange data anytime. The request form is started in the same browser mode as the entire application. This applies, for example, to the request scenarios where HR master data is changed (Personnel Change Requests, HCM Processes and Forms).

Section 9.7.3, "Usage Options in SAP NetWeaver Portal," describes the technical details of the application options in the portal.

9.2.3 Applicant Role

This section uses the scenario, *Create Cost Center* (technical name: SMC1), as an example to illustrate the functionality of the ISR from making an order to creating the cost center in the system.

In the BUSINESS UNIT ANALYSIS role of the BUA business package, you can call the request form for the CREATE COST CENTER scenario directly as a service link (see Figure 9.2, left column, below the SERVICES folder) and context-dependently from the cost center monitor of the BUA (see Figure 9.2; MASTER DATA iView). In both cases, the QISR_UI_FORM Web Dynpro application is started in the iView (see Section 9.7.3). You can reproduce the complete scenario in your system.

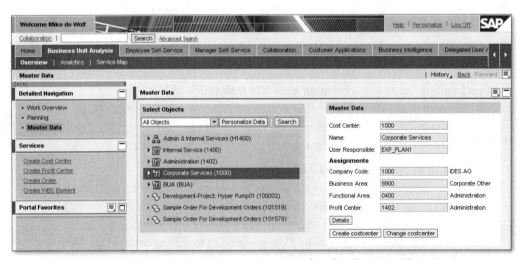

Figure 9.2 Calling Create Cost Center as a Service Link and in the Master Data Monitor

The service request consists of three steps. The Roadmap Web Dynpro screen element above the form displays the current step of the three request steps.

- In the first step, the form is filled out.

- In the second step, the completed form can be checked and then printed before it is submitted.

- In the third step, you're informed that your request was sent successfully.

However, this roadmap has nothing to do with the downstream process of the service request implementation.

> **Three Steps**
>
> If you use the QISR_UI_FORM Web Dynpro application, these three steps are mandatory. However, if you integrate the ISR request form with your own Web Dynpro application (see Section 9.2.2, "Calling the Request Form in the Portal", and Section 9.7.3), you don't have to use this roadmap.

1. Step 1: Process Form

Figure 9.3 shows a request form that consists of some input fields that are required for requesting a new cost center and some display fields. The personal data of the applicant (name, user data, etc.) is determined and displayed automatically.

The applicant can copy an existing cost center as the template for the new cost center using the COPY TEMPLATE button. The cost center number 1000 and the controlling area 1000 were copied into the form as templates from the currently selected cost center of the master data monitor.

By clicking on this button, the master data of cost center 1000 is copied into the corresponding input field for the new cost center in the form. This makes it easier for the applicant to complete the form, because—at least in this business context of the business unit analyst—he can refer to an existing cost center.

In contrast to this, the context of the template cost center is missing if the request form is started via a service link. In this case, the applicant must enter the template cost center manually, which seems to be no problem in this simple example. However, the applicant can also implement a complex data initialization from the context of a surrounding application. Therefore, it depends on the requirements for the request scenario how you call the scenario. You could also use a (programmable) input help here.

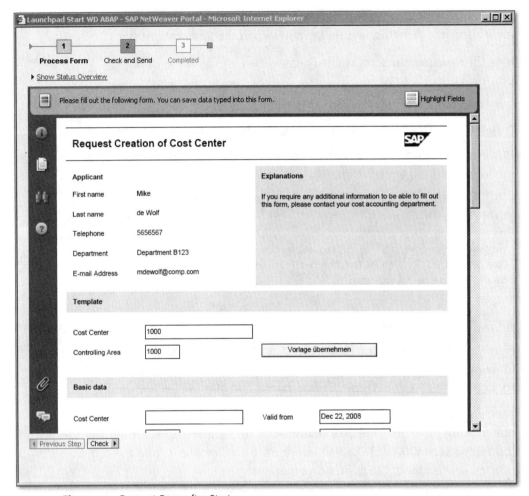

Figure 9.3 Request Form after Start

Programmable Form Process Logic with the QISR1 BAdI

A function carried out by a button is programmed in the QISR1 BAdI. Besides buttons and data initializations, additional functions in a form include programmable input helps, events in input fields, and form data checks (see Section 9.6).

At the end of the form, you can enter additional specifications or comments into a long text field without having to stick to a format (see Figure 9.4).

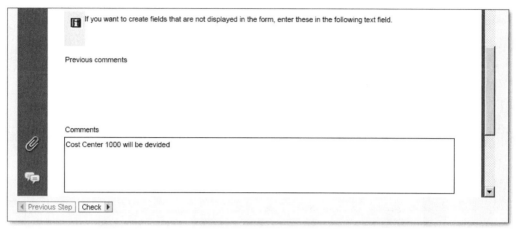

Figure 9.4 Entering Comments and Checking the Form in the First Step

After having completed the form, click on the CHECK (or Next Step) button below the form. At this point, you can have the system check to see if the form data is correct. These checks are programmed in the QISR1 BAdI (see Section 9.6.3, "Programming Examples"). If one or more entries in the form contain errors, the processing of the request may be put on hold; for this reason, you can have the system output error messages, which are displayed above the form. In this case, the request remains at step 1 (see Figure 9.5). After the incorrect field values have been corrected, the request changes to step 2 of the form, CHECK AND SEND.

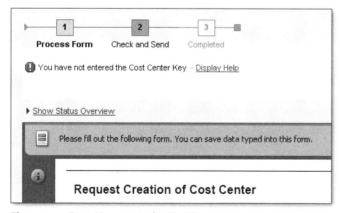

Figure 9.5 Error Message in the First Step

2. Step 2: Check and Send

In step 2, the form is displayed again but can no longer be changed. You can print the form for documentation purposes using the Adobe Reader function. If the applicant wants to change entries, you can return to step 1 via the PREVIOUS STEP button (see Figure 9.6).

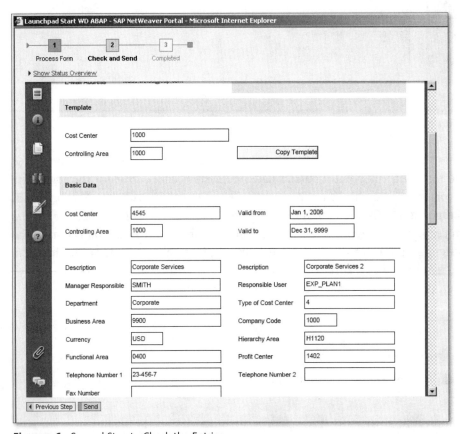

Figure 9.6 Second Step to Check the Entries

If the data is correct according to the system check and the applicant, you can submit the request by clicking the SEND (or Submit) button.

3. Step 3: Completed—Output of the Request Number

After the system has generated the request, the request number that corresponds to the notification number in the SAP ERP system (see Figure 9.7) is confirmed in step 3. You can also call the request via a link (QISR_UI_DISPLAY_ONLY Web Dynpro application).

Figure 9.7   Third Step with Notification Number of the Request

Additional Steps after the Creation of the Request

The applicant can now track the status of his service request using the ISR status overview (QISR_UI_STATUSOVERVIEW Web Dynpro application), which is mapped as a separate iView (see Figure 9.8). However, the applicant can also open the status overview via the SHOW STATUS OVERVIEW link within the request form (see Figure 9.3). From here, you can call the form in the display mode and print it anytime.

Service Request: Status Overview											
Internal Service Requests Status Overview											
Description	Notification	Status	Created on	Changed on	Req. start	Required End	Additional Column 1	Additional Column 2	Warning		Reverse
Cost center 1000 has to be devided	1005410	Open / For Approval	22.12.2008		22.12.2008	20.02.2009	4545	Corporate Services			Reverse
Die Kostenstelle 1000 wird aufgeteilt	1005201	Open / For Approval	26.08.2008		26.08.2008	25.10.2008	1050	Corporate Services	End of processing exceeded since:58 Day(s)		Reverse
Die Kostenstelle 1000 wird aufgeteilt	1005183	In Process / Approved	22.08.2008	22.08.2008	22.08.2008	21.10.2008	9896	Corporate Services 2	End of processing exceeded since:62 Day(s)		Reverse
Bitte bis Ende des Monats liefern.	1005181	Open	21.08.2008		21.08.2008	20.10.2008			End of processing exceeded since:63 Day(s)		Reverse
Report 123456	1005180	Open	21.08.2008		21.08.2008	20.10.2008			End of processing exceeded since:63 Day(s)		Reverse

Row 1 of 5

Data from: 22.12.2008 Time: 13:41:44 Refresh

Figure 9.8   Status Overview of all Requests of the Applicant

Depending on the settings, it is at least technically possible that the applicant can modify the request retroactively. This is not possible in this example, however. But the applicant can always view the current status of his request form when starting the form in the status overview. That means, for example, that he can also view the corresponding comment of the approver. The status of the request is OPEN until a processor or approver has processed the request. You can reverse requests with this status anytime via the appropriate function in the ISR status overview. When the status changes to IN PROCESS, the request can no longer be reversed. In additionally configurable columns, you can display up to five selected values of a form (see Section 9.4.5, "Characteristics"). For request 1005183 in Figure 9.8, the new cost center number and its description are displayed.

9.2.4 Approver Role

After the successful creation of the request, the system generates a notification with the OPEN status. Because the usage of SAP Business Workflow is defined in the Customizing of the corresponding notification type and the ISR, the request creation involved the creation of the corresponding workflow item. The *Create Cost Center* example requires an approval procedure. The system displays this workflow item in the Customizing of the defined approver both in the Universal Worklist (UWL) in SAP NetWeaver Portal and in the inbox of SAP Business Workplace (Transaction SBWP) in SAP ERP.

The approver can process the request via one of these two inboxes. However, when you open the workflow item, you're provided with various user interfaces. It depends on the workflow template used which request processing type the approver can use (see Section 9.4.8, "Processor Determination (BAdI QISR3) and Workflow").

▶ **UWL: starting the form in the portal with approval functions**
If the approver receives the request in the UWL, the original request form is started in a new browser window (see Figure 9.9). The approver can now make a decision for the request using the APPROVE, REJECT, or BACK TO AUTHOR functions—mapped as buttons below the form (see Figure 9.10).

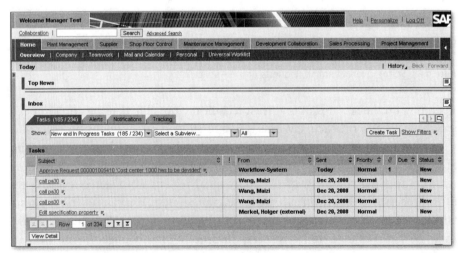

Figure 9.9 Workflow Item in the UWL of the Approver

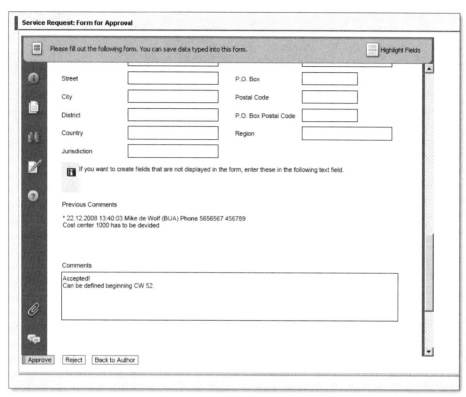

Figure 9.10 Comment Entry and Functions for the Approver in the Form

In this scenario, the approver can comment on his decision; however, he cannot change the request data. If the approver selects the REJECT option, the system automatically closes the notification. In contrast, selecting the BACK TO AUTHOR option leads to a new workflow item in the applicant's inbox. The applicant can now modify and resend the request.

The ISR framework also enables the approver to change the request data (see Section 9.7.4, "ISR_PROCESS_EVENT Remote Function Call"). It depends on the request scenario whether this makes sense. The applicant can view the status change due to the decision of the approver and the comments in the ISR status overview.

▶ **Workplace: starting Transaction IQS22 from the workflow item**
If the approver receives the request in the workplace inbox, Transaction IQS22 (see Figure 9.11) is called. Here, the approver can also approve or reject the request. However, the BACK TO AUTHOR function is not supported.

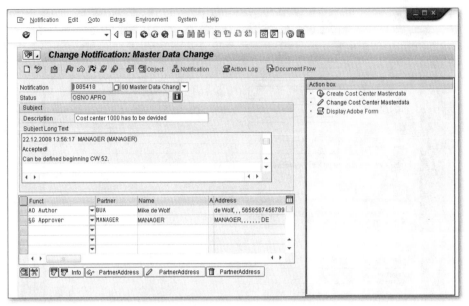

Figure 9.11 IQS22 Notification Transaction

If the approver approves the request, a new workflow item is generated for the processor who then only uses Transaction IQS22 to process the request.

9.2.5 Processor Role

The processor can call and check the form with the original data through an activity in Transaction IQS22 and view the form data as a table (see Figure 9.12).

Unlike the approver, the processor is now provided with the means to implement the request service in the system. In this scenario, these include:

▶ **Display Adobe Form**
This activity calls the QISR_UI_DISPLAY_ONLY Web Dynpro component in a browser window. In this context, consider the Customizing in Section 9.4.6, "Activities and Automatic Updates in Notifications."

▶ **Create Cost Center Master Data**
This activity executes a Business Application Programming Interface (BAPI) to create a cost center; the data for the BAPI is copied from the form data.

▶ **Change Cost Center Master Data**
This activity leads to the change transaction of the cost center.

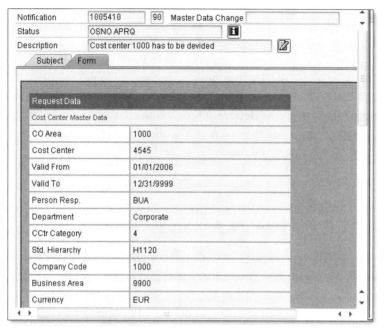

Figure 9.12 Table View of the Form Data in the Notification

These activities were defined in the scenario Customizing and programmed in the QISR4 BAdI (see Section 9.4.6). To display the activity, a text for the link has been defined in the scenario Customizing. The main setting for the activity is the entry of a function module that executes the activity.

Automatic Execution of an Activity

You can configure the ISR scenario in such a way that the activity for creating the required cost center in the backend system is automatically executed when the request is approved in the form. In doing this, the notification would be closed automatically, and the role of the processor would be obsolete.

Tip: Program the submission of an email as an automatic notification of the applicant in the QISR4 BAdI implementation of the activity (see Section 9.4.6).

After the processor has successfully executed the activity (activities) for creating the cost center, he completes the notification via a menu function. He also has the option of entering a comment into the long text field. The status changes to Completed; thus, the service has been successfully executed and completed. The applicant can check this status in the status overview (see Figure 9.8).

9.2.6 Workflow or Worklist?

By using the notification as the data medium of the request, you can forward the request to the responsible departments or persons via SAP Business Workflow; however, you don't have to use the SAP Business Workflow module. Together with Transaction IQS8 and IQS9, the notification provides so-called worklists, which processors or approvers can use to determine the requests that are relevant to them. From here, the processors or approvers can access the corresponding transaction (IQS22 or IQS23) to process the request. Figure 9.11 displays the user interface of processor Transaction IQS22.

9.3 Getting Started—Creating a Plain Scenario

Now that you know what you can achieve with ISR scenarios, the following section explains the necessary preliminary considerations and procedures for creating your own scenario. Afterward, it describes the ISR wizard for generating a plain scenario. After this section, you'll know how to design and implement your own scenarios.

9.3.1 Preliminary Considerations for a New ISR Scenario

Prior to creating an ISR scenario, you must answer some questions on the business background of the service request. Table 9.1 can help you describe your preliminary considerations in detail. You should first consider what the overall process should look like. Don't make any detailed considerations until you have a better idea of the process.

Subject Area	Preliminary Considerations
Request form	▸ What input fields (characteristics) should be displayed in the request form? What fields are necessary for completing the service request?
	▸ What checks, data initializations, input helps, or specific functions are required by applicants or other roles in the form?
	▸ What does the layout for the form look like?
	▸ Does a form already exist?

Table 9.1 Checklist for the Creation of a Scenario

Subject Area	Preliminary Considerations
Roles, worklist, and workflow	▶ What roles are provided for the execution of the service? ▶ Do you want to use SAP Business Workflow to process the notification, or do you want to have the processor select his notifications from a worklist? ▶ Are approval steps necessary, and if so, how many? ▶ Do multiple processors have to be involved simultaneously, or can the processors become active one after the other? ▶ What criteria should be used for the determination of the processor (fixed processor or depending on request fields, organizational structures, costs, last name of the applicant, and so on)?
Request in the backend (notification)	▶ What activities (transaction calls, response email, and so on) should be provided to the processors in the activity list of the notification transaction? ▶ Should individual activities be executed automatically (for example, by the applicant or approver)?
Evaluation	▶ Do you want to create detailed reporting of your request scenario?
Service costs	▶ Do you want to record and evaluate the service costs of your request scenario? ▶ Are plain blanket costs sufficient, or do you want to calculate differentiated service costs?

Table 9.1 Checklist for the Creation of a Scenario (Cont.)

After having answered all of these questions, you can start creating your own ISR scenario. However, before you begin implementing the ISR Customizing directly, you can use the ISR wizard instead. It is particularly helpful if you work with the ISR framework for the first time.

9.3.2 ISR Wizard

The ISR wizard enables you to create a scenario step by step. You can find the ISR wizard in the Implementation Guide (IMG) (Transaction SPRO • Execute Project or the SAP menu path Tools • Customizing • Img) of the SAP ERP system menu path CROSS-APPLICATION COMPONENTS • INTERNET/INTRANET SERVICES • INTERNAL SERVICE REQUEST • SCENARIO DEFINITION • ISR WIZARD. The Define Scenario with ISR Wizard IMG activity (Transaction QISRCONF) serves to define a scenario. The Overview of the Scenarios Created in the ISR Wizard IMG activity (Transaction QISRLIST) displays all current scenarios created with the ISR wizard.

Within the wizard, you come across basically the same questions as listed in Table 9.1. In this context, the wizard tries to draft the questions from a business perspective and avoid questions on technical details as much as possible. That means that detailed technical knowledge about the ISR components (notification, workflow, Adobe form, and so on) is not required. The ISR wizard "translates" the answers from the subwizards into technical settings that are later used to generate the Customizing settings for the actual ISR scenario.

Subwizards

The ISR wizard consists of seven individual subwizards for different subject areas; all steps of the subwizards are displayed with a status. Figure 9.13, for example, illustrates the current status of the ISR wizard with all subwizards and their statuses for a scenario that has only been partly processed.

The individual subwizards are partly based on each other and therefore depend on each other. A dependent subwizard cannot be called until the required previous subwizards have been completed. This is indicated accordingly. The interdependencies are explained within every subwizard. Apart from that you can execute the wizards in any order you like.

> **Postprocessing a Subwizard**
>
> If you postprocess a subwizard—which can be done anytime—you must also carry out the steps in the subsequent, dependent subwizards again to make the necessary adaptations.

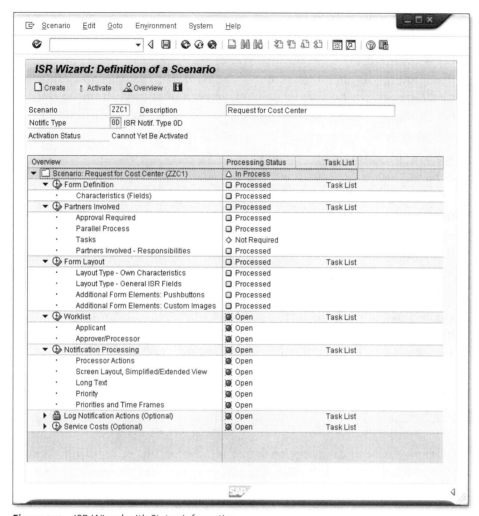

Figure 9.13 ISR Wizard with Status Information

The following subwizards are available. One wizard always covers a specific subject area of the ISR. The Customizing or form settings that each subwizard generates are explained in Section 9.4 or 9.5.

▸ **Form Definition** (can be executed independent of the other subwizards)
Here, you define the characteristics of the form.

▸ **Partners Involved** (can be executed independent of the other subwizards)
Here, you define the roles and partners that are involved in the business pro-

cess of the service request and assign user or workflow rules for the determination of the processors at runtime.

▶ **Form Layout** (depends on the first wizard)
Here, you specify the rough layout of the form. For example, you define the characteristics' positioning. In addition, you can select fields from the General ISR Fields pool (see Section 9.4.5) and define for which role the characteristic is ready for input.

▶ **Worklist** (depends on the second wizard)
Here, you define how the processors can find their service requests. You can also configure the ISR status overview here.

▶ **Notification Processing** (can be executed independent of the other sub-wizards)
Here, you specify the functions of the notification transactions (for example, IQS22) for processing the service request, for example, activities for the processor.

▶ **Log Notification Actions** (depends on the second and fifth wizard; optional)
Here, you configure whether and how activities of the notification processing are documented in the notification. These settings are critical for evaluations in notification reporting.

▶ **Service Costs** (can be executed independent of the other subwizards; optional)
Here, you define how the costs of a service request are recorded.

The last two subwizards are optional, that is, you don't have to execute them to activate the scenario. If a subwizard has not been processed yet, its status is Open. If a subwizard has been partly processed but is not completed yet, its status is In Process. If a wizard is completed, its status is Processed. After having completed all subwizards that are not optional, you can activate the scenario.

Activation

The current settings of the subwizards are initially only buffered in the ISR wizard, even though all of the subwizards are not completed yet. You can modify and postprocess any subwizard as long as the scenario is not activated. Not until you activate the entire scenario in the ISR wizard are the settings transferred to the corresponding Customizing tables as a scenario that can be actually used.

However, you cannot generate the Customizing settings for the scenario until all mandatory subwizards have been completed. To do this, you must execute the Activate function. Only then will the actual ISR scenario be created with the name of the scenario defined in the ISR wizard and the Customizing transferred to the respective Customizing tables. In addition, the system generates a notification type with the corresponding Customizing settings. The Activation Status (Cannot Yet Be Activated or Can Be Activated) indicates whether the scenario is active.

This activation also involves generating a functional interactive Adobe form with all of the required input fields and technical properties—interface, context, data view, script, field binding, and so on (see Figure 9.14). The generated form can then be edited by designing the layout or retroactively extending it with additional fields (see Section 9.5), for example.

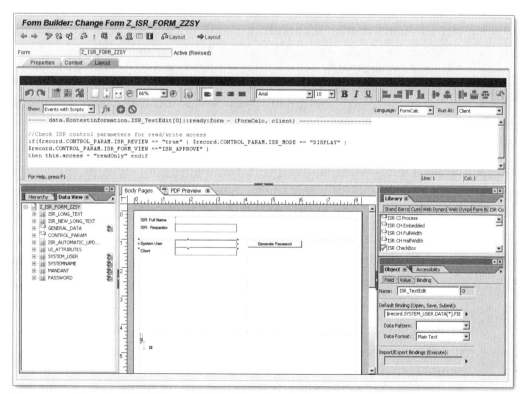

Figure 9.14 Generated Adobe Form with Data View, Data Binding Layout of the Fields, Script

The name of the form or interface is composed as follows (xxxx refers to the name of the scenario):

- ► Form: Z_ISR_FORM_xxxx
- ► Interface: Z_ISR_IF_xxxx

The Customizing settings and the generated Adobe form are collected in the requests that you provided and can therefore be transferred to other systems. For the activation, you need one Customizing and one workbench request each (for SAP Interactive Form by Adobe). In addition, you are prompted to specify the package assignment for the Adobe form and its interface. You must also activate the corresponding workbench objects in the respective dialog box.

Worklist

After activation, additional changes may have to be made to the Customizing when implementing the new ISR scenario. For this reason, the Worklist provides an overview of all generated Customizing settings in an Adobe Portable Document Format (PDF) print form (see Figure 9.15, the example refers to the settings of the ZZSY sample scenario). Among other things, it describes which control functions the respective generated Customizing entry is responsible for and where in the IMG you can find it.

This list is also used for documentation purposes for the subwizards to track all entries in the wizards, because you can no longer process the scenario in the wizard after it has been activated. You can only process it in the actual IMG activities of the ISR. The worklist displays the current processing status of a partly completed and not activated scenario.

It also describes any necessary or optional Customizing settings that cannot be executed by the wizard and must be carried out manually after the scenario has been activated.

For example, you must assign the number range of the notification type in the required target system in each client and for each notification type separately. This setting cannot be transferred. The components of the ISR scenario that have to be programmed, for example, the implementation of the QISR1 BAdI, are also not generated by the ISR wizard.

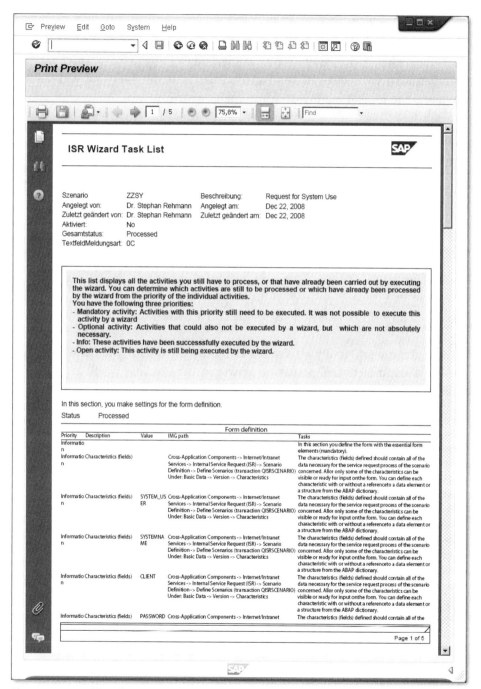

Figure 9.15 Worklist of the ISR Wizard

ISR Wizard Overview

The SCENARIO LIST of the ISR wizard provides an overview of all of the scenarios that were created in the system via the ISR wizard (see Figure 9.16). This overview distinguishes between activated and open scenarios. In this overview, you can create new scenarios and modify or delete open scenarios.

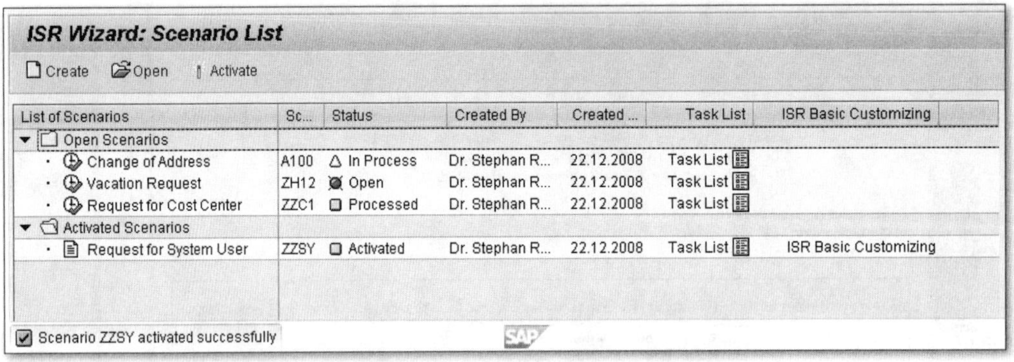

Figure 9.16 List with Open and Activated Scenarios of the ISR Wizard

Because you cannot modify activated scenarios in the wizard, the ISR wizard cannot be called for activated scenarios. However, the Worklist is still available for activated scenarios. In addition, you can navigate directly to the BAdI Builder module for the QISR1 BAdI (see Section 9.6) and basic ISR Customizing, Define Scenarios IMG activity (see Section 9.4). Here, you can view which settings the system has transferred to the Customizing tables during the activation of the scenario and modify them, if necessary.

> **Activated Scenario**
>
> Only activated scenarios are in the basic ISR Customizing (Transaction QISRSCENARIO). These can no longer be modified or deleted with the ISR wizard but are still listed in the ISR wizard overview (Transaction QISRLIST).

Defining a Scenario

To define a scenario with the ISR wizard, use the following work steps as a guide. The *Request for System User* sample scenario (ZZSY) illustrates this process.

1. Create the ZZSY scenario with Transaction QISRCONF. Subwizards with the CLOCK icon can be executed, subwizards with the LOCK icon cannot. The system automatically determines the NOTIFIC TYPE number (see Figure 9.17).

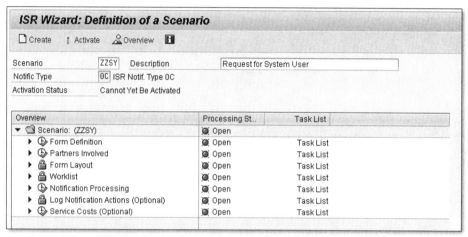

Figure 9.17   ISR Wizard for a New Scenario

2. Process all of the required subwizards until the entire scenario's status is Processed. All subwizards have the same structure and usually provide a default value for plain scenarios. That means that you can create a scenario very quickly by accepting the default values in the subwizards.

   The first step includes preliminary explanations on the subject area. The definition of the form is shown in Figure 9.18.

3. Next, configure the settings. In the CHARACTERISTICS (FIELDS) step, you can specify the characteristics of the scenario (see Figure 9.19). If you know the reference of a characteristic in the Data Dictionary, enter it here. In Figure 9.19, SYSTEM USER, SYSTEM NAME, CLIENT, and PASSWORD are defined as characteristics.

4. The final step is to COMPLETE the subwizard. No specific settings are made in this step.

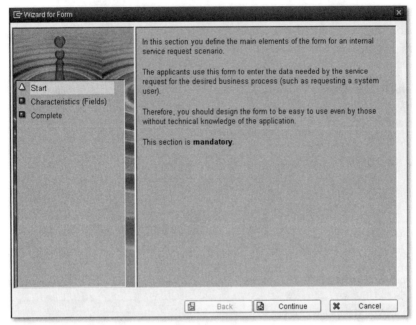

Figure 9.18 Step 1 of the Form Definition Subwizard

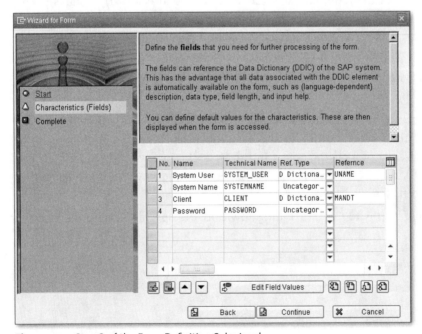

Figure 9.19 Step 2 of the Form Definition Subwizard

5. Perform the same steps for the other subwizards with an identical structure. After executing all relevant subwizards (see Figure 9.20), click the ACTIVATE button.

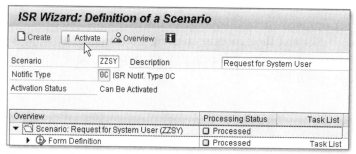

ISR Wizard: Definition of a Scenario

☐ Create | ⬆ Activate | ⌂ Overview | ⓘ

Scenario	ZZSY	Description		Request for System User
Notific Type	0C	ISR Notif. Type 0C		
Activation Status	Can Be Activated			

Overview	Processing Status	Task List
▼ Scenario: Request for System User (ZZSY)	☐ Processed	
▶ Form Definition	☐ Processed	Task List

Figure 9.20 Activation of the ISR Scenario

6. Carry out the two additional tasks that are described in the worklist.

9.4 Customizing and Programming a Scenario

You have now created the framework of your ISR scenario using the ISR wizard. You can use the following IMG activities to postprocess and refine the *scenario Customizing* and scenario-specific programming of available BAdIs.

You can also create ISR scenarios without the wizard. If you're familiar with the ISR, or if you want to use your own or an already-existing ISR scenario as a template, use the following IMG activities.

9.4.1 General Details

The *Define Scenario* IMG activity (Transaction QISRSCENARIO) provides central access to the Customizing of ISR scenarios. The Customizing of these scenarios is often referred to as basic ISR Customizing. It can be found via the menu path CROSS-APPLICATION COMPONENTS • INTERNET/INTRANET SERVICES • INTERNAL SERVICE REQUEST • SCENARIO DEFINITION.

Here, you can view a list of scenarios. Select a scenario, and go to BASIC DATA and Version. This brings you to the basic ISR Customizing. From here you can configure the settings for the following subject areas (see Figure 9.21):

▶ **General details**
The general details include the scenario description, the version, and the application (see Section 9.4.2, "Application and Version").

▶ **Notification type**
The notification type includes the Customizing for the notification transactions of the (optional) approver and the processor and their functions. The notification type enables you to define the structure process steps of the service (see Section 9.4.3, "Notification Type").

▶ **Entry type**
Here, you define the interactive Adobe form as the entry interface for the applicant (see Section 9.4.4, "Entry Type").

▶ **Characteristics**
They enable you to define the input and display fields of the form and any additional fields for processing the service request (see Section 11.4.5).

▶ **Activities**
You define the activities for the roles involved in the process (such as processor and approver) that can be executed manually or automatically (see Section 9.4.6 and Section 9.4.7, "The Processor's Activities from the Form").

▶ **Processor determination**
If you want to use SAP Business Workflow, you can specify the responsible processor(s) or rules for a system-based determination of one or more processors (see Section 9.4.8, "Processor Determination (BAdI QISR3) and Workflow").

▶ **Costs**
You can configure whether or not the internal costs of the service request should be determined in Controlling of the SAP ERP system (see Section 9.4.9, "Service Costs and BAdI QISR2").

▶ **Form flow logic**
Here, you specify how the QISR1 BAdI affects the form flow logic. Programmable form flow logic is one of the central functions for ISR and is therefore described separately in Section 9.6.

The central concept, *scenario*, comprises all Customizing settings and programming for a request service.

ISR Scenario

The technical identifier of the ISR scenario is a four-digit, alphanumeric code, ZZSY in this example. The customer namespace is defined by the first character and comprises all characters except for S and all digits from 0 to 9. The scenarios provided by SAP all start with S. The technical key field, SCENARIO, serves to identify the ISR scenario in the entire ISR framework.

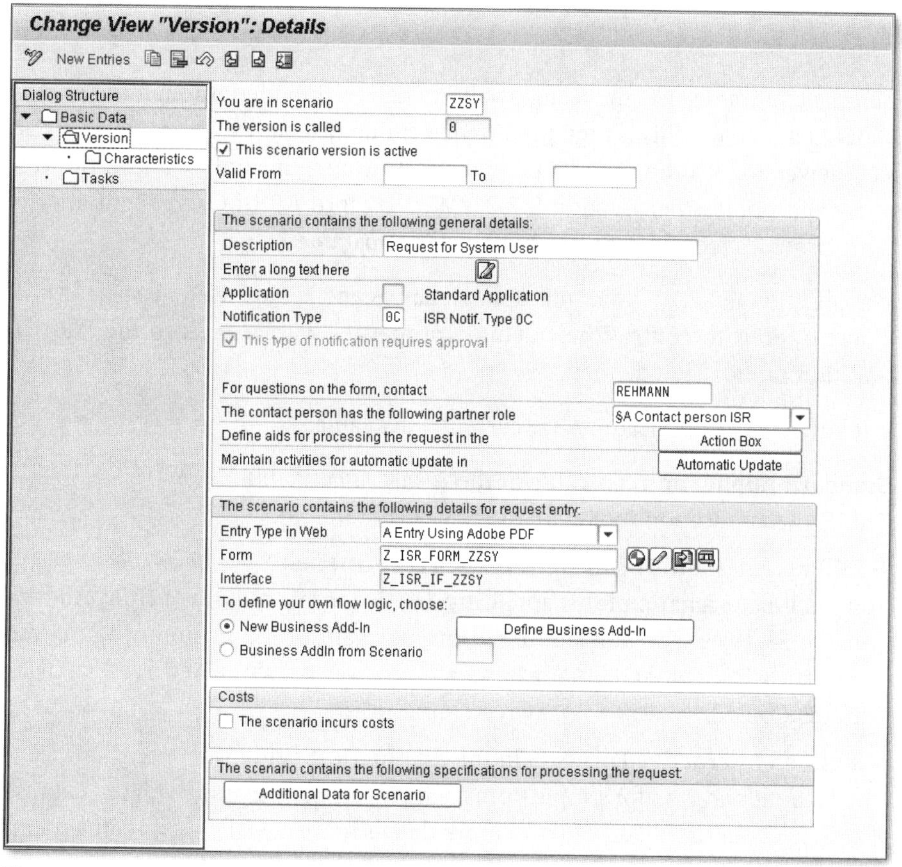

Figure 9.21 Basic ISR Customizing

9.4.2 Application and Version

The scenario may consist of multiple versions of which only one is active. The system automatically determines the version number (starting with 0), and you can define a validity period for every scenario version. This validity period of the version must be unique and must not overlap with the validity period of another version (see Figure 9.22). Provided scenarios are always version 0.

Dialog Structure	Version				
▼ ☐ Basic Data	Scenario	Version	Actv.	Valid From	Valid To
▼ ☐ Version	ZMC1	0	☑		12/31/2009
· ☐ Characteristics	ZMC1	1	☐	01/01/2010	12/31/2999
· ☐ Tasks					

Figure 9.22 Two Versions of a Scenario

When the applicant starts the form, a validity date is provided through the VALID-ITY_DATE parameter. This is then used to determine the valid version. You can also select the version via the VERSION parameter. However, this only works if the version is valid (local time). Section 9.7.2, "Web Dynpro ABAP Component and Its Usage," provides more details on the transfer of parameters.

The application tends to group multiple scenarios and is only used by specific SAP ERP applications to control their defined properties with respect to the ISR. An application cannot be redefined.

The following SAP applications are currently available:

▶ **Standard Application** (no value in the APPLICATION field)
This is the application for standard scenarios of the ISR.

▶ **HCM Processes and Forms** (H in the APPLICATION field)
You can link a scenario of this application with a form scenario of HCM Administrative Services. For more information, navigate to the Customizing via the menu path PERSONNEL MANAGEMENT • HR ADMINISTRATIVE SERVICES • FORM/PROCESS CONFIGURATION • FORM CONFIGURATION.

▶ **Simplified Interactive Forms** (S in the APPLICATION field)
This is the application for simple forms, which you can integrate with the Express Planning application. You can find more details in the SAP Library via the menu path CROSS-APPLICATION COMPONENTS • EXPRESS PLANNING • PLANNING SERVICES • PLANNING SERVICES WITH CLOSE LINKAGE • ADOBE FORM SERVICE.

▶ **Manual Correspondence** (MC in the APPLICATION field)
This is the application for the public sector.

▶ **Tax and Revenue Management (TRM)** (T in the APPLICATION field)
This is the application for the public sector to process tax forms.

You only need to enter an application if the scenario should be integrated with a special SAP ERP application. Note that such scenarios can only function smoothly within these applications, because certain functions are lost or added when specific applications are selected.

If you want to use an application, first get information on the specific documentation of the respective SAP ERP application. If you want to use a request scenario without a connection to an application, you can ignore this setting (see Figure 9.23). The application is usually not needed for customer-specific scenarios. Furthermore, the scenario description is entered here.

Figure 9.23 Access to the Basic ISR Customizing

9.4.3   Notification Type

The notification type is assigned to the scenario (see Figure 9.22). The notification type itself includes the Customizing for the different components of the notification. The Customizing for the notification type can be found via the menu path CROSS-APPLICATION COMPONENTS • INTERNET/INTRANET SERVICES • INTERNAL SERVICE REQUEST • SCENARIO DEFINITION • PREPARE GENERAL NOTIFICATION.

SAP provides a notification type for each subject area mentioned in Section 9.2.1, and comprises several scenarios. If the settings of one of these notification types are not sufficient, you should define your own notification type.

The following settings are linked to the notification type:

▶ Whether or not the scenario requires an approval

▶ The definition of the layout for the notification transaction that is used by the processor to process the service request

▶ The available activities

For simple scenarios, you can use the 01 ("ISR: Incurs Costs"; subject to approval) or 02 ("General"; not subject to approval) notification type. If you need to use your own notification type, you should copy the 01 or 02 notification type and set up your scenarios with your own notification type. The IMG activity can be found via the menu path CROSS-APPLICATION COMPONENTS • INTERNET/INTRANET SERVICES • INTERNAL SERVICE REQUEST • SCENARIO DEFINITION • PREPARE GENERAL NOTIFICATION • NOTIFICATION CREATION • NOTIFICATION TYPE • DEFINE NOTIFICATION TYPES. If your client doesn't include the 01 or 02 notification type, you can copy these settings from the 000 client using Transaction QISR_SM29.

You should use a provided notification type as a template for defining your own notification type. If you used the ISR wizard to generate an ISR scenario, the system has already generated a new notification type.

Number Range Assignment for the Notification Type

You must assign the notification type in every system to a number range. This Customizing cannot be transferred. Navigate to Transaction IW20 or the IMG via the menu path CROSS-APPLICATION COMPONENTS • INTERNET/INTRANET SERVICES • INTERNAL SERVICE REQUEST • SCENARIO DEFINITION • PREPARE GENERAL NOTIFICATION • NOTIFICATION CREATION • NOTIFICATION TYPE • DEFINE NUMBER RANGES.

If no number range has been assigned, the system outputs one of the following error messages when you send the form: "An error occurred whilst processing the notification" or "An unexpected error occurred during the processing...."

9.4.4 Entry Type

The entry type enables you to define which input screen the applicant should use to enter the service request (see Figure 9.21). Due to the fact that SAP R/3 4.6C already provided the ISR the first time, there are many entry types available. As of SAP ERP 5.0, the actual recommended entry type is "Entry Using Adobe PDF." Therefore, the additional entry types are listed but are not detailed further:

- Text Entry Only
- Entry Using Internet Transaction Server (ITS) Service
- Entry Using Notification Transaction
- Entry Using JavaServer Page (JSP) iView
- Entry Using Business Server Pages (BSP)
- Entry Using Adobe PDF

After selecting the Entry Using Adobe PDF option, specify the name of the interactive form. The system then displays the corresponding interface of the form for information purposes. You can regenerate, modify, display, or test the Adobe form from this interface (see Section 9.5). These functions are made available in the form via buttons next to the field, which enables you to navigate to Form Builder by clicking on the respective buttons. It is absolutely necessary that the form has some ISR-specific properties so that it can be used in the ISR framework. This is ensured when you process the form using the functions of the basic ISR Customizing.

For each scenario, use a specific form with its own interface. Otherwise, the form or interface may become unusable for other scenarios if you implement changes retroactively. Section 9.5 describes the form definition in more detail.

9.4.5 Characteristics

A main aspect of the definition of a service request is the definition of the characteristics (fields) that the service request requires. The necessary input or display fields in the request form should be mentioned first. They are defined as characteristics in the scenario Customizing. Basically, you must define every field as a characteristic that contains data, for example, fields that need to be populated by the applicant.

However, this also includes fields that are only required to display data from the backend or that are populated during the processing of the service. Fields that should not be available to all roles involved, but are required to further process the service request, must also be defined. For example, the form of a request for a system user doesn't require the technical field for the initial password. The value of this field is generated by the processor.

The characteristics of the ISR Customizing can also have a reference to the Data Dictionary or be freely defined as follows (see Figure 9.24):

▶ Characteristics with reference to a data element of the ABAP Dictionary

▶ Characteristics with reference to a structure of the ABAP Dictionary

▶ Uncategorized characteristics; they have an implicit type, CHAR250, without input or output conversion and can thus have a maximum length of 250 characters.

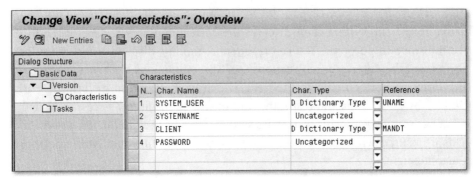

Figure 9.24 Scenario Customizing with the Characteristics List

The following basic conditions apply to the definition of characteristics:

▶ The names of the characteristic or structure fields must be unique within the scenario.

▶ The length of the characteristic or structure field names should not exceed 28 characters.

▶ The data length of the characteristic or structure field names should not exceed 250 characters.

▶ The names of the characteristic or structure fields must not start with "ISR_."

▶ The description of the characteristics can contain up to 40 characters.

In addition to these scenario-specific characteristics, you're provided with numerous default characteristics that can be automatically initialized and displayed in the request form. This also includes the general ISR fields (see Section 9.5.2, "Structure of the Interface and Form Context").

General ISR Fields

For each scenario and form, the ISR framework provides a pool of so-called *general fields* that the system determines automatically at runtime. The list mainly contains address characteristics of the involved processors and technical values, such as scenario, the time of entry of the notification, and so on. You can find the complete list in the QISRSGEN-ERAL_PARAM DDIC structure.

You can also use the characteristic definition to define additional functions:

▶ **Programmed input help**

The characteristic should be provided with a programmed input help. To do this, you must define for the characteristic which technical name you use for the key value and description for the programming of the SCENARIO_SET_ADDI-TIONAL_VALUES BAdI method of the QISR1 BAdI (see Section 9.6).

▶ **Long text formatting**

The characteristic should be mapped as a long text field where plain text can be entered. In this case, select the LONG TEXT checkbox (see Figure 9.25). You can also use the ISR_NEW_LONG_TEXT standard ISR field (see Section 9.6.2, "Default Values for the MODE, USER_COMMAND, and FORM_VIEW Parameters").

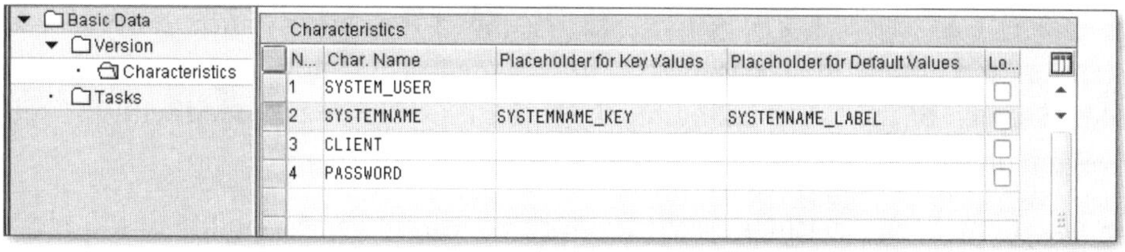

	Characteristics				
N...	Char. Name	Placeholder for Key Values	Placeholder for Default Values	Lo...	
1	SYSTEM_USER			☐	
2	SYSTEMNAME	SYSTEMNAME_KEY	SYSTEMNAME_LABEL	☐	
3	CLIENT			☐	
4	PASSWORD			☐	

(Tree: ▼ ☐ Basic Data → ▼ ☐ Version → · ☐ Characteristics, · ☐ Tasks)

Figure 9.25 Customizing for Programmed Input Help and Long Text Formatting

Define the characteristics for the additional columns in the ISR status overview (see Figure 9.8) via the Additional Data for Scenario to which you can navigate via the Customizing of the button with the same description in the basic ISR Customizing. All of the characteristics are available for the definition of up to five columns (see Figure 9.26).

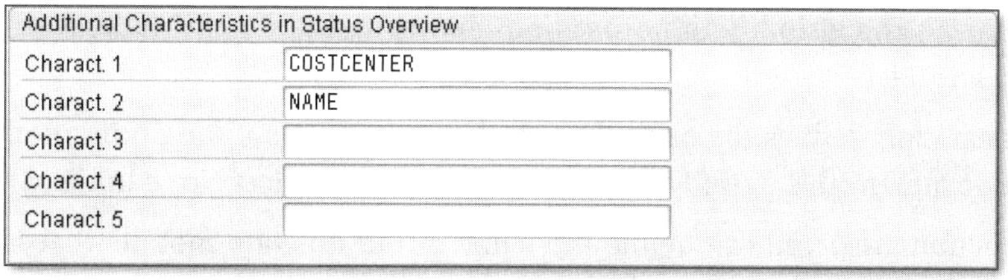

Additional Characteristics in Status Overview	
Charact. 1	COSTCENTER
Charact. 2	NAME
Charact. 3	
Charact. 4	
Charact. 5	

Figure 9.26 Characteristics for the Additional Columns of the Status Overview

9.4.6 Activities and Automatic Updates in Notifications

This section describes the activities that approvers or processors can perform within the scope of the notification transactions. Section 9.4.7, "The Processor's

Activities from the Form," introduces the activities that processors can carry out from the form. These two activity types involve different technical requirements and require different Customizing.

The Processor's or Approver's Activities in the Notification Transaction

You can distinguish between manual activities for the processor of the service request using notification transactions and activities for automatic updates without using notification transactions. The automatic activity is not performed or triggered by the processor but automatically executed by the system at a specific time.

To define the two activity types, click the Action Box button in the basic ISR Customizing (see Figure 9.21). Activities are defined for each notification type and can be used within all scenarios that are assigned to this notification type. In the detail screen of the Customizing for the activities, you are provided with the following options:

- ► The Control data settings are critical for the visibility and usability of the activity within the notification transaction.
  - ► Scenario controls the visibility of the activity in the respective scenarios that belong to the notification type.
  - ► Sort Number controls the order in which the activities are provided in the activity bar of the notification transactions.
  - ► Usage controls the visibility of the activities in the notification; default value: Any View (Create, Change, Display).
  - ► And controls the visibility in notifications and/or tasks; default value: Notification and Task.
  - ► Documentation defines the execution of an activity to see if the notification should document this. (Tip: For the sake of simplicity, select None initially.)
- ► In the Function area, you can define the name of the function module that is processed when the activity is called. The provided scenarios contain some examples of such function modules.
  - ► In the User Interface area, you specify the icon and the text that is displayed in the activity bar.
  - ► In the Rules area, you define the order and dependencies for the execution of the activities.

Define one of the following generic function modules as a Function if the activity is programmed with the "ISR: Execution of a Function in the Action Box" BAdI. The FUNCTION key word of the activity is required for the implementation of the QISR4 BAdI.

▶ ISR_ACTIVITY_EXECUTE_TASKDOC

▶ ISR_ACTIVITY_EXECUTE_ACTIONDOC

▶ ISR_ACTIVITY_EXECUTE

All three modules can be used the same way and call the same method, EXECUTE_FUNCTION, of the QISR4 BAdI. It depends solely on the specification in the Documentation field which function module you use. You can use ISR_ACTIVITY_EXECUTE if Documentation = None is selected.

Programming an Activity

The function module of an activity must have a defined interface. Because the interface is designed for the requirements of the notification, it makes sense to enter the ISR_ACTIVITY_EXECUTE function module and perform the actual programming in the QISR4 BAdI. The benefit of this approach is that the necessary data for executing the activity is provided in the ISR-typical form for transfer structures. Thus, you can program the activity in the same way as the form flow logic in the QISR1 BAdI.

Activities for Automatic Updates

If you want to use automatic updates, click on the Automatic Update button. Basically, all activities of the scenario are available for automatic updates. Only activities that are follow-up activities or dependent activities, that is, that require a previous activity, are not provided. You define whether the applicant or the approver performs individual activities for automatic updates, that is, either by submitting or approving the request.

Programming an Activity in the QISR4 BAdI

The automatic activity must be executed without interaction in the backend, that is, without being output or displayed on dynpros. The call should be implemented via the QISR4 BAdI through BAPIs or SELECT commands, for example, and no error message should be output via the RETURN parameter.

The interface of the EXECUTE_FUNCTION method in the QISR4 BAdI provides the corresponding parameters, which are listed in Table 9.2.

Parameters	Type	Description
FLT_VAL	Importing	Scenario name
QMART	Importing	Notification type
FUNCTION	Importing	Key of a function of the activity bar (action box) from the ISR Customizing
RETURN	Exporting	Error message
GENERAL_DATA	Changing	General data
SPECIAL_DATA	Changing	Data of the scenario-dependent fields

Table 9.2 Interface of the QISR4 BAdI

Depending on the selected function (FUNCTION), the required activity is usually executed after the evaluation of the scenario. Let's look at a programming example: The MC1 function creates a cost center via a BAPI. In addition, this function should be executable as an automatic function. The MC3 function executes a transaction and therefore cannot be used as the automatic activity; nevertheless, both functions can be programmed in one implementation (see Listing 9.1). The correct application of the functions must be ensured in the ISR Customizing.

```
METHOD if_ex_qisr4~execute_function.
  DATA: ls_change_data   TYPE fcom_isr_cc,
        lt_return        TYPE TABLE OF bapiret2,
        lt_costcenter    TYPE TABLE OF
                           bapi0012_ccinputlist.

* move form data to local structure
  CALL FUNCTION 'ISR_SPECIAL_DATA_TO_STRUC'
      EXPORTING
          it_special_data = special_data
      CHANGING
          cs_data         = ls_change_data.

  CASE function.
* Create cost center automatically
    WHEN 'MC1'.
* move special data to BAPI structure
*     ...
* Call BAPI to create Cost Center
      CALL FUNCTION 'BAPI_COSTCENTER_CREATEMULTIPLE'
          EXPORTING
```

```
          controllingarea = ls_change_data-co_area
          testrun         = space
      TABLES
          costcenterlist  = lt_costcenter
          return          = lt_return.
    IF lt_return[] IS INITIAL.
      COMMIT WORK.
    ENDIF.

*   Call transaction to change cost center
      WHEN 'MC2'.
        SET PARAMETER ID:
            'CAC' FIELD ls_change_data-co_area,
            'KOS' FIELD ls_change_data-costcenter.
        CALL TRANSACTION 'KS02' AND SKIP FIRST SCREEN.
      WHEN OTHERS.
    ENDCASE.
ENDMETHOD.
```

Listing 9.1 Programming the QISR4 BAdI for Activities

9.4.7 The Processor's Activities from the Form

The processor of a request can carry out multiple activities from the form using the corresponding buttons. The activities are provided as buttons (see Figure 9.27) in the service request (above the form) and can be hidden and displayed via the HIDE ACTIVITY LIST link.

Figure 9.27 The Processor's Activity List above the Form

Define the activities in the Customizing of the Report Launchpad. These activities can be useful when the processor processes the service request only in SAP NetWeaver Portal and doesn't use notification transactions.

Technical requirements for using the activities are SAP ERP 6.0 SP 12 and SAP NetWeaver Portal. For more information on these requirements, refer to SAP Note 1103969. In addition, you also need one of the following Web Dynpro applications: QISR_FORM or QISR_UI_FORM_DISPLAY_ONLY.

The form is called via the URL parameter, IFV=P. You can also set the FORM_VIEW = ISR_PROCESS container parameter in the workflow. The parameterized URL for a request with the notification number, 000600000110, of the SRCR scenario that is started by the processor in the CHANGE mode, may look as follows:

http://<server>:<port>/sap/bc/Web Dynpro/sap/qisr_ui_form?sap-language= DE&SCENARIO=SRCR&MODE=CHANGE&NOTIF_NO=000600000110&IFV=P.

You can configure the activities in the Customizing of the Report Launchpad using Transaction LPD_CUST.

1. To use the Report Launchpad correctly, the LPD_EXPERT parameter of your system user must be set to 'X.'

2. Call Transaction LPD_CUST and create a new launchpad.

3. The role must always be QISR. The instance corresponds to your scenario.

4. Select the ACTION LAUNCHPAD flag (see Figure 9.28). In the launchpad itself, you can define activities with various application categories.

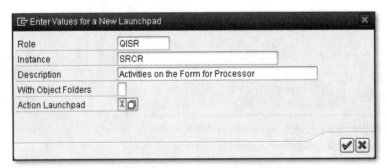

Figure 9.28 Customizing of a New Launchpad for Activities

5. Figure 9.29 shows simple examples for application categories. For a detailed explanation of the Report Launchpad, refer to the corresponding documentation.

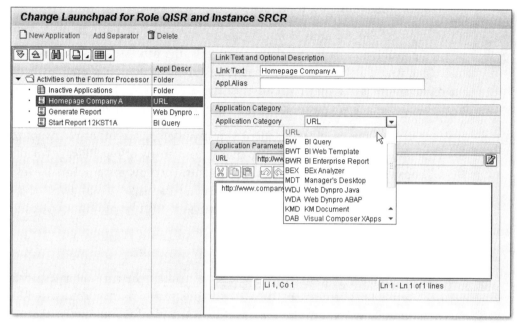

Figure 9.29 Customizing for the Activities of the Form

Analogous to the activities of the notification transaction from Section 9.2.5, "Processor Role," or Section 9.4.6, you can also use the QISR4 BAdI.

1. To do this, define an activity with the Transaction application category.

2. Include a variant of the QISRACTIVITY report in the launchpad with a customer-specific transaction.

3. The ISR framework automatically transfers the QMNUM and SCENARIO parameters for the notification number and the scenario.

4. Use the report variant to control the FUNCTION key value of the selected activity. Use Transaction QISRACTIVITY as an orientation point.

9.4.8 Processor Determination (BAdI QISR3) and Workflow

There are several ways to determine the responsible processor or approver of the service request. The use of SAP Business Workflow enables you to have the system automatically determine the processor.

If you don't use SAP Business Workflow, the processor can find the service request he is responsible for via the worklist. To do this, the processor can use Transaction IQS8, which is the variant with the lowest implementation effort. However, the disadvantage is that the processor must actively search for his requests. In this case, the system doesn't ensure that all service requests are provided.

If you don't use the provided standard workflow templates and if you want to use your own workflow template, you must create an event type linkage for the BUS7051 object category, the CREATED event, and its workflow pattern. For all event type linkages of this combination, you must enter the QGN01_EVENT_NOTIF_CRE-ATED_ISR function module as the Check Function.

WS03100019 Standard Workflow Template

The BUS7051 business object is responsible for generating the runtime object (previously referred to as *notification*) of the request and provides integration with SAP Business Workflow. You can use the WS03100019 standard workflow template of the notification. This workflow template supports the integration of any number of processors, and you can choose whether you want to use an approval step or not.

In the Customizing of the workflow, you must activate the event type linkage for the BUS7051 object category. You can define the responsible processors either directly in the Customizing of the workflow or use the rules of the workflow (Transaction PFAC) to have the system determine them automatically. For approvals, the workflow template only supports the variant with Backend Transaction IQS22.

WS31000009 ISR Workflow Template

If you want to perform *more* than one approval step, the standard workflow template of the notification is not sufficient. As an alternative, you can use the WS31000009 workflow template provided with the ISR framework, which also supports the two request processing options of the approver, that is, in the SAP ERP backend system and in the portal (see Section 9.2.4, "Approver Role"). This template must be defined in the basic Customizing of the ISR in Additional Data For Scenario (see Figure 9.30).

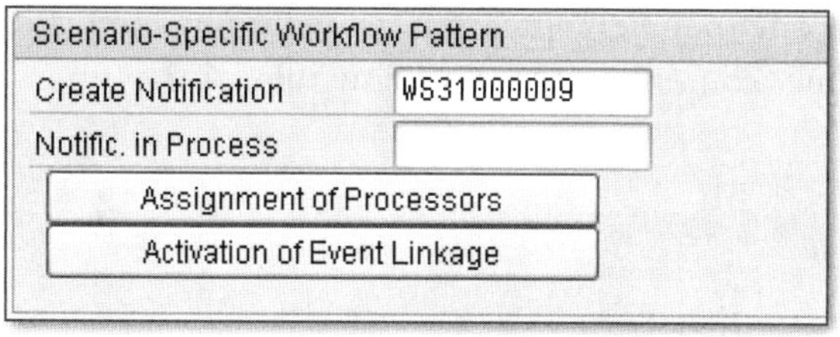

Scenario-Specific Workflow Pattern	
Create Notification	WS31000009
Notific. in Process	
Assignment of Processors	
Activation of Event Linkage	

Figure 9.30 Advanced ISR Customizing for the Workflow

You can call the event type linkage in the same screen via the ACTIVATION OF EVENT LINKAGE button. The names of the processors or workflow rules for the automatic determination of processors or approvers must be defined in the ISR Customizing (see Figure 9.31). To do this, click on the ASSIGNMENT OF PROCESSORS button. You should use the WS31000009 ISR workflow template, because it is more flexible and can be configured more easily.

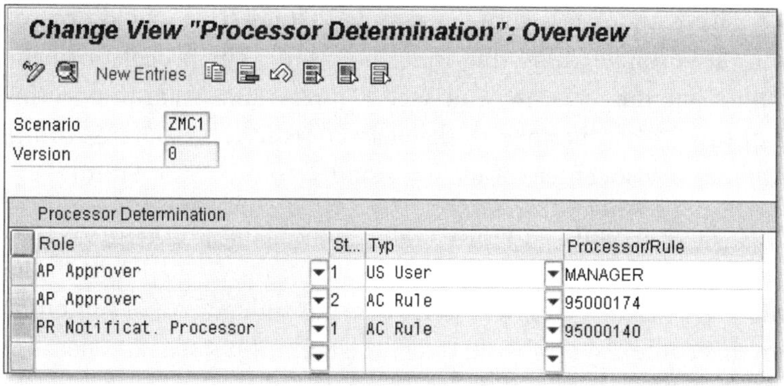

Change View "Processor Determination": Overview

New Entries

Scenario	ZMC1
Version	0

Processor Determination

Role	St...	Typ	Processor/Rule
AP Approver	1	US User	MANAGER
AP Approver	2	AC Rule	95000174
PR Notificat. Processor	1	AC Rule	95000140

Figure 9.31 Processor Assignment to ISR Roles

In addition to the central Customizing, by using the WS31000009 workflow template the current workflow container can be changed for every processor determination by means of a rule for a scenario-specific implementation of the QISR3 BAdI. The rule enables you to determine the responsibilities based on the form data, and the QISR3 BAdI also enables you to control the processor determination. This BAdI has only one method.

Table 9.3 describes the interface of the single method, CONTAINER_FOR_ACTOR_DET_FILL. The IS_VIQMEL, IS_TQ80 and IS_VIQMSM parameters provide information on the current notification at runtime, IT_SPECIAL_DATA contains the form data. You can now use this data to adapt the CT_ACT_CONTAINER workflow container. IT_CONT_DEF contains the list of the container elements from the workflow template. Thus, you can evaluate the container content using a workflow rule for the processor determination.

Parameter	Type	Description
IT_CONT_DEF	Importing	Workflow container elements
IS_VIQMEL	Importing	Notification
IS_TQ80	Importing	Notification type
IS_VIQMSM	Importing	Task
IT_SPECIAL_DATA	Importing	Form data
CT_ACT_CONTAINER	Tables	Workflow container

Table 9.3 Interfaces of CONTAINER_FOR_ACTOR_DET_FILL

In this context, let's have a look at a simple example that describes the processor determination with a workflow rule using the QISR3 BAdI. The processor of the request is determined via the 95000140 rule (see Figure 9.32). According to this rule, all requests of the SMC1 scenario with the characteristic value A* to L* of the persons responsible for a cost center should be assigned to processor Smith.

If the characteristic value is within the interval M* to Z*, the processor MSS1 is determined (see Figure 9.33). This already works without the QISR3 BAdI. In the BAdI, for example, you can still change the person responsible for a cost center for specific criteria. In this context, you should query the current ISR scenario because this BAdI implementation is used for all scenarios that deploy the so-called workflow templates (see Listing 9.2).

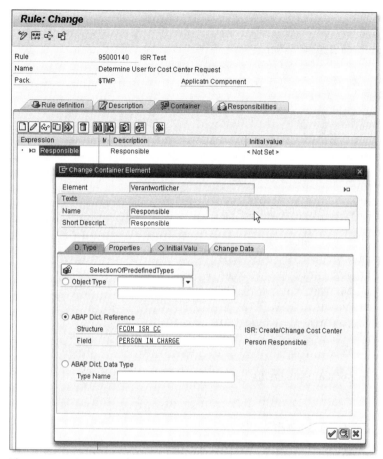

Figure 9.32 Container Element of the Rule with Reference to a Characteristic

Name	Priority	Status	Code	Assigned a...	Assigned u...
▼ 📇 M bis Z		☐ Res...	M bis Z		
· 📇 Peter Smith			Smith	11/13/2006	12/31/2030
▼ 📇 A bis L		☐ Res...	A bis L		
· 📇 MSS1			MSS1	08/26/2008	12/31/2030

Figure 9.33 Definition of the Responsibilities of the Rule

```
METHOD if_ex_qisr3~container_for_actor_det_fill.
DATA: ls_change_data   TYPE fcom_isr_cc,
      ls_act_container TYPE swcont.

* Only Scenario SMC1
  CHECK is_viqmel-auswirk = 'SMC1'.

* Form data in local structure
  CALL FUNCTION 'ISR_SPECIAL_DATA_TO_STRUC'
    EXPORTING
      it_special_data = it_special_data
    CHANGING
      cs_data         = ls_change_data.

* Adaptation of the WF container
  IF ls_change_data-department = 'A123'.
    READ TABLE ct_act_container INTO ls_act_container
        WITH KEY element = 'PERSON_INCHARGE'.
    ls_act_container-value = 'STANDARD_RESPONSIBLE'.
    MODIFY ct_act_container FROM ls_act_container.
  ENDIF.
ENDMETHOD.
```

Listing 9.2 Programming of the QISR3 BAdI

9.4.9 Service Costs and BAdI QISR2

The ISR integrates with the Overhead Cost Controlling function of SAP ERP 6.0. This function allows for a cost-related control of the available service requests in the enterprise. If a department in your enterprise provides one or more services to employees, you can internally allocate the overhead costs that were incurred in this department.

The ISR provides three options for cost determination:

▶ **Template allocation of Easy Cost Planning**
Easy Cost Planning enables you to link a complex cost determination process with the service request. The options and functions of this tool are not explained in detail here, because this would go beyond the scope of this chapter.

▶ **Estimated costs**
Estimated costs result in an entry of the costs into the notification. However, these costs are not transferred to Overhead Cost Controlling.

▸ **Price list**

The price list determines the cost of a request. This section describes the price list procedure.

Costs are automatically posted to a cost object, such as an internal order or cost center of the applicant, when the notification that was created with the ISR is completed. The cost center of this service department accepts these costs as an activity based on a price that you can define.

You can implement the automatic cost determination by configuring only a few settings (see Figure 9.34):

1. In the basic ISR Customizing, select the THE SCENARIO INCURS COSTS flag.

2. Then, enter the CONTROLLING AREA.

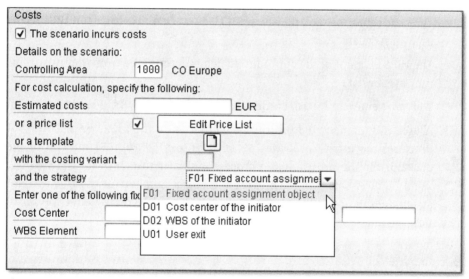

Figure 9.34 Basic ISR Customizing for Service Costs

3. Use the PRICE LIST to determine the cost sender. To do this, select the PRICE LIST flag and click on EDIT PRICE LIST.

4. In the price list, define the combination of the cost center and the activity type of the service provider (for example, cost center of the service department). Enter the "costs" of a service request into the ISR Price field.

5. You can also create multiple prices. The Default flag controls which price is used (see Figure 9.35).

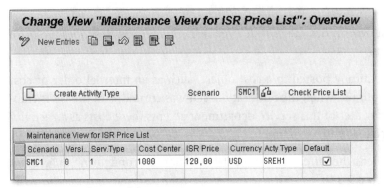

Figure 9.35 Definition of the Price List

6. Determine the cost collector (strategy) by selecting the *account assignment object*. The following options are available:

   ▶ The cost center of the applicant, which is determined from the HR-specific user master data.

   ▶ The WBS element of the applicant, which is determined from the HR-specific user master data.

   ▶ You must enter an internal order, a cost center, or a WBS element.

   ▶ A user exit, namely, the BAdI implementation of the QISR2 BAdI. Table 9.4 describes the interface of the ISR_ACCOUNT_ASSIGNMENT_GET method of the QISR2 BAdI. The programming process is similar to that of the QISR1 BAdI. OBJNR_REAL enables you to provide the object number for the true account assignment in Controlling (CO). OBJNR_STAT enables you to define the statistical account assignment object.

Parameter	Type	Description
FLT_VAL	Importing	Scenario name
GENERAL_DATA	Importing	General ISR data
SPECIAL_DATA	Importing	Form data
OBJNR_REAL	Exporting	True CO account assignment
OBJNR_STAT	Exporting	Statistical CO account assignment

Table 9.4 ISR_ACCOUNT_ASSIGNMENT_GET Method

7. After defining your own notification type, check to see if an implementation for the NOTIF_EVENT_POST BAdI with the notification type of your scenario exists. If there is no such implementation, create a new one with your notification type as the filter value. You should use the ISR_CHECK_AT_POST implementation as the template.

9.4.10 Testing the Scenario

The Test function next to the Form field in the basic ISR Customizing (see Figure 9.22) enables you to quickly call the form to check any changes made to the form or the Customizing.

1. To do this, you must navigate to the Additional Data for Scenario Customizing and enter the corresponding server via the SERVER button.

2. If there is no entry for the entry type in the Web (A – Entry Using Adobe PDF), create a new entry.

3. Enter the URL for the server into the Server for Call the ISR Forms field as follows:

   http://<myserver>:<port>/sap/bc/Web Dynpro/sap/

   Replace the *<myserver>* placeholder with your server, and enter the corresponding port for *<port>*.

4. Furthermore, implement the settings from SAP Note 1110677 for activating the testability with the Web Dynpro ABAP component of the ISR in the Customizing.

5. To test the Adobe form, click the TEST button. The system automatically inserts the necessary URL parameters (for example, the scenario). The form for creating a request is started in a browser window.

6. The ISR_PROCESS_EVENT function module is another alternative for testing. It enables you to test all backend settings without an Adobe form: the scenario Customizing, the Workflow, and the BAdI implementation. Section 9.7.4 provides a detailed description of the function module.

9.5　Request Forms as Adobe Forms

The interactive Adobe form within the ISR framework must meet specific technical requirements with regard to the interface, the context of the form, and the individual screen elements. Therefore, the basic ISR Customizing provides additional definition and generation aids.

9.5.1　Specific Properties

You define the characteristics in the ISR Customizing as described in Section 9.4.5. The fields in the Adobe form, however, are bound to the context of the form and not to the Customizing of the ISR. So how can you ensure that the form contains the appropriate characteristics?

The interface and the context of the form must meet specific criteria. The options provided by Form Builder for defining the form interface cannot be fully used within the ISR. The reason for this restriction is that the definition of the form context is outsourced to the ISR Customizing. This means that the interface and context must correspond to the characteristics of the Customizing.

The following conditions apply to the usage of interfaces in the ISR:

▶ You can only use DDIC interfaces. It is not possible to use XML interfaces.

▶ The interface must have an ISR-specific data structure.

▶ Only import parameters are used.

▶ It is not possible to link single elements to specific DDIC elements or advanced Form Builder functions. Initializations and form routines are not supported, for example.

▶ You must program data initializations in the appropriate implementation of the QISR1 BAdI (see Section 9.6).

The following conditions apply to the usage of forms in the ISR:

▶ The layout type must be Zero Client Installation (ZCI) Layout.

▶ The data context has an ISR-specific data structure and must be copied from the interface on a one-to-one basis.

▶ To use programmed input helps, the script of the screen elements from the ISR library is mandatory. The same holds true for the usage of form events and standardized approval forms.

> **ZCI in the ISR**
>
> Along with the introduction of ZCI technology, all of the provided Adobe forms of the ISR were set from the previous ACF technology to ZCI. The delivery in SAP ERP 6.0 was implemented in SP 5 (see SAP Note 947675). You should use the ZCI Layout type for customer-specific forms within the ISR.
>
> The ZCI technology is described in detail in Section 8.5.2.

9.5.2 Structure of the Interface and Form Context

The ISR framework ensures that the contents of the fields of the Adobe form are transferred to the backend and that field contents that are determined in the backend are correctly mapped in the form. Here, it is critical that the form context meets the ISR criteria. The context only corresponds to the assigned interface. If you only use the functions of the ISR Customizing to generate new and adapt existing forms, this requirement is automatically met.

To ensure correct data binding of the Adobe form at runtime, every characteristic must use the generic table types of the ISR in the context of the Adobe form (see Figure 9.36):

▶ **QISR_TAB_TYPE_DATE**
Characteristics of the Date type (DDIC data type: DATS)

▶ **QISR_TAB_TYPE_TEXT**
Characteristics for plain text

▶ **QISR_TAB_TYPE**
All other characteristics

All three table types have the same data structure: `<characteristic>-<DATA>-<FIELD>`. The `<characteristic>` placeholder stands for the name of the characteristic from the ISR Customizing. Due to the generic programming of the ISR Web Dynpro component, this tabular data structure is necessary and must not be changed.

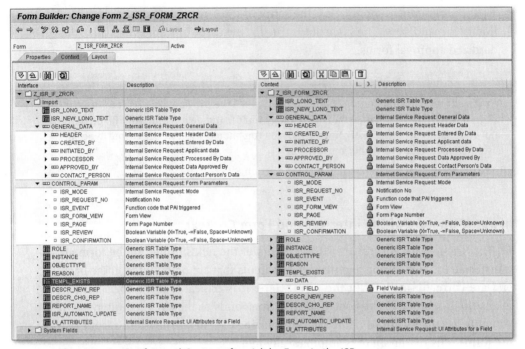

Figure 9.36 Interface and Context of an Adobe Form in the ISR

The following ISR-specific structures constitute the exception to this rule, because they exist in all forms and interfaces of the ISR and thus don't have to be generated in the Web Dynpro component.

▶ **General ISR data** (structure: GENERAL_DATA)
The structure provides information on the processors involved and technical information (see Section 9.4.5).

▶ **Form parameters** (structure: CONTROL_PARAM)
The structure provides technical information that can be used for script programming. The attributes correspond to those from Section 9.6.2. The ISR_REVIEW attribute indicates whether the user is in the second step (Check and Send) of the request form, and the ISR_CONFIRMATION attribute provides the information that the user is currently in the third and last step (Completed) of the request form.

▶ **UI attributes of a field** (structure: UI_ATTRIBUTES)
This structure contains the layout information from the QISR1 BAdI.

> **Creating the Context and the Interface**
>
> You should only use the Generate and Change Adobe Form functions of the ISR Customizing to adapt the context of a form. The interface is automatically modified.

9.5.3 Generating Adobe Forms from Characteristics

During the generation of an Adobe form, the system automatically copies the characteristics of the scenario to the interface and context of the form. For the creation of an Adobe form, a number of configurations are possible:

▶ **You have defined an ISR scenario with characteristics, but the form has not been created yet.**
You generate the form via the GENERATE button (see Figure 9.37). You then have the following options:

  ▶ A blank form

  ▶ A form in the SAP standard (the ISR_FORM_STANDARD form is used as the template)

  ▶ The form with the template of another scenario

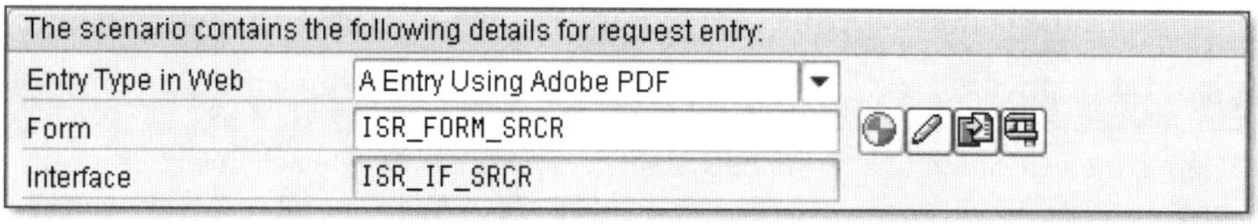

Figure 9.37 Functions for the Generation and Processing of an Adobe Form in the Basic ISR Customizing

In Form Builder, you then design the layout. To define fields with ISR-specific script programming (see Section 9.5.5, "ISR Library—Special Screen Elements"), use the ISR library—at least at the beginning. Finally, generate the data binding between the layout elements and the context fields. If you use Form Builder to define new fields in the layout for which no characteristics exist, Form Builder asks you when you exit it whether these characteristics should be created (see Section 9.5.4, "Generating New Characteristics from the Form").

► **You have defined an ISR scenario with characteristics and have a PDF form, but no Form Builder form.**
In this case, you can perform the same steps as described previously. The only difference is that, after the generation, you load the PDF into Form Builder and then edit the layout. Then, you implement the data binding.

► **You have a form defined in Form Builder. This form has the appropriate form fields in the layout but doesn't have the appropriate context for the ISR.**
There are two "useful" alternatives to customize the form for the ISR:

  ► If you have defined the corresponding characteristics in the ISR Customizing, enter the name of the form into the ISR Customizing and click on the Change Adobe Form button. This brings you to Form Builder, and the system generates the appropriate interface and context. Note that the previous context is overwritten. Now, you need to manually implement the data binding between the layout and context.

  ► If you haven't defined the corresponding characteristics in the ISR Customizing yet, enter the name of the form into the ISR Customizing, and click on the Import Form Fields button. Now the system reads the technical names of all layout elements of the form that can be used for data input and generates the characteristics in the ISR Customizing. In addition, it automatically generates the context and the data binding in the form (see Section 9.5.4).

What Happens During the Generation?

During the generation of a form, the system generates the Workbench object of a form and of an ABAP Dictionary-based interface (DDIC). XML-based interfaces cannot be used within the ISR.

You can specify the technical name of the form and interface in the fields of the ISR Customizing with the same name in advance. You can freely select the name within the framework of the customer namespace of Workbench objects. If you don't specify the names, the system automatically determines these names. To do this, the following logic is used in the customer system; xxxx refers to the four-digit name of the scenario:

► Form: ZISR_FORM_xxxx

► Interface: ZISR_IF_xxxx

The system automatically copies the characteristics of the scenario that are defined in the ISR Customizing to the DDIC interface and context of the form. The standard fields described in Section 9.5.2 are copied in the same way.

9.5.4 Generating New Characteristics from the Form

If you first define a form without having created an ISR scenario with characteristics in advance, or if you have defined new fields in the layout, you can proceed as follows to make the form usable in the ISR.

1. Call Form Builder via the Change Adobe Form button. If you have defined new fields in the layout, these fields are automatically copied as characteristics to the scenario Customizing when you exit Form Builder. During this process, the system automatically defines the data binding of the new fields in the layout. To achieve this, confirm the corresponding dialog box.

2. You can also implement this at a later stage. Click the corresponding button to carry out the Import Form Fields function in Customizing. The system then uses the technical names of all screen elements that are defined in the form to generate the corresponding characteristics. In addition, it also adapts the corresponding interface and context in the form. Finally, the system generates the data binding between the context elements and the corresponding screen elements of the form; so far, everything has been done automatically. Answer Yes in the dialog box to confirm activation of the form.

3. The generated characteristics are declared as Uncategorized. Therefore, you need to postprocess the Customizing of the characteristics, for example, to create the reference to the Data Dictionary for individual characteristics.

4. If you created the form outside the scenario Customizing, navigate to the Customizing and enter the required form into the Form field. Then, click on the Import Form Fields button to the right of the input field.

9.5.5 ISR Library—Special Screen Elements

You should use the screen elements from the ISR library for forms with ZCI Layout (see Figure 9.38). In this context, the script is important and not the layout, which you can customize as required.

The library is provided with the SAP GUI. SAP Note 947633 contains current updates for the ISR library, and the entire ISR library is documented in SAP Note 741381.

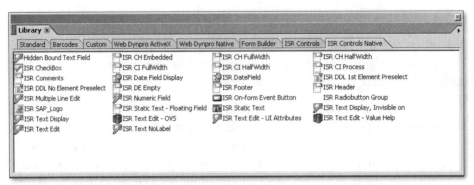

Figure 9.38 ISR Library for Forms with the ZCI Layout Type

The advantage—or preferably, the requirement—of the ISR library is that an ISR-specific script (FormCalc or JavaScript) with specific functions is already assigned to the individual elements. For example, if you plan to implement programmed input helps for a form field, you must use this script.

The critical special screen elements with a specific script include:

▶ **ISR DDL 1st Element Preselect (input help)**
The first value pair of the programmed value list is automatically copied for the field value. Section 9.6.3 contains a programming example for a dropdown list box.

▶ **ISR DDL No Element Preselect (input help)**
The field can only be populated via a manual selection from the dropdown list box.

▶ **ISR On-form Event Button (button)**
Here, the system generates a button with an event. This button can be evaluated in the QISR1 BAdI.

▶ **ISR Text Edit — Object Value Selector (OVS) (input help)**
You define the input and output fields of the OVS in Customizing Transaction QISRSCENARIO_OVS. You program this input help in the SET_ADDITIONAL_DATA method of your BAdI implementation, QISR1.

▶ **ISR Text Edit — Value Help (input help)**
SAP Note 1035630 provides detailed information on this DDIC-related input help.

► **ISR Text Edit — UI Attributes (script template)**

SAP Note 925657 contains details on how to control layout properties of individual fields, such as mandatory field, visibility, and ready-for-input status using the QISR1 BAdI.

► **ISR Multiple-Line Edit (multiple-line long text field)**

If you use this field, you must select the Long Text flag for the respective characteristic in the ISR Customizing (see Section 9.4.5).

You can also bind the form field to the standard ISR element for comments, ISR_NEW_LONG_TEXT, from the form context (see Figure 9.39). Here, every newly entered text is transferred to the subject long text of the notification. It can be viewed and changed in Transaction IQS22. In this case, you should define a second long text field and bind it to the second standard ISR element for comments on the ISR_LONG_TEXT display. Now the system displays already-entered texts. The form in Figure 9.39 shows an example for both long text fields.

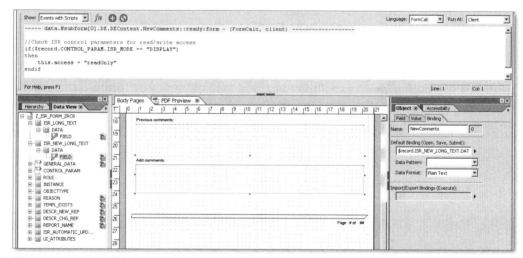

Figure 9.39 Usage of the Standard Long Text Fields, ISR_NEW_LONG_TEXT and ISR_LONG_TEXT, in Form Builder

The following sections introduce simple examples of ISR-specific scripts.

Using the Script to Control the Ready-for-Input Status of Fields

You can easily make the fields editable by adapting the script programming of individual fields in Form Builder. The standard ISR script for controlling the ready-for-input status is defined in the `ready:form - (formcalc,client)` event of a field (see Listing 9.3).

```
//Check ISR control parameters for read/write access
if($record.CONTROL_PARAM.ISR_MODE == "DISPLAY" |
    $record.CONTROL_PARAM.ISR_FORM_VIEW =="ISR_APPROVE" )
then
        this.access = "readOnly"
endif
```

Listing 9.3 Script for the Ready-for-Input Status

For example, if you remove the query for equality with the ISR_APPROVE event, the corresponding field is ready for input for the approver.

If you have complex requirements for the layout properties, use the dynamic script of the ISR Text Edit – UI Attributes script template from the ISR library.

Using the Script to Generate an Event

You can link a button to an event by modifying the script programming of the button. If you click on this button, the BAdI implementation of the QISR1 BAdI is executed, and the system transfers the EVENT of the form to the USER_COMMAND parameter. The standard ISR script for the name of the event is defined in the `mouseDown - (FormCalc, client)` event of the button (see Listing 9.4).

```
//Set ISR_EVENT for BAdI processing in backend
$record.CONTROL_PARAM.ISR_EVENT = "CUSTOM_EVENT"
```

Listing 9.4 Script for the CUSTOM_EVENT Event

You must also define the mechanism of the event of the Adobe form in the `click - (JavaScript, client)` event of the field (see Listing 9.5).

```
//Trigger call to backend for
//BAdI user command processing
ContainerFoundation_JS.SendMessageToContainer(event.
  target, "submit", "", "", "", "");
this.access = "readOnly"
```

Listing 9.5 Script for an Event

Enhanced Input Help

SAP ERP 6.0 SP 12 (SAP_APPL) enables you to provide an enhanced input help (Object Value Selector (OVS)) to one or more fields in an Adobe form in the ISR. SAP Note 906950 provides detailed information on the OVS. You must carry out the following steps to implement an enhanced input help.

1. **Corresponding ISR Customizing**
   You need to define the attributes for the input help in Customizing Transaction QISRSCENARIO_OVS (see Figure 9.40). Select a scenario and navigate to CHARACTERISTICS WITH ENHANCED SEARCH HELP. Define a characteristic as the start field for an input help and check the Active flag.

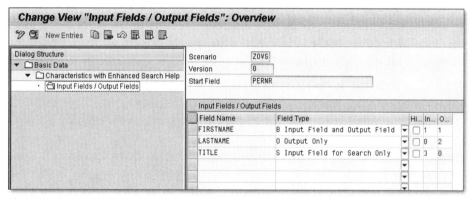

Figure 9.40 Customizing of the Enhanced Input Help

   Define the input and output fields for the selected start field (you can use all characteristics of the scenario), and specify which type and position the respective field should have:

   ▶ B INPUT FIELD AND OUTPUT FIELD

   ▶ S INPUT FIELD FOR SEARCH ONLY

   ▶ O OUTPUT ONLY

   Output fields can be hidden. That means the results list of the input help does not display the field. After the selection of the user in the dialog box of the input help, the value of this field is transferred to the form just like the other selected values.

2. **Screen element in the form**

Use the ISR Text Edit – OVS or ISR Text Edit – Value Help screen element from the ISR library for enhanced input help.

Note that you need to enter the corresponding field name in the `Click` action handler in addition to the common data binding and the script of the input help. Find the following line:

```
var fieldName = "FieldNameToBeReplaced";
```

Replace the `FieldNameToBeReplaced` variable with the field name, which you can find in the lower-level Binding tab of the Object tab. Here, the field name is listed as Name.

If the system is supposed to automatically check the value entered in the SAP ERP backend system after the user has made an entry in the input help, insert the following lines in the `Exit` event of the screen element via the script editor of the Adobe form (see Listing 9.6).

```
xfa.record.CONTROL_PARAM.ISR_EVENT.value =
  "<EVENT_NAME>";
xfa.record.GENERAL_DATA.HEADER.EXT_REF_NUMBER.value =
  "VALUE_HELP";
```

Listing 9.6 Additional Script for the Input Help

Replace the `<EVENT_NAME>` placeholder with any event name. You can also use the `CHECK` standard event.

3. **Programming the input help**

You can program the input help in the scenario-specific implementation of the `QISR1` BAdI in the `SCENARIO_SET_ADDITIONAL_VALUES` or `INT_SERVICE_REQUEST_INIT` method.

Insert all output values of the output fields in the `ADDITIONAL_DATA` transfer table. This data is then used as the basis of the search. Based on the input, the system delivers the results list to the OVS search fields as a subset of the entries from the `ADDITIONAL_DATA` table at runtime. The table contains the following fields:

- `FIELDINDEX` field: counter, starting with 1
- `FIELDNAME` field: characteristic name
- `FIELDVALUE` field: value

4. **Tips for the implementation in the QISR1 BAdI**

The sorting of the rows in the results list is controlled via the FIELDINDEX counter. In the FIELDNAME field, you must enter the exact characteristic name, without additional ending, such as _KEY, as it is required for the programming of the dropdown list box (see Section 9.6.3).

Other fields in the form can be programmed as dropdown list boxes. The ISR_CUST_SCENARIO_VALHLP_GET function module provides all of the information from the Customizing of the enhanced input help.

Listing 9.7 illustrates a programming example of the SCENARIO_SET_ADDITIONAL_VALUES method from the QISR1 BAdI for an enhanced input help. The PERSON characteristic is defined as an OVS, and the maximum results list consists of the FIRSTNAME, LASTNAME, and TITLE output fields. The entries in the ADDITIONAL_DATA table could look as follows; the list contains two data records.

```
METHOD if_ex_qisr1~SCENARIO_SET_ADDITIONAL_VALUES
  DATA: ls_additional_value TYPE qisrsspecial_param.
  ls_additional_value-fieldindex = 1.
  ls_additional_value-fieldname  = ,FIRSTNAME'.
  ls_additional_value-fieldvalue = ,Jim'.
  APPEND ls_additional_value TO additional_data.
  ls_additional_value-fieldname  = ,LASTNAME'.
  ls_additional_value-fieldvalue = ,Smith' .
  APPEND ls_additional_value TO additional_data.
  ls_additional_value-fieldname  = ,TITLE'.
  ls_additional_value-fieldvalue = ,Mr.'.
  APPEND ls_additional_value TO additional_data.
  CLEAR ls_additional_value.

  ls_additional_value-fieldindex = 2.
  ls_additional_value-fieldname  = ,FIRSTNAME'.
  ls_additional_value-fieldvalue = ,Linda'.
  APPEND ls_additional_value TO additional_data.
  ls_additional_value-fieldname  = ,LASTNAME'.
  ls_additional_value-fieldvalue = ,Green' .
  APPEND ls_additional_value TO additional_data.
  ls_additional_value-fieldname  = ,TITLE'.
  ls_additional_value-fieldvalue = ,Mrs.'.
  APPEND ls_additional_value TO additional_data.
  CLEAR ls_additional_value.
```

Listing 9.7 Programming for an Enhanced Input Help (OVS)

9.6 Form Flow Logic

In addition to the definition of the Customizing and the Adobe form, you can now start using programs to control the flow logic of the form with the QISR1 BAdI. An essential aspect of the ISR is its flexibility in manipulating the flow logic of the request form. The ISR framework enables you to control the flow logic of the request form in the backend via the predefined QISR1 BAdI definition. This section uses simple programming examples to show how you can use the BAdI implementation.

To add your own processing logic to a form, select Define Business-Add-In in the basic ISR Customizing. Now you can create, modify, or delete implementations. You can assign a specific BAdI implementation of the QISR1 BAdI definition to each scenario by default. However, if required, you can also use one BAdI implementation for multiple scenarios. You either assign the additional scenario directly to a BAdI implementation as an additional filter value or you enter the scenario into Business Add-In from Scenario whose BAdI implementation you want to use for the current scenario. This configuration only applies to the QISR1 BAdI.

> **Multiple Assignment of a BAdI Implementation to the Scenario**
> You can use the BAdI implementation in multiple scenarios. However, you should link a scenario to the BAdI implementation of another scenario in the basic Customizing if you have many similar scenarios or if you don't want to modify the existing BAdI implementation.

Figure 9.41 shows a diagram of the form flow logic with the times of the calls of individual methods of the QISR1 BAdI. For more information, refer to SAP Note 105505.

In total, nine BAdI methods are available:

▶ **INT_SERVICE_REQUEST_INIT** (initialization)
This method is executed once as the first method when a request form is called for a new request and is used for data initializations in the form. The following parameter values are already defined here:

  ▶ MODE = "CREATE"

  ▶ FORM_VIEW = "ISR_REQUEST"

  ▶ EVENT (empty)

SAP Note 883718 describes how you can also use the method in the Change or Display mode.

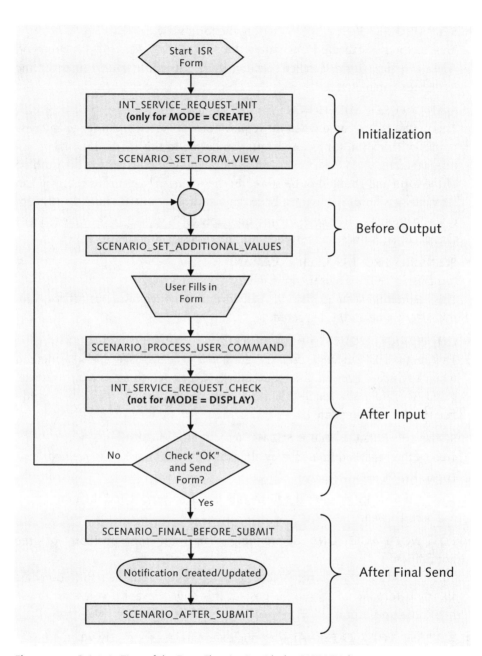

Figure 9.41 Points in Time of the Form Flow Logic with the QISR1 BAdI

▶ **SCENARIO_SET_FORM_VIEW** (setting the form view)
This method is executed once after the `INT_SERVICE_REQUEST_INIT` method when a request form is called. Section 9.6.2 lists the default values for the `FORM_VIEW` parameter.

▶ **SCENARIO_SET_ADDITIONAL_VALUES** (input helps)
This method is executed when the request form is started and prior to any new output of the form, for example, after an `EVENT`. In this method, populate the internal table, `ADDITIONAL_DATA`, with values that you only need at the runtime of the form and should not be stored in the request. That means that you can set value lists for dropdown list boxes and control parameters here. The system doesn't automatically delete the internal table, `ADDITIONAL_DATA`, which means that data that is once set is stored until the form is submitted.

▶ **SCENARIO_PROCESS_USER_COMMAND**
(processing your own user commands)
This method is executed first when any event in the request form (Check, Submit, User Command) is triggered.

▶ **INT_SERVICE_REQUEST_CHECK** (check)
This method is executed after the `SCENARIO_PROCESS_USER_COMMAND` method when a standard event in the request form (Check or Submit of a form) is triggered. Therefore, the request data is always checked before the new or modified notification is updated.

▶ **SCENARIO_FINAL_BEFORE_SUBMIT** (check prior to the submit event)
This method is called immediately after the notification has been created.

▶ **SCENARIO_AFTER_SUBMIT** (exit after the submit event)
This method is called after the form data has been posted and the notification has been created.

▶ **POST_NOTIF_POSITION** (determining data for the position of the notification)
This method serves to derive the notification position from the notification data shortly before the notification is posted. It is only relevant if you want to use notification positions.

▶ **REVERSE_NOTIF_EXTERNAL** (deleting external data separately when a notification is reversed)
This notification is an exception, because it is not processed via the form. Instead, it is used when a service request is reversed in the ISR status overview

to allow for request-specific and scenario-specific data changes outside of the actual request.

This is the case, for example, if you entered additional information on the request in a customer-specific table when creating the request in your scenario to use it for later evaluations. By reversing the request, you can adapt this data.

9.6.1 Data Structures within the ISR Framework

Table 9.5 lists the most important data structures for implementing the BAdI methods. They are provided in most of the methods of the QISR1 BAdI and in the other BAdIs of the ISR (see Section 9.4). However, this list is not complete, because the other parameters are not relevant for most of the applications. Their relevance is described in the documentation of the QISR1 BAdI.

Parameter	Type	Description
FLT_VAL	QSCENARIO	Current scenario
MODE	QISRDMODE	Describes the edit mode
FORM_VIEW	QISRDFORMVIEW	Current form view
USER_COMMAND	SYUCOMM	Event (standard events and scenario-specific events)
RETURN	BAPIRET1	Return structure for error messages
MESSAGE_LIST	QISRTRETURN	List with messages of various error categories
UI_ATTRIBUTES	QISRTUI_ATTRIBUTES	UI properties of a form field
GENERAL_DATA	QISRSGENERAL_PARAM	General ISR data (applicant, and so on)
SPECIAL_DATA	QISRTSPECIAL_PARAM	Form data
ADDITIONAL_DATA	QISRTSPECIAL_PARAM	Values for input helps

Table 9.4 Interface Parameters of Methods of the QISR1 BAdI

9.6.2 Default Values for the MODE, USER_COMMAND, and FORM_ VIEW Parameters

The following list describes some critical parameters of the BAdIs and the relevance of the corresponding permitted values.

- ▶ **MODE**

  MODE describes the current edit mode. The MODE parameter enables you to design your program logic based on the current mode:

  - ▶ CREATE if the ISR form is called for a new request
  - ▶ CHANGE if the ISR form with the notification number is called to be modified
  - ▶ DISPLAY if the ISR form with the notification number is called to be displayed

- ▶ **FORM_VIEW**

  FORM_VIEW describes the current processor role.

  - ▶ ISR_APPROVE if the approver is processing the form
  - ▶ ISR_REQUEST if the applicant is processing the form
  - ▶ ISR_PROCESS if the processor is processing the form or the notification

- ▶ **USER_COMMAND**

  The standard ISR events in USER_COMMAND are defined as follows:

  - ▶ SEND if the form is sent for a new request/notification
  - ▶ SAVE if the form is saved for an existing request/notification
  - ▶ CHECK if the Check button is clicked in the form
  - ▶ ACCEPT if the Approved button is clicked in the approval form
  - ▶ REJECT if the Reject button is clicked in the approval form
  - ▶ BACK if the Back to Author button is clicked in the approval form

  In your customer-specific form, you can define any number of events that can be queried in the methods of the QISR1 BAdI via the USER_COMMAND parameter at runtime (see Section 9.6.3).

9.6.3 Programming Examples

This section provides some simple programming examples. They are designed to introduce you to the programmed form flow logic and illustrate the basic options of the QISR1 BAdI.

Programming Example for a Field Initialization

The NEW_COSTCENTER characteristic is initialized via the INITIATED_BY-MASTER_CCTR standard ISR parameter (see Listing 9.8).

```
METHOD if_ex_qisr1~int_service_request_init
* local data
  DATA: ls_special_data TYPE qisrsspecial_param.

  LOOP AT special_data INTO ls_special_data.
      CASE ls_special_data-fieldname.
    WHEN 'NEW_COSTCENTER'.
      ls_special_data-fieldvalue =
                 general_data-initiated_by-master_cctr.
        WHEN OTHERS.
    ENDCASE.
      MODIFY special_data FROM ls_special_data.
  ENDLOOP.
```

Listing 9.8 Field Initialization

Programming Example for a Check

The system returns an error message after a check (see Listing 9.9).

```
METHOD if_ex_qisr1~int_service_request_check
  IF general_data-initiated_by-lastname is initial.
    return-type   = 'E'.
    return-id     = 'QISR'.
    return-number = '046'.
    EXIT.
  ENDIF.
```

Listing 9.9 Programming of an Error Message

Programming Example for a Form Event

The USER_COMMAND or EVENT URLB of the form is processed if it is a new request (see Listing 9.10).

```
METHOD if_ex_qisr1~scenario_process_user_command.
  DATA:      ls_special_data type qisrsspecial_param.
  DATA:      lv_vacation(1)   type c.

* only for new requests
   CHECK mode = 'CREATE'.

* process user commands
     CASE user_command.
    WHEN 'VACA'.
```

527

```
* read special data VACATION
      LOOP AT special_data INTO ls_special_data.
        IF ls_special_data-fieldname = 'VACATION'.
          lv_vacation = ls_special_data-fieldvalue.
      ENDLOOP.
      READ TABLE special_data INTO ls_special_data
          WITH KEY fieldname = 'ESS_COSTS'.
      IF sy-subrc EQ 0 AND lv_vacation eq 'X'.
*     delete 'ESS_COSTS' if leave is selected
        CLEAR ls_special_data-fieldvalue.
      ENDIF.
      MODIFY special_data FROM ls_special_data
                          INDEX sy-tabix.
   ENDCASE.
```

Listing 9.10 Programming of an Event (User Command)

Programming Example for an Input Help

To implement an input help for a characteristic (for example, SYSTEMNAME) in the QISR1 BAdI, you must populate the internal table, ADDITIONAL_DATA, of the SCE-NARIO_SET_ADDITIONAL_VALUES method for the key value (for example, SYSTEM-NAME_KEY) and the corresponding description (for example, SYSTEMNAME_LABEL). You implement multiple entries in the input help via the sequential numbering in the FIELDINDEX field.

You must define the technical name and the description of the key value in the Customizing of the characteristics (see Figure 9.25). The technical names are used to correctly assign the input values. The ADDITIONAL_DATA table can therefore contain the values of several input helps at the same time.

Either use the ISR_DDL_NoSelected or ISR_DDL_1stSelected layout element from the ISR library (see Section 9.5.5). Figure 9.42 displays the result of the programming example in the Adobe form using the ISR_DDL_NoSelected element. SAP Note 1133359 describes how you can map the dropdown list box as an Extended Value Selector (EVS).

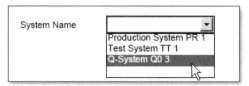

Figure 9.42 Programmed Input Help in the Adobe Form at Runtime

To define an enhanced input help, use the separate Customizing transaction, QISRSCENARIO_OVS, instead of the basic ISR Customizing. The value list is programmed in the `SCENARIO_PROCESS_USER_COMMAND` method. You can find a programming example in SAP Note 906950. In the Adobe form, use the ISR Text Edit – OVS layout element from the ISR library.

You don't have to implement this method to use the ISR Text Edit – Value Help input help. This input help automatically provides domain-fixed values or an input help that is assigned to a data item. The prerequisite here is that the characteristic in the ISR Customizing is assigned to the respective data item.

An input help with two selection values for the `System` characteristic is programmed as in Listing 9.11.

```
if_ex_qisr1~scenario_set_additional_values
  DATA: ls_additional_value TYPE qisrsspecial_param.

* first DDLB entry
  ls_additional_value-fieldindex = 1.
  ls_additional_value-fieldname  = 'SYSTEMNAME_KEY'.
  ls_additional_value-fieldvalue = 'PR1'.
  APPEND ls_additional_value TO additional_data.
  ls_additional_value-fieldname  = 'SYSTEMNAME_LABEL'.
  ls_additional_value-fieldvalue = 'Produktive System PR 1'.
  APPEND ls_additional_value TO additional_data.

* second DDLB entry
  ls_additional_value-fieldindex = 2.
  ls_additional_value-fieldname  = 'SYSTEMNAME_KEY'.
  ls_additional_value-fieldvalue = 'TT1'.
  APPEND ls_additional_value TO additional_data.
  ls_additional_value-fieldname  = 'SYSTEMNAME_LABEL'.
  ls_additional_value-fieldvalue = 'Test System TT 1'.
  APPEND ls_additional_value TO additional_data.
```

Listing 9.11 Programming of an Input Help for a Dropdown List Box

9.6.4 Reading and Setting the Special Request Fields in BAdI Methods

You can easily access the general request data within the BAdI implementations, because it is transferred with the GENERAL_DATA structure to the methods. In contrast, the special request data that is defined as a characteristic in the ISR Customizing is provided as a table, and the table SPECIAL_DATA contains one row for each characteristic.

As you saw in the previous examples, the code can quickly become confusing for more complex programming tasks if you always need to find single field values via the LOOP AT special_data ABAP command. Therefore, SAP provides two function modules to move this tabular data to the corresponding local structures at the beginning of a BAdI method and write it back to the table at the end of the method.

▶ **ISR_SPECIAL_DATA_TO_STRUC**
This function module serves to move the special request data from the SPECIAL_DATA table to a structure. In this process, only the request data is transferred from the table to the structure (see Listing 9.12).

```
DATA: ls_master_data TYPE bapi2075_7.
* move special request data to structure
  CALL FUNCTION 'ISR_SPECIAL_DATA_TO_STRUC'
      EXPORTING
          it_special_data = special_data
      CHANGING
          cs_data         = ls_master_data.
* addtional processing steps
* ...
* return the special request data
  CALL FUNCTION 'ISR_STRUC_TO_SPECIAL_DATA'
      EXPORTING
          is_data         = ls_master_data
      CHANGING
          ct_special_data = special_data.
```

Listing 9.12 Programming the Data Transfer

▶ **ISR_STRUC_TO_SPECIAL_DATA**
This function module works similar to ISR_SPECIAL_DATA_TO_STRUC, only the other way round.

You can use the same function modules to read and write the ADDITIONAL_DATA transfer table for the input help.

As an alternative to these two function modules, you can use the methods of the CL_ISR_DATA help class. In addition to the already-mentioned options for transferring data to the local structure, this class also provides the option to manipulate the data, for example, by adding, inserting, and deleting data (see Listing 9.13).

```
METHOD if_ex_qisr1~int_service_request_check.

  DATA: BEGIN OF ls_characteristics,
          company_code   TYPE bukrs,
          cost_center    TYPE kostl,
        END OF ls_characteristics.

* copy the form data to class storage
* CL_ISR_DATA
  CALL METHOD cl_isr_data=>set
    EXPORTING
      it_data = special_data.

* read the form data in local structure
  CALL METHOD cl_isr_data=>read
    EXPORTING
      id_index      = 1
    IMPORTING
      es_data_record = ls_characteristics.

* data changes
  IF ls_characteristics-cost_center = '12345678'.
    ls_characteristics-company_code = '1000'.
  ELSE.
    ls_characteristics-company_code = '0001'.
  ENDIF.

* replace the data
  CALL METHOD cl_isr_data=>insert
    EXPORTING
      is_data_record = ls_characteristics
      id_index      = 1
    RECEIVING
      rt_data       = special_data.

ENDMETHOD.
```

Listing 9.13 Programming with the CL_ISR_DATA Help Class

9.6.5 Error Handling During Checks

You can output error messages within the INT_SERVICE_REQUEST_CHECK and SCE-NARIO_PROCESS_USER_COMMAND methods to prevent the processing of the service request. To do this, fill the RETURN transfer structure with the respective error message. If you want to output multiple messages, use the MESSAGE_LIST transfer table.

Error Handling Controls the Processing of the Request

If you use Web Dynpro applications in the ISR, you can control the processing of a request by the applicant. If the MESSAGE_LIST transfer table contains one or more messages, an error message from the RETURN structure that was output at the same time is not displayed; however, the messages of MESSAGE_LIST are always displayed. The error message in the RETURN structure prevents the system from sending the request. If the RETURN structure remains empty, the request can be sent despite the messages in the MESSAGE_LIST transfer table, independent of their message category.

9.6.6 Controlling the Field Layout

You can control the layout properties of individual form fields, such as mandatory field, visibility, and ready-for-input status, in the ISR framework. A requirement for this is Support Package 4 of SAP ERP 6.0. SAP Note 925657 provides more information on this. You can control the layout properties in the following methods:

▶ INT_SERVICE_REQUEST_CHECK

▶ INT_SERVICE_REQUEST_INIT

▶ SCENARIO_SET_ADDITIONAL_VALUES

▶ SCENARIO_PROCESS_USER_COMMAND

They have the UI_ATTRIBUTES interface parameter. Like the ADDITIONAL_DATA table, this table is usually empty at the ISR runtime and must be filled for the respective characteristics (FIELDNAME). You can assign the following properties to any field of the form using the UI_ATTRIBUTE field:

M Mandatory Field and Ready for Input

I Ready for Input

R Visible and not Ready for Input

H Not Visible

You can adapt this property after any standard event or an action in the form for which an event is executed.

9.7 ISR Architecture

This section illustrates the architecture of the ISR framework and provides an overview of the SAP technologies used and their integration with the ISR framework. In addition, it describes the communication between the individual frontend and backend components and the critical interfaces of the ISR, particularly the Web Dynpro applications.

9.7.1 ISR as a Toolset

As described earlier, the ISR uses various applications from SAP NetWeaver and SAP ERP and combines them to form a framework that allows for form-based request scenarios and the involved process for the execution of the required service. To process the process, that is, forward the request to the processor responsible, it can be integrated with SAP Business Workflow. This is achieved by using the BUS7051 business object of the quality notification—or simply notification—as the runtime object of the service request.

Furthermore, the request scenario is integrated with SAP CO to determine direct and indirect overhead costs of the service request. ISR links these different applications and provides various interfaces so that you can use programs to flexibly control the request form and process.

Figure 9.43 illustrates the communication between the QISR_UI_FORM Web Dynpro component and the backend. The Web Dynpro component communicates with the ISR runtime in the backend via the ISR_PROCESS_EVENT Remote Function Call (RFC). During ISR runtime, the methods of the QISR1 BAdI (see Section 9.6.1, "Data Structures within the ISR Framework") are called at different times.

When the form is sent, the form data is stored separately in the Business Document Service (BDS), that is, the document management of the Knowledge Provider, and the notification is created. Thus, the data is not stored with the form as a PDF. This program design is also the reason why the ISR cannot support the process of entering requests offline. Within the ISR, the Adobe form only serves as the interface layout for entering the request and is always merged with the current data at runtime.

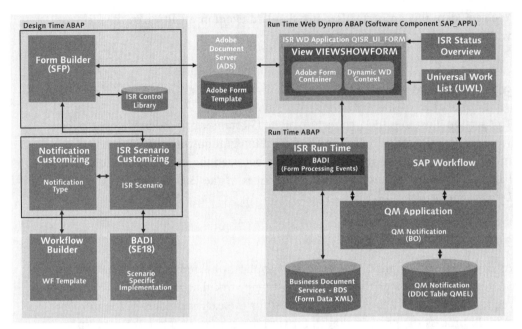

Figure 9.43 Communication between ABAP Design Time and ABAP Runtime

Data Storage Separated from the Layout

Only the form data is stored, not the PDF. Technically, the interactive Adobe form serves solely as the input screen. Users can still store a current PDF in Adobe Reader.

When the notification is created, the CREATED event of the business object is triggered and the system generates the corresponding work item in the UWL (in the portal) or in SAP Business Workplace (Transaction SBWP).

9.7.2   Web Dynpro ABAP Component and How to Use It

As described in Section 9.4.4, the UI technology to enter the request is interchangeable. In addition to the interactive Adobe form (available as of SAP ERP 5.0), you can use other form technologies, such as ITS Services, BSP forms, or JSP forms. However, for all request forms as of SAP ERP 5.0, the Adobe form is the standard solution of the ISR and embedded in a Web Dynpro component (see Figure 9.44).

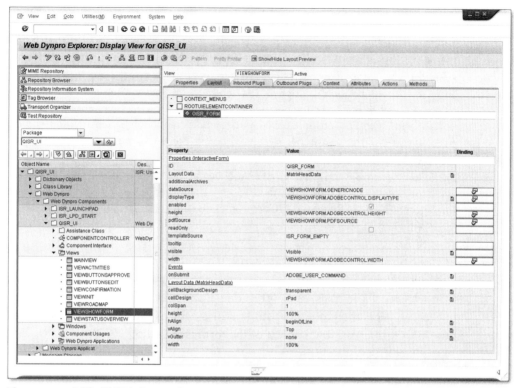

Figure 9.44 QISR_UI Web Dynpro Component

Basic Principles of the Web Dynpro Component of the ISR

For integration of the Adobe form, the following Web Dynpro applications, based on Web Dynpro ABAP and Web Dynpro Java, are available:

▶ QISR_UI Web Dynpro ABAP component

▶ PCUI_GP~ISR Web Dynpro ABAP component

Both solutions provide the same functions, particularly for displaying the form — there are no differences.

Both technologies have four Web Dynpro applications each with identical parameters. The QISR_UI Web Dynpro ABAP component is available as of Support Package 8 of SAP ERP 6.0. However, you should at least use SAP ERP SAP_APPL SP 12. The Web Dynpro Java component has been available as of SAP ERP 5.0 and is provided in the PCUI_GP software component.

Selection Options for Web Dynpro ABAP or Java

You may have wondered why the ISR Customizing provides the Adobe PDF entry type but no selection options for Web Dynpro ABAP or Java.

Every scenario that deploys the Adobe PDF entry type in the Customizing, and to which an interactive Adobe form is assigned, can be used with both Web Dynpro UI technologies—without having to configure additional settings in the backend. For this reason, no Customizing entry is possible or required for a differentiation between Web Dynpro ABAP and Web Dynpro Java. You decide with your iView or Web Dynpro component which type of Web Dynpro technology you want to use.

The following sections only describe the Web Dynpro ABAP solution—most of the provided ISR scenarios are started via the QISR_UI Web Dynpro ABAP component. Only the Personnel Change Request (PCR) application uses the Web Dynpro Java component of the ISR in SAP ERP 6.0.

The basic principle of the ISR framework is that the form data is processed and stored separately from the form. At runtime, the interactive form serves solely as the input screen. The basis for a correct data transfer between the various components of the ISR is therefore the definition of the form fields with identical names in the ISR Customizing and context of the form (see Section 9.5.2).

The QISR_UI Web Dynpro component uses InteractiveForm as the screen element. Both the dataSource attribute for the form data and the pdfSource attribute are bound to a context element of the Web Dynpro component, which is not filled until the component is started.

The system generates the context of the Web Dynpro component for the data of the form. The basis for the generation is the list of characteristics from the ISR Customizing. This list is read via an RFC, from which the appropriate context for the form is generated. At the beginning of the form runtime, the name of the form (for example, ISR_FORM_SRCR) is determined via an appropriate Web Dynpro interface and transferred to the InteractiveForm Web Dynpro screen element. Adobe Document Services (ADS) read the corresponding interactive PDF and display it together with the data of the context.

Web Dynpro Applications of the ISR

The standard interface of the ISR is provided by four Web Dynpro applications, which you can independently integrate with your portal environment. Note that all applications must be started with specific parameters.

▶ **QISR_UI_FORM**

The `QISR_UI_FORM` Web Dynpro application in the form of a roadmap consisting of three steps and SAP Interactive Forms by Adobe is used for request creation (see Figure 9.3). Required parameters include:

 ▶ `SCENARIO`
  ISR scenario, must always be specified

 ▶ `NOTIF_NO`
  Notification number

 ▶ `MODE`
  Mode

Only specify the notification number if an existing request is changed (`MODE = CHANGE` parameter) or displayed (`MODE = DISPLAY` parameter). For new requests (`MODE = CREATE` parameter), `NOTIF_NO` remains empty.

▶ **QISR_UI_FORM_APPROVE**

The `QISR_UI_FORM_APPROVE` application only consists of SAP Interactive Forms by Adobe and is used to approve the request. No roadmap is used here.

However, it makes sense to deploy this application if you use a notification type with approval. The approver is provided with the APPROVE, REJECT, and BACK TO AUTHOR buttons (see Figure 9.10). The only required parameter is:

 ▶ `WF_ID`
  Technical number of the workflow item of the approver

In the standard version of the ISR scenarios, none of the form fields of this application are ready for input. However, by adapting the script programming of individual fields in Form Builder, you can make them ready for input (see Section 9.5.5).

▶ **QISR_UI_FORM_DISPLAY_ONLY**

The `QISR_UI_FORM_DISPLAY_ONLY` application only serves to display the current status of an ISR form. It only contains the form without input options, roadmaps, or functions in the form of buttons. Required parameters include:

 ▶ `SCENARIO`
  ISR scenario

 ▶ `NOTIF_NO`
  Notification number

▶ **QISR_UI_STATUSOVERVIEW**

The QISR_UI_STATUSOVERVIEW application provides the applicant with an overview of all of his requests for the last 365 days and their status (see Figure 9.8). This application can be called without additional parameters.

ISR_SCENARIO_PARAMS for Any Parameters

The ISR_SCENARIO_PARAMS parameter enables you to initialize single or multiple characteristics that are defined in the scenario. This parameter is also used, for example, to define the version of the scenario (see Section 9.4.2).

To initialize multiple fields, use the dollar sign ($) to separate the field and value combinations. Do not leave blanks between these combinations, transfer the values as a continuous string. The prerequisite here is that the parameter must be defined as a characteristic in the ISR Customizing; however, it doesn't have to be a form field. Depending on the technology, you can use ISR_SCENARIO_PARAMS for all three usage options of the ISR in SAP NetWeaver Portal (see Section 9.7.3) either as a URL parameter (iView) or via the corresponding interface methods of the ISR (Web Dynpro component).

Let's look at an example: The ORDER characteristic should be initialized with the value 000000123456 and the ACCOUNT characteristic with the value 400100. Therefore, the assembled parameter for ISR_SCENARIO_PARAMS is as follows: ISR_SCENARIO_PARAMS =ORDER=000000123456$ACCOUNT=400100.

9.7.3 Usage Options in SAP NetWeaver Portal

The forms of the ISR are available to the user in different ways in SAP NetWeaver Portal:

▶ Direct usage of an ISR Web Dynpro application (for example, QISR_UI_FORM) via a link

▶ ISR Launchpad, embedded in a specific Web Dynpro component

▶ Component use of the QISR_UI Web Dynpro component

ISR Web Dynpro Application in an iView

If you use an ISR Web Dynpro application, you can provide the request as a callable service in the portal. This corresponds to a link to an iView that starts the application in Web Dynpro ABAP (or Web Dynpro Java) of the ISR. The application must be started with the SCENARIO and MODE parameters. Here, SCENARIO corresponds to the four-digit scenario name, for example, SMC1. For a new request, you must specify MODE = CREATE. Section 9.6.2 provides more information on the valid values for the MODE parameter.

A display option in the portal should include one of the corresponding Web Dynpro applications in an iView. Both the Web Dynpro component of the ISR status overview and the UWL access this Web Dynpro application of the ISR (see Figure 9.45).

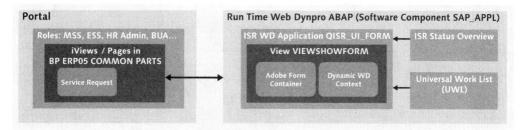

Figure 9.45 Communication between SAP NetWeaver Portal and Web Dynpro Runtime

You can find generic iViews of the ISR in SAP NetWeaver Portal via the menu path PORTAL CONTENT • ERP COMMON PARTS.

ISR Launchpad

You can call one or more request forms via buttons within your own component in Web Dynpro ABAP (see Figure 9.46). The advantage of the ISR Launchpad is that, when starting the request form, you can transfer any URL parameters that can be evaluated in the initialization method of the QISR1 BAdI implementation. In addition, a check can be executed in the backend before the form is started, for example, to check if the user is authorized to start the request form.

The SCENARIO_CHECK method of the QISR6 BAdI is called in the ISR_LAUNCH-PAD_SCENARIO_CHECK function module. This function module is executed prior to the start of the request form in the ISR Launchpad. This applies to both the Web Dynpro Java variant and the Web Dynpro ABAP variant of the ISR. This check enables you to prevent the start of the form, for example, due to missing authorizations.

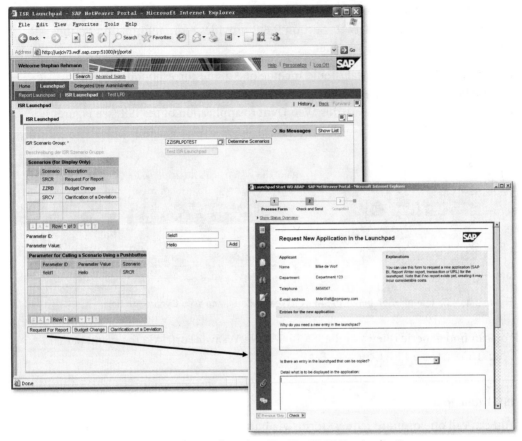

Figure 9.46 Start of an ISR Form from the ISR_LPD_START Test Application

If you use the third variant of the ISR integration (QISR_UI as a component use), you may also integrate this check option with your own Web Dynpro component. To do this, simply integrate the ISR_LAUNCHPAD_SCENARIO_CHECK function module.

Integrating the ISR Launchpad with Programs

This integration type of the ISR application (see Figure 9.47) is programmed in the ISR_LPD_START Web Dynpro component as an example and can be started via the application in Web Dynpro ABAP that has the same name.

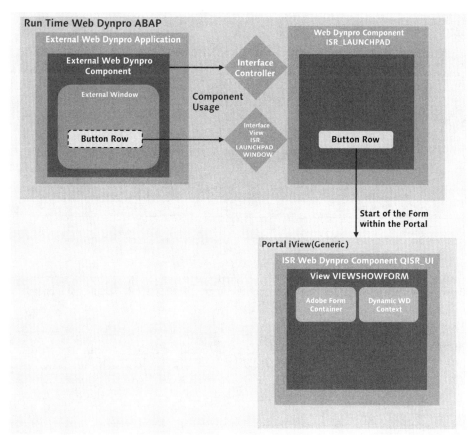

Figure 9.47 Schematic Diagram of the ISR Launchpads in Your Own
Web Dynpro Application

The following section describes the steps for integrating the ISR Launchpad:

1. First, specify the ISR_LAUNCHPAD Web Dynpro component as the COMPONENT USE in Transaction SE80 in the surrounding Web Dynpro component (see Figure 9.48).

2. Integrate the ISR_LAUNCHPAD_WINDOW interface view into the VIEWCONTAINER of the appropriate WINDOW (see Figure 9.49).

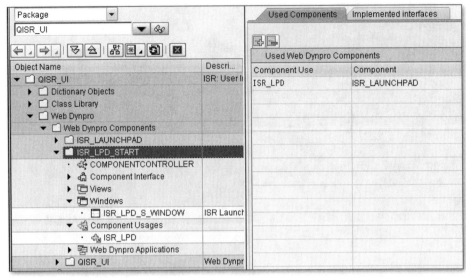

Figure 9.48 ISR_LAUNCHPAD as Component Use in the ISR_LPD_START Sample Component

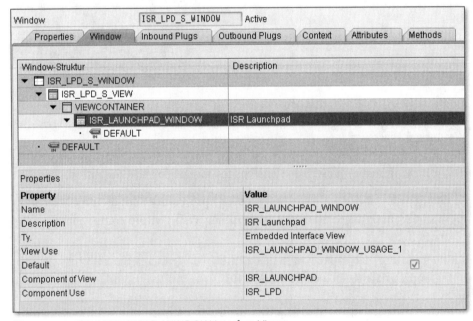

Figure 9.49 ISR_LAUNCHPAD_WINDOW Interface View

3. Create a new ABAP class (provider class) that implements the IF_ISR_LPD_PRO-
   VIDER interface. You need this class to start the launchpad with the required
   parameters (see Figure 9.50).

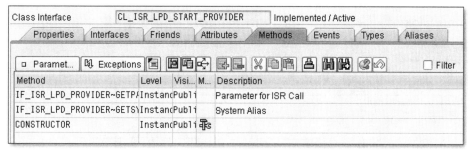

Figure 9.50 Provider Class with Interface

Then, generate an instance of the provider class and initialize the ISR Launchpad
with the necessary scenario group in the view of the surrounding application. For
this reason, the INIT method was created in COMPONENTCONTROLLER in the sample
Web Dynpro component, ISR_LPD_START. This method is called in the WDDOMODIFY
method of the ISR_LPD_S_VIEW view. You can also define the implementation of
the INIT method in your Web Dynpro component in the WDDOINIT method in
COMPONENTCONTROLLER if the scenario group is not changed during the execution
(see Figure 9.51).

4. Implement the IF_ISR_LPD_PROVIDER~GET_PARAMETERS method to transfer the
   required call parameters to the ISR request. The method has the EXPORTING
   parameter, ET_PARAMS, of the QISRTLPD_SCEN_PARAM type which contains the
   SCENARIO field. This field, in turn, contains a table with the following fields:

   ▶ PARAM_INDEX

   ▶ PARAM_KEY

   ▶ PARAM_VALUE

   Therefore, you can specify a list with parameters you defined yourself for one
   or more scenarios. PARAM_KEY corresponds to the technical name of the parameter and PARAM_VALUE to the value of the parameter. If you want to transfer one
   parameter value, enter ‚1' for PARAM_INDEX.

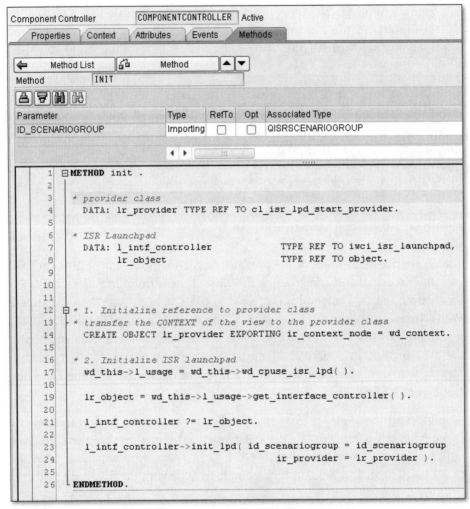

Figure 9.51 Initializing the ISR Launchpad in COMPONENTCONTROLLER

Customizing the ISR Launchpad

Proceed as follows in the Customizing of the ISR Launchpad:

1. First, define an ISR SCENARIO GROUP (see Figure 9.52).

2. Based on this group, define the list of the ISR scenarios that can be started for your ISR Launchpad (see Figure 9.53).

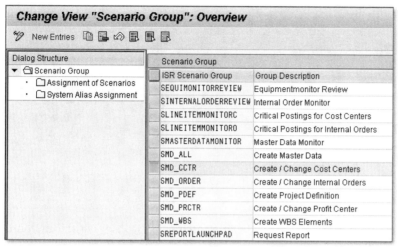

Figure 9.52 Customizing the Scenario Group for the ISR Launchpad

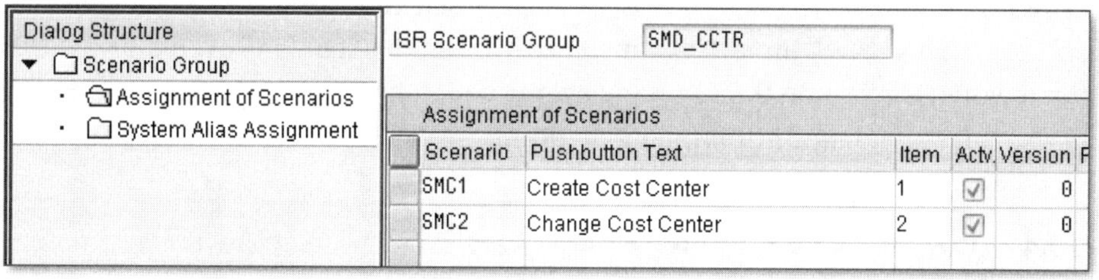

Figure 9.53 Assigned Scenarios of a Scenario Group

3. Finally, specify the order and the text of the buttons. The Customizing for the ISR Launchpad can be found via the menu path CROSS-APPLICATION COMPONENTS • INTERNET/INTRANET SERVICES • INTERNAL SERVICE REQUEST • SCENARIO DEFINITION • DEFINE SCENARIO GROUPS or directly via the VC_ISRGRP view cluster.

QISR_UI Web Dynpro Component as the Component Use

The third option for using the ISR Web Dynpro component is direct integration with your own Web Dynpro component. In this case, the QISR_UI Web Dynpro component is defined as the USED COMPONENT (see Figure 9.54).

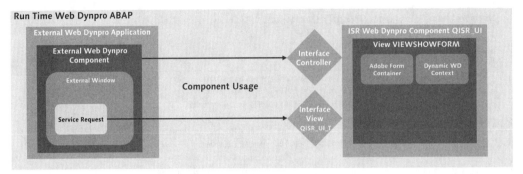

Figure 9.54 Schematic Diagram of the QISR_UI Web Dynpro Component as a Direct Component Use

The communication with the QISR_UI component takes place via the methods of the InterfaceController. It provides numerous SET/GET methods to determine or modify the data of the form and additional technical control parameters. The central method, CALL_ISR_PROCESS_EVENT, is used to call the ISR framework via an EVENT. This EVENT import parameter processes the standard events of the ISR framework (see Section 9.6.2) or any events you defined yourself that are queried in the corresponding BAdI implementation.

9.7.4 ISR_PROCESS_EVENT RFC

In addition to the mentioned Web Dynpro interfaces, there are other technical interfaces that can also be useful for the implementation of a scenario. In addition, some service modules are available that are useful for the implementation of BAdIs.

RFC ISR_PROCESS_EVENT is the central communication interface of the ISR framework between the ISR frontend and the backend. It can be used to simulate the processes of creating, changing, or reading a service request *without* deploying the ISR frontend (Web Dynpro application, Adobe form). In this context, the QISR1 BAdI is also implemented. Table 9.6 describes the meaning of the individual fields of the interface.

Parameter	Type	Values	Description
SCENARIO	Importing		Four-digit scenario name
MODE	Importing	CREATE, CHANGE, DISPLAY	Describes the edit mode

Table 9.6 Interface of RFC ISR_PROCESS_EVENT

Parameter	Type	Values	Description
EVENT	Importing	SEND, SAVE, CHECK, APPROVE, etc.	Event (standard events and scenario-specific events)
NOTIF_NO	Importing		Notification number if MODE = CHANGE or MODE = DISPLAY
NOTIF_NO_OUT	Exporting		Notification number is output if notification was created
RETURN	Exporting		Error message
DATA	Tables		Form data and general data
ADDITIONAL_DATA	Tables		Values for input helps

Table 9.6 Interface of RFC ISR_PROCESS_EVENT (Cont.)

You don't have to consider the FLAG_INOUT_CONVERSION, FLAG_RESET, ISR_PAGE_IN, ISR_PAGE_OUT, or ISR_FORM_VIEW parameters or additional table parameters for the simulation.

DATA and ADDITIONAL_DATA Table Parameters

The DATA and ADDITIONAL_DATA table parameters have a generic structure and each contain the following fields:

► FIELDINDEX
► FIELDNAME
► FIELDVALUE

DATA contains a list of all characteristics (FIELDNAME) with the corresponding characteristic values (FIELDVALUE). Because a characteristic can include multiple values, each combination of FIELDNAME and FIELDVALUE has a counter in the FIELDINDEX field, which starts with '1.'

ADDITIONAL_DATA contains the values for the input helps. The data formatting is described in Section 9.6.3.

The following examples describe the possible or necessary parameterization of the ISR_PROCESS_EVENT RFC for various application cases.

Example 1: Starting a Request

To simulate the start of a new service request, start the RFC with the SCENARIO = xxxx (xxxx refers to the scenario name) and MODE = CREATE parameters. The EVENT parameter remains empty. The DATA and ADDITIONAL_DATA tables now contain the initialized characteristics and possible values for the programmed input helps.

Example 2: Submitting a Request

If you want to submit a service request, start the RFC with the SCENARIO = xxxx, MODE = CREATE and EVENT = SEND parameters. In the DATA table, transfer the data that the service request is supposed to contain. The NOTIF_NO_OUT return parameter contains the notification number.

If you want to check the data before it is submitted, simply enter EVENT = CHECK for the parameter. If the data is not correct, the system outputs an error message with the RETURN return structure. This also applies to Example 3.

Example 3: Reading an Existing Request

If you want to read a service request, start the RFC with the SCENARIO = xxxx, MODE = DISPLAY, and NOTIF_NO parameters, including the corresponding notification number. The EVENT parameter remains empty. The DATA and ADDITIONAL_DATA tables now contain the list of the characteristic values and possible values for the programmed input helps.

Example 4: Changing an Existing Request

If you want to change a service request, start the RFC with the SCENARIO = xxxx, MODE = CHANGE, EVENT = SAVE, and NOTIF_NO parameters, including the corresponding notification number. In the DATA table, transfer the data that the service request should contain. Note that the transfer of characteristics without characteristic value results in a deletion of an existing characteristic value.

9.7.5 Additional Interfaces and Auxiliary Functions

Table 9.7 lists additional function modules and an ABAP class that are useful for the programming within the BAdI implementation.

Interface	Description
ISR_GENERAL_DATA_GET	Reads general, scenario-specific, and request-specific data of a request from the database or the internal function group storage.
ISR_SPECIAL_DATA_GET	Reads scenario-specific and request-specific characteristic data of a request from the database or the internal function group storage.
Class: CL_ISR_DATA	This help class can be used to facilitate the programming based on the relatively general interface parameters of the BAdI methods for the specific characteristics of a scenario. Section 9.6.4, "Reading and Setting Special Request Fields in BAdI Methods," contains a programming example.
ISR_SPECIAL_DATA_TO_STRUC	The function module serves to move the form data from the generically formatted transfer tables of the BAdIs to an appropriate, scenario-specific table or structure. This facilitates the subsequent programming, which is based on the form data. The function module can be used as an alternative to the CL_ISR_DATA class.
ISR_STRUC_TO_SPECIAL_DATA	If you want to change the form data in a BAdI method, this module can be used to move the data from the scenario-specific table or structure to the generic transfer table of the BAdIs.
ISR_NOTIF_REVERSE	This function module is used to reverse ISR requests. This is possible as long as the status of the notification is Open. The function module changes the status to Completed. The ISR status overview also displays the Reversed status. You can carry out your own processings in an implementation of the REVERSE_NOTIF_EXTERNAL method of the QISR1 BAdI. The function module is also used in the ISR status overview.
ISR_REQUEST_GET_RFC	The function module outputs a list of all service requests of any applicant with the current status information. The function module is also used in the ISR status overview.

Table 9.7   Useful Interfaces for the BAdI Implementation

Interface	Description
ISR_ACTOR_FOR_ROLE_GET	This function module can be used, for example, to determine the current processor in a customer-specific workflow template by means of rules. In addition, the CONTAINER_FOR_ACTOR_DET_FILL method of the QISR3 BAdI is implemented to change the data of the workflow container.
Function group: QISR5	The function modules of the QISR5 function group can be used to determine the Customizing settings for a scenario.

Table 9.7 Useful Interfaces for the BAdI Implementation (Cont.)

The BAdI interfaces listed in Table 9.8 can be used within the ISR and were described in detail using programming examples in this chapter. BAdI QISR5 does exist but is usually not used.

BAdI Interface	Purpose	Where Is It Explained?
QISR1	Form programming interface	Section 9.6
QISR2	Account assignment determination	Section 9.4.9
QISR3	Fills the container to determine the processor	Section 9.4.8
QISR4	Executes a function of the activity bar (action box)	Section 9.4.6
QISR6	ISR: Calls in the ISR Launchpad (Web Dynpro)	Section 9.7.3

Table 9.8 BAdI Interfaces of the ISR

9.8 Summary

This chapter introduced you to the concept of the ISR as an application of the interactive Adobe forms within SAP ERP. You now know that the ISR is a framework that you can flexibly configure and that links several SAP components, and you know the prerequisites to use the ISR. A sample scenario was used to illustrate the usage options of the ISR. This chapter also described how you can use the ISR wizard to create a simple ISR scenario together with an Adobe form.

In addition, it introduced the Customizing and BAdI interfaces as the modeling tools of the scenario. Now you can implement complex requirements for the scenario. You learned how you can generate and extend an interactive Adobe form for the ISR framework. This is particularly critical, because the ISR framework requires a specific interface and context structure. Furthermore, this chapter illustrated the purpose of the ISR library.

The last sections outlined the basic technical architecture of the ISR. The ABAP interfaces are considerably useful for making the programming of the BAdI implementation of a scenario more efficient.

Chapter 10, "ABAP PDF Object," which mainly addresses advanced form developers, provides more information on the ABAP PDF object.

The ABAP PDF object is the interface to Adobe Document Services (ADS). It provides access to various functions that can be used in ABAP programs and provides a high level of flexibility, particularly in offline scenarios.

10   ABAP PDF Object

So far, you've only used ADS in conjunction with form output and interactive online scenarios. You've used a function module interface that automatically calls the required functions of ADS and processes the result in the system. However, you have not communicated with ADS directly—this task is assumed by the form runtime environment.

In addition, you were introduced to different frameworks, such as Web Dynpro ABAP and Internet Service Request (ISR). All of these frameworks have been specially designed for their respective application and provide functions that are relevant for the appropriate scenarios. However, individual frameworks don't provide all of the functions of ADS. For example, Web Dynpro ABAP doesn't offer a connection to the SAP spool system and the form runtime environment has no interface for digital signatures.

10.1   Overview

This chapter discusses the ABAP Portable Document Format (PDF) object that provides you with comprehensive functions for processing PDF documents. It is an interface that uses the methods of ADS, which enables you to implement your requirements very flexibly.

In some cases, however, you must handle some details that are otherwise assumed by the frameworks. This, in turn, increases the programming effort. For example, if you want to create a PDF, you must provide an XML data stream and the form in binary format or via a URL. Otherwise, this is done by the form runtime environment. However, there are several options to retrieve this information.

You can also use the PDF object to create a print output. Because you then must assume the administration of spool requests and the communication with the spool system yourself, it is recommended to use the function module interface as described in Chapter 6, "Form Output." Therefore, this chapter focuses on the options for calling ADS in offline scenarios.

Section 10.2, "Instantiating the PDF Object," provides a general overview of the PDF object and describes its basic functioning. This is followed by the steps required to develop an offline scenario with interactive PDF forms. Here, the focus is on the processing steps that require a functionality of ADS and how you can use them via the PDF object.

The creation of interactive PDF documents as the first step is detailed in Section 10.3, "Creating a PDF Document." Section 10.4, "Processing an Interactive PDF Document," describes how you can process a filled-out PDF document after it has been received in the SAP system. This section also discusses the extraction of data (see Section 10.4.2, "Data Extraction") and the validation of digital signatures (see Section 10.4.3, "Validation of a Digital Signature"). Finally, the chapter is rounded off with a brief overview of additional methods for the PDF object (see Section 10.5, "Additional Methods of the PDF Object").

> **Note**
>
> For the sake of simplicity, local files are used in this chapter to focus the examples on the essential aspects.

10.2 Instantiating the PDF Object

IF_FP_PDF_OBJECT is the central interface for the PDF object and provides all of the methods that you need for accessing ADS. The implementing class of this interface is CL_FP_PDF_OBJECT.

You can create an instance of this class via the factory class, CL_FP (see Listing 10.1). You need this coding in all of the programs that work with the PDF object. After that, you can access all methods of the PDF object via the l_pdfobj reference.

```
DATA: l_fp      TYPE REF TO if_fp,
      l_pdfobj  TYPE REF TO if_fp_pdf_object,
      l_fpex    TYPE REF TO cx_fp_runtime,
```

```
      l_err      TYPE string.
* Get FP reference.
l_fp = cl_fp=>get_reference( ).
TRY.
*    Create PDF Object.
     l_pdfobj = l_fp->create_pdf_object( ).
   CATCH cx_fp_runtime_internal
         cx_fp_runtime_system
         cx_fp_runtime_usage INTO l_fpex.
     l_err = l_fpex->get_errmsg( ).
     MESSAGE l_err TYPE 'E'.
ENDTRY.
```

Listing 10.1 Instantiating the PDF Object

If you don't specify a connection to ADS, the system uses the standard connection with the name ADS. If you have created additional connections in your system, you can transfer them when creating the reference. The CREATE_PDF_OBJECT method has an optional parameter, CONNECTION, via which you can transfer the connection.

Because errors can occur during the method calls, you must catch multiple exceptions. The three following exception classes derive from CX_FP_RUNTIME. In Listing 10.1, all exceptions are processed collectively:

▶ **CX_FP_RUNTIME_INTERNAL**
The exception class, CX_FP_RUNTIME_INTERNAL, is intended for internal errors of the PDF object and you will hardly ever come across it.

▶ **CX_FP_RUNTIME_SYSTEM**
The exception class, CX_FP_RUNTIME_SYSTEM, is primarily used if a serious error occurs in the processing done by ADS.

▶ **CX_FP_RUNTIME_USAGE**
The CX_FP_RUNTIME_USAGE exception is triggered if you call the PDF object incorrectly or provide insufficient information for a scenario.

The PDF object contains a lot of methods. Therefore, you are first provided with a brief overview of the different types of methods.

▶ The methods of the PDF object are subdivided into different groups. For example, you can use the SET methods to set different data—an example would be the SET_DATA method to specify XML data.

▶ Another group is formed by the SET_TASK methods that communicate the tasks to the PDF object. Here, you can specify, for example, whether you want to create a PDF document (SET_TASK_RENDERPDF) or extract the data from a PDF (SET_TASK_EXTRACTDATA).

▶ The EXECUTE method is the method that calls ADS. You must set all data and specify the task of the PDF object prior to this call.

▶ GET methods deliver results that are provided depending on the task, for example, a PDF document or an XML data stream.

▶ You need the RESET method to reuse the instance of the PDF object after a call to ADS. This method resets the internal data.

When you call the EXECUTE method, the system checks the input data for completeness and creates the work instructions for ADS. Then, the actual call is implemented via the Web service interface. If the call was successful, that is, no exception was triggered, you can call the result via different GET methods. For example, if you requested a PDF document, you can receive it via the GET_PDF method. If you schedule another call to ADS and want to reuse the instance of the PDF object, you must reset the PDF object via the RESET method.

The following sections of this chapter describe the different application scenarios of the PDF object, including sample programs that are provided as test programs by SAP (a test program exists for each method). You can use these programs to familiarize yourself with and test the options of the PDF objects. After that, you can copy the method calls into your own programs. The basic structure is always identical:

1. Creating the instance
2. Setting the data
3. Specifying the task
4. Calling ADS
5. Retrieving results

10.3 Creating a PDF Document

The creation of a PDF document is the primary function of Adobe Document Services. Chapter 6 described how you can create a PDF document via the function module interface and return it to the application. In this process, you can define various properties, for example, whether the PDF is interactive, whether additional usage rights are assigned, or whether it is a dynamic interactive PDF document. The data for the form was provided either as Dictionary objects or as XML data stream.

To create a PDF document, you need a form and a data stream. However, you can also create a PDF document without transferring a data stream. This is particularly useful for interactive scenarios; however, values are frequently predefined here.

The PDF object includes methods in its interface that you can use to control the PDF creation. This can be important, for example, if the functions are not provided via the superordinate interfaces.

Let's first look at the form: Where can you obtain a form for document creation? The PDF object can't access the form repository that was described in Chapter 4, "Interface and Form Context." You can use Transaction SFP to maintain forms that are evaluated by the form runtime environment and provided to the PDF object. If you use the PDF object directly, you must retrieve the form yourself.

1. For simplicity, let's assume that the form is saved locally on your computer. You can find a sample form and a corresponding data record relative to the installation directory of Adobe LiveCycle Designer \EN\Samples\Purchase Order\Schema. There you'll find two folders called *Forms* and *Data*. The *Forms* folder includes the form, *Purchase Order.xdp;* and the *Data* folder contains the XML data record, *Purchase Order.xml.*

2. To create a PDF from these two files, use the test program, FP_PDF_TEST_01. Enter the complete path of the *Purchase Order.xml* file as the XFD FILENAME via the input help. Select the *Purchase Order.xdp* file under XFT FILENAME. You can leave the other fields as they are.

3. Select EXECUTE to display the finished PDF.

Now, take a closer look at the test program to better understand the methods of the PDF object. Listing 10.2 shows the relevant part. The other parts of the program deal with importing files, error handling, and PDF display.

```
l_pdfobj = l_fp->create_pdf_object( ).
l_pdfobj->set_template( xftdata = l_xft locale = l_locale ).
l_pdfobj->set_data( formdata = l_xfd ).
l_pdfobj->set_task_renderpdf( ).
l_pdfobj->execute( ).
l_pdfobj->get_pdf( IMPORTING pdfdata = pdfresult ).
```

Listing 10.2 Creating a PDF Document

▶ After the instantiation of the PDF object, the system calls the `SET_TEMPLATE` method to transfer the content of a form. You will learn how you can transfer a form via a reference later on. In this process, the system also sets the locale—a combination of language and country, for example, `de_DE` or `en_US`.

▶ The XML data is specified via the `SET_DATA` method.

▶ A PDF creation is requested by calling the `SET_TAST_RENDERPDF` method to communicate the task to be sent to the PDF object.

▶ Now, all information for creating a document is available; this is done via the call of the `EXECUTE` method. Only now is ADS called and contents transferred.

▶ Retrieve the result—the finished PDF document—via the `GET_PDF` method. This method also returns the number of pages created; the parameter is called `RENDERPAGECOUNT` and is an integer type.

10.3.1 Retrieving a Form

In a real-life scenario, the form and the data stream aren't available on your local PC and you must retrieve the form from the respective storage. If the form was created using Transaction SFP, you can use an Application Program Interface (API) to read the form. This chapter doesn't detail the complex API of the `SAFPAPI` package, which provides comprehensive functions for form processing. You need this package if you want to generate forms via API. But because you only want to determine the form content at runtime, you can also use a help class for access.

This help class is called `CL_FP_WB_HELPER` and offers interesting methods for accessing interfaces and forms. The method used to read a form at runtime is called `FORM_LOAD_FOR_RUNTIME`. However, this method doesn't provide the content of the form, only a reference to a form workbench object. The code fragment from Listing 10.3 shows how you can retrieve the form content.

```
DATA: l_wb_form TYPE REF TO if_fp_wb_form,
      l_form    TYPE REF TO if_fp_form,
      l_layout  TYPE REF TO if_fp_layout,
      l_content TYPE FPCONTENT.
l_wb_form = cl_fp_wb_helper=>form_load_for_runtime(
              i_name = l_name i_language = l_language ).
l_form ?= l_wb_form->get_object( ).
l_layout = l_form->get_layout( ).
l_content = l_layout->get_layout_data( ).
```

Listing 10.3 Reading the Form Content

The FORM_LOAD_FOR_RUNTIME method expects the name (FPNAME data type) and language (LANGU data type) as parameters. The result—a reference to IF_FP_WB_FORM— is used to determine the reference to a form object (IF_FP_FORM). This object, in turn, provides the GET_LAYOUT method to access the layout object (IF_FP_LAYOUT); the actual form content is now available in binary form via the GET_LAYOUT_DATA method (the FPCONTENT data type corresponds to the XSTRING ABAP data type).

> **Note**
>
> This example doesn't contain any error handling. Therefore, note that you must catch the corresponding exceptions of the method, for example, if the required form doesn't exist.

You can transfer the form that you read as shown in Listing 10.3 to the PDF object via the SET_TEMPLATE method (see Listing 10.2).

10.3.2 Transferring a Form via a Reference

If you provide the forms separately and enable HTTP access, you can transfer a link to the form instead of the form itself. To do this, select the XFTFILE parameter instead of XFTDATA when calling the SET_TEMPLATE method. You can transfer HTTP or FILE references, which may refer to a file in a directory.

Note, however, that ADS must have access via the specified URL. This is the task of the form runtime environment because only a logical connection can be transferred. ADS retrieves the logon data via a Destination service (the configuration is described in Chapter 3, "Installation and Configuration").

Therefore, the simplest way is to read the form separately and transfer it to the PDF object as content; however, no caching options are available this way. Therefore, the creation of the PDF document via the function module interface is preferred.

10.3.3 Creating an Interactive PDF Document

To ensure that the PDF is created as an interactive document, only a minor modification for calling the SET_TEMPLATE method is necessary. To do this, set the FILL-ABLE parameter to 'X.' If you want to create a dynamic interactive PDF, also set the DYNAMIC parameter to 'X' when calling the SET_TASK_RENDERPDF method.

You can use the `PRINTABLE` and `CHANGESRESTRICTED` parameters to restrict the change options. By default, you always create a PDF document that you can print from Adobe Reader. But if you set the `PRINTABLE` parameter to its initial value, you can't print the PDF any longer. The `CHANGESRESTRICTED` parameter controls whether you may fill or sign a PDF document; you can also restrict the sticky note function with this parameter.

These functions are activated by default. Table 10.1 contains a list of the possible values.

Value	Allowed Functions
space	All changes
A	Only additional contents
F	Filling and signing
N	Filling, signing, and annotations
X	No changes allowed

Table 10.1 Values for the Change Options of a PDF Document

Now let's create a small program with which you can create different types of PDF documents for testing purposes and that enables you to create an interactive PDF document that is optionally dynamic. An XML file with data is supposed to be optional so that you can receive an empty interactive PDF document. This is needed in Section 10.4 for simulating an offline scenario.

Listing 10.4 shows the program's code.

```
PROGRAM z_ifba_book_pdf.
TYPE-POOLS abap.
INCLUDE fp_utilities.
PARAMETERS:
    p_xfd  TYPE localfile VISIBLE LENGTH 64,
    p_xft  TYPE localfile VISIBLE LENGTH 64 OBLIGATORY,
    p_pdf  TYPE localfile VISIBLE LENGTH 64 OBLIGATORY,
    p_int  TYPE abap_bool DEFAULT abap_true AS CHECKBOX,
    p_dyn  TYPE abap_bool AS CHECKBOX.
DATA: l_fp      TYPE REF TO if_fp,
      l_pdfobj  TYPE REF TO if_fp_pdf_object,
      l_xft     TYPE xstring,
      l_xfd     TYPE xstring,
```

```
       l_pdfresult TYPE xstring,
       l_fpex      TYPE REF TO cx_fp_runtime,
       l_error     TYPE string.
AT SELECTION-SCREEN ON VALUE-REQUEST FOR p_xfd.
  PERFORM value_help_for_file USING 'XML' CHANGING p_xfd.
AT SELECTION-SCREEN ON VALUE-REQUEST FOR p_xft.
  PERFORM value_help_for_file USING 'XDP' CHANGING p_xft.
AT SELECTION-SCREEN ON VALUE-REQUEST FOR p_pdf.
  PERFORM value_help_for_output_file USING 'PDF'
                                     CHANGING p_pdf.
START-OF-SELECTION.
  IF p_xfd IS NOT INITIAL.
    PERFORM load_file USING p_xfd CHANGING l_xfd.
  ENDIF.
  PERFORM load_file USING p_xft CHANGING l_xft.
* Get FP reference.
  l_fp = cl_fp=>get_reference( ).
  TRY.
*    Create PDF Object.
    l_pdfobj = l_fp->create_pdf_object( ).
*    Set template.
    l_pdfobj->set_template( xftdata = l_xft
                            fillable = p_int ).
*    Set data.
    IF l_xfd IS NOT INITIAL.
      l_pdfobj->set_data( formdata = l_xfd ).
    ENDIF.
*    Tell PDF object to create PDF.
    l_pdfobj->set_task_renderpdf( dynamic = p_dyn ).
*    Execute, call ADS.
    l_pdfobj->execute( ).
*    Get result.
    l_pdfobj->get_pdf( IMPORTING pdfdata = l_pdfresult ).
    CATCH cx_fp_runtime_internal
          cx_fp_runtime_system
          cx_fp_runtime_usage INTO l_fpex.
      l_error = l_fpex->get_errmsg( ).
      MESSAGE l_error TYPE 'E'.
  ENDTRY.
  PERFORM download_file USING l_pdfresult p_pdf.
```

Listing 10.4 Flexibly Creating Interactive PDF Documents

For testing purposes, you can create any forms that you created using Adobe Live-Cycle Designer. If you define an XML file, the XML structure must suffice for the schema of the form design.

> **Interactive Forms can also be Created via the Form Interface**
>
> You can also create an interactive or dynamic form with restricted change options via the function module interface.

Listing 10.5 shows an example of how you must change Listing 6.6 from Section 6.4.2, "Returning Documents," to receive a dynamic interactive PDF document that you may only fill out and sign.

```
...
* Request PDF document.
  gs_outputpar-nodialog = abap_true.
  gs_outputpar-getpdf   = abap_true.
..gs_outputpar-pdfchangesrestricted = 'F'.
  CALL FUNCTION 'FP_JOB_OPEN'
    CHANGING
      ie_outputparams = gs_outputpar
    EXCEPTIONS
...
* Set language and country.
  gs_docparams-langu        = p_langu.
  gs_docparams-country      = p_ctry.
  gs_docparams-fillable     = abap_true.
  gs_docparams-dynamic      = abap_true.
* Call generated function module (form).
  CALL FUNCTION gv_fmname
    EXPORTING
...
```

Listing 10.5 Example for Restricted Change Options

10.3.4 Usage Rights

When an interactive PDF document is created via ADS, usage rights are added to the document by default. This enables the user not only to change values in an interactive PDF document, but also to save them or send them via email. In addition, the user can also add a digital signature or annotations to the document.

There are many different usage rights that are summarized in categories and are available as attributes in the IF_FP_PDF_USAGE_RIGHTS interface. Most of the following usage rights are added to the interactive PDF document by default; if not, this is indicated in the text.

▶ **DOCRIGHTS**
The FULLSAVE usage right enables you to save the document with all changes. This usage right is not set by default and is the only usage right from the DOCRIGHTS category.

▶ **FORMRIGHTS**
The usage rights, FILLIN, ADD, and DELETE, enable you to fill out, add, and delete fields. IMPORT or EXPORT enable the import or export of form data. SUBMIT-STANDALONE enables the offline transfer, while SPAWNTEMPLATE enables the creation of new pages. ONLINE is required for calling Web services from the form and BARCODE activates a 2D bar code functionality. The usage rights, IMPORT and BARCODE, are not set by default.

▶ **SIGNRIGHTS**
For working with digital signatures, you must set the usage right, MODIFY.

▶ **ANNOTRIGHTS**
The usage rights, CREATE, DELETE, MODIFY, COPY, IMPORT, and EXPORT, are available for working with annotations. The usage right, ONLINE, for uploading and downloading annotations, is not set by default.

▶ **EMBEDFILERIGHTS**
To work with file attachments, you must set the usage rights, CREATE, DELETE, MODIFY, and IMPORT.

▶ **No usage rights**
If you don't want to set usage rights during the creation of interactive PDF documents, you must call the SET_USAGERIGHTS method prior to the call to ADS.

Here, you can use the DEFAULT_RIGHTS parameter to control whether or not you want to use the standard rights. If you set the parameter to ABAP_FALSE, no rights are set.

▶ **Individual usage rights**
If you only want to use some rights, set the parameter to ABAP_FALSE and transfer the desired rights together with the RIGHTS table parameter.

The structure of the table consists of two fields, RIGHT and VALUE. In the RIGHT field, you can transfer the IF_FP_PDF_USAGE_RIGHTS=>ANNOTRIGHTS value and in the VALUE field the IF_FP_PDF_USAGE_RIGHTS=>ANNOTRIGHT_CREATE value, for example. Note that the usage rights, BARCODE and ONLINE, are not part of the credential and can therefore not be used presently.

Listing 10.6 shows how you can extend Listing 10.4 so that the user can only add and change annotations to an interactive PDF document. Insert the lines directly before calling the EXECUTE method.

```
* No default usage rights
* Only allow create/modify annotations
DATA: l_right   TYPE sfpuright,
      lt_rights TYPE tfpuright.
l_right-right = if_fp_pdf_usage_rights=>annotrights.
l_right-value = if_fp_pdf_usage_rights=>annotright_create.
APPEND l_right TO lt_rights.
l_right-right = if_fp_pdf_usage_rights=>annotrights.
l_right-value = if_fp_pdf_usage_rights=>annotright_modify.
APPEND l_right TO lt_rights.
CALL METHOD l_pdfobj->set_usagerights
  EXPORTING
    default_rights = abap_false
    rights         = lt_rights.
```

Listing 10.6 Defining Usage Rights

When you execute the changed program, you can only add or change annotations in the PDF; you can't change the values in the form.

Default usage rights are also assigned to interactive PDF documents that are created via the function module interface. This is done automatically when you set the FILLABLE parameter to ABAP_TRUE during the creation of the documents (see Section 6.4.2). If you want to create a document without usage rights via the function module interface, set the FILLABLE parameter to 'N.'

When you've created an interactive PDF document, you can add usage rights later on. To do this, refer to the FP_PDF_TEST_27 test program that can read an existing PDF file, add a usage right, and save the new PDF.

10.4 Processing an Interactive PDF Document

The Web Dynpro ABAP and ISR frameworks presented in this book are specialized in processing online scenarios. However, interactive PDF documents also support numerous functions that are required in offline scenarios. The complete implementation of an interactive offline scenario would go beyond the scope of this book because many different options for interactive PDF documents can be received in the system. Furthermore, the requirements of how to handle data are characterized by different aspects. Therefore, this chapter focuses on the essential points and presents the functions of the PDF object that support you in the processing of interactive PDF documents.

The core functions for processing are always identical regardless of how documents were received in the system. Therefore, for better understanding, it is sufficient to simulate an offline scenario based on examples. The concepts presented can be found in every implementation.

An offline scenario consists of three steps:

1. An interactive PDF document is provided. It can contain prepopulated data and be sent to a user via email or is provided for download on an Internet page.
2. The user fills the form with data and adds a digital signature, if necessary.
3. The completed and possibly signed form is sent via email or uploaded in a portal to the system for processing.

We've already discussed the necessary functions of ADS for the first step, that is, providing an interactive PDF document. You can create such a document either via the generated function module interface or directly via the PDF object (see Section 10.3.3, "Creating an Interactive PDF Document"). Here, you can also influence the usage rights (see Section 10.3.4, "Usage Rights").

During the creation, you can partially predefine data. The finished PDF document is then sent via email or provided for download. If your scenario requires unique identification when it is received, you can generate hidden data in the PDF document. Here, it is sufficient to transfer the data in the form context (or simply in the XML data stream if you work with the PDF object directly) during document creation; the fields don't have to be bound to the form. The hidden data can be read later on, which enables an identification of the scenario and a unique assignment of the document. However, the exact implementation depends on the specific requirements.

10.4.1 Filling Out an Interactive PDF Document

Now we'll create an interactive PDF document as described in Section 10.3, using the purchase order example. You can find all of the required data in the installation directory of Adobe LiveCycle Designer.

1. Start the Z_IFBA_BOOK_PDF program and specify the sample form and the data record.

2. As PDF FILENAME, specify the target file in which the finished PDF document is to be saved. The checkboxes for an interactive or dynamic document are set so that an interactive, not dynamic, document is created.

3. If you open the created PDF document with Adobe Reader, you can change the field values. For example, change the quantities in the purchase order. You can see that the total is adapted automatically.

4. At the bottom left, there is a signature field. Simply click on it to sign the document digitally. Select a DIGITAL ID and click on SIGN (see Figure 10.1). In the figure, some fields are grayed out for security reasons.

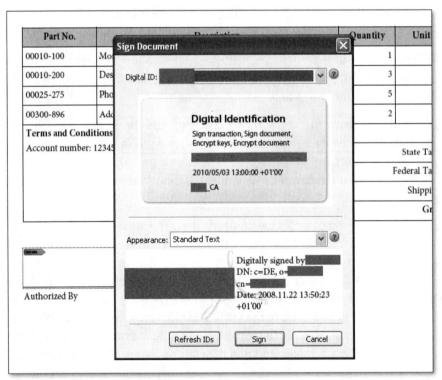

Figure 10.1 Signing a PDF Document

5. Adobe Reader now prompts you to save the document. Enter a file name and save the document. The document is now digitally signed and displayed accordingly by Adobe Reader (see Figure 10.2).

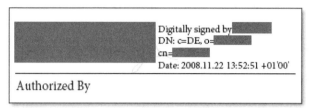

Figure 10.2 Signature in a PDF Document

6. The completed and signed PDF document can now be sent via email.

The following descriptions focus on the processing of the document after it has been received by the system. The following sections detail how to extract data from a PDF document and check the digital signature.

10.4.2 Data Extraction

An important functionality for processing interactive PDF documents is the option to extract data provided in XML format. The PDF object offers methods to transfer a PDF document and to read the XML data from it by calling ADS. To do this, a complete application program must perform the following tasks:

1. Extracting data from the PDF document

2. XML processing

3. Identifying the document

4. Starting a process for further processing

This book details the first task, that is, the data extraction from a PDF document. The XML processing and the assignment of documents are strongly characterized by the application and the scenario and must be implemented accordingly depending on the respective requirement.

Listing 10.7 shows the basic steps of data extraction:

▶ Transfer an existing document to the PDF object via the SET_DOCUMENT method.

▶ Select the data extraction by calling the SET_TASK_EXTRACTDATA method.

▶ ADS is called via the EXECUTE method.

▶ Then, the data of the document is available and can be retrieved using the GET_DATA method.

```
l_pdfobj = l_fp->create_pdf_object( ).
l_pdfobj->set_document( pdfdata = l_pdf ).
l_pdfobj->set_task_extractdata( ).
l_pdfobj->execute( ).
l_pdfobj->get_data ( formdata = l_data ).
```
Listing 10.7 Calling the PDF Object for Data Extraction

The complete program (FP_PDF_TEST_03) is available in your system. In the selection screen, select a PDF file and specify a target file to save the XML data. If you create an interactive PDF document via the program from Listing 10.4, you can extract the data with the FP_PDF_TEST_03 program.

1. Specify the file as the PDF document that contains the changed values and the signature from Section 10.4.1, "Filling Out an Interactive PDF Document."
2. Open the created XML file and check to see if it contains the changed values. Now this data can be processed by an application. The values are not saved in the local files.
3. The PDF object returns the data directly to the calling application. The test program saves the files locally to make working with the PDF object as easily as possible.
4. A real application would now receive the data and start a workflow for further processing, if necessary.
5. For processing the XML data, use the XML processor in ABAP to map the values from the XML data stream to the Dictionary fields.

Data Extraction from Interactive PDF Documents Only

If you try to extract data from a noninteractive PDF document, ADS triggers an error message that is forwarded as an exception to the calling program via the PDF object.

You can only extract data from interactive PDF documents based on the XML Forms Architecture (XFA) technology by Adobe.

10.4.3 Validation of a Digital Signature

To exclude or recognize data manipulations, the document was digitally signed in Section 10.4.1. If the data is changed later on, the signature becomes invalid. The PDF object provides a method to check all signatures of a PDF document.

A unique identification of the sender is also necessary to ensure that the signature was done by the person responsible. This task is not covered by ADS; instead, ADS validates the signatures and then detects manipulations. The assignment between the signature and the user must be carried out separately.

Listing 10.8 provides the methods required for determining the signature:

▶ Transfer the signed PDF document to the PDF object, as described in Section 10.4.2, during data extraction by calling the SET_DOCUMENT method.

▶ Use SET_TASK_GETSIGNATURES to activate the signature determination.

▶ After you call ADS via EXECUTE, you are provided with the signature information via the GET_SIGNATURES method.

```
l_pdfobj = l_fp->create_pdf_object( ).
l_pdfobj->set_document( pdfdata = l_pdf ).
l_pdfobj->set_task_getsignatures( ).
l_pdfobj->execute( ).
l_pdfobj->get_signatures( IMPORTING signatures = l_sigs ).
```

Listing 10.8 Calling the PDF Object for Determining the Digital Signatures

SAP provides a test program for determining signatures. This is the FP_PDF_TEST_12 program that only tests PDF files and outputs information about the contained signatures on the screen.

> **A Secure Connection is Required for Processing Digital Signatures!**
>
> Up to now, you haven't had to consider the connection to ADS for the instantiation of the PDF object. If you don't specify any connection, the system automatically selects the connection with the name ADS.
>
> If you implement security-relevant operations, for example, signature determination, the system checks whether a Secure Socket Layer (SSL) connection is used. If the connection is only secured with a standard authentication (user name and password), an error message is created when the SET_TASK_GETSIGNATURES method is called.
>
> To work with digital signatures, you must either secure the ADS connection or set up a second secure connection, for instance, ADS_SSL, which you configure accordingly. You must explicitly notify the connection name to the PDF object. This is done using the following call:
>
> `l_pdfobj = l_fp->create_pdf_object(connection = 'ADS_SSL' ).`

Now, run the FP_PDF_TEST_12 program and enter the document from Section 10.4.1 as the PDF file that you digitally signed (see Figure 10.1). The result is shown in Figure 10.3.

Short text	Value
Field Name	SignatureField1
Status	All Checks OK
Signatory	
Date and Time	Sat Nov 22 2008 13:52:51 GMT+0100
Location	
Information About Contact	
Legal Attestations	
Rights (See Interface IF_FP_PDF_SECURITY_PERMISSIONS)	All
Reason	null
Version	1
Highest Version Still Valid for This Version	1

Figure 10.3 Result of the Signature Check

▶ The STATUS field indicates whether the signature is valid. If the message "Cannot check signature" is displayed in the status field, you must check the configuration of the Trusted Anchors as described in Section 3.6.2, "Credentials, Trusted Anchors, Certificate Revocation Lists."

▶ If you change and save the PDF with Adobe Reader after signing it, a new version is created internally that is also displayed in Adobe Reader. As a result, the signature is no longer valid in version 2. If you rerun the FP_PDF_TEST_12 test program, the result remains as shown in Figure 10.3. Version 1 is still specified as the highest version.

▶ The test program doesn't show that there is a second version. The GET_SIG-NATURES method of the PDF object returns the table with the signatures and a numeric value, NUMVERSIONS, which specifies the number of versions contained in the PDF document. To determine whether no changes have been made to the document after signing it, you must check that the signature itself is valid and that it is valid for the highest version.

▶ If there are multiple signature fields on a form, you receive information for each signature about the validity and the versions of the document.

These are the essential functions of ADS for processing interactive PDF documents in offline scenarios. Some additional information in the next section shows which functions are available with regard to PDF documents.

10.5   Additional Methods of the PDF Object

The PDF object provides many more functions that are described in the online help. Just start Transaction SFP and follow the menu path HELP • APPLICATION HELP.

▶ Under Reference, you can find the entry, Runtime API of the PDF Document Object. There, all methods, including their parameters, are displayed.

▶ Take a look at the section, "Example and test programs." Here, you can find more than 20 test programs that you can use to test the individual methods of the PDF object. Some of the test programs, for example, PDF creation, data extraction, or check of digital signatures, have already been presented in this chapter.

▶ FP_PDF_TEST_15 is another interesting program that you can use to determine file attachments of a PDF document.

▶ You can add files to a PDF document using the methods in the FP_PDF_TEST_16 program.

▶ The FP_PDF_TEST_20 program details how you can influence the initial display of a PDF document when it is opened in Adobe Reader.

▶ If a user added annotations to a PDF document, you can display them using the FP_PDF_TEST_14 program.

▶ Check your system to find out which test programs exist according to the FP_PDF_TEST_* pattern. Some of the functions may be useful in your application scenarios.

10.6   Summary

This chapter presented the ABAP PDF object that provides you with all of the functions of ADS in an ABAP environment. You learned the basic functioning of the PDF object and can now create PDF documents interactively. You also learned how to access forms from the form storage.

You were introduced to the most important steps for an offline scenario. A completed PDF document that is possibly prepopulated with values is signed digitally and sent to ADS for processing. In addition, this chapter described how you can determine the XML data that have been entered or changed by a user. This chapter also detailed checking digital signatures. There are additional functions of the PDF object that you can view based on test programs delivered by SAP.

Chapter 11, "Offline Scenarios via Web Services," presents an example of how you can implement an offline scenario using a Web service.

This chapter describes how you can implement offline scenarios using Web services and details two variants — the use of Web service-based data connections and the Simple Object Access Protocol (SOAP) object in JavaScript — based on examples.

11 Offline Scenarios via Web Services

The query and transmission of data via a Web service is an alternative to processing interactive Portable Document Format (PDF) forms in the backend, which was described in Chapter 10, "ABAP PDF Object." The Web service reads and updates business data in the SAP system. This chapter provides the basics and usage options for integrating interactive PDF forms with Web services.

11.1 Overview

An interesting alternative for processing a PDF document in SAP systems is by direct link via Web services. In PDF forms, you have the option to call a Web service and to transfer data at the same time; you can also use the return values of Web services to update form fields and tables, for example.

There are two variants for using Web services:

▶ **Web Service Definition Language (WSDL)–based data connections**
In this procedure, you define a data connection for a Web service. Request and response parameters are then available via the data view. The parameters can be used for form generation via the known graphical-visual methods. The disadvantage of this procedure is that transport authentication is not supported.

▶ **Usage of the SOAP object in JavaScript**
Using the SOAP object in JavaScript enables you to write script programs that call Web services. These programs must read and update form fields themselves, which is a disadvantage compared to the WSDL-based data connection. However, this approach has the advantage of supporting transport authentication via user name and password.

This chapter is not aimed at developing complex scenarios, but rather to introduce you to the procedure for the two implementation approaches. This enables you to decide for yourself whether Web services are an option for implementing a connection to an SAP system.

11.2 Using WSDL Data Connections

This section considers the first example of WSDL data connection. To do this, first generate a Web service from a Business Application Programming Interface (BAPI). Then, create a form template that uses this Web service via a WSDL data connection. After you've generated an interactive PDF form from the form template, you can test it in Adobe Reader.

11.2.1 Creating a Web Service Based on a BAPI

For the first example, we'll generate a Web service for a BAPI of the flight customer database; here, only one function for querying all customers through the Web service is provided.

> **Generating Web Services in this Book**
>
> The procedure presented in this chapter isn't a general introduction to the generation and usage of Web services for SAP systems. It is rather a simple and quickly reproducible instruction to obtain a Web service that can be called to illustrate the PDF form techniques presented here.
>
> The Web services were generated on an SAP system based on SAP NetWeaver 7.0 SP 12. The dialogs may appear different in other release versions.

Creating a Web Service for BAPI

1. Log on to your SAP system and start the ABAP Development Workbench using Transaction SE80.

2. Have the system display all local objects for your user. Select LOCAL OBJECTS from the dropdown list and click on the button for updating the display (the glasses icon). The screen should now look as illustrated in Figure 11.1.

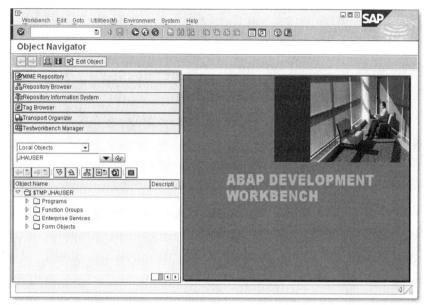

Figure 11.1 Display of Local Objects

3. To start the creation of a Web service, right-click the $TMP node in the object hierarchy to open the context menu. Follow the menu path CREATE • ENTERPRISE SERVICE/WEB SERVICE • WEB SERVICE.

   Then, a wizard opens that helps you create a service definition. To set up the service, proceed as follows:

4. Read the first screen of the wizard and then click on the Continue button.

5. Fill out the second screen (CREATE SERVICE) as follows (see Figure 11.2): Enter Z_IFBA_BOOK_CUSTOMERS as the name of the service definition and "Returns customer list." as the short text. Choose BAPI as the ENDPOINT TYPE and confirm this step by clicking on the CONTINUE button.

6. In the third screen (CHOOSE ENDPOINT) enter BC-DWB as the application (see Figure 11.3). Choose FLIGHTCUSTOMER for the BAPI; to do this, select SCUSTOMER in the input help. Click on CONTINUE.

7. In the following screen (CHOOSE OPERATIONS), select the GETLIST operation as illustrated in Figure 11.4. Deselect the other operations, if required. Choose CONTINUE to go to the next screen.

8. In the CONFIGURE SERVICE screen (see Figure 11.5), select the RELEASE SERVICE FOR RUNTIME. Click on CONTINUE to confirm.

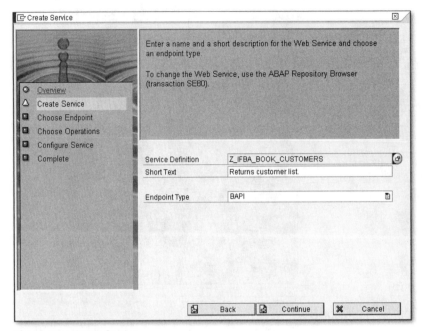

Figure 11.2 Create Service

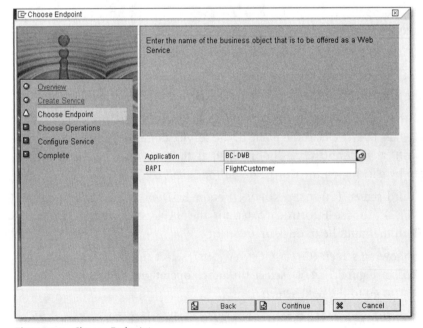

Figure 11.3 Choose Endpoint

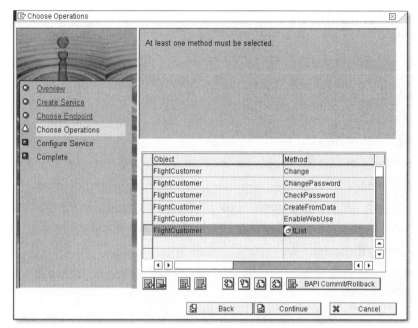

Figure 11.4 Choose Operations

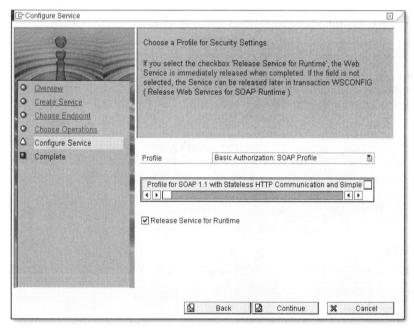

Figure 11.5 Configure Service

9. Confirm the last step, Complete, by clicking the Continue button. In the next dialog, Create Object Directory Entry, select Local Object for the $TMP package.

You have now created a Web service. To use it as a data connection for the form design, you now must specify that the Web service can be called without authentication.

Configuring the Web Service

Start Transaction WSCONFIG to configure the Web service you created previously. Proceed as follows:

1. Select the previously created Web service (Z_IFBA_BOOK_CUSTOMERS) as the Service Definition and Variant; it is recommended to use the input help here.

2. Then, REFRESH the screen.

3. Double-click the Web service that appears below Released Web Services. This opens a new screen.

4. In this screen, you can find the ICF DetailS BUTTON. Click on this button to go to the next screen.

5. There, double-click the (Web) service. You must expand the hierarchy tree under Virtual Hosts/Services.

Communication User

If you want to, and have the appropriate rights, you can create a communication user and use it instead of your own user data throughout this chapter. Communication users can't log on to an SAP system and therefore should be used for security reasons.

The screen shown in Figure 11.6 should now appear. In the figure, the LOGON DATA tab has already been selected and the changes described in the following have been implemented for defining a user for the Web service.

1. Switch to change mode.

2. Enter a client, user, and password (for example, your logon data or a communication user).

3. Then, save the changes. Because no productive scenario is developed here, you can ignore the message to not use a dialog user.

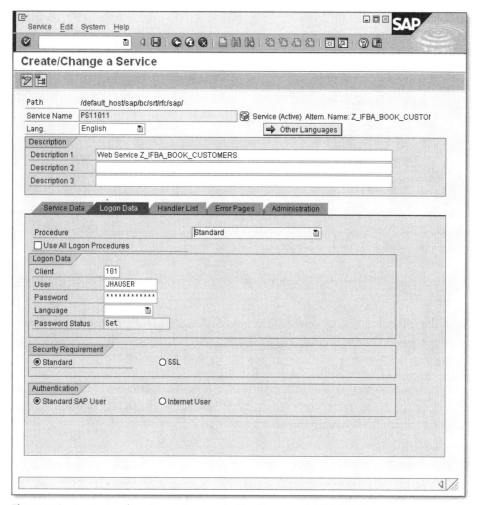

Figure 11.6 Processing the Internet Communication Framework (ICF) Details

Accessing the WSDL File of the Web Service

To create a WSDL-based data connection, you need the URL for the Web service. This can be called using Transaction WSADMIN.

1. At this point, start Transaction WSADMIN.

2. In the screen that opens expand the hierarchy tree for Soap Application For Bapis until you reach the Web service you just created (see Figure 11.7).

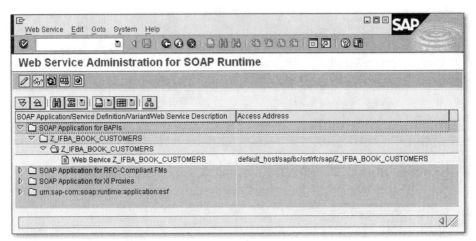

Figure 11.7 Administration Web Services for SOAP Runtime

3. Select your Web service, go to the WEB SERVICE menu, and choose the WSDL menu item.

4. In the following dialog, select Document Style so that the parameters are transferred in document format; confirm your selection. Displaying the content of the WSDL file is started externally in the default browser.

You should continue with the creation of a form template (see Section 11.2.2, "Creating the Form Template") when the WSDL file is displayed as illustrated in Figure 11.8, without having to enter a user name and password.

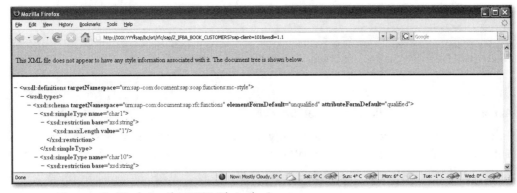

Figure 11.8 Displaying the WSDL File in the Browser

11.2.2   Creating a Form Template

After you've created the Web service, you can continue with the creation of the form template that uses the Web service. To do so, use Transaction SFP to start Form Builder.

Creating a Form Interface

First, you need an interface for the form template. Proceed as follows:

1. Create a new interface called Z_IFBA_BOOK_WS_INTERFACE1.

2. Add a parameter to the interface and call it CUSTOMERS. The type assignment is TYPE and the type name is TY_CUSTOMERS.

3. Save the interface and activate it in the last step.

The interface should now appear as illustrated in Figure 11.9.

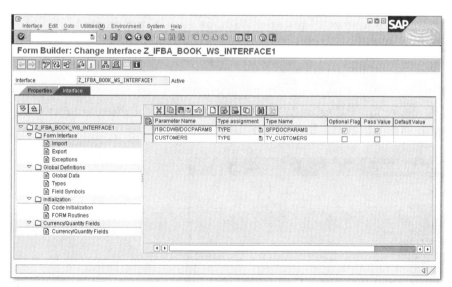

Figure 11.9   Z_IFBA_BOOK_WS_INTERFACE1 Interface

Creating the Form Design

After you've created the interface, you can create the form. Proceed as follows:

1. Create a new form called Z_IFBA_BOOK_WS_FORM_01. You can enter "test form for Web service" as the description.

2. Select the previously selected interface, Z_IFBA_BOOK_WS_INTERFACE1, and save the form as a local object.

3. Add the CUSTOMERS parameter to the context of the form. The context should now appear as illustrated in Figure 11.10.

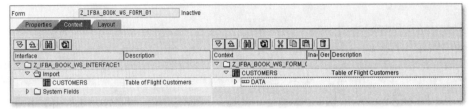

Figure 11.10 Context for the Form

4. When this is done, switch to the LAYOUT view and take a look at the data view. Below the Z_IFBA_BOOK_WS_FORM_01 node, you can find the CUSTOMERS table structure for storing customer information.

Next, proceed as follows to create the WSDL-based data connection:

1. Right-click the data view to open the context menu and follow the NEW DATA CONNECTION... menu path.

2. In the following dialog, enter "IFBA_BOOK_WebService" as the name of the data connection and select WSDL FILE as the option for the data description. This is shown in Figure 11.11. Click NEXT.

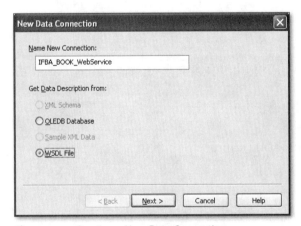

Figure 11.11 Creating a New Data Connection

3. In the next step, enter the URL for the WSDL file of the Web service. You can copy it from the browser window that you opened for displaying the WSDL file. Then, click NEXT.

4. In the following step, you must select one operation—namely the operation that you've provided via the Web service in "Creating a Form Interface" in Section 11.2.2. Select the operation and click FINISH.

The Web service now appears in the data view. It has its own icon to differentiate itself from the other data connections. Below the new data connection, you can find the structure for the request and the response of the Web service. In addition, there is a button for calling the Web service. Adobe LiveCycle Designer has automatically generated a button that you can add to a form template via the data view.

Next, customize the data view so that it appears as illustrated in Figure 11.12. To do this, expand or collapse the corresponding node in the data view using the plus (+) and minus icons (-).

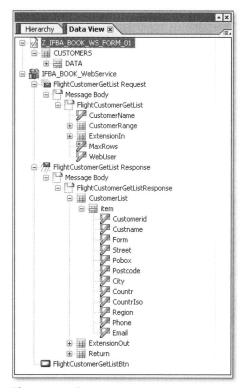

Figure 11.12 Data View

> **WSDL-Based Data Connection**
>
> WSDL-based data connections are active only at runtime. They are not part of the data's structure description that is based on the form.

After you've set up the data connection for the Web service, you can supplement the form template for the use of the Web service. Proceed as follows:

1. First, insert the button for calling the Web service (FlightCustomerGetListBtn) from the DATA VIEW in the top-left corner of the first page.

2. Then, drag and drop the MAXROWS field, which you can find under FLIGHTCUS-TOMERGETLIST REQUEST. Position it on the right-hand side of the button and set the default binding to None, because the value of this field is not supposed to be saved.

3. Click on the button for the Web service call and navigate to the Object palette. There, on the EXECUTE tab, you can find information about the Web service and operation saved for the button.

   In addition, the Re-merge Form Data option is available. Select this option. This results in the re-merge of the form after the call of the Web service and is required because a table structure is expected as the return of the Web service and because the table in the form is to be organized according to the received structure.

4. Next, drag and drop the table from the data view. To do this, select the table structure, which you can find under the node for FLIGHTCUSTOMERGETLIST RESPONSE. The name of the table node is CUSTOMERLIST and the individual table rows are ITEM nodes.

5. Position the table below the button and as close to the left border as possible.

6. Then, delete the columns COUNTRYISO, REGION, POBOX, and EMAIL from the table. To do so, highlight the respective column and remove it via the menu path TABLE • DELETE • COLUMN. You must do this because you require more space for the columns CUSTOMERID, CUSTNAME, STREET, and CITY to fit the corresponding text later on.

7. Finally, enlarge the four columns just mentioned.

Figure 11.13 shows what the form template is supposed to look like at this point. If the screen also shows warnings (the yellow exclamation marks) you can ignore them because they will be fixed with the next steps, because the data binding of the table hasn't been specified yet.

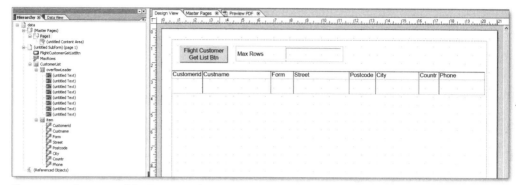

Figure 11.13 Structure of the Form Template

Now select any cell of the table's data row and navigate to the BINDING tab of the Object palette. In this tab, you can find an area for the Import/Export Bindings. Enter some text in the first text field, for example, "Street" if you selected the cell of the STREET column. According to this, the import/export binding is used instead of the default binding for the binding to Web services.

Import/Export Binding of Form Fields

The import/export binding is a runtime property. At runtime, a form field can be bound to multiple Web services at the same time and have both import and export bindings (for example, a response parameter of a Web service can be used as a request parameter of another Web service).

Don't confuse import/export binding with the default binding to the form's data structure.

Because the import/export binding is a runtime property, you must implement the binding to the data structure in the next step. To do this, you specified a structure in the interface and in the context at the beginning of this example. Navigate to the hierarchy and carry out the following steps:

1. Select the CustomerList table and set the default binding to None.

2. Select the Item row under CustomerList. Then, set the default binding to `$record.CUSTOMERS.DATA[*]`.

3. Navigate to the data view and expand it so that you can view all nodes under the menu path Z_IFBA_BOOK_WS_FORM_01 • CUSTOMERS • DATA.

585

4. Specify the data binding for all cells of the table. To do so, drag and drop the respective data node from the data view to the respective cell.

5. All warnings with regard to the data binding have disappeared and the form template is now complete. Finally, you must save and activate the form so that you can test it in the next step.

11.2.3   Testing the Form Template

To test the form template you must create a PDF file for the form in the next step. The PDF preview of Adobe LiveCycle Designer can't be used because you first must add corresponding usage rights to the PDF for calling the Web services.

Creating a Program for Generating a PDF

Section 10.3.1, "Retrieving a Form," already described the basics for creating the program. Here, Listing 11.1 references a program that outputs a form, created using Transaction SFP as an interactive PDF form.

Use Transaction SE38 (ABAP Editor) to create a new test program called Z_IFBA_BOOK_SFP_PDF and utilize Listing 11.1 as the program code. The program has been developed especially for the testing purposes of this chapter whereas the form is referenced via a name from the form storage of the SAP system. It doesn't use data for generating the PDF form. Run the program and select Z_IFBA_BOOK_WS_FORM_01 as the form template and enter "Z_IFBA_BOOK_WS_FORM_01.PDF" as the name of the PDF to be created.

```
PROGRAM z_ifba_book_sfp.pdf.
TYPE-POOLS abap.
INCLUDE fp_utilities.
PARAMETERS:
    p_frm TYPE fpwbformname OBLIGATORY,
    p_pdf TYPE localfile VISIBLE LENGTH 64 OBLIGATORY,
    p_int TYPE abap_bool DEFAULT abap_true AS CHECKBOX,
    p_dyn TYPE abap_bool AS CHECKBOX.
DATA: l_fp TYPE REF TO if_fp,
    l_pdfobj TYPE REF TO if_fp_pdf_object,
    l_xftref TYPE xstring,
    l_pdfresult TYPE xstring,
    l_fpex_api TYPE REF TO cx_fp_api,
    l_error TYPE string.
```

```
AT SELECTION-SCREEN ON VALUE-REQUEST FOR p_pdf.
  PERFORM value_help_for_output_file USING 'PDF' CHANGING p_pdf.

START-OF-SELECTION.
* Determine the URL for the form.

  TRY.
      cl_fp_wb_helper=>form_layout_exists( i_name = p_frm ).
    CATCH cx_fp_api_usage. "#EC NO_HANDLER
    CATCH cx_fp_api_repository INTO l_fpex_api.
      IF l_fpex_api->textid =
         cx_fp_api_repository=>object_already_exists.
        l_xftref = cl_fp_wb_helper=>form_layout_url(
                                   i_name = p_frm
                                   i_dest_path = 'X' ).
      ELSE.
        MESSAGE ID 'FPRUNX' TYPE 'E' NUMBER '050'
                WITH sy-langu.
      ENDIF.
  ENDTRY.
* Get FP reference.
  l_fp = cl_fp=>get_reference( ).
  TRY.
*    Create PDF Object.
     l_pdfobj = l_fp->create_pdf_object( ).
*    Set template.
     l_pdfobj->set_template( xftfile = l_xftref
                             fillable = p_int ).
*    Tell PDF object to create PDF.
     l_pdfobj->set_task_renderpdf( dynamic = p_dyn ).
*    Execute, call ADS.
     l_pdfobj->execute( ).
*    Get result.
     l_pdfobj->get_pdf( IMPORTING pdfdata = l_pdfresult ).
    CATCH cx_fp_runtime_internal
          cx_fp_runtime_system
          cx_fp_runtime_usage INTO l_fpex.
      l_error = l_fpex->get_errmsg( ).
      MESSAGE l_error TYPE 'E'.
  ENDTRY.
  PERFORM download_file USING l_pdfresult p_pdf.
```

Listing 11.1 Test Program for Generating Interactive PDF Forms

Offline Test of the Generated PDF

In the previous section, you generated a PDF file that you can now test offline. Proceed as follows:

1. Double-click the PDF file, Z_IFBA_BOOK_WS_FORM_01.PDF, to open it in Adobe Reader. The table for the customer information doesn't show rows.

2. In the MAXROWS field, enter the number of table rows to be returned. Only select a small number (for example, ten) because pagination has not been specified in the form template. As an exercise, you can first implement the pagination and then test the form with larger tables.

3. Click on the button for calling the Web service.

4. A security warning appears because the PDF wants to call a Web service. At this point, you can decide whether you want to allow or block this for the PDF.

   Because the created Web service is to be called, you can allow it. You can also specify that Adobe Reader remembers this for the Web service. Then, the warning isn't displayed if you want to test different values for the number of rows returned.

Figure 11.14 illustrates what the result of a test run can look like. Note that the MAXROWS text field has no data binding and therefore doesn't contain any value after the remerge.

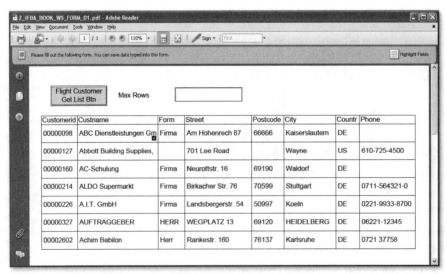

Figure 11.14 Test of the Form Template in Adobe Reader

You should implement another test to check whether the data received from the Web service has been merged with the PDF form. To do that, carry out the following steps:

1. Open the PDF form and fill the table for the customer information by calling the Web service.

2. Save the PDF form and exit Adobe Reader.

3. Reopen the PDF form and check to see if the table for the customer information is empty.

To work properly, you specify the default binding for the table during the creation of the form template.

11.3 Using the SOAP Object in JavaScript

This section describes the use of the SOAP object based on a second example.

To obtain Web services with very simple interfaces, you must first create function modules and then generate the corresponding Web services for these function modules. Then, you create a form template and program script programs that call the previously created Web services via the SOAP object.

11.3.1 Creating a Web Service on the Basis of a Function Module

In this section, we'll create the Web services that are used in a PDF form later on. First, let's look at two of the Web services that can be called without a transport authentication and one that can be called with a transport authentication. To do this, you must carry out the following three steps sequentially:

1. Create a function group

2. Create two function modules

3. Create three Web services for the function modules

Creating a Function Group

Proceed as follows to create a function group:

1. Start Transaction SE80 to open the Object Navigator.

2. Have the system display the local objects from the $TMP package.

589

3. Right-click on it to open the context menu of the $TMP package in the object hierarchy. Follow the menu path, CREATE · FUNCTION GROUP.

4. In the following dialog, enter Z_IFBA_BOOK_FCT_GROUP as the name of the function group and "A function group for the IFBA book" as the short text.

5. Save the function group and specify it as a local object.

You have now created a function group. In the next step, we'll add two function modules to this group.

Creating Two Function Modules

To create the Z_IFBA_BOOK_SUQARE function module, proceed as follows:

1. Open the context menu for the Z_IFBA_BOOK_FCT_GROUP function group and follow the CREATE · FUNCTION MODULE menu path.

2. In the following dialog, enter Z_IFBA_BOOK_SQUARE as the name and "Returns the square of the input parameter." as the short text. Then, save the function module.

3. In the screen of the function module, first go to the ATTRIBUTES tab and select the REMOTE-ENABLED MODULE option for the processing type so that you can create a Web service from this module (see Figure 11.15).

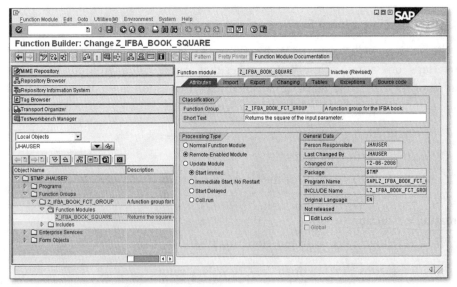

Figure 11.15 Properties of a Function Module

4. Go to the IMPORT tab to determine an input parameter. Create a parameter called INPUT, specify TYPE as the typing and I as the associated type, and select the PASS VALUE option (see Figure 11.16).

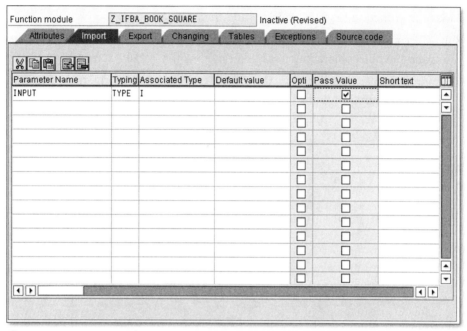

Function module	Z_IFBA_BOOK_SQUARE			Inactive (Revised)			

| Attributes | Import | Export | Changing | Tables | Exceptions | Source code |

Parameter Name	Typing	Associated Type	Default value	Opti	Pass Value	Short text	
INPUT	TYPE	I		☐	☑		▲
				☐	☐		▼
				☐	☐		
				☐	☐		
				☐	☐		
				☐	☐		
				☐	☐		
				☐	☐		
				☐	☐		
				☐	☐		
				☐	☐		
				☐	☐		▲
				☐	☐		▼

Figure 11.16 Determining the Import Parameter

5. Go to the EXPORT tab to determine a return parameter. Create a parameter called OUTPUT, with TYPE as the typing and I as the associated type. Then, select the PASS VALUE option.

6. Go to the SOURCE CODE tab and supplement the source code analog with Listing 11.2. The function from Listing 11.2 calculates the square of an input parameter and returns it.

```
FUNCTION Z_IFBA_BOOK_SQUARE.
*"----------------------------------------------------------
*"*"Local interface:
*"  IMPORTING
*"     VALUE(INPUT) TYPE  I
*"  EXPORTING
*"     VALUE(OUTPUT) TYPE  I
*"----------------------------------------------------------
```

```
OUTPUT = INPUT * INPUT.
ENDFUNCTION.
```

Listing 11.2 Source Code of the Z_IFBA_BOOK_SQUARE Function Module

7. Save the function module, check it, and then activate it.

8. It is recommended to test the function module in the last step. To do that, expand the object hierarchy until you can view the Z_IFBA_BOOK_SQUARE node.

9. Open the context menu, follow the TEST • TEST menu path, and test the function module. If everything runs smoothly, that is, if a square is returned for an input (see Figure 11.17), you have created the first function module successfully. We will set up a Web service for the function module later on.

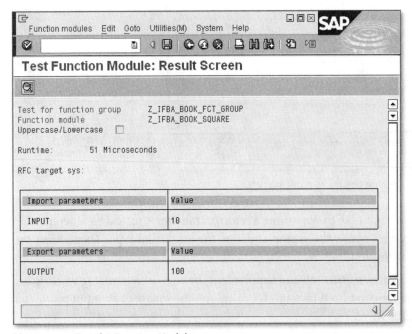

Figure 11.17 Test the Function Module

Repeat the procedure to create a second function module. In doing so, note the following:

1. The name of the second function module is Z_IFBA_BOOK_TIME and the short text is "Returns a random value between 0 and 9."

2. The function module has no import parameters.

3. The name of the export parameter is L_INT.

4. The listing of the source code is shown in Listing 11.3.

5. Remember that it must be a remote-enabled module.

```
FUNCTION Z_IFBA_BOOK_TIME.
*"----------------------------------------------------------
*"*"Local interface:
*"  EXPORTING
*"     VALUE(L_INT) TYPE  I
*"----------------------------------------------------------
DATA: l_time TYPE syuzeit.
GET TIME FIELD l_time.
l_int = l_time+5(1).
ENDFUNCTION.
```

Listing 11.3 Source Code of the Z_IFBA_BOOK_TIME Function Module

Don't continue with the following section until you've successfully created and tested the two function modules.

Creating a Web Service Based on a Function Module

To create a Web service for the Z_IFBA_BOOK_TIME function module, proceed as follows (the procedure is analog to the one described in Section 11.2.1, "Creating a Web Service-Based on a BAPI"):

1. Open the context menu for the Z_IFBA_BOOK_TIME function module. Follow the menu path CREATE • WEB SERVICE.

2. Click on Continue to confirm the first screen of the wizard, Create Service Definition.

3. In the second screen for creating the service, enter Z_IFBA_BOOK_TIME as the name of the service definition and "Returns a random value between 0 and 9." as the short text. The Endpoint Type has already been selected correctly; confirm your entries with Continue.

4. In the Choose Endpoint screen, the correct function module has already been selected. You only need to select the Name Mapping option and click on Continue to confirm.

5. In the configure Service screen, select Release Service for Runtime and click Continue to confirm.

6. Click on the Complete button of the wizard and create the Web service as a local object.

7. Configure the Web service as described in "Configuring the Web Service" in Section 11.2.1.

8. Repeat this procedure for the `Z_IFBA_BOOK_SQUARE` function module. Enter "Returns the square of the input parameter." as the short description.

9. Ultimately, you need another Web service that requires a transport authentication. To do this, use the `Z_IFBA_BOOK_SQUARE` function module again. You must take the following aspects into account during the creation of this Web service:

   ▶ The name of the service definition is `Z_IFBA_BOOK_SQUARE_SEC`.

   ▶ The last step—the configuration of the Web service—is not implemented.

As a reference, Figure 11.18 illustrates the object hierarchy in the ABAP Development Workbench. Compare it with your hierarchy:

▶ Below FUNCTION MODULES, there is a function group called `Z_IFBA_BOOK_FCT_GROUP`.

▶ Below this function group, the two function modules, `Z_IFBA_BOOK_SQUARE` and `Z_IFBA_BOOK_TIME`, should be available.

▶ In the ENTERPRISE SERVICES category, you should find the four created Web services under SERVICE DEFINITIONS (three for the function modules and one for the BAPI).

Call the WSDL file in the web browser for all three Web services using Transaction WSADMIN so that you can copy the URL of the individual Web services later on. The procedure is described in "Accessing the WSDL File of the Web Service" in Section 11.2.1. You can find the Web services for the function module under "SOAP Application for RFC-Compliant FMs" in Figure 11.7, section 11.2.1. If you call the WSDL file for the `Z_IFBA_BOOK_SQUARE_SEC` Web service, the system will prompt you for a user name and password. Enter a user that is valid for the client used.

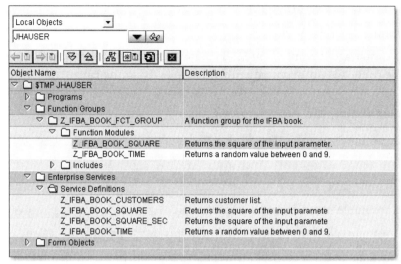

Figure 11.18 Object Navigator of the ABAP Development Workbench

11.3.2 Creating a Form Template

To create a form template that uses the previously created Web services, start Transaction SFP in the next step.

Creating a Form Interface

This section describes a very simple example for testing the Web services. For this reason, the interface remains empty. Proceed as follows:

1. First, create a new interface called Z_IFBA_BOOK_WS_INTERFACE2. Enter "Interface for the function module test." as the short description. Leave the interface type as ABAP Dictionary-based Interface.

2. Then, save the interface as a local object.

3. Finally, activate the interface.

Creating the Form Design

Proceed as follows to create the form design.

1. Create a new form called Z_IFBA_BOOK_WS_FORM_02; the short description is "Form for a function module test."

2. Use the newly created interface, `Z_IFBA_BOOK_WS_INTERFACE2`.

3. Save the form as a local object.

4. Because the interface is empty, you can't create a context. This isn't a problem because the context is not required in this example. Go to the Layout tab.

11.3.3 Implementing the Web Service Calls

The following sections describe the call to a Web service by means of the SOAP object in JavaScript.

▶ The first example processes a return parameter.

▶ The second example uses a parameter for the call.

▶ The third example calls a Web service that requires transport authentication.

▶ The last example transfers a user name and password in an authentication object so that the user is not asked for it.

You can find a figure of the finished form template as a reference at the end of this section. You can test each example individually or summarize all examples in one form template and then test them. The test of the form is described in Section 11.3.4, "Testing the Form Template."

Calling the Z_IFBA_BOOK_TIME Web Service

This first example introduces you to using the SOAP object and calling the `Z_IFBA_BOOK_TIME` Web service. The return result is copied to a text field. Carry out the following steps to create the form templates:

1. The first page of the form is untitled. Rename the page to "Page1."

2. Add a button to the form. Position this button in the top-left corner of the first page and change the label to "Call TIME."

3. Then, add a text field to right of the button. Change the label to "Result."

4. Click the button and have the system display the script for the `click` event; it should be empty. Change the language to JavaScript.

5. Enter Listing 11.4 as the script for the `click` event.

```
// URL pointing to the WSDL
var cURL =
```

```
"http://XXX.com:YYY/sap/bc/srt/rfc/sap/
  Z_IFBA_BOOK_TIME?sap-client=101&wsdl=1.1";
// Connect to web service
var service = SOAP.connect(cURL);
// Call operation "ZIfbaBookTime" and keep the result in
// a variable
var result = service.ZIfbaBookTime();
// Update textfield on form with the result returned from
// the web service
xfa.resolveNode
  ("data.Page1.TextField2").rawValue = result;
```

Listing 11.4 Calling the Z_IFBA_BOOK_TIME Web Service

> **Note**
>
> These listings contain line breaks within the strings for formatting reasons. Leave these line breaks out when entering the listings.

6. Replace the URL for the Web service (cURL variable) by copying the URL from the browser that displays the WSDL file for the Z_IFBA_BOOK_TIME function module and inserting it into the script.

7. You can add another line in the area below the button and the text field to separate this area.

The script in Listing 11.4 establishes a connection to the Web service. To do that, the connect method of the SOAP object is used. This method requires a URL that points to the WSDL of the Web service as a parameter. The return value is a proxy object for the Web service that provides a method for each operation of the Web service. In this example, you can call the ZIfbaBookTime method because this is the operation provided by the Web service. In this first and rather simple example, the return value of the Web service call can be directly assigned to the text field.

Calling the Z_IFBA_SQUARE Web Service

The second example transfers a request parameter for the call of the Z_IFBA_BOOK_SQUARE Web service. In comparison to the previous example, this example considers the creation and processing of the request and response structures.

1. Add another button to the form template and change the label to "Call SQUARE."

2. Then, insert two more text fields to the right of the button you just inserted. Change the label of the first text field to "Input" and the label of the second text field to "Output."

3. Click the button and have the system display the script for the `click` event. Change the language to JavaScript.

4. Copy the script from Listing 11.5 and adapt the URL for the Web service just as in the previous example. However, this example uses the `Z_IFBA_BOOK_SQUARE` Web service.

```
// URL pointing to the WSDL
var url = "http://XXX.com:YYY/sap/bc/srt/rfc/sap/
  Z_IFBA_BOOK_SQUARE?sap-client=101&wsdl=1.1";
// Create request structure, read Input out of text field
var request = {
        "urn:sap-com:document:sap:soap:functions:
         mc-style:ZIfbaBookSquare" :
        {Input:
          xfa.resolveNode("data.Page1.TextField2").
          rawValue}
};
// Call web service using SOAP object
var response = SOAP.request ({
        cURL: url,
        oRequest: request,
        cAction:
          "urn:sap-com:document:sap:soap:functions:
          mc-style"
});
// Now update the text field with the response
// access response array
// see WSDL/web service definition for identifiers
var result =
response["urn:sap-com:document:sap:soap:functions:
  mc-style:ZIfbaBookSquareResponse"]["Output"];
// Set rawValue of corresponding text field
xfa.resolveNode("data.Page1.TextField3").rawValue
                                        = result;
```

Listing 11.5 Calling the Z_IFBA_BOOK_SQUARE Web Service

5. You can also add another line to separate the area.

The second example (see Listing 11.5) doesn't use the `connect` method for the SOAP object, but instead calls the `request` method. For this reason, a `request` object was created; it is important to know the structure and the names of the request's fields. You need to look at the WSDL file to determine the namespaces. There you can find the namespace, `urn:sap-com:document:sap:soap:functions:m c-style`, which is used in the example. Other parameters are the URL of the WSDL for the Web service and the `cAction` string that is written in the SOAP header and is an optional parameter. Due to the fact that it is in the SOAP header, it can be read by a firewall, for example.

Finally, the return value (`result`) is read from the returned structure (`response`). Here, it is important again to know the structure and the name of the fields. In the present example, `Output` is a field below the `ZIfbaBookSquareResponse` response structure. The namespace is the same as for the request structure.

Calling the Z_IFBA_BOOK_SQUARE_SEC Web Service

This example is a variant of the previous example: A Web service is called that requires authentication at transport level. The difference doesn't become apparent until runtime when you test the form.

To create the appropriate form template, repeat the example from "Calling the Z_IFBA_SQUARE Web Service" in Section 11.3.3. However, note the following:

1. Enlarge the button and change the label to "Call SQUARE_SEC."

2. Use the `Z_IFBA_BOOK_SQUARE_SEC` Web service instead of the `Z_IFBA_BOOK_SQUARE` Web service when you determine the URL (see Listing 11.5).

Automatic Authentication for Calling a Web Service

In contrast to the previous example, the fourth example doesn't prompt for the authentication in a dialog, but transfers the required information, that is, the user name and the password, already in the script program for the call to the SOAP object. Repeat the second example and note the following:

1. Enlarge the button and change the label to "Call SQUARE_SEC Auth Obj."

2. Use the `Z_IFBA_BOOK_SQUARE_SEC` Web service instead of the `Z_IFBA_BOOK_SQUARE` Web service when you determine the URL.

3. Replace the Web service call in the script (`SOAP.request`) by the script shown in Listing 11.6.

4. In the script program, rename both text fields to `TextField6` and `TextField7`.

5. For the `oAuthenticator` object, adapt the values for `<user-id>` and `<password>` according to your system. Utilize a valid user name and password for the client you use.

```
// Create object for authentication
var oAuthenticator =
{
Username: "<user-id>",
Password: "<password>"
};
// Call web service using SOAP object
var response = SOAP.request ({
        cURL: url,
        oRequest: request,
        cAction: "urn:sap-com:document:sap:soap:
          functions:mc-style",
        oAuthenticate: oAuthenticator
});
```

Listing 11.6 Extension to the Use of an Authentication Object

The script program for the fourth example (Listing 11.6) combines an object for authentication (`oAuthenticator`) and contains a user name and a password. The object is transferred as an additional parameter for the call of the `request` method.

Note here that the password and the user name don't have to be contained in the script program. They can also originate from fields of the form (for example, you can use the Password field).

Finished Form Template

If you've completed and followed all of the examples sequentially, the form template should appear as illustrated in Figure 11.19. The figure shows the positioning of the individual form fields and the script for the `click` event of the first example.

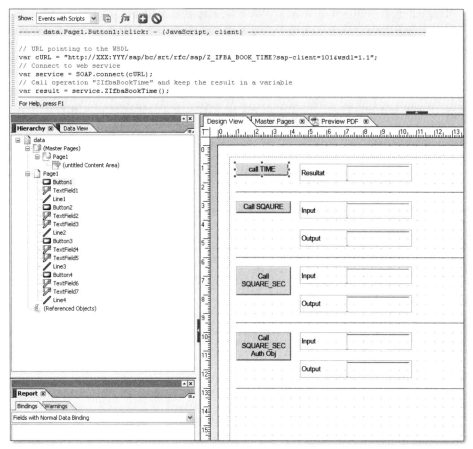

Figure 11.19 Structure of the Form Template

11.3.4 Testing the Form Template

To test a form template, you must first create a PDF and save it as described in Section 11.2.3, "Testing the Form Template." You can then open the PDF file in Adobe Reader and test the Web service calls.

The following describes the test results you can expect for the four examples:

▶ **Calling the Z_IFBA_BOOK_TIME Web service**
After you click the Call TIME button, a security warning is displayed because you called an external Web service. You must allow it for the test. After a short period of time, a number between 0 and 9 is displayed in the Result text field.

This example deliberately uses a Web service that returns different results—so if you click on the button repeatedly, you can see that the Web service has really been called multiple times.

▶ **Calling the Z_IFBA_BOOK_SQUARE Web service**
To test the second example, enter a figure in the INPUT field. Then, click the Call SQUARE button. Then, permit access to the Web service. After a short period of time, the Output field shows the square of the figure entered in the Input field.

Note that no error handling has been implemented for the examples. You can repeat the call with different values in this example as well.

▶ **Calling the Z_IFBA_BOOK_SQUARE_SEC Web service**
This example behaves like the previous one. The only difference is that the dialog for the transport authentication is displayed (see Figure 11.20). To continue, you must enter a valid user and the corresponding password for the selected client. If required, uncheck the SAVE THIS INFORMATION option.

Figure 11.20 Dialog for the Authentication

▶ **Automatic authentication for calling a Web service**
This example behaves exactly like the second example. By using an authentication object the authentication is implemented automatically. Although you use the Web service that requires authentication, you can't draw any distinction to the second example.

Now you know the most important procedures for using Web services. The next section provides some remarks for frequently asked questions.

11.4   Tips for Using Web Services

This section summarizes tips and procedures for the use of Web services.

11.4.1   Calling the Web Service in the Click Event

You don't have to use the button generated by Adobe LiveCycle Designer to call a Web service. You can implement this yourself in a script. Listing 11.7 shows what the script line must look like in JavaScript to call the Web service that you created in Section 11.2, "Using WSDL Data Connections," and used in the form template. Note that the name of the data connection is used for the Web service. In this example, the name is IFBA_BOOK_WebService.

```
xfa.connectionSet.IFBA_BOOK_WebService.execute(1);
```

Listing 11.7 Calling the Web Service of a Data Connection

The parameter specifies whether the form is remerged (value 1) or not (value 0) after the call to the Web service. If the form is remerged, the execution of the script program aborts at this point.

11.4.2   Calling the Web Service Automatically When Opening the Form

A Web service doesn't always have to be called as a reaction to a user interaction; it can also be implemented automatically by a script in the form:ready or Layout:ready event, for example. This way, the form can request data before it is displayed to the user or it can be checked to see if the required SAP system can be accessed, for example.

11.4.3   Calling Multiple Web Services Using a Button

There are cases in which multiple Web services are called consecutively (for example, to read details for a business partner that is not determined until the call of the first Web service). Here, you can use the procedure described in Section 11.4.1, "Calling a Web Service in the Click Event."

You can also implement multiple calls of different Web services consecutively in a single script. Here, you must note that—as soon as the form must be re-merged by setting the parameter to 1—the execution of the script program is aborted accordingly.

11.5 Summary

Web services are a simple and elegant method to connect interactive PDF forms with an SAP system; for this reason, two different approaches are available:

- On one hand, you can use the WSDL-based data connection. In this approach, the request and response parameters are provided via the data view together with a ready-to-use button. They can also be used for the graphical interactive procedure of creating form templates.

- At present, however, the WSDL-based data connection doesn't support authentication when calling Web services. This is supported by the second approach, the use of the SOAP object in JavaScript. The SOAP object enables an authentication at transport level by means of user name and password. The request and the processing of the responses must be programmed in JavaScript.

You got to know both approaches based on examples in this chapter.

The Authors

Dr. Jürgen Hauser has worked for Adobe Systems since 2005. His responsibilities include representing Adobe at SAP AG in Walldorf, Germany; product management for SAP Interactive Forms by Adobe, and additional duties, such as local contact for Adobe Flex and Adobe AIR. He has presented SAP Interactive Forms by Adobe at numerous conferences worldwide. He previously worked as a project manager and system architect for a large German consulting firm. After finishing his studies in computer science, with a minor in mathematics, he participated in the Distributed Systems research group. He earned his doctorate in multimedia systems from the University of Stuttgart, Germany.

Andreas Deutesfeld studied physics with computer science at the Johannes Gutenberg University in Mainz, Germany. After finishing his studies, he joined SAP AG in Walldorf, Germany, in 1996. His work focused on form technologies in the development of SAP NetWeaver. He has conducted numerous workshops and classes and consulted for many projects on this topic. Since 2003, he has been heavily involved as a development architect in the design and implementation process of the new form solution, SAP Interactive Forms by Adobe. He lives in a small town on the Rhine with his wife and son.

Dr. Stephan Rehmann holds a PhD in low-temperature physics from the University of Bayreuth, Germany. He joined SAP AG in 1998 and worked in the development division of the overhead cost-controlling product team. At present, he is responsible for the ISR framework for SAP ERP, among other things.

Thomas Szücs was senior software developer at SAP AG for the Web Dynpro ABAP division where he was in charge of Adobe integration, among other things. After almost nine years at SAP working on SD, CRM, and SAP NetWeaver, he now works as a senior solution architect at Corporate Business Solutions GmbH in Heidelberg, Germany. He is married and lives near Bruchsal, Germany, with his wife.

Philipp Thun studied media system design, with a focus on computer science, at the University of Applied Sciences Darmstadt, Germany. After he finished his studies, he worked as a project coordinator for a public data center. Since 2003 he has been a developer at SAP AG in Walldorf, Germany, and has concentrated on form technologies. His work focuses on SAP Interactive Forms by Adobe. He is primarily responsible for the integration of runtime components (Adobe Document Services) with SAP NetWeaver in a joint project with Adobe.

Index

E

Q

T

U

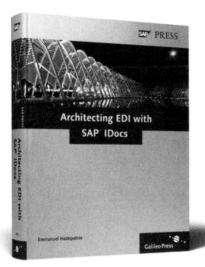

Covers the requirements, standards, and capabilities of EDI and IDocs

Teaches how to design the architectural blueprint of the EDI systems

Provides a sample scenario for implementing order-to-cash in a real-world project

Emmanuel Hadzipetros

Architecting EDI with SAP IDocs

This book is your project-based guide to architecting Enterprise Data Interchange (EDI) with SAP IDocs. Following a large sample scenario of an order-to-cash process from blueprint to code, you'll get an A-to-Z explanation of what an EDI system or architecture looks like. The book explains the basics of the process, shows a real-life implementation, and introduces utilities, test strategies, monitoring and troubleshooting activities. Following the sample project, you'll learn everything you need to know about SAP EDI.

approx. 600 pp., 69,95 Euro / US$ 69.95

ISBN 978-1-59229-227-1, July 2009

>> www.sap-press.de/1850

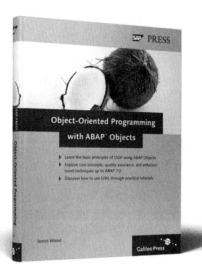

Learn the basic principles of OOP using ABAP Objects

Explore core concepts, quality assurance and enhancement techniques up to ABAP 7.0

Discover how to use UML through practical tutorials

James Wood

Object-Oriented Programming with ABAP Objects

This book provides a gentle (and yet, comprehensive) start to programming object-oriented ABAP! What are objects? How to define and write classes? What's polymorphism all about? The book helps you to venture the switch to object-oriented programming, and brings your skills up to date: First learn about all essential OO concepts, then see examples from daily development work. Exception handling, object debugging and unit testing are demystified here, plus, you get advice on enhanced techniques and tools in ABAP 7.0.

357 pp., 69,95 Euro / US$ 69.95
ISBN 978-1-59229-235-6

>> **www.sap-press.de/1859**

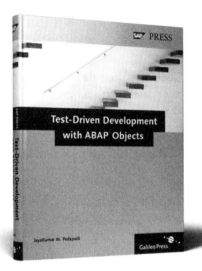

Provides a complete guide to the basic principles, design, and realization of TDD

Covers how to use ABAP Unit, test doubles, mock objects, legacy code testing, and more

Teaches how to develop a variety of applications from testing your first "Hello World" to highly customized tools

JayaKumar M. Pedapudi

Test-Driven Development with ABAP Objects

This practical handbook teaches you how to perform test-driven development using ABAP Objects (release 7.0) and the ABAP Unit tool. You will learn how to improve your development style and gain the skills needed to develop quality software products. The main chapter of the book shows five cases with step-by-step procedures on writing TDD programs. These practical cases increase in complexity, from simple to expert, so that you will clearly understand the TDD approach. After reading the book you will not only know the methodology behind TDD, but be able to use ABAP Unit for writing and testing new applications and enhancing existing legacy systems.

approx. 330 pp., 69,95 Euro / US$ 69.95
ISBN 978-1-59229-248-6, July 2009

>> www.sap-press.de/1969

Master the implementation, development, and configuration of end-to-end process integration in B2B scenarios

Explore the adapter framework, industry-standard support, BPM capabilities, and more

Learn from comprehensive best practices and real-life test scenarios with SAP NetWeaver PI 7.1

Sam Raju, Claus Wallacher

B2B Integration Using SAP NetWeaver PI

Using SAP NetWeaver Process Integration (PI) for the implementation of B2B scenarios differs greatly from the implementation of other scenarios. This comprehensive guide for B2B process integration provides in-depth coverage: If you are an advanced to professional administrator, developer, or consultant in the PI area, you'll learn new ways to exploit SAP NetWeaver PI's integration functionality to optimize connectivity with your (global) trading partners by setting up a reliable, secure, and low-effort data exchange.

608 pp., 2008, 69,95 Euro / US$ 69.95
ISBN 978-1-59229-163-2

>> www.sap-press.de/1591

Second edition, updated and expanded to cover SAP NetWeaver Application Server Java (release 7.1)

Covers new topics, such as Java EE 5, EJB 3.0, SAP NetWeaver CE, and more

Includes sample applications on Web Dynpro, Visual Composer, CAF, and Developer Studio

Includes the SAP NetWeaver CE 7.1 Trial Version on DVD

Karl Kessler et al.

Java Programming with SAP NetWeaver

Explore all the innovations in SAP NetWeaver AS Java (release 7.1) with this completely updated and extended second edition of our standard work. You'll get profound insights into all topic areas linked to Java programming for SAP applications: business logic, persistence, scalability, maintainability, development in teams, and UI design. Three completely new chapters show you the development of composite applications with the Composition Environment. All other chapters have been revised and updated to Java EE 5.

696 pp., 2. edition 2008, with DVD 5, 69,95 Euro / US$ 69.95
ISBN 978-1-59229-181-6

>> www.sap-press.de/1657

Develop your own enterprise services

Benefit from in-depth descriptions of standard services usage

Increase your knowledge through recommendations on service enabling

Martin Huvar, Timm Falter, Thomas Fiedler, Alexander Zubev

Developing Applications with Enterprise SOA

With this book, application developers and software architects finally have at their disposal a thorough introduction to software development with SAP's enterprise service-oriented architecture (enterprise SOA).
The book provides an in-depth description of all enterprise SOA components and methodologies, as well as the metadata model, and it explains how to develop your own enterprise services, and combine them into applications in different scenarios (service consumer). The book covers user interface scenarios as well as process and integration scenarios.

329 pp., 2008, 69,95 Euro / US$ 69.95, ISBN 978-1-59229-178-6

>> www.sap-press.de/1604

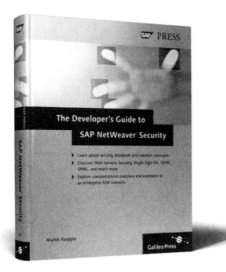

Learn about security standards and solution concepts

Discover Web Services Security, Single Sign-On, SAML, SPML, and much more

Explore comprehensive exercises and examples in an Enterprise SOA scenario

Martin Raepple

The Developer's Guide to SAP NetWeaver Security

This practical guide for developers, system integrators, and software architects, describes security technologies in conjunction with SAP NetWeaver Application Server up to and including Release 7.0. In addition to covering the basic principles of Web Service Security, Single Sign-On, SAML, SPML, the book focuses on providing practical exercises and examples to help you establish a profound understanding of the standards used. To accomplish this, a cross-enterprise scenario is used in which system components (based on various technologies) are integrated with each other using different standards (Open Source, Microsoft .NET, J2EE, Legacy). This exclusive sample scenario focuses on key areas of the application layer, such as communication and data security as well as identity management, and it provides readers with numerous screenshots as well as volumes of sample code.

548 pp., 2008, with CD, 69,95 Euro / US$ 69.95, ISBN 978-1-59229-180-9

>> www.sap-press.de/1656

Planning and implementing new, self-contained SAP applications

Developing flexible application architectures with SAP NetWeaver Application Server ABAP

Best practices for optimum usage of all potentials in an existing infrastructure

Thorsten Franz, Tobias Trapp

ABAP Objects: Application Development from Scratch

Developing completely new ABAP applications – separate from the SAP standard – represents a very challenging task even for experienced developers. To help you master this challenge, this comprehensive programming guide for ABAP Objects provides an overview of the overall software development process. It describes the basic principles of designing and implementing an application in ABAP Objects, and how you can ensure that the application remains extensible for customer processes and sufficiently flexible for further development. The book describes from scratch all process steps to be carried out during programming, and illustrates these steps with numerous code examples and screenshots.

505 pp., 2008, 69,95 Euro / US$ 69.95
ISBN 978-1-59229-211-0

>> **www.sap-press.de/1790**